D1411390

Patriotic Holidays
of the United States

Patriotic Holidays

of the United States

An Introduction to the History, Symbols, and Traditions Behind the Major Holidays and Days of Observance

By Helene Henderson

Foreword by Matthew Dennis

Omnigraphics

615 Griswold • Detroit, MI 48226

Omnigraphics, Inc.

Cherie D. Abbey, *Managing Editor*
Laurie Lanzen Harris, *Editor*
Amy Marcaccio Keyzer, *Copyeditor*
Allison A. Beckett, Mary Butler, and Linda Strand, *Research Staff*

* * *

Peter E. Ruffner, *Publisher*
Frederick G. Ruffner, Jr., *Chairman*
Matthew P. Barbour, *Senior Vice President*
Kay Gill, *Vice President — Directories*

* * *

Elizabeth Barbour, *Research and Permissions Coordinator*
David P. Bianco, *Marketing Director*
Leif A. Gruenberg, *Development Manager*
Kevin Hayes, *Operations Manager*

Barry Puckett, *Librarian*
Cherry Stockdale, *Permissions Assistant*
Shirley Amore, Kevin Glover, Martha Johns, and Kirk Kauffman, *Administrative Staff*

Library of Congress Cataloging-in-Publication Data

Henderson, Helene, 1963-
    Patriotic holidays of the United States : an introduction to the history, symbols, and traditions behind the major holidays and days of observance / by Helene Henderson ; foreword by Matthew Dennis.
        p. cm.
    Summary: "Provides information about the history and celebration of American patriotic holidays and days of observance. Features include narrative overviews, primary source documents, chronology, and print and web sources for further study"—Provided by publisher.
    Includes bibliographical references and index.
    ISBN 0-7808-0733-2 (hardcover : alk. paper)
    1. Holidays—United States—History. 2. Special days—United States—History. 3. Patriotism—United States—History. I. Title.
    JK1761.H46 2005
    394.26973—dc22

                                                   2005024870

Table of Contents

Patriotic Holidays of the United States

Appendix: Primary Sources

Foreword

The old adage that "time waits for no man" is not exactly true. Human societies often agree to pause in their regular calendars, not merely to rest, but to recognize and commemorate important historical moments. We call these pauses holidays. Humans and nations need such breaks to reflect on who they are, to remember their successes and failures, to express gratitude to forebears or higher powers, to chart their course in life, and sometimes just to relax or let off steam.

Holidays are like peaks in a nation's terrain. Without them, the landscape would be flat and monotonous; with them, we find places that rise above the everyday world and give us lofty views and broader perspectives. They are special places, enjoyable to inhabit briefly, that give us the lay of the land. Holidays thus punctuate national life and help give it meaning. America's patriotic holidays, as this informative and engaging book shows, are the extraordinary annual events that help define the United States and its people. On such occasions, Americans tell themselves and the world who they are. They commemorate their origins, call attention to their basic values and ideals, celebrate their good fortune, and express thanks to those who created, nurtured, and protected their nation.

Patriotism is difficult to define, but its essence is devotion and service to one's country. This volume offers a fascinating introduction to American patriotism by showing how Americans have expressed that devotion through holiday occasions, in symbols and ceremonies, picnics and parades, solemn rites, such as silent graveside vigils, and raucous rituals, such as the exploding fireworks of the Fourth of July. The book encompasses the country's oldest patriotic fete—Independence Day—and its newest—Patriot Day, observed on September 11—and the myriad occasions that emerged in the American calendar in-between. Readers will learn essential, sometimes surprising facts about American patriotic holidays that will inform their understanding of American history, culture, society, and politics. And each entry invites readers to probe more deeply, to ask new questions about the United States and its people, guided by the book's excellent list of book and web resources.

Patriotic holidays can be moments that combine both festivity and deeper reflection. We might ask, what is an American? And what does it mean to be patriotic? In fact, virtually all Americans are patriots, yet they understand and love their country in different ways and have different ideas about how their nation might best fulfill its ideals and principles. Patriotic holidays can be times for dissension as well as celebration, moments when some Americans stop, not merely to hail the country's triumphs, but to challenge the country to do better. Controversies are not inherently bad; they can prod Americans to think more clearly about their country, to examine its promise and performance in a more careful and informed fashion.

American patriotic holidays are dynamic works-in-progress. As this book shows so well, they are American "democracy in action." They have emerged and endured not because they were mandated by a king or president, but because they have been embraced by ordinary American people. They will continue to change as the United States changes. American patriotic holidays exist because they are celebrated, because they have meaning and purpose, and because they are often great fun.

Matthew Dennis
Professor of History, University of Oregon
Author of *Red, White, and Blue Letter Days:*
An American Calendar (2002)

Preface

The history of patriotic holidays in the United States is also a history of democracy in action — the first holiday, Independence Day, perhaps most dramatically illustrates this. Historians write about how the United States celebrated itself into nationhood in the summer of 1776. And Americans have continued to do so.

The story of American holidays is largely the story of how ordinary Americans took steps to initiate observances that reflected their convictions — from the Fourth of July to the birthday of Martin Luther King Jr. This is not surprising, because the United States is a nation founded on the idea that the people — not a tyrant, not a king, not a dictator — should govern themselves.

In the establishment of their holidays, Americans have continued to define what it is to be American. They did not, in all cases, create the events observed — as, for example, in commemorating Pearl Harbor and September 11 — but they did create the observances of those events. In so doing, Americans have woven such events into the national collective memory and common culture and determined how they will remember them. The pages of this book tell their stories.

Audience

Patriotic Holidays of the United States: An Introduction to the History, Symbols, and Traditions Behind the Major Holidays and Days of Observance is intended for a general audience, including students and teachers, as well as interested adults and civic groups.

Scope

This book provides information about holidays that are central to the United States' identity as a nation. Given that the most basic definition of "patriotism" is love of country, the holidays covered in this book are those dealing with aspects of democratic civic rights, responsibilities, and values consistent with ideals laid out in the nation's founding documents. They include major American federal secular holidays and other days of national significance.

The following holidays, which are covered in this volume, are designated as legal public holidays by U.S. law:

Columbus Day—second Monday in October
Independence Day—July 4
Labor Day—first Monday in September
Martin Luther King Jr. Birthday—third Monday in January
Memorial Day—last Monday in May
Thanksgiving—fourth Thursday in November
Veterans Day—November 11
Washington's Birthday (Presidents' Day)—third Monday in February

Of the legal public holidays above, only Independence Day and Veterans Day are celebrated on the same date every year. In 1968 Congress passed Public Law 90-363, popularly known as the Uniform Monday Holiday Law, which became effective on January 1, 1971. This law moved the observances of several holidays—Washington's Birthday (February 22), Memorial Day (May 30), and Veterans Day—to a nearby Monday. (In 1975 Congress moved Veterans Day back to its original date, November 11, because of popular protest.) Public Law 90-363 also created the Columbus Day federal holiday and set the precedent for scheduling the Martin Luther King Jr. observance on a Monday when it became a public holiday in 1983.

The days listed below, which are also covered in this volume, are not legal public holidays:

Armed Forces Day—third Saturday in May
Citizenship Day—September 17
Election Day—the Tuesday after the first Monday in November
Emancipation Day—January 1
Flag Day—June 14
Inauguration Day—January 20
Juneteenth—June 19
National Pearl Harbor Remembrance Day—December 7
Patriot Day—September 11

Armed Forces Day was established by a presidential proclamation. Citizenship Day, Flag Day, National Pearl Harbor Remembrance Day, and Patriot Day are officially designated in the U.S. Code as "patriotic and national observances." Election Day is a holiday in 10 states. Inauguration Day is a legal public holiday only in the metropolitan area of the District of Columbia, according to law. Emancipation Day and Juneteenth have no federal legal status, but several states have officially recognized them.

Organization

The first entry, Patriotism in the United States, provides an overview of issues related to patriotism and holidays. It discusses patriotism, considers the role that holidays play in fostering citizenship and national identity, provides information on the U.S. form of government, outlines major political parties, and describes several national symbols and mottoes.

The remaining entries are arranged alphabetically by the official name of the holiday as designated in the U.S. Code. Each entry begins with the following elements: 1) the name of the holiday; 2) the date on which the holiday was established; and 3) the date on which the holiday is celebrated. The main body of each entry contains: 1) an introductory paragraph outlining what or who the holiday commemorates, when it became a holiday, whether it is a legal public holiday or day of observance, and when the holiday is celebrated; 2) a historical overview of the event or person commemorated; 3) information about the process by which the holiday was created; and 4) descriptions of major observances of the holiday and important traditions.

The date on which a holiday was established is defined by various rubrics, according to its legal status:

- Date Established as a Federal Holiday: the date on which a holiday was established as a federal holiday by law
- Date Established as a Patriotic and National Observance: the date on which the U.S. Congress officially designated the holiday as a "patriotic and national observance" in the U.S. Code, Title 36
- Date Established by Presidential Proclamation: this rubric appears in entries for holidays that have not been officially established as either a federal holiday or a patriotic and national observance, but only by a presidential proclamation

For each holiday, brief descriptions of, and contact information for, numerous other observances around the country are keyed to a U.S. map at the end of each entry. Boxes and sidebar articles provide additional information about people, customs, songs, foods, and other miscellany associated with each holiday.

Each entry concludes with listings of helpful web sites and suggestions for further reading.

Cross References

Within each entry, terms in boldface type and see-also references guide the reader to holidays featured in other entries in the book as well as to relevant primary sources in the Appendix.

Other Features

Appendix: Primary Sources

The Appendix contains a variety of primary sources that illuminate the history and observance of America's patriotic holidays. These include both official documents and more personal accounts. Taken together, they provide rare insight into the holidays' historical significance for all Americans.

The primary sources, which are arranged according to the date of the observance described or the date of the document, fall into the following general categories:

- Official documents, including the Mayflower Compact (Thanksgiving); the Declaration of Independence (Independence Day); the Constitution of the United States (Citizenship Day); the Emancipation Proclamation (Emancipation Day); and Flag Laws and Regulations (Flag Day).

- Speeches, including President Franklin D. Roosevelt's address after the attack on Pearl Harbor; the "I Have a Dream" speech by Martin Luther King Jr. at the 1963 March on Washington for Jobs and Freedom; President George W. Bush's speech to Congress and the nation after the attacks of September 11, 2001; U.S. Representative William Lacy Clay's remarks on the 40th anniversary of the 1963 March on Washington; and U.S. Representative John Conyers's comments on the significance of the Martin Luther King Jr. Birthday.

- Personal accounts, letters, and articles, including excerpts from Christopher Columbus's journal on the landfall; diary excerpts from Sarah Ridg [Schuyler] describing Washington's Birthday and Inauguration Day in 1809; Sarah Josepha Hale's 1863 letter to President Abraham Lincoln requesting the creation of Thanksgiving; an excerpt from an article by African Methodist Episcopal Bishop H. M. Turner recalling the celebratory events following the issuance of the Emancipation Proclamation; excerpts from interviews with early Oregonians remembering Independence Day observances in the 1860s and 1870s; excerpts describing Memorial Day ceremonies in Washington, D.C., in the late 19th century; an 1892 Columbus Day school program by Francis Bellamy containing the original Pledge of Allegiance; and an exchange of correspondence regarding the 1894 Pullman workers' strike, which led the U.S. Congress to create Labor Day as a federal holiday.

Bibliography

The Bibliography contains a complete list of books and articles consulted in the preparation of this volume.

Web Sites

This section includes all web sites listed in the entries in alphabetical order by the name of the sponsoring organization.

Index

The Index includes people, places, customs, symbols, foods, musical and literary works, and other subjects mentioned in the entries.

Acknowledgments

We are indebted to the many individuals, institutions, and organizations that allowed us to reprint images and text in this volume, especially Bradford Baker, Public Affairs Officer, USS Arizona Memorial; Steve Blando, Deputy Chief, Community Relations Branch, U.S. Coast Guard Public Affairs; Kim Curtis at Monticello; Brian Distefano, Consumer Marketing Manager, Galveston Park Board of Trustees; the Dwight D. Eisenhower Library; Thomas Featherstone, Detroit News Collection, Walter P. Reuther Library, Wayne State University; Jay Godwin, Heraldry Archivist, U.S. Air Force Historical Research Agency; Sinclair Hitchings and Jane Winton, Print Department of the Boston Public Library; Renee Hylton, U.S. National Guard Bureau; Allan Kujala of Sussex County Return Day, Inc.; Ricardo E. Magdaleno, Event Coordinator, City of Houston, Texas; Lynford Morton, Public Affairs, U.S. Coast Guard Public Affairs; Bob Renner, Commandant of the U.S. Marine Corps; Rich Sale, Account Executive, Bennett Graphics, and the Georgia Veterans Day Parade Association of Atlanta; Phil Sheridan, Public Affairs Officer, Independence National Historic Park; Cecil Stoughton, Lyndon Baines Johnson Library and Museum; James Talley; Robert Thompson, National Flag Day Foundation, Inc.; Terri Tremblay, American Antiquarian Society; Gina Uriarte at Hamilton Ink; the U.S. Department of Defense; Timothy Warnock, Chief, Organizational History Branch, U.S. Air Force Historical Research Agency; and Andy Wilkinson.

A full list of illustration and text credits appears at the back of the book.

In addition, special thanks go to Matthew Dennis, professor of history at the University of Oregon, for generously contributing his insightful foreword to this volume; to Laurie Lanzen Harris for her wise editorial counsel; and to Mary Ann Stavros for her appealing page design and typesetting.

Comments and Suggestions

We welcome your comments on *Patriotic Holidays of the United States* and any suggestions for other issues that warrant treatment in Omnigraphics' series on holidays, religion, and culture. Correspondence should be addressed to:

Editor, *Patriotic Holidays of the United States*
Omnigraphics, Inc.
615 Griswold
Detroit, MI 48226
E-mail: editorial@omnigraphics.com

Chronologies

Chronology of the Historical Events Commemorated by Holidays and Observances

October 12, 1492: Columbus's landfall in the Bahamas

Autumn 1621: Pilgrims' Thanksgiving at Plymouth Colony, Massachusetts

February 22, 1732: Birth of George Washington

July 4, 1776: Declaration of Independence approved by Continental Congress

June 14, 1777: Flag established by Continental Congress

September 17, 1787: U.S. Constitution signed

January 1, 1863: Emancipation Proclamation issued

June 19, 1865: Emancipation Proclamation announced in Galveston, Texas (Juneteenth)

September 5, 1882: First Labor Day observance in New York City

November 11, 1918: Armistice of World War I (Veterans Day)

January 15, 1929: Birth of Martin Luther King Jr.

December 7, 1941: Attack on Pearl Harbor

September 11, 2001: Attacks in New York and Washington, D.C.

Chronology of the Establishment of Holidays and Observances

1845: Election Day, as a uniform day throughout the United States

October 3, 1863: Thanksgiving, as observance by presidential proclamation

May 5, 1868: Memorial Day (first "official" observance designated by Union General John A. Logan)

June 28, 1870: Independence Day, as a holiday in D.C.

January 31, 1879: Washington's Birthday, as a legal holiday in D.C.

1885: Washington's Birthday, as a legal holiday for federal offices in every U.S. state

August 1, 1888: Memorial Day, as Decoration Day, a holiday in D.C.

1892: Columbus Day, as observance by presidential proclamation

June 28, 1894: Labor Day, as a legal public holiday

June 14, 1916: Flag Day, as observance by presidential proclamation

January 23, 1933: Inauguration Day (changed date from March 4 to January 20 by 20th Amendment to the Constitution)

April 30, 1934: Columbus Day, as a patriotic and national observance

May 13, 1938: Armistice Day, as a legal public holiday

May 13, 1938: Independence Day, as a legal public holiday

May 13, 1938: Memorial Day, as a legal public holiday on May 30

May 13, 1938: Washington's Birthday, as a legal public holiday on February 22

December 26, 1941: Thanksgiving, as a legal public holiday

August 3, 1949: Flag Day, as a patriotic and national observance

February 27, 1950: Armed Forces Day, as observance by presidential proclamation

February 29, 1952: Citizenship Day, as a patriotic and national observance

June 1, 1954: Veterans Day (changed name from Armistice Day)

January 11, 1957: Inauguration Day, as a legal public holiday in D.C. and metro area

June 28, 1968: Columbus Day, as a legal public holiday

June 28, 1968: Memorial Day (changed date from May 30 to last Monday in May)

June 28, 1968: Washington's Birthday (changed date from February 22 to third Monday in February)

November 2, 1983: Birthday of Martin Luther King Jr., as a legal public holiday

August 23, 1994: National Pearl Harbor Remembrance Day, as a patriotic and national observance

December 18, 2001: Patriot Day, as a patriotic and national observance

Patriotic Holidays
of the United States

We the People

insure domestic Tranquility, provide for the common def... and our Posterity, do ordain and establish this Constitut...

Section. 1. All legislative Powers herein granted shall...

... 2. The House of Representatives shall be comp...

Patriotism in the United States: An Introduction to American Patriotism, Holidays, Government, Political Parties, National Symbols, and Mottoes

The history of American patriotic holidays is one in which "We, the people"—ordinary Americans—have decided what should be celebrated, what should be memorialized, and how that should be done. Several European explorers landed on what became the United States' portion of the North American continent before 1492, but some Americans decided that Christopher Columbus should be commemorated as the founding explorer. So October 12—the date he landed on an island in the Bahamas in 1492—became a patriotic holiday (*see* **Columbus Day**). For years during and after the Civil War, American women decorated the graves of fallen soldiers on both sides, but ordinary Americans demanded that a day be set aside to officially commemorate them all, instigating the creation of the federal **Memorial Day** holiday in 1938. The armistice, or peace agreement, ending World War I occurred on November 11, 1918, on a boxcar in western Europe. But it was an ordinary American who, in the early 1950s, urged that that date should commemorate all American veterans of all wars. Enough other Americans thought so, too, and **Veterans Day** was the result. And the list goes on.

This entry provides background information on American patriotism, holidays, government, political parties, national patriotic symbols, and mottoes. It is divided into three main sections: Patriotism and Holidays; U.S. Government and Major Political Parties; and America and Its Patriotic Symbols.

Patriotism and Holidays

The basic dictionary definition of a patriot is "a person who loves his country and defends and promotes its interests." Patriotism can be based on love for one's country's principles and ideals, love for one's country's history and heritage, love for one's country's natural beauties and treasures, a general love for one's countrymen, or a combination of these. What is unique about the United States is its foundation not on shared blood ties, long attachment to a piece of land, or allegiance to a king or queen, but on particular ideals, namely, the right to life, liberty, and the pursuit of happiness through government of the people, by the people, and for the people.

> *"The spirit of resistance to government is so valuable on certain occasions, that I wish it to be always kept alive. It will often be exercised when wrong, but better so than not to be exercised at all. I like a little rebellion now and then. It is like a storm in the atmosphere."*
>
> —Thomas Jefferson to Abigail Adams, 1787

Patriotism further calls for action that demonstrates love of country, including a willingness to sacrifice one's personal fortunes, preferences, or life for the greater good of the nation. As one of the Founding Fathers and second president, John Adams, put it: "Public Virtue is the only Foundation of Republics. There must be a positive Passion for the public good, the public Interest . . . and this public Passion, must be Superior to all private Passions."

As long as the United States remains a free and open society, Americans will disagree on what policies the government should pursue, how it should handle problems, and even on what it means to be patriotic. This situation often makes for uncomfortable uncertainties in American society, but it is also true to American principles as outlined in the Constitution, Bill of Rights, and the Declaration of Independence.

In this way, it can be patriotic to support an American government's policies when one decides they reflect the principles stated in the Constitution or Declaration of Independence. It can also be patriotic to protest an American government's policies when one thinks that they betray the ideals expressed in those documents. The Founding Fathers, for example, considered themselves patriotic British citizens when they challenged British policies in America before finally breaking away and creating the nation (*see* **Independence Day**).

Patriotism: Points of View

"To be an American is not . . . a matter of blood; it is a matter of an idea—and history is the image of that idea."
—Robert Penn Warren, American writer

"Our country! In her intercourse with foreign nations, may she always be in the right; but our country, right or wrong."
—Stephen Decatur, U.S. Navy commander

"Our country, right or wrong. When right, to be kept right; when wrong, to be put right." —Carl Schurz, U.S. general and senator

"To announce that there must be no criticism of the president, or that we are to stand by the president, right or wrong, is not only unpatriotic and servile, but is morally treasonable to the American public." —Theodore Roosevelt, U.S. president

"Patriot: The person who can holler the loudest without knowing what he is hollering about." —Mark Twain, American writer

"True patriotism hates injustice in its own land more than anywhere else." —Clarence Darrow, American attorney

"I venture to suggest that what we mean is a sense of national responsibility which will enable America to remain master of her power—to walk with it in serenity and wisdom, with self-respect and the respect of all mankind; a patriotism that puts country ahead of self; a patriotism which is not short, frenzied outbursts of emotion, but the tranquil and steady dedication of a lifetime. These are words that are easy to utter, but this is a mighty assignment. For it is often easier to fight for principles than to live up to them." —Adlai E. Stevenson, Illinois governor and presidential candidate

"In America, our origins matter less than our destination, and that is what democracy is all about."
—Ronald Reagan, U.S. president

Many Americans express patriotism by observing national civic holidays, just as members of religious groups express faith by observing major religious holy days.

Historian David Waldstreicher writes about how American nationalism and identity were nurtured from the beginning by the very act of celebrating new events in holidays like the Fourth of July, battle anniversaries, and other notable occasions. This was even more important in the country's early years because the nation was composed of people from a variety of backgrounds and traditions. It was not a very diverse group in the beginning (most were from the British Isles), but it would become more so. Moreover, Europeans', and Africans', roots in North America did not reach nearly as deep or firmly into the earth as they did in Europe, Africa, and other lands around the world. To compensate for the lack of historical time of settlement and the absence of ancient local heroes, the invention of traditions and the marking of important occasions in the life of the new nation were crucial in creating a shared bond of tradition and a sense of common belonging to a relatively new homeland through the shared experience of celebrating common holidays. As more and diverse peoples migrated to the United States, it became even more important to celebrate significant annual anniversaries.

U.S. Government and Major Political Parties

According to a document titled *Our American Government*, the United States is "a federal, representative, democratic republic, an indivisible union of 50 sovereign states. With the exception of town meetings, a form of pure democracy, we have at the local, state, and national levels a government which is: 'federal' because power is shared among these three levels; 'democratic' because the people govern themselves and have the means to control the government; and 'republic' because the people choose elected delegates by free and secret ballot."

The earliest influences on the U.S. form of government—a democratic republic—come from ancient Greece and Rome. The ancient capital of Greece, Athens, employed a system of government called *demokratia*— from *demos*, meaning "people," and *kratos*, meaning "power." From this derives American democracy, though Athenian democracy was quite different. In ancient Athens, every citizen—every adult man, that is—was expected not only to vote, but also to take a direct role in the government at some point in his life. Instead of electing people to represent them in the legislature, for example, citizens chose government leaders from amongst themselves by lottery. In comparison, the U.S. system of representative democracy is more like an oligarchy—rule by an elite few. The Founding Fathers preferred the example of the Greek city-state of Sparta, whose government consisted of two kings whose powers were limited by councils called *ephors* (meaning "overseers"), and whose members were citizens elected each year. *Ephors* had executive, legislative, and judicial powers. The kings generally served as military commanders and religious heads as well.

The Founding Fathers framed the republican aspect of the government from the model of the ancient Roman Republic. The term "republic" comes from the Latin *res publica*, which means "public affair." The Roman Republic provided the Fathers the closest historical analogy to what they hoped to create—a governmental system that balanced the separated powers of the executive, legislative, and judicial branches with the powers of the individual state and local governments.

The Fathers looked not just to ancient examples of government, but also to the English form of government with which, after all, they were most familiar. England had its own revolution in 1688 which resulted in a Bill of Rights and a more powerful Parliament, including a House of Commons to represent ordinary Englishmen. The framers of the Constitution borrowed aspects of that system and created the legislative branch of government, Congress, which consists of the Senate and the House of Representatives.

The term "Founding Fathers" refers to the men who drafted and signed the Constitution of the United States. (See the Appendix for a list of their names.)

An overriding influence was the ideals of the Enlightenment, or Age of Reason. Scientific and philosophical developments in 17th- and 18th-century Europe and America created an intellectual climate in which such ideas as rationalism (the use of human reasoning ability to understand the world and improve the human condition), religious toleration, and secularism (separating church and state) were dominant. Some of the most important Enlightenment ideas that informed the framers included English philosopher John Locke's view that government should be a social contract among the people. Locke influenced the political philosophy of French statesman and philosopher Charles Montesquieu, who proposed the separation of powers in a government, which found practical expression in the Constitution. (*For more on American government since Independence, see* **Citizenship Day**.)

Seat of Government

The first seat of American government was Independence Hall in Philadelphia, Pennsylvania, where the Continental Congress approved the Declaration of Independence in 1776 and the Constitution in 1787. The government moved to New York during the Revolutionary War, then back to Philadelphia before moving to its new home, the District of Columbia.

It wasn't until 1800, 17 years after America won independence from Britain, that the new country had a permanent capital city. In 1791 President George Washington approved the plan for the 100-square-mile city to be located along the Potomac River, borrowing land from the states of Maryland and Virginia. Washington hired Pierre Charles L'Enfant, who had served under him as a major during the Revolutionary War, to design the city that became Washington, D.C.

Major Political Parties — Brief History and Symbols

In the early years of the United States, political parties quickly evolved into a hallmark of U.S. democracy. They are organizations that people join on the basis of their opinions about the best way to govern the country. The Democratic Party and the Republican Party have been the two most powerful political parties in the United States since the 1860s, though the Green Party, the Reform Party, and independents—people who don't align themselves with any political party—also represent the voting public.

The United States has the distinction of being the first country in the world to elect its national leaders from people belonging to nationwide political parties. Today modern democracies around the world typically operate through the competition—and sometimes coalition—of a number of political parties. While there have been dozens of political parties in the United States, the sections below offer a brief history of the parties that have elected members to the presidency throughout American history.

Federalist Party

The first Federalists were members of the Constitutional Convention of 1787-88. They favored a Constitution that would provide a strong federal government and encourage the development of industry. Alexander Hamilton, James Madison, and John Jay detailed their case in *The Federalist Papers*, which originally appeared as 85 essays in newspapers between 1787 and 1788. The party formed after the Federalists were largely successful in drafting the Constitution they envisioned. By the 1820s, however, the Federalist Party had lost power to the Democratic-Republican Party.

Only the first two presidents were members of the Federalist Party: George Washington (1789-97) and John Adams (1797-1801).

Democratic-Republican Party

The men who eventually formed this party opposed the Federalists' Constitution and policies. Early on, they were known as Anti-Federalists or Republicans, and they included Patrick Henry and George Clinton. Thomas Jefferson became the leader of this movement, whose philosophy is known as Jeffersonian democracy. The Democratic-Republicans favored a more decentralized government that provided more state and local control. This, in Jefferson's thinking, would give more political power to the small farming communities to which the majority of American citizens belonged. In 1798 the party settled on the name Democratic-Republicans. By the 1830s they were known as Democrats.

Four presidents were members of the Democratic-Republican Party: Thomas Jefferson (1801-09), James Madison (1809-17), James Monroe (1817-25), and John Quincy Adams (1825-29).

Democratic Party

The Democratic Party is the continuation of the anti-Federalist Democratic-Republicans; members officially changed its name in the 1840s. The Democrats have been known as the party of the "common man," a phrase that illustrates members' concerns with working people and minorities.

Fifteen presidents have been members of the Democratic Party. The first was Andrew Jackson (1829-37). The most recent Democratic president was Bill Clinton (1993-2001).

Symbols of Major American Political Parties — Elephant and Donkey

The symbols of the Republican and Democratic Parties came about in the 19th century. Both the Democratic donkey and Republican elephant were popularized by the political cartoonist Thomas Nast (1840-1902), a contributor to *Harper's Weekly*. Nast is credited with *creating* only the Republican elephant, however.

The donkey symbol first appeared as a Democratic mascot nearly 50 years before Nast's cartoons. It was the 1828 presidential campaign of Democrat Andrew Jackson, whose campaign slogan was "Let the people rule." Jackson had a reputation for stubbornness—a trait not lost on those who disagreed with him. Jackson's political opponents called him a jackass. In response, Jackson gamely adopted the donkey as his campaign symbol. Jackson won the presidency that year, and the label stuck. Newspapers and political commentary continued to employ the donkey as a symbol of Jackson during his tenure.

In 1874 Thomas Nast brought the Republican elephant and Democratic donkey to life together in his drawings for *Harper's*. Their first joint appearance was in a cartoon based on a wild hoax. That year the *New York Herald* published a story that claimed all the animals in the Central Park Zoo had broken out and were roaming freely all over the park. It so happened that the *Herald* sympathized with the Democratic Party and had been printing editorials warning of the dangers if Republican president Ulysses S. Grant ran for a third term. (This was before the 22nd Amendment to the Constitution limited a president to two terms.)

Nast was a Republican. He drew a cartoon depicting the zoo animals running around Central Park. In the cartoon, a donkey wearing a lion skin scares and chases the other animals, including an elephant wearing a sign "Republican voters." Nast's audience knew from his other cartoons that the donkey stood for the Democratic-leaning *Herald* newspaper. The association between the elephant and the Republicans and between the donkey and the Democrats lingered in readers' minds, and soon other cartoonists began using the symbolism as well.

Eventually both parties accepted the animal symbols created by Nast. The Republican Party even took the step of officially designating the elephant its symbol.

STRANGER THINGS HAVE HAPPENED.
HOLD ON, AND YOU MAY WALK OVER THE SLUGGISH ANIMAL UP THERE YET.

One of Thomas Nast's political cartoons depicts the Democratic donkey and the Republican elephant. It appeared in the December 27, 1879, issue of Harper's Weekly.

Whig Party

The Whig Party organized in the 1830s in opposition to Democrat Andrew Jackson's presidency. Members adopted the name of the major political party in England that advocated more rights for British citizens and less power for the king. The American Whigs hoped to win more rights for the states, prevent the National Bank of the United States from being dissolved, and secure government programs to develop the West and build more infrastructure, such as roads and canals. The Whig Party collapsed by the 1850s, and its members joined other parties.

Four presidents were members of the Whig Party: William H. Harrison (1841), John Tyler (1841-45), Zachary Taylor (1849-50), and Millard Fillmore (1850-53).

Republican Party

Although known as the "Grand Old Party" (GOP), the Republican Party is actually the youngest of the major American political parties. It formed in the mid-1850s as a coalition of abolitionists, former Whig Party members, proponents of free settlement of the West, and others. Historically, the Republican Party has stood for less government interference in corporate life and the lives of individual people.

The party's birthplace is a matter of some dispute. According to the Republican Party, the first "official" Republican meeting took place in Jackson, Michigan, on July 6, 1854. The first "unofficial" gathering occurred in Ripon, Wisconsin, on March 20, 1854. Other towns claiming status as the birthplace of the party include Crawfordsville, Iowa, and Exeter, New Hampshire.

Twenty presidents have been members of the Republican Party. The first member of the party to be elected president was Abraham Lincoln (1861-65). The most recent Republican president was George W. Bush (2001-).

America and Its Patriotic Symbols

The American's Creed

I believe in the United States of America as a government of the people, by the people, for the people; whose just powers are derived from the consent of the governed; a democracy in a republic, a sovereign nation of many sovereign states; a perfect union, one and inseparable; estab-

lished upon those principles of freedom, equality, justice, and humanity for which American patriots sacrificed their lives and fortunes.

I therefore believe it is my duty to my country to love it, to support its Constitution; to obey its laws; to respect its flag; and to defend it against all enemies.

Less well known than the Pledge of Allegiance (*see* **Flag Day**), the Creed contains the basic ideas in the Declaration of Independence and the Preamble to the Constitution. It was the winning entry in a national contest in 1918. William Tyler Page of Maryland, an employee at Congress, was the author. Page served in the elected post of Clerk of the House of Representatives from 1919 to 1931.

Cornucopia

The cornucopia, or horn of plenty, is more often associated with the fall harvest and **Thanksgiving**. But the horn filled with fruits and vegetables frequently appeared in early American prints and paintings symbolizing the material and spiritual abundance of the new nation.

Eagle

The American bald eagle is the national bird. Congress officially designated it as such in 1782 when it finalized the design of the Great Seal. Eagles have served as a symbol of strength and nobility for many peoples around the world. Members of Congress agreed that the national bird should be one that is native to this land. Thus, the bald eagle was proposed. Benjamin Franklin famously suggested the turkey, a

The American bald eagle is the national bird.

"more respectable" bird than the eagle, which he asserted to be "a bird of bad moral character," because it robs food from other birds and animals.

The bald eagle is not "bald" in the modern sense of the word as "hairless"; its name comes from the word "piebald," which means "marked with white." Experts estimate that from 25,000 to 50,000 bald eagles flourished when European settlers first came to North America in the

1600s. By 1967, however, there were so few eagles, they were placed on the endangered species list. Because of its protected status, the number of eagles increased from 417 in 1963 to more than 13,000 in 2000.

Flag

The first official U.S. flag had 13 stars arranged in a circle on a blue field and 13 alternating red and white stripes. The 13 stars and stripes symbolize the 13 colonies. Congress approved this flag on June 14, 1777, a date now commemorated as **Flag Day**. A popular misconception is that the colors of the flag have official meanings. Actually, Congress designated symbolic values to the red, white, and blue colors in the Great Seal (*see below*), which many transfer to the flag.

The Great Seal of the United States

The Great Seal of the United States took nearly six years and the handiwork of several designers to complete. The first committee began work on July 4, 1776, and the finishing touches were put on the final design on June 20, 1782, when Congress approved it. The Great Seal is officially in the care of the Secretary of State, who makes sure its imprint appears on treaties with foreign countries and other important documents, especially those pertaining to international relationships, the facades of U.S. embassies and consulates around the world, and on all U.S. coins and the $1 bill. The Great Seal affixed onto a document is intended to ensure that it is a genuine and official document of the United States.

This is the obverse of the first official Great Seal of the United States, approved by Congress on June 20, 1782.

The obverse, or front, of the Great Seal shows an American bald eagle holding 13 arrows in its left talon, symbolizing Congress's powers of war, and an olive branch with 13 olives and leaves in its right talon, symbolizing its powers of peace. The number 13 refers to the original 13 colonies. The eagle faces to his right, in accordance with heraldic tradition. The U.S. motto *E Pluribus Unum* is written on a banner which the eagle clutches in his beak. Over the eagle's chest is a red, white, and blue shield. In 1782, Secretary of Congress Charles Thomson explained that the red and white stripes "represent the several states . . . supporting a Chief [the blue background of the shield] which unites the whole and represents Congress." It was for the Great Seal that Congress approved symbolic meanings for the national colors: white for "purity and innocence," red for "valor and strength," and blue for "vigilance, perseverance, and justice." Above the eagle's head is the "constellation"—the cloud encircling 13 stars on a blue field. As in the starred field on the U.S. flag, the constellation indicates the United States as a new nation among nations, as a metaphorical new constellation in the sky. The front of the Great Seal also serves as the nation's coat of arms.

The reverse, or back, of the Great Seal has a mysterious single eye inside a triangle surrounded by light rays, hovering above an unfinished pyramid. This is the Eye of Providence alluded to in the motto above it: *Annuit Coeptis*, Latin for "It (the Eye of Providence, or God) is favorable to our undertakings" or "He favors our undertakings." The base of the pyramid is inscribed with the year of the nation's founding in Roman numerals. The banner along the bottom of the reverse reads *Novus Ordo Seclorum*, which is Latin for "a new order of the ages." Because of its more mystical symbolism, the reverse of the Seal has been called the Seal's spiritual side.

Liberty Bell

The Pennsylvania Assembly commissioned a bell for its State House in 1751 to mark the 50th anniversary of William Penn's Charter of Privileges. Craftsmen in London, England, made the bell and delivered it to Philadelphia, where officials hung it in the tower on June 7, 1752. The Liberty Bell was rung to summon members of the Assembly to meetings as well

The Liberty Bell has been moved several times, most recently in 2004 to a new specially built pavilion called the Liberty Bell Center at Independence National Historic Park.

as for patriotic occasions, such as **Independence Day** and George **Washington's Birthday**.

This beloved symbol, weighing in at 2,080 pounds and designed to sound an E-flat note, has been mostly silent since 1846, when it was rung to commemorate Washington's birthday and promptly cracked. But inscribed on the Bell is a message that carries without sound: "Proclaim liberty throughout all the land unto all the inhabitants thereof." This message comes from the biblical book of Leviticus (25:10).

Liberty Cap

This medallion, *Libertas Americana, depicts the American Liberty goddess with a small* pileus*-style liberty cap atop a pole. In 1783, Benjamin Franklin asked French artist Augustin Dupré to design the medallion in commemoration of the American Revolutionary War victories at Saratoga and Yorktown.*

Though largely forgotten today in the United States, the liberty cap was one of the most popular icons of the Revolutionary era. The liberty cap that appeared in colonial America usually resembled a Phrygian cap. In ancient Greek art this hat was often drawn on the heads of people from Phrygia, a land in what is now west central Turkey. Sometimes, too, the liberty cap looked more like a *pileus*, a cap dating from ancient Rome used to signify the freeing of a slave. Classical images such as these were familiar to educated colonials. Paul Revere was one, and he is likely to have been the first American to include the liberty cap in popular illustrations. From the 1760s through the Revolution, Americans put the liberty cap on flags, seals, and coins, and set it atop liberty trees and poles.

The liberty cap's fall from favor in the United States began after French radicals used it as a symbol in the French Revolution of 1789-93 and it became associated with the brutal violence of that era. Later, in the years after independence, the issue of slavery became a growing source of tension between the new states in the North and the South. With the war against British tyranny won, the association of the liberty cap with freedom from slavery grew more evident, particularly to pro-slavery Americans. As a result, the liberty cap as an American symbol became scarce.

One of the few contemporary reminders of this early American symbol is a natural formation in Yellowstone National Park. A hot spring cone at Mammoth Hot Springs is named "Liberty Cap" for its marked resemblance to the old cap. (To see a photo, go to http://www.nps.gov/yell/tours/mammoth/librtcap.htm)

RAISING THE LIBERTY POLE.
1776.

This engraving, titled Raising the Liberty Pole, shows some colonists raising a liberty pole while others in the background take down an image of King George III (left) and conduct a militia drill (center). John C. McRae created this engraving around 1875. He based it on a painting by Frederick A. Chapman.

Liberty Tree and Pole

In the heavily wooded lands of New England, trees have often been imbued with symbolic significance. Early colonists incorporated certain trees into important events in their shared political life. In 1683, for example, William Penn arranged peace with local Indians at what became known as the Treaty Elm tree. Around the same time, the colony of Massachusetts chose a design for a flag that featured a pine tree. In 1687, legend has it, colonists in Hartford, Connecticut, stowed their charter—which contained the laws by which they governed themselves—in an oak tree to protect it from the British; that tree became famous as the Charter Oak.

The first liberty tree as such emerged in the next century. On the morning of August 14, 1765, citizens hung a likeness of the devil on a tree in the Boston Commons. The "devil" held a copy of the new Stamp Act, which most colonists considered an unjust tax imposed by the British. Nearby hung an effigy of local resident Andrew Oliver. Oliver was to be the stamp distributor in Boston for the British. (*See* **Independence Day** *for more on the Stamp Act and the American Revolution.*)

The idea of using trees to protest against the British caught on throughout the colonies. Some used an actual tree, and some used a pole, reminiscent of the old maypole. Sometimes the colonists active in preserving their freedoms used the tree or pole as a gathering place to discuss strategy. Sometimes they hung effigies to make a symbolic public point. When war broke out, the British often purposely destroyed liberty trees and poles.

Some scholars have suggested ancient Roman origins for the liberty pole as well as a relationship to maypoles. Whatever the ultimate origins, liberty trees and poles were ubiquitous symbols of colonial resistance and freedom throughout the Revolutionary era and beyond. To this day the governor of Massachusetts issues a proclamation every year declaring August 14 as Liberty Tree Day to commemorate the Sons of Liberty meeting under the tree. And, though the Charter Oak died in 1856, legislators in Connecticut preserved its memory by designating it the state tree.

Some Americans have revived this tradition by planting new liberty trees as memorials to those who died in or responded to the attacks on September 11, 2001, as well as those serving in the armed forces (see **Patriot Day**).

Mottoes: E Pluribus Unum *and* In God We Trust

E Pluribus Unum is a Latin phrase meaning "out of many, one," referring to the union of the original 13 colonies. The motto appears in the Great Seal and on U.S. coins and currency. Historians trace the earliest occurrence of this motto to a magazine called the *Gentleman's Journal,* which was published in England from 1692 to 1694. It was adopted later by the *Gentleman's Magazine.* This magazine was published in London from 1731 to 1922, and was popular in the colonies.

Congress passed a joint resolution designating "In God we trust" as the U.S. national motto in 1956, and President Dwight D. Eisenhower signed it into law. The national motto also appears on coins and currency. The origin of the phrase is found in the national anthem, "The Star-Spangled Banner" (see below): "And this be our motto—'In God is our trust'."

Mount Rushmore

From 1927 to 1941 sculptor Gutzon Borglum, his son Lincoln, and almost 400 other people labored to create Mount Rushmore, a national monument to four presidents, carved out of a mountainside in the Black

Mount Rushmore contains the likenesses of George Washington, Thomas Jefferson, Theodore Roosevelt, and Abraham Lincoln. The sculpture is 60 feet high.

Hills of South Dakota. It was an incredibly dangerous job, but no lives were lost. Gutzon Borglum died in 1941, before his full vision for the site was completed. It was also to have included a Hall of Records, a chamber carved out of the mountain to hold the nation's most precious documents. In 1998 the National Park Service partially fulfilled Borglum's aim by installing at the entry to the incomplete chamber a vault containing porcelain enamel panels upon which are inscribed the words to the Declaration of Independence and the Constitution as well as a history of the monument's creation.

Borglum was chosen for the project in 1923, when Doane Robinson, state historian for South Dakota, proposed an idea to attract more tourists to the Black Hills. Robinson's plan was to carve likenesses of famous people from the Old West out of the Needles, tall granite formations in the area. After surveying the area, Borglum recommended instead that Mount Rushmore be the site of a larger monument with national, rather than local, significance.

Borglum decided to carve the images of four presidents who represented the birth and growth of the United States: George Washington for his leadership as the first president and commander of the Revolutionary War; Thomas Jefferson for organizing the Louisiana Purchase, which expanded the nation's boundaries; Abraham Lincoln for preserving the union and abolishing slavery; and Theodore Roosevelt, for his role in steering the country onto the 20th-century world stage.

The Name "America"

A little-known German clergyman was responsible for naming the newly discovered continents. Martin Waldseemüller (c. 1470-c.1518) was part of a small group of men in Saint-Dié, France, who published works with the new invention of the day, the printing press. One of the group read the *Mundus Novus* (c. 1502), a fantastical account of an exploration to the New World, and they all set out to publish a map that included the new lands. Waldseemüller decided that the new southern continent should be named "America," after the writer of the account, Amerigo Vespucci (1454-1512).

Vespucci began his career as a business manager for the powerful Renaissance Italian family, the Medicis. He moved to Seville, Spain, in the pivotal year of 1492, where his maritime interests took on new urgency. Scholars disagree on when Vespucci actually made his first voyage to the New World—he claimed to have landed in Brazil in 1497, before Christopher Columbus reached the continent—but most acknowledge that he was on a ship that sailed to Brazil in 1501 (*see also* **Columbus Day**).

In any case, Vespucci's sensational stories about the new southern continent reached all over Europe, thanks to the printing press. The Saint-Dié group's map—better known as the Waldseemüller map—reached thousands as well. Shortly afterward, Waldseemüller reconsidered naming the new continent after Vespucci and left off the name "America" from three later versions of the map. By that time, however, people had already accepted the name. In 1538 Gerardus Mercator produced his acclaimed world map. He showed the two new continents with the names "North America" and "South America."

Why "America" rather than "Amerigo"? It was customary to name things after women, and "America" is the feminine version of the name "Amerigo."

Martin Waldseemüller printed this map of the New World in 1507.

The National Anthem

The United States did not have an official national anthem until March 3, 1931, when President Herbert Hoover signed a congressional act into law that designated Francis Scott Key's "The Star-Spangled Banner" as the national anthem. What took so long? For one thing, "The Star-Spangled

Banner" was not especially popular around the country until the Civil War era. Songs such as "America the Beautiful," "Yankee Doodle," and "Hail Columbia" held firm places in the hearts of Americans. In 1889, however, the United States Navy made "The Star-Spangled Banner" its official song for morning flag-raisings. In 1917 the Army also incorporated the anthem into its ceremonies. The lobbying effort to make "The Star-Spangled Banner" the national anthem was led by the United States Daughters of 1812 and Congressman J. Charles Linthicum of Baltimore, Maryland. It took about 20 years of wrangling among competing favorites before "The Star-Spangled Banner" won out as the national anthem.

Francis Scott Key wrote the words to accompany the melody of an old English song, "To Anacreon in Heaven." Composed during the War of 1812, the poem was written by Key in the early morning hours of September 14, 1814, after he watched the battle at Fort McHenry, near Baltimore, Maryland.

Key was an attorney who had gone aboard a British ship to try to negotiate the release of an American prisoner. The British detained Key along with his companion, American officer John Skinner, to keep them out of the way because they planned to bomb Fort McHenry. Key watched the bombardment all night and was inspired to write the poem when he saw the flag flying over the still-standing fort at dawn.

Here are the complete lyrics:

> O say can you see, by the dawn's early light,
> What so proudly we hail'd at the twilight's last gleaming,
> Whose broad stripes and bright stars through the perilous fight
> O'er the ramparts we watch'd were so gallantly streaming?
> And the rocket's red glare, the bombs bursting in air,
> Gave proof through the night that our flag was still there,
> O say does that star-spangled banner yet wave
> O'er the land of the free and the home of the brave?
>
> On the shore dimly seen through the mists of the deep
> Where the foe's haughty host in dread silence reposes,
> What is that which the breeze, o'er the towering steep,
> As it fitfully blows, half conceals, half discloses?
> Now it catches the gleam of the morning's first beam,

In full glory reflected now shines in the stream,
'Tis the star-spangled banner—O long may it wave
O'er the land of the free and the home of the brave!

And where is that band who so vauntingly swore,
That the havoc of war and the battle's confusion
A home and a Country should leave us no more?
Their blood has wash'd out their foul footstep's pollution.
No refuge could save the hireling and slave
From the terror of flight or the gloom of the grave,
And the star-spangled banner in triumph doth wave
O'er the land of the free and the home of the brave.
O thus be it ever when freemen shall stand.

Between their lov'd home and the war's desolation!
Blest with vict'ry and peace may the heav'n rescued land
Praise the power that hath made and preserv'd us a nation!
Then conquer we must, when our cause it is just,
And this be our motto—"In God is our trust,"
And the star-spangled banner in triumph shall wave
O'er the land of the free and the home of the brave.

Statue of Liberty

The Statue of Liberty stands in New York Harbor on what was originally Bedloe's Island (in 1956 it was renamed Liberty Island). The statue itself is 151 feet tall, but the whole structure, including the pedestal, reaches 305 feet into the sky. The statue's grayish-green color comes from the fact that its surface was constructed using bright, gleaming copper sheets. Over time, weather turned the copper into the color seen today.

The people of France presented the people of the United States with the gift of the Statue of Liberty in 1886. The French wanted to commemorate the friendship between the two countries with a centennial anniversary present marking the American Declaration of Independence. Difficulties in fund-raising, however, delayed the gift by ten years. The statue's designer was Frédéric-Auguste Bartholdi. He called it *Liberty Enlightening the World*. Alexandre-Gustave Eiffel, who built the famous tower in Paris, constructed the iron framework for the statue.

The Statue of Liberty

The Statue of Liberty is 305 feet high from the ground to the tip of the torch. The date of American independence is inscribed in the tablet in her left hand. Her feet step upon the broken chains of bondage. Her crown's seven rays stand for the seven continents and seas of the earth. The Statue of Liberty stands in New York Harbor in view of Ellis Island, the first stop for millions of immigrants to the United States from 1892 to 1954. On the statue's pedestal is a plaque engraved with the words of poet Emma Lazarus's inspiring and hopeful "New Colossus":

Not like the brazen giant of Greek fame,
With conquering limbs astride from land to
    land,
Here at our sea-washed, sunset-gates shall stand
A mighty woman with a torch, whose flame
Is the imprisoned lightning, and her name
Mother of Exiles. From her beacon-hand
Glows world-wide welcome, her mild eyes
    command
The air-bridged harbor that twin-cities frame.

"Keep, ancient lands, your storied pomp!"
    cries she,
With silent lips. "Give me your tired, your poor,
Your huddled masses yearning to breathe free,
The wretched refuse of your teeming shore;
Send these, the homeless, tempest-tost to me,
I lift my lamp beside the golden door!"

November 2, 1883
Emma Lazarus

Artists have used figures of women to represent abstract ideals, such as purity or freedom, since ancient times. In fact, Liberty was an ancient Roman goddess of freedom—called Libertas in Latin. Earlier European artists also depicted America as an Indian woman. Later ones portrayed the nation as an idealized European woman. They have also called her Columbia (the female form of the last name of Christopher Columbus and Liberty (*see also* **Columbus Day**).

The Statue has been closed to the public twice: when it was restored in 1984-86 for its 100th anniversary, and after the attacks on September 11, 2001 (*see* **Patriot Day**), when officials feared it might be a terrorist target. The Statue of Liberty reopened in August 2004, but a glass enclosure now separates visitors from the crown and torch at the very top of the statue.

Uncle Sam

Uncle Sam has been an American symbol ever since his name was made up out of the initials "U.S." stamped onto meat barrels during the War of 1812. Samuel Wilson and his brother Ebenezer had a meat-packing business in Troy, New York. During the war they provided meat for the troops. It was delivered in barrels stamped "U.S." One of Wilson's workers enthusiastically spread the story that the "U.S." stood for "Uncle Sam," and the moniker stuck.

Around 1917, James Montgomery Flagg created this famous Army recruiting poster of the World War I era that depicted Uncle Sam.

Artist James Montgomery Flagg drew the most well known Uncle Sam—the tall, thin, white-haired and bearded man wearing a top hat and red, white, and blue suit. Flagg used himself as the model for his depiction.

Some historians believe that an earlier American folkloric character—Brother Jonathan—was the prototype for Uncle Sam. Jonathan, according to legend, is the son of John Bull, a personification of Britain.

"Yankee Doodle"

Scholars disagree about the exact origins of "Yankee Doodle," and it is likely the product of strands of folk songs from the Netherlands and England. The long-standing explanation for the song known today as "Yankee Doodle" is that it was a British song intended to denigrate Americans.

The Chorus from "Yankee Doodle"

Yankee doodle keep it up,
Yankee doodle dandy,
Mind the music and the step,
And with the girls be handy.

Many of the lyrics are attributed to Dr. Richard Schackburg, an English surgeon who served during the French and Indian Wars (1754-63). According to traditional lore, Schackburg wrote lyrics to the old folk tune in 1755. Twenty years later, British soldiers sang "Yankee Doodle" on their march toward Lexington and Concord, the first battle of the Revolutionary War in 1775. Americans, in turn, adopted the song after their first successes of the war.

Yellow Ribbons

Americans first tied yellow ribbons around trees during the hostage crisis of 1979-81. On November 4, 1979, Iranian revolutionary students took all personnel of the U.S. Embassy in Tehran hostage. From all accounts, it was Penne Laingen, the wife of the Embassy's chargé d'affaires Bruce Laingen, who began the custom by tying a yellow ribbon around a large oak tree in their yard, then spread the idea through television interviews, newspaper columns, and a newsletter for the families of the hostages. Soon yellow ribbons dotted the American landscape.

The idea came from a song popular during the 1970s, "Tie a Yellow Ribbon 'Round the Ole Oak Tree," written by Irwin Levine and L. (Larry) Russell Brown in 1972 and recorded by Tony Orlando and Dawn in 1973. Historians have found earlier songs with similar themes and images, for example, "Round Her Neck She Wears a Yeller Ribbon (For Her Lover Who Is Fur, Fur Away)," copyrighted by George A. Norton in 1917. A variation of this song provided the theme song for the 1949 film, *She Wore a Yellow Ribbon*, directed by John Ford and starring John Wayne.

The story in the song "Tie a Yellow Ribbon," and the earlier versions of the story, have a newly released prisoner riding home on a bus or a train. The prisoner has asked his family, or girlfriend, to tie a ribbon or handkerchief around a nearby tree if they will welcome him back home. How a symbol for forgiving a loved one for his transgressions became a symbol for holding vigil for innocent loved ones being held hostage or brave loved ones off at war remains unclear. But the theme common to both situations is resolve in the face of captivity, whether just or unjust.

The ribbons returned in the winter of 1990-91 when the United States led a U.N. coalition in a war to force Iraq's Saddam Hussein to retreat after his

invasion of neighboring Kuwait. In 2003 yellow ribbons once again began appearing on trees—as well as on homes, businesses, and vehicles—across the country as Americans waited for their loved ones to return from wars in Afghanistan and Iraq. These days the ribbons are also red, white, and blue, in addition to yellow. There are also now signs and magnets in ribbon shape.

Since the hostage crisis in Iran from 1979 to 1981, Americans have used yellow ribbons as a symbol of holding vigil for loved ones in dangerous situations overseas.

Web Sites

American Folklife Center of the Smithsonian Institution has a web page on yellow ribbons at http://www.loc.gov/folklife/ribbons/

Democratic Party's official web site is at http://www.democrats.org/

Independence Hall Association gives information about Independence Hall and the Liberty Bell at http://www.ushistory.org

Library of Congress online exhibits:

"American Women: 'With Peace and Freedom Blest!' Woman as Symbol in America, 1590-1800" at http://memory.loc.gov/ammem/awhhtml/aw05e/aw05e.html

"The Star-Spangled Banner" and "Yankee Doodle" at http://www.loc .gov/rr/perform/ihas/ihashome.html (click "Patriotic Melodies")

LOC.GOV (Library of Congress) Wise Guide. "How Did America Get Its Name?" July 2003. Online at http://www.loc.gov/wise guide/america.html

National Anthem Project, sponsored by the National Association for Music Education, promotes "The Star-Spangled Banner" at http://www .thenationalanthemproject.org

National Park Service offers web sites on U.S. national parks and monuments, including:

Fort McHenry at http://www.nps.gov/fomc/

History of Washington, D.C., at http://www.cr.nps.gov/nr/travel/wash/lenfant.htm

Independence Hall at http://www.nps.gov/inde/home.htm

Mount Rushmore at http://www.nps.gov/moru/

Republican Party's official web site is at http://www.gop.com

Smithsonian Institution's National Museum of American History has an online exhibit on the Flag and "The Star-Spangled Banner" at http://americanhistory.si.edu/ssb/

"Symbols of U.S. Government" pages at Ben's Guide to U.S. Government, a web site of the U.S. Government Printing Office at http://bensguide.gpo .gov/3-5/symbols/index.html

U.S. State Department's Bureau of International Information Programs provides numerous articles by experts on American history and political system at http://usinfo.state.gov/products/pubs/election04/ and at http://usinfo.state.gov/products/pubs/democracy/

White House Historical Association produces educational materials, programs, online exhibits, videos, the *White House History Journal*, and a book, *The White House: An Historic Guide* (20th edition, 1999) at http://www.whitehousehistory.org

Sources for Further Reading

Bateman, Teresa. *Red, White, Blue, and Uncle Who? The Stories Behind Some of America's Patriotic Symbols*. New York: Holiday House, 2003. For young adults.

Bodnar, John, ed. *Bonds of Affection: Americans Define Their Patriotism*. Princeton, N.J.: Princeton University Press, 1996.

Harden, J. David. "Liberty Caps and Liberty Trees." *Past & Present* 146 (February 1995): 66-102.

Horwitz, Elinor Lander. *The Bird, the Banner, and Uncle Sam: Images of America in Folk and Popular Art*. Philadelphia: J. B. Lippincott, 1976.

Kennedy, Caroline. *A Patriot's Handbook: Songs, Poems, Stories and Speeches Celebrating the Land We Love*. New York: Hyperion, 2003.

Ketchum, Alton. "The Search for Uncle Sam." *History Today* 40, 4 (April 1990): 20-26.

Kroll, Steven. *By the Dawn's Early Light: The Story of the Star Spangled Banner*. New York: Scholastic, 2000. For young adults.

Marcovitz, Hal. *The Liberty Bell*. Philadelphia: Mason Crest Publishers, 2003. For young adults.

Molotsky, Irvin. *The Flag, the Poet and the Song: The Story of the Star-Spangled Banner*. New York: Dutton, 2001.

Murray, Stuart. *America's Song: The Story of 'Yankee Doodle'*. Bennington, Vt.: Images from the Past, 1999.

Our Flag [52-page booklet]. Washington, D.C.: Joint Committee on Printing, U.S. Congress, 2003. Online through the Federal Citizen Information Center at http://www.pueblo.gsa.gov/cic_test/misc/ourflag/titlepage.htm

Patriotism in America. Issue of *CQ Researcher* 9, 24 (June 25, 1999): 547-67.

Schlesinger, Arthur M., Jr., ed. *History of U.S. Political Parties*. 5 vols. Philadelphia: Chelsea House Publishers, 2002. For young adults.

Trachtenberg, Marvin. *The Statue of Liberty*. London: Penguin Books, 1976.

U.S. Department of State, Bureau of Public Affairs. *The Great Seal of the United States*. Washington, D.C., September 1996. Online in PDF format at http://www.state.gov/www/publications/great_seal.pdf

U.S. House of Representatives. Joint Committee on Printing. *Our American Government*. 106th Congress, 2d sess., 2000. H. Doc. 106-216. Online at http://www.access.gpo.gov/congress/house/

Armed Forces Day

Date Established by Presidential Proclamation: February 27, 1950

Date Observed: Third Saturday in May

Armed Forces Day was established as a national observance by President Harry S. Truman in his presidential proclamation of February 27, 1950. Truman's proclamation designated one day each year to honor all branches of the U.S. military: the National Guard, the Army, the Navy, the Marine Corps, the Coast Guard, and the Air Force. The purpose of the new day was to remember the unification of all the military branches under the Department of Defense in 1949. Before that, each branch of the military had had its own day of commemoration. The Army, Navy, Marines, and the Coast Guard continue to mark their individual days in addition to Armed Forces Day. In 1999 Congress designated May as National Military Appreciation Month.

Overview of the Armed Forces

National Guard

The National Guard's roots go back to the Massachusetts Bay Colony, where the first organized volunteer militia was established on December 13, 1636. The famed Minute Men of the Revolutionary War evolved out of these early New England militias. The militias, or national guards, were established in the U.S. Constitution under Article 1, Section 8 (*see Appendix*). In 1903 Congress passed a law establishing the National Guard as the Army's main reserve force. In 1916 the National Defense Act provided regular paychecks for the force, which until then had been largely volunteer.

The National Guard formally became part of the U.S. Army in 1933. The Air National Guard was instituted in 1947 as part of the U.S. Air Force. Today National Guard troops serve in the Army and the Air Force, and each state has its own National Guards.

To the Guards is entrusted a unique double role among the armed forces, as established in the U.S. Constitution and protected in the Second Amendment. When the nation is at peace, the state governors are the commanders-in-chief of their respective Guard units. State governors may activate National Guards in times of local disasters, such as devastating storms and large riots. But when the nation is at war, the president of the United States assumes command of the National Guard, and National Guard units must be prepared to fight overseas with full-time Army and Air Force troops. The Air National Guard has the additional mission of protecting U.S. air space.

Creed: "I Am the Guard"

Civilian in Peace, Soldier in War . . . of security and honor for three centuries I have been the custodian . . . I am the Guard!

At Concord's bridge, I fired the fateful shot heard 'round the world. I bled on Bunker Hill. My footprints marked the snows at Valley Forge. With Washington on the heights of Yorktown, I saw the sword surrendered . . . I am the Guard. These things I know—I was there! I saw both sides of the War Between the States—I was there! The hill at San Juan felt the fury of my charge; the far plains and mountains of the Philippines echoed to my shout. In France the dark forests of the Argonne blazed with my barrage; Chateau-Thierry crumbled to my cannonade.

I am the Guard. I bowed briefly on the grim road at Bataan. Through the jungles and on the beaches I fought the enemy . . . beat, battered, and broke him. I scrambled over Normandy's beaches—I was there! I flew MiG Alley to the Yalu—I am the Guard! I fought in the skies above Vietnam—I was there! In the skies and on the ground, I made the Arabian desert feel the fury of the storm. I am the Guard!

Civilian in peace, soldier in war . . . the stricken have known the comfort of my skill. I have faced forward to the tornado, the typhoon, and the horror of the hurricane and the flood. I saw the tall towers fall—I was there!

"I Am the Guard," Courtesy National Guard Bureau

*I am the Guard. For three centuries the custodian of security and honor,
   now and forever . . . I am the Guard.*

Song: "I Guard America"

The National Guard song, "I Guard America," was written by country
music artist James Rogers in 1990 in honor of the Tennessee National
Guard, in which he served during the 1970s. In August 1998, the Enlisted
Association of the National Guard of the United States designated "I
Guard America" its official song. The chief of the National Guard and the
directors of the Army and Air National Guards have also endorsed the
song for its reflection of the Guards' heritage since the Revolutionary War.

Active Duty: *See under* Army and Air Force

Army

The U.S. Army was originally known as the Continental
Army. The Continental Congress established the Army
on June 14, 1775—the same day it designated the American flag—and called on George Washington to be its
first general and commander-in-chief (*see also* **Flag Day**).
With this act, the colonies joined to provide a unified
defense against the British (*for more on the Revolution,
see* **Independence Day**). The special mission of the Army
is to conduct military operations on land.

The Army Seal

In addition to observing Armed Forces Day, the Army has its
own annual commemoration. Army Day was originally May 1 in
1928; that date was intended to counter the May Day holiday created in the
former Soviet Union to celebrate communism. In 1929, however, Army Day
was changed to April 6, the date the United States entered World War I.

Army Birthday

Many bases celebrate the Army's birthday on or around June 14 each year.
Senior officers hold a twilight "tattoo" (a festive military evening event
with music and drills), a wreath-laying ceremony at Arlington National
Cemetery, and a cake-cutting ceremony at the Pentagon, in which the oldest and youngest soldiers join with senior staff in cutting the cake. There
is also a formal Birthday Ball at a Washington hotel. Bases around the
nation and the world hold their own events, which can include formal

balls, cake-cutting ceremonies, sporting events, concerts, and other special activities.

Creed: "The Soldier's Creed"

I am an American Soldier.

I am a Warrior and a member of a team. I serve the people of the United States and live the Army Values.

I will always place the mission first.

I will never accept defeat.

I will never quit.

I will never leave a fallen comrade.

I am disciplined, physically and mentally tough, trained and proficient in my warrior tasks and drills. I always maintain my arms, my equipment and myself.

I am an expert and I am a professional.

I stand ready to deploy, engage, and destroy the enemies of the United States of America in close combat.

I am a guardian of freedom and the American way of life.

I am an American soldier.

Song: "The Army Goes Rolling Along"

This song was written in 1908 by a young first lieutenant serving in the Philippines. Edmund Louis "Snitz" Gruber came up with the lyrics while marching through the Zambales mountains with his battalion. Gruber was a descendant of Franz Gruber, who co-wrote "Silent Night." The original title of this song was "The Caissons Go Rolling Along." A caisson was a horse-drawn wagon used to carry ammunition. Gruber's field composition proved immediately popular with the troops. In 1917 some army officers commissioned John Philip Sousa to turn the song into a march. In 1956 some lyrics were changed. It was retitled "The Army Goes Rolling Along," and the Army adopted it as its official song.

Active Duty

495,472 (as of April 30, 2005)
  73,343 were women (as of September 30, 2004)
127,585 were Army National Guard and Army Reserve
      (as of June 15, 2005)

"The Soldier's Creed," Courtesy U.S. Army

Navy

The Continental Congress created the Continental Navy on October 13, 1775. Its first mission was to send two ships to scout and intercept British munitions supply ships. Congress disbanded the Continental Navy after the Revolutionary War. But a few years later, in 1789, the Constitution authorized the reestablishment of the Navy. The Navy's mission is to maintain forces on the seas.

The Navy Emblem

Navy Birthday

The Navy celebrates the Navy Birthday on October 13. In addition, in 1922 the Navy League began a Navy Day observance on October 27 to commemorate the birthday of President Theodore Roosevelt, a former Assistant Secretary of the Navy and advocate for the branch.

Naval bases around the United States and the world hold their own events for the Navy Birthday. Events often include a formal ball and dinner and the cutting of the traditional Navy birthday cake, shared by the youngest and oldest sailors present. Other ceremonies include a flag raising, the playing of the national anthem, and the placing of uniform hats from all branches of the military on a table to symbolize those who have lost their lives in service. The attack on the Navy destroyer USS *Cole* occurred the day before the Navy Birthday in 2000, cancelling planned events. The celebration in 2001 came a month after the September 11 attacks (*see* **Patriot Day**). Commemorations that year were not cancelled, but they were subdued and less formal.

Fleet Week

Several ports along the East and West coasts of the United States hold Fleet Week around the Navy's birthday in October. These events pay tribute to sailors, and they also help familiarize civilians with naval life.

(*For more details, see Observances map below. For Fleet Week in New York, see* **Memorial Day** *observances.*)

Creed: "The Sailor's Creed"

I am a United States Sailor.

I will support and defend the Constitution of the United States of America and I will obey the orders of those appointed over me.

I represent the fighting spirit of the Navy and those who have gone before me to defend freedom and democracy around the world.

I proudly serve my country's Navy combat team with Honor, Courage and Commitment.

I am committed to excellence and the fair treatment of all.

Song: "Anchors Aweigh"

The Navy's official song was originally written to be a football fight song. Midshipman Alfred Hart Miles and his fellow students at the Naval Academy wanted a new cheering song for the upcoming Army-Navy football game in December 1906. Miles asked Naval Academy Band leader Lieutenant Charles A. Zimmerman for his help, and the two wrote "Anchors Aweigh." Navy won the game that year.

The expression "anchors aweigh" refers to the lifting of a ship's anchor from the bottom of the sea, enabling it to sail.

Active Duty

364,504 (as of April 30, 2005)
  54,248 were women (as of September 30, 2004)
    3,338 were Naval Reserve (as of June 15, 2005)

Marine Corps

The Continental Congress established the Continental Marines on November 10, 1775. After the Revolutionary War, Congress relieved the Marines, along with the Navy, of duty, only to reinstitute the force on July 11, 1798, as the United States Marine Corps.

The Marines are called "the few" because they are the smallest force of the U.S. military. They are also, however, usually the first to be deployed. Their mission is to be ever battle ready as a U.S. expeditionary force on land, air, and sea.

"The Sailor's Creed," Courtesy U.S. Navy

Marine Corps Birthday

The Marine Corps observed its birthday on the July 11 date with little or no fanfare until 1921, when officers decided to change the date back to the date of its founding, November 10, and to do so with special events. Like other branches of the military, a favorite custom is the cutting of the birthday cake. In the Marines the youngest and oldest present share in the cutting honors after which the oldest gets the first piece of cake and the youngest gets the second. What is unique about the Marine cake is its shape: it is designed to look like the Tun Tavern in Philadelphia, the traditional birthplace of the Marines.

Many commands hold a formal birthday ball at which a Marine reads the original orders for the commemoration, a band plays "The Marines' Hymn," and all enjoy a banquet and the cake. During times of war, however, the celebrations are more somber.

The Marine Corps Emblem

Motto

Semper Fidelis or *Semper Fi*, Latin for "always faithful."

Creed: "My Rifle — The Creed of a United States Marine"

1. *This is my rifle. There are many like it, but this one is mine.*

2. *My rifle is my best friend. It is my life. I must master it as I must master my life.*

3. *My rifle, without me, is useless. Without my rifle, I am useless. I must fire my rifle true. I must shoot straighter than my enemy who is trying to kill me. I must shoot him before he shoots me. I will . . .*

4. *My rifle and myself know that what counts in this war is not the rounds we fire, the noise of our burst, nor the smoke we make. We know that it is the hits that count. We will hit . . .*

5. *My rifle is human, even as I, because it is my life. Thus, I will learn it as a brother. I will learn its weaknesses, its strength, its parts, its accessories, its sights and its barrel. I will ever guard it against the ravages of weather and damage as I will ever guard my legs, my arms, my eyes and my heart against damage. I will keep my rifle clean and ready. We will become part of each other. We will . . .*

"My Rifle — The Creed of a United States Marine," Courtesy U.S. Marine Corps

6. Before God, I swear this creed. My rifle and myself are the defenders of my country. We are the masters of our enemy. We are the saviors of my life.

7. So be it, until victory is America's and there is no enemy, but peace!!

Song: "The Marines' Hymn"

According to the Marine Corps, the lyricist of the Marines' official song is unknown, but tradition has it that a Marine serving in the Mexican-American War of 1846-48 wrote the first verse. A Library of Congress article attributes at least one verse to a Colonel Henry C. Davis in the early 20th century. The famous opening line evokes the Mexican-American War—"the halls of Montezuma"—and the Tripolitan War of 1801-5—"the shores of Tripoli." The melody was adapted from a comic opera *Genevieve de Brabant*, composed by Jacques Offenbach (1819-1880), which debuted in a Paris theater in 1859. It is customary for Marines to pen a new verse for the Hymn for each military mission they are assigned.

Active Duty

177,380 (as of April 30, 2005)
  10,779 were women (as of September 30, 2004)
   9,291 were Marine Corps Reserve (as of June 15, 2005)

Coast Guard

On August 4, 1790, Congress established what eventually became the U.S. Coast Guard. In those days, it was called the Revenue Service, the Revenue Marine, or the system of cutters. The force's mission was to thwart smugglers and ensure that merchant ships paid customs fees. In 1915 Congress passed a law that officially created the U.S. Coast Guard and moved the U.S. Life-Saving Service into its domain. Today the Coast Guard's mission is to provide maritime safety and rescue as well as the national defense of U.S. waterways. It also contributes to the protection of natural marine resources.

Coast Guard Day

The Coast Guard celebrates its birthday on August 4 with birthday cake, band music, speeches, and giving awards for notable service. In Grand

Haven, Michigan, citizens honor the Coast Guard each year on its birthday with what is reputed to be the largest civilian festival for any branch of the military. Located on the shores of Lake Michigan, Grand Haven was home to an early Coast Guard life-saving station and the cutter *Escanaba* (lost during World War II) and has been celebrating the Guard since 1924. For more details, see under Observances below.

Creed: "Creed of the United States Coast Guardsman"

I am proud to be a United States Coast Guardsman.

I revere that long line of expert seamen who by their devotion to duty and sacrifice of self have made it possible for me to be a member of a service honored and respected, in peace and in war, throughout the world.

I never, by word or deed, will bring reproach upon the fair name of my service, nor permit others to do so unchallenged.

I will cheerfully and willingly obey all lawful orders.

I will always be on time to relieve, and shall endeavor to do more, rather than less, than my share.

I will always be at my station, alert and attending to my duties.

I shall, so far as I am able, bring to my seniors solutions, not problems.

I shall live joyously, but always with due regard for the rights and privileges of others.

I shall endeavor to be a model citizen in the community in which I live.

I shall sell life dearly to an enemy of my country, but give it freely to rescue those in peril.

With God's help, I shall endeavor to be one of His noblest Works . . .

A United States Coast Guardsman.

Song: "Semper Paratus"

Latin for "always ready," "Semper Paratus" is also the branch's motto. In 1927 the Coast Guard organized a competition to find a branch anthem. A Coast Guardsman serving in the Bering Sea Forces composed the winning entry, "Semper Paratus." Legend has it that Captain Francis Saltus Van Boskerck pounded out the tune on what was the only piano in Alaska. Two

The Coast Guard Emblem

"Creed of the United States Coast Guardsman," Courtesy U.S. Coast Guard

friends, dentists Alfred E. Nannestad and Joseph O. Fournier, helped Van Boskerck write the lyrics. Over the years, a few Coast Guardsmen have changed some of the lyrics, but "Semper Paratus" remains the Coast Guard song, motto, "pledge," and "guide."

Active Duty

40,173 (as of April 30, 2005)
(figures for women not provided by U.S. Coast Guard or
      Department of Defense)
  579 were Coast Guard Reserve (as of June 15, 2005)

Air Force

On July 27, 1947, President Harry S. Truman signed the National Security Act into law. That law officially created a separate Department of the Air Force and became effective on September 18, 1947. Prior to that, the U.S. aviation force was part of the Army and called the Army Air Force. The earliest military air program began in 1907 with an Aeronautical Division under the U.S. Army Signal Corps. This division possessed eight balloons and one small dirigible. American aviation power developed gradually over the 20th century, from its first plane in 1908 to the sophisticated air fleet of today. The mission of the Air Force is to defend the United States and its interests through forces in air and space.

Air Force Coat of Arms

President Truman designated August 1 as Air Force Day in 1947, but the observance was short-lived. After the creation of Armed Forces Day in 1949, the Air Force no longer commemorated Air Force Day.

Song: "U.S. Air Force Song (Off We Go)"

The "U.S. Air Force Song," like the Coast Guard song, was the result of a nationwide competition. In 1938 the magazine *Liberty* sponsored the song-writing contest. The wives of airmen chose the "U.S. Air Force Song" from among some 600 entries. The composer was Robert Crawford (1899-1961), a singer and pilot. The *Apollo 15* flight in 1971 carried Crawford's sheet music to the moon and back.

Active Duty:

360,578 (as of April 30, 2005)
  73,786 were women (as of September 30, 2004)
  12,343 were Air National Guard and Air Force Reserve
      (as of June 15, 2005)

Reserves

Like the National Guard, the Reserve forces are also citizen soldiers, but unlike the National Guard, the Reserves' role is to supplement the federal U.S. military branches.

Observances

Many military bases around the nation open their doors to the public on Armed Forces Day in an effort to familiarize civilian Americans with the U.S. defense system. The president of the United States issues a presidential proclamation at least once a term to encourage Americans to attend Armed Forces Day activities and events and to appreciate the service of the men and women in uniform. The president also may visit a military base on this day to give a speech conveying the nation's recognition of its armed forces.

A Sampling of Observances

1. **San Francisco, California:** Fleet Week takes place during the second week in October. The celebration, held since the 1980s, includes an air show, usually featuring the Navy's Blue Angels, a parade of ships (which visitors can tour), fireworks, and concerts. Contact Fleet Week San Francisco at SFFLEETWEEK@aol.com, http://fleetweek.us/fleetweek

2. **Torrance, California:** Since 1960 the city has organized an Armed Forces Day Parade. Other events include flyovers and military displays. Contact City of Torrance Traffic and Special Events Division, 310-618-5695.

3. **San Diego, California:** Fleet Week events occur from late September to late October and include ship and plane parades, ship tours, salutes, concerts, fireworks, and special ceremonies. Contact Fleet Week San Diego at 800-FLEETWEEK (353-3893), http://www.fleetweeksandiego.org

4. **Grand Haven, Michigan:** In early August, "Coast Guard City USA" hosts the annual week-long Coast Guard Festival celebrating the town's long relationship with the Coast Guard. Events include a National Coast Guard Memorial Service, a Miss Coast Guard Pageant, parades, concerts, ship tours, the traditional birthday picnic at Mulligan's Hollow, and much more. Contact the Coast Guard Festival, 113 N. Second St., Grand Haven, MI 49417, 888-207-2434, 616-846-5940, fax: 616-846-2509, contact@ghcgfest.org, http://www.ghcgfest.org/

5. **Lexington, Kentucky:** A parade and picnic mark Armed Forces Day. Contact Lexington-Fayette Urban County Government, 859-258-3014.

6. **New Orleans, Louisiana:** The National D-Day Museum hosts special events for Armed Forces Day including military displays, drills, living history, and military band concerts. Contact the Museum, 945 Magazine St., New Orleans, LA 70130, 504-527-6012, fax: 504-527-6088, info@ddaymuseum.org, http://www.ddaymuseum.org

7. **Greenville, South Carolina:** Armed Forces Day Parade and flyover. Contact Greenville County Schools, 864-241-3462.

8. **Norfolk, Virginia**: Fleet Week spans the second week in October and features concerts, a chili cookoff, golf tournament, and other activities. Contact Hampton Roads Council Navy League, 5700 Lake Wright Dr., Ste. 107, Norfolk, VA 23502, 757-486-7654, fax: 757-486-7803, navyleague@earthlink.net, http://www.fleetweekhamptonroads.com

Web Sites

Air Force official web site at http://www.af.mil

Air Force Historical Research Agency at http://afhra.maxwell.af.mil

Air National Guard official web site at http://www.ang.af.mil/

Army official web site at http://www.army.mil

Army National Guard official web site at http://www.arng.army.mil/

Coast Guard official web site at http://www.uscg.mil

Library of Congress's "I Hear America Singing" pages contain lyrics, sheet music and other information about military songs at http://lcweb2.loc.gov/cocoon/ihas/html/patriotic/patriotic-home.html

Marine Corps official web sites at http://www.marines.com and http://www.usmc.mil/

Marine Corps History and Museums Division offers details about customs and traditions at http://hqinet001.hqmc.usmc.mil/HD/

National Guard Bureau official web site at http://www.ngb.army.mil/

National Military Appreciation Month web site at http://www.nmam.org

Naval Historical Center's web site provides information about the history of the Navy and Navy Day at http://www.history.navy.mil

Navy official web site at http://www.navy.mil

U.S. Department of Defense at http://www.defenselink.mil

Related Organizations

Air Force Association at http://www.afa.org/

Air Force Sergeants Association at http://www.afsahq.org/

Army and Navy Union, USA at http://www.armynavy.net/

Fleet Reserve Association at http://www.fra.org/

Marine Corps League at http://www.mcleague.org/

National Guard Association of the United States at http://www.ngaus.org/

Navy League at http://www.navyleague.org/

Non-Commissioned Officers Association at http://www.ncoausa.org/

Reserve Enlisted Association at http://www.reaus.org/

Reserve Officers Association at http://www.roa.org/

Sources for Further Reading

Bartlett, Merrill L., and Jack Sweetman. *The U.S. Marine Corps: An Illustrated History*. Annapolis, Md.: Naval Institute Press, 2001.

Boyne, Walter J. *Beyond the Wild Blue: A History of the United States Air Force, 1947-1997*. New York: St. Martin's Press, 1997.

Connell, Royal W., and William P. Mack. *Naval Ceremonies, Customs, and Traditions*. 6th ed. Annapolis, Md.: Naval Institute Press, 2004.

Doubler, Michael D., and John W. Listman, Jr. *The National Guard: An Illustrated History of America's Citizen-Soldiers*. Washington, D.C.: Brassey's, 2003.

Harmon, Daniel E. *The U.S. Armed Forces*. Philadelphia: Chelsea House, 2001. For young adults.

Hoffman, Jon T., ed. *USMC: A Complete History*. Quantico, Va.: Marine Corps Association; [s.l.]: H. L. Levin Associates, 2002.

Hogan, David W. *Centuries of Service: The U.S. Army, 1775-2004*. Washington, D.C.: Center of Military History, United States Army, 2004.

Holland, W. J., Jr., ed. *The Navy*. Washington Navy Yard, D.C.: Naval Historical Foundation; [s.l.]; Hugh Lauter Levin Associates, 2000.

Johnson, Robert Erwin. *Guardians of the Sea: History of the United States Coast Guard, 1915 to the Present*. Annapolis, Md.: Naval Institute Press, 1987.

Mahon, John K. *History of the Militia and the National Guard*. New York: Macmillan, 1983.

The National Guard: Defending the Nation and the States. Washington, D.C.: U.S. Advisory Commission on Intergovernmental Relations, April 1993.

Wright, Robert. *The Continental Army*. Washington, D.C.: Center of Military History, 1983.

Citizenship Day

Date Established as a Patriotic and National Observance: February 29, 1952

Date Observed: September 17

Citizenship Day is a patriotic and national observance celebrating the signing of the Constitution of the United States on September 17, 1787, and recognizing new U.S. citizens—immigrants who have been naturalized as well as those who were born in the United States and have reached the age of 18. On February 29, 1952, President Harry S. Truman signed the law establishing Citizenship Day as an official observance. On August 2, 1956, Congress passed a law designating Constitution Week—September 17 through September 23—as a patriotic and national observance. Each year the president of the United States issues a proclamation calling on Americans to mark Citizenship Day and Constitution Week with events geared toward educating and reminding citizens of their rights and responsibilities.

New U.S. Citizens Sworn in from 1971 to 2003:

From 1971 to 1980: 1.5 million
From 1981 to 1990: 2.2 million
From 1991 to 2000: 5.6 million
From 2001 to 2003: 1.4 million

History of the U.S. Constitution

The Constitution created the *United* States of America and its government. The Constitution unified the states by providing a basic structure for a national government that all the states agreed upon in ratifying the document. It laid out the three branches of federal government: the executive (the presidency), the legislative (the Congress), and the judicial (the Supreme Court), along with a system of checks and balances to prevent any branch from acquiring too much power. All three of these were national extensions of what already existed in the states themselves. Each state

Opposite page: Every Fourth of July, a naturalization ceremony is held at Monticello, Thomas Jefferson's home.

had a governor (the executive branch), a body of representatives who made the state's laws (the legislative branch), and judges who decided disputes about laws (the judicial branch). Although subject in some ways to the power of the federal government, the states retain the power to write their own budgets, create their own educational systems, and make and enforce many of their own laws.

Before the Constitution was written, the nation was governed under the Articles of Confederation. Congress approved the Articles on November 15, 1777, after independence was declared and during the Revolutionary War. Formally known as the Articles of Confederation and Perpetual Union, the Articles went into effect on March 1, 1781, and designated Congress to take charge of the military, commerce between the states, and taxes, but did not require states to provide troops or money. This situation caused George Washington great trouble in raising money for the troops fighting the British for independence. Moreover, once the war was won, Congress lacked the authority to even summon state representatives to approve the peace treaty of 1783. Months went by before they all assembled to approve it.

Early on, then, it was apparent to many that the Articles of Confederation weren't sufficient to govern the confederation of states. By the mid-1780s some began calling to revise the Articles.

The members of the Constitutional Convention met between May 25, 1787, and September 17, 1787. Altogether, 12 state legislatures designated 74 delegates, but only 55 participated. Rhode Island distrusted the project and sent no delegates. James Madison, an avid proponent of a strong federal government, led the effort to draft the new constitution. Several delegates proposed various plans over the months, some granting more, some less, power to a central government. The Convention appointed a committee to draft a constitution, which was presented on August 6, 1787. After much heated debate and modification, the delegates voted unanimously to approve the Constitution on September 15, 1787. (*See the Appendix for the text of the Constitution, the Bill of Rights, and the Amendments.*)

The Convention's president, George Washington, presented the Constitution to Congress on September 17. According to the document, at least 9 of the 13 states had to approve it in order for the Constitution to become effective. At this time, not surprisingly, the debate between the Federalists

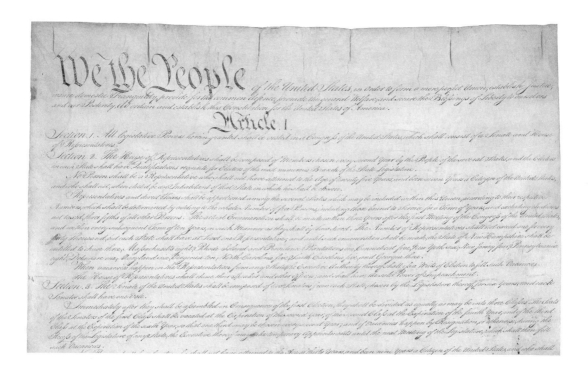

Detail of the Preamble to the U.S. Constitution.

and Anti-Federalists intensified as each side tried to influence the states. The men who pushed for the Constitution and national government to govern all the states beyond their own individual jurisdictions, were known as the Federalists. Alexander Hamilton, Madison, and John Jay led the Federalist faction by writing newspaper articles arguing in its favor. These became known as *The Federalist Papers.*

The Federalists were concerned that, without a strong central government, the states—which had diverse interests and loyalties—would lapse into endless conflicts with one other, maybe even wars. (Reflecting this, a historian titled his recent book about the Constitution "Peace Pact.") The Federalists argued that the states needed to be united into something greater than an alliance, or confederation, of states. They also saw urgency in creating a national government to represent the states to the world. Because Britain and Spain were growing military powers, the Federalists believed America had to have a strong central government in order to provide a national military defense, as well as a united front more powerful than any individual European nation could display.

Opponents, who feared a tyrannical central government, were known as the Anti-Federalists. Thomas Jefferson and others opposed the Constitution because it did not contain a section clearly ensuring freedoms, such as those of speech and religion. (A series of amendments, the Bill of Rights, was added after the Constitution was adopted by the states; see below.) Anti-Federalists also were against the idea of a central government imposing taxes and believed the states would lose their sovereignty.

When the States Ratified the Constitution

Delaware . . . . December 7, 1787
Pennsylvania . . . . December 12, 1787
New Jersey . . . . December 18, 1787
Georgia . . . . January 2, 1788
Connecticut . . . . January 9, 1788
Massachusetts . . . . February 6, 1788
Maryland . . . . April 28, 1788
South Carolina . . . . May 23, 1788
New Hampshire . . . . June 21, 1788
Virginia . . . . June 25, 1788
New York . . . . July 26, 1788
North Carolina . . . . November 21, 1789
Rhode Island . . . . May 29, 1790

For two years the two camps debated how the nation would proceed in its grand experiment of self-governance. They also sought to sway public opinion, and there were sometimes violent demonstrations.

In December 1787, the states began to vote. Each state assembled a special convention of its leading statesmen to decide the issue. As noted above, at least 9 of the 13 states had to ratify, or approve, the Constitution before it would become the foundation of the national government. On December 7, 1787, Delaware became the first state to approve the Constitution. Pennsylvania was the second state to vote to ratify the Constitution, on December 12, 1787. Throughout that winter, four more states approved it: New Jersey on December 18, Georgia on January 2, 1788, Connecticut on January 9, 1788, and Massachusetts on February 6, 1788. On June 21, 1788, the ninth state — New Hampshire — voted to approve, or ratify, the Constitution. The new United States government officially came into being on March 4, 1789.

Some states held elaborate parades, dubbed "Federal Processions," to celebrate their ratification of the Constitution. On July 4, 1788, for example, a Grand Federal Procession took place in Philadelphia, combining the constitutional achievement with the **Independence Day** holiday.

The Bill of Rights

As mentioned above, the Bill of Rights was not part of the original Constitution approved by the states. The Congress presented the first ten amendments to the Constitution to the states for ratification in 1790.

After three-quarters of the states voted their approval, Congress approved the Bill of Rights on December 15, 1791. The Constitution guarantees Americans rights and liberties, but the Bill of Rights spells out what those rights and liberties are. They include freedom of religion, speech, assembly, and the press, freedom from unreasonable searches and seizures, the right to form a "well-regulated militia," own private property, and the right to a speedy and public trial and legal representation. (*See the Appendix for the text of the Bill of Rights.*)

In 1941 President Franklin D. Roosevelt named December 15 Bill of Rights Day and called upon Americans to observe it with appropriate activities. On December 10, 1948, the United Nations adopted the Universal Declaration of Human Rights. Today the president of the United States issues an annual proclamation declaring December 10 as Human Rights Day, December 15 as Bill of Rights Day, and the week beginning December 10 as Human Rights Week.

> *"Eternal vigilance is the price of liberty."*
>
> — Abolitionist Wendell Phillips in an 1852 speech to the Massachusetts Anti-Slavery Society. Though some believe Patrick Henry or Thomas Jefferson first spoke this famous sentence, scholars have not yet uncovered it in any of their documents.

Citizenship

There are three ways in which people become U.S. citizens: 1) all persons born on U.S. soil are considered citizens; 2) all persons born in another country to parents who are U.S. citizens are considered citizens; and 3) persons born outside the United States may apply for citizenship (the process is outlined below).

U.S. citizens have civil and human rights that are envied by many other people in the world. But those rights did not come cheaply, nor are they forever guaranteed. "Eternal vigilance is the price of liberty," said abolitionist Wendell Phillips in an 1852 speech. Americans are familiar with this warning in the context of living in an age of terrorism. But throughout U.S. history, it has also meant that if Americans do not participate actively in their democracy, they may lose some rights. The Founding Fathers knew that the history of human civilization has long demonstrated the temptation to abuse power. So, even though the United States developed one of the fairest systems of government in the world, it cannot reach its potential for justice and equality without the participation of its citizens.

In addition to rights, American citizens have certain responsibilities: to obey laws, to vote, to serve on juries if requested, and to pay taxes.

Naturalization: How to Become a United States Citizen

Someone who has legally moved to the United States from another country but is not a citizen is officially referred to as an alien. Legal aliens enjoy many of the rights of citizenship, but not all — most notably, they can't vote.

Sample Questions from the Civics Test

1. What are the colors of our flag?
2. What is the Constitution?
3. What are the duties of the Supreme Court?
4. When was the Declaration of Independence adopted?

Answers below.

A person wishing to become a U.S. citizen must go through a process administered by the U.S. Citizen and Immigration Services. This process is called naturalization, and it can take up to nine months. The first step is filing an application for citizenship and paying an application fee (which was $320 in 2004, plus a $70 fee for processing the fingerprints each applicant must provide). Persons serving in the armed forces who apply for citizenship are not required to pay any fees, however.

Next, applicants go through an interview with an immigration official and take tests to determine their command of the English language and knowledge of American history and principles of government. Many officials and Americans have expressed dissatisfaction with the civics test for various reasons. Some note that it can be unfairly given because examiners choose only 10 questions out of a possible 100, and the questions vary greatly in difficulty. The U.S. Citizen and Immigration Services plans to adopt a new civics test by 2006.

Naturalization Ceremony

Once applicants have met all the requirements and passed the tests, only one thing is left: attending a naturalization ceremony and taking the Oath of Allegiance. Many ceremony organizers throughout the United States endeavor to make this a memorable occasion for the country's newest citizens.

Answers:
1. Red, white, and blue.
2. The supreme law of the land.
3. To interpret and explain laws.
4. July 4, 1776.

At naturalization ceremonies, all new citizens take the following Oath of Allegiance:

> I hereby declare, on oath, that I absolutely and entirely renounce and abjure all allegiance and fidelity to any foreign prince, potentate, state or sovereignty, of whom or which I have heretofore been a subject or citizen; that I will support and defend the Constitution and laws of the United States of America against all enemies, foreign and domestic; that I will bear true faith and allegiance to the same; that I will bear arms on behalf of the United States when required by the law; that I will perform noncombatant service in the armed forces of the United States when required by the law; that I will perform work of national importance under civilian direction when required by the law; and that I take this obligation freely without any mental reservation or purpose of evasion; so help me God.

In 2004 some 28,000 people became new American citizens in Citizenship Day naturalization ceremonies around the country, held on or around September 17.

Observances

Aside from the Grand Federal Processions mentioned above, the earliest celebration marking the signing of the Constitution took place in Philadelphia in 1861. In 1887 Philadelphia marked the 100th anniversary with a reenactment of the Grand Federal Procession.

During the early 20th century, as more immigrants came to the United States, observances of the anniversary grew in number. Today Citizenship Day is a popular time for naturalization ceremonies nationwide. In addition, some locales host observances celebrating the Constitution.

A Sampling of Observances

1. **Mesa, Arizona:** Held since the 1970s, the Constitution Week Celebration includes musical performances and historical programs. Contact City of Mesa, Parks and Recreation Dept., 480-969-7094, http://www.ci .mesa.az.us/

2. **Mount Rushmore, South Dakota:** Visitors can sign the Constitution at the Lincoln Borglum Museum during Constitution Week. Contact

Naturalization Oath of Allegiance, courtesy U.S. Citizenship and Immigration Services

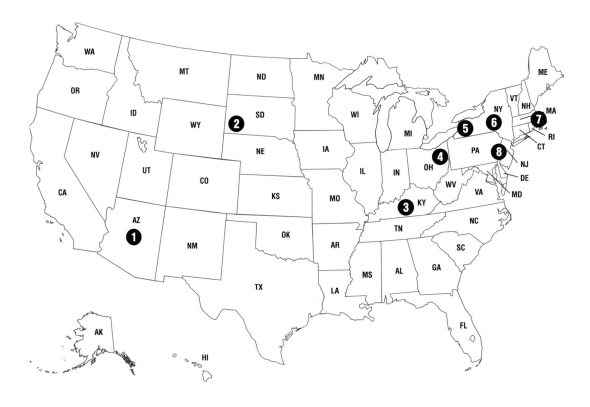

Mount Rushmore National Memorial, 13000 Highway 244, Bldg. 31, Ste. 1, Keystone, SD 57751-0268, 605-574-2523, fax: 605-574-2307, http://www.nps.gov/moru/

3. **Hodgenville, Kentucky:** Visitors to the Abraham Lincoln Birthplace National Historic Site during Constitution Week can put their signatures on a giant Constitution. Contact Abraham Lincoln Birthplace National Historic Site, 2995 Lincoln Farm Rd., Hodgenville, KY 42748, 270-358-3137, fax: 270-358-3874, http://www.nps.gov/abli/

4. **Louisville, Ohio:** Held since 1952, Constitution Week includes a parade, sporting events, banquets, music, pageants, and special ceremonies. Contact Constitution Week Committee, P.O. Box 143, Louisville, OH 44641

5. **Buffalo, New York:** A naturalization ceremony, dinner, and citizens awards at the Theodore Roosevelt Inaugural National Historic Site are combined with the annual commemoration of Roosevelt's inauguration

there on September 14, 1901, after President William McKinley was assassinated. Contact the Historic Site at 641 Delaware Ave., Buffalo, NY 14202, 716-884-0095, fax: 716-884-0330, http://www.nps.gov/thri/

6. **Rome, New York:** Annual Naturalization Ceremony is scheduled near Citizenship Day. Contact Fort Stanwix National Monument, 112 E. Park St., Rome, NY 13440, 315-336-2090, fax: 315-334-5051, http://www.nps.gov/fost/

7. **Quincy, Massachusetts:** The Constitution Day Celebration at the Old House Carriage House is a reenactment of the Constitutional Convention. People are invited to be delegates for their states and participate in the reenactment. Contact Adams National Historical Park, 135 Adams St., Quincy, MA 02169-1749, 617-770-1175, fax: 617-472-7562, http://www.nps.gov/adam/

8. **Philadelphia, Pennsylvania:** The National Constitution Center offers numerous events during Constitution Week, including a reading of the Constitution, a naturalization ceremony, musical and dance performances, a citizens awards dinner, a mock election for Americans of all ages, and more. Contact the Center at 525 Arch St., Independence Mall, Philadelphia, PA 19106, 215-409-6600, http://www.constitutioncenter.org

Web Sites

Ben's Guide to U.S. Government, a service of the U.S. Government Printing Office, provides information about the rights and responsibilities of citizenship at http://bensguide.gpo.gov/6-8/citizenship/index.html

Bill of Rights Institute develops educational programs about early U.S. documents at http://www.billofrightsinstitute.org/

Library of Congress presents information about the Constitution at http://memory.loc.gov/ammem/today/sep17.html

Library of Congress provides an online exhibit about the history of immigration at http://memory.loc.gov/learn/features/immig/introduction .html

National Archives offer an online exhibit, "The Charters of Freedom," at http://www.archives.gov/national_archives_experience/charters/charters.html

U.S. Citizen and Immigration Services gives information about how to become a U.S. citizen as well as educational resources on immigration at http://uscis.gov/

Sources for Further Reading

Berkin, Carol. *A Brilliant Solution: Inventing the American Constitution.* New York: Harcourt Brace & Company, 2002.

Brownstone, David M. *Facts about American Immigration.* New York: H. W. Wilson, 2001.

Daniels, Roger. *American Immigration: A Student Companion.* Oxford: Oxford University Press, 2001. For young adults.

Freedman, Russell. *In Defense of Liberty: The Story of America's Bill of Rights.* New York: Holiday House, 2003. For young adults.

Hendrickson, David C. *Peace Pact: The Lost World of the American Founding.* Lawrence: University Press of Kansas, 2003.

Kammen, Michael. *A Machine That Would Go of Itself: The Constitution in American Culture.* New York: Alfred A. Knopf, 1986.

Kielburger, Marc, and Craig Kielburger. *Take Action! A Guide to Active Citizenship.* Hoboken, N.J.: John Wiley & Sons, 2002. For young adults.

Maddex, Robert L. *The U.S. Constitution A to Z.* Washington, D.C.: CQ Press, 2002.

Schudson, Michael. *The Good Citizen: A History of American Civic Life.* Cambridge, Mass.: Harvard University Press, 1999.

Siemers, David J. *Ratifying the Republic: Antifederalists and Federalists in Constitutional Time.* Stanford, Calif.: Stanford University Press, 2002.

Vile, John R. *Encyclopedia of Constitutional Amendments, Proposed Amendments, and Amending Issues, 1789-2002.* 2nd ed. Santa Barbara, Calif.: ABC-CLIO, 2003.

Columbus Day

Date Established as a Federal Holiday: June 28, 1968

Date Observed: Second Monday in October

Columbus Day is a national public holiday commemorating Christopher Columbus, whose voyages to the New World spurred Europeans to explore and settle in North and South America. It was originally observed on October 12, the date Columbus made landfall on a small island in the Bahamas chain. In 1892 Benjamin Harrison was the first president to issue a proclamation calling for national observances of Columbus Day to mark the 400th anniversary of Columbus's landfall. On April 30, 1934, Congress passed a law designating Columbus Day a patriotic and national observance. In 1968 President Lyndon B. Johnson signed the bill that made Columbus Day a federal holiday to be observed on the second Monday of October. The law went into effect in 1971.

Columbus's Life and Travels

Columbus was born Cristoforo Colombo in 1451, but scholars have not determined the exact date of his birth. His father was a weaver, and Columbus learned the family trade. He grew up in the city of Genoa, Italy, in a region of Europe in which an age of exploration was just beginning. Columbus wanted to be part of it, so as a young man, he found jobs on ships. Genoa lies along the north central coast of the Mediterranean Sea. The coast of Spain marks the eastern border of the Mediterranean. And just over Spain's western border lies Portugal, which in the 15th century led the Age of Exploration and Discovery.

No one is certain what Columbus looked like, since historians know of no portrait done during his lifetime. An artist painted this portrait sometime between 1890 and 1940.

73

Columbus married Felipa Perestrello e Moniz around 1479. They had one son, Diego. A few years after his wife died, Columbus had another son, Ferdinand, with Beatriz Enríquez de Harana. Ferdinand accompanied his father on his fourth voyage to the New World.

For years Columbus appealed to European royalty to fund a westward voyage to Asia, also known to Mediterranean Europeans as the Indies. The journals Columbus left behind reveal his motivations: a desire to find gold and possibly other riches, and then to return to fame and adulation. In 1484 Columbus approached King John II of Portugal to finance what he called his Enterprise of the Indies voyage. The king declined. A year later Columbus went to Spain and lobbied King Ferdinand and Queen Isabel of Spain, known as the Catholic monarchs. In 1492 they agreed to supply him with three ships and crews.

According to historian Matthew Dennis, "Within fifty years of 1492 . . . the Greater Antilles and Bahamas saw their population reduced from an estimated million people to about five hundred."

Columbus was confident about the trip because he was convinced that only about 2,400 miles separated Europe from the Indies. In fact, the distance is 10,000 miles. Many geographers of the time correctly estimated the distance. Contrary to modern myth, educated Europeans of the time did not believe the earth was flat. Though some of Columbus's crewmen were experienced and knowledgeable mariners who believed the earth was round, others probably thought the earth was flat.

The *Pinta*, *Niña*, and *Santa María* departed on August 3, 1492. A sailor on the *Niña* spotted land early in the morning of October 12. That day they went ashore and Columbus named the island San Salvador. The native peoples' name for the island was Guanahani. It is not certain which island they landed on, and over the years historians have come up with various theories about which Bahamian island it was. Between 1493 and 1504 Columbus made three more voyages across the Atlantic Ocean. (*See the Appendix for excerpts from the journal of Christopher Columbus.*)

Columbus died on May 20, 1506, in the city of Valladolid, Spain. It is interesting to note that Columbus died never believing that he had reached the New World; instead, he always claimed to have reached Asia. Yet even after death, his body crossed the Atlantic. Although Columbus had directed in his will that he wished to be buried in Hispaniola, he was first buried at the church of San Francisco in Valladolid. Three years later his body was moved to the cathedral in Seville. Then in 1537 after his eldest son Diego died, Diego's wife María Colón y Toledo arranged a journey to Santo Domingo on the island of Hispaniola to bury the remains of her husband and father-in-law. In 1795 Spain lost control of Hispaniola to the French, so Columbus's remains were exhumed and sent to Havana, Cuba. When the Spanish lost Cuba in the Spanish-American War of 1898, they took what they believed to be Columbus's remains for burial to the cathedral in Seville. According to officials in the Dominican Republic, however, those remains may not be Columbus's at all. In 2002 scientists obtained samples from some of the remains in question plus those of another relative of Columbus's, and began DNA testing in an effort to determine whether Columbus is really buried in Seville or in Santo Domingo.

Consequences of Contact

To the people living in the Americas, Columbus's voyages amounted to catastrophic invasion. Their world and way of life would never be the same. The Tainos inhabited the Bahamas when Columbus arrived. He called them "Indians" because he believed he was in the Indies, that is, Asia.

According to historian Matthew Dennis, "Within fifty years of 1492, for example, the Greater Antilles and Bahamas saw their population reduced from an estimated million people to about five hundred." Many died of diseases for which they had no immunities. Others perished in violent clashes with the newcomers.

Two days after landing on the Bahamian island, Columbus and his men captured native people to take back to Spain to display and sell as slaves. The Catholic monarchs reproached Columbus, freed the native peoples, and warned him not to capture or enslave any more people. Yet during the second voyage of 1493-96 he kidnapped yet more people to take to Spain.

By practicing slavery, Columbus clearly violated the Catholic monarchs' instructions to him. Queen Isabel especially held firm to the policy that the people living on the Caribbean islands Columbus claimed for Spain were Spanish subjects. Since the monarchs prohibited the enslavement of Spanish subjects, the native peoples could not be taken as slaves.

On October 7, 2000, protesters blocked the Italian Pride Columbus Day Parade in Denver, Colorado. Since the early 1990s people have attended peaceful demonstrations against the Denver parade because of its identification with Columbus.

On his third trip, Columbus stayed at his colony in Hispaniola from 1498 to 1500. The monarchs, troubled by the reports of his mismanagement of the colonists and maltreatment of the native people, sent Francisco de Bobadilla to inspect conditions at the colony. They also gave him the power to arrest Columbus. Bobadilla sent Columbus, along with his brother Diego, back to Spain in chains. Indeed, Columbus spent the last years of his life trying to regain the esteem of the monarchs. He did manage one more voyage, but returned to Spain out of favor.

Columbus as National Symbol

Many historians note that Columbus is as much a symbol as he was a man. Throughout U.S. history, Americans have attached different meanings to Columbus, generally based on the cultural climate of the day and the state of historical knowledge and perspective about his actions.

Until the mid-18th century, Columbus was a fairly obscure figure to most Americans. At that time he began to loom large as the hero who discovered a New World—America. Revolutionary-era Americans adopted the nickname Columbia for their land. Columbia also became an American goddess—the image of an idealized European woman—who appeared on coins and in illustrations and paintings. Columbia replaced the Indian goddess, who previously represented America, and was later transformed into the Liberty goddess—the ultimate expression of which is the Statue of Liberty (*see section on the Statue of Liberty in* **Patriotism in the United States**).

When the United States of America was created by the Constitution of 1789, Americans decided to name the new capital city the District of Columbia. More places in the United States are named after Columbus than anyone else, except George Washington. Columbus the symbol helped Americans to create a national identity that was distinct from Britain. As one writer put it, "the New World needed new ancestors."

In addition, Columbus's name evoked dreams of a nation growing in self-determination, power, and territory, which suited the actual expansion of European settlements across the continent over the next century.

When American writer Washington Irving's *The Life and Voyages of Christopher Columbus* was published in 1828, many thousands of readers devoured its mixture of fact and legend. The book, for example, attributed to Columbus the "proof" that the earth was round. Irving's book established Columbus's reputation as mythical American hero, for a time.

In the late 20th century, as the 500th anniversary of Columbus's first voyage approached, radical reassessments of Columbus and his effect on the New World appeared in the popular and academic press. The cultural and historical climate had changed. Many people questioned the validity of giving Columbus credit for "discovering" America.

In particular, the American Indian movement of the 1960s and 1970s did much to present a long-neglected side of the Columbus story—the perspectives of the peoples who lived on the continents for centuries before Europeans arrived. Thus, the 500th anniversary proved to be another instance when the actions of this pivotal figure from American history galvanized the interest of the public.

Why Columbus?

Columbus never set foot on North America, though other explorers did shortly after he sailed. These other explorers are celebrated in the regions they travelled. Juan Ponce de León arrived in Florida in 1513. Alonzo Alvarez Piñeda sailed into Corpus Christi Bay off Texas in 1519. Giovanni Verrazano reached New York Harbor, Narragansett Bay, and numerous islands off the northeastern coast in 1524.

Furthermore, the Norse Vikings were the first Europeans who are known to have reached North America. Norse sagas describe Leif Ericson's journey around the year 1000 to a previously unknown land he called Vinland. Experts don't know exactly where Vinland was, but they agree that it refers to North America and that Vikings explored some portion of the North American east coast. Archaeologists have found remains of Viking settlements in Newfoundland, Canada, dating 500 years before Columbus set sail. But experts still don't know how long those settlements survived. A saga tells that they wearied of problems with the native inhabitants and moved to Greenland. So why is there a national holiday for Columbus?

For one thing, the lasting popularity of Irving's book about Columbus, combined with the Revolutionary-era legacy, cemented Columbus's accomplishments for many Americans.

In addition, the Knights of Columbus (a Roman Catholic men's society) and many Italian Americans celebrated October 12 each year. Between 1880 and 1924 about four million Italians emigrated to the United States, adding to an already considerable Italian-American population. In the 1890s they began urging that Columbus Day be a holiday as a celebration of their heritage as Roman Catholic Italian-Americans. They encountered prejudiced resistance by other Americans, however, particularly Protestants who feared and mistrusted Roman Catholics. Still, it was during this time that President Harrison proclaimed Columbus Day a day of national observance.

In 1905 Colorado was the first state to declare a holiday for Columbus. Within five years, fourteen other states followed suit.

Around this time Spanish Americans began to challenge Italian Americans over which group could claim Columbus. In many Latin American countries and Hispanic-American communities, Columbus Day is also known as Día de la Raza or "Day of the Race," a celebration of their Hispanic heritage marked with parades and other festivities.

Later in the century, Norwegian Americans antagonized members of both groups, as well as broader popular opinion, by asserting that it was one of their own—Leif Ericson—who was the first European to come to the New World. By the 1980s Native American groups and other Americans expressed outrage that Columbus continued to be honored with a national holiday.

These disputes reflect the struggles for ethnic identity and recognition throughout the nation, especially among those not represented by the predominant English-American population, to legitimize their status as Americans.

Observances

Historians trace the first observance of Columbus's 1492 landfall to 1792 in New York City. That year the Society of St. Tammany organized a banquet for the 300th anniversary celebration that included the raising of a 14-foot-high monument to Columbus.

Commemorations at the 400th anniversary were much more widespread. President Benjamin Harrison proclaimed October 12, 1892, a national hol-

A scene from San Francisco's annual Italian Heritage Parade.

iday for Americans to observe with appropriate activities and programs (*see the Appendix for a Columbus Day school program from 1892*). To mark the occasion Chicagoans put on the World's Columbian Exposition in 1893, and festivals were held in New York, Boston, and New Haven, Connecticut.

Today it remains a day of protest and mourning for some, commemoration of an ancestor for others. The Transform Columbus Day Alliance is a coalition of groups that participate in annual protests at Denver's Columbus Day Parade. They urge the abolition of the Columbus Day holiday and instead "[advocate] a celebration that is much more inclusive and more accurately reflective of the cultural and racial richness of the Americas." Some cities have changed their observances from focusing on Columbus to celebrating Italian heritage, while others continue to identify with Columbus and his accomplishment. In the words of an organizer for the annual festival in Baltimore, "Columbus Day is a celebration of the vision of democracy in the new world. His voyages created opportunities that still exist today."

A Sampling of Observances

1. **San Francisco, California:** Italian Heritage Parade, held for more than 130 years, is a highlight of weekend festivities that also offer a formal ball, food and wine tasting, Italian music, selection of Queen Isabella and her court, and other events. Contact Columbus Day Celebration, Inc., info@sfcolumbusday.org, http://www.sfcolumbusday.org

2. **Reno, Nevada:** Great Italian Festival: food, bocce ball, and contests, including grape stomping, since 1981. Contact Eldorado Hotel Casino, 345 N. Virginia St., Reno, NV 89501, 800-648-5966 or 775-786-5700, http://www.eldoradoreno.com/events/italian_festival.php

3. **Denver, Colorado:** A coalition of American Indian organizations and supporters hold peaceful protest demonstrations at the city's annual Columbus Day parade. Contact Transform Columbus Day Alliance, info@ transformcolumbusday.org, http://www.transformcolumbusday .org

4. **New York, New York:** Annual parade on Fifth Avenue, one of the nation's largest. Contact Columbus Citizens Foundation, 212-249-9923, fax: 212-737-4413, http://www.columbuscitizensfd.org/

5. **Boston, Massachusetts:** Annual Columbus Day Parade, held on the Sunday closest to October 12, proceeds downtown in odd-numbered

years, in Revere/East Boston in even-numbered years. Contact City of Boston, Mayor's Office of Arts & Cultural Development, City Hall Pl., Boston, MA 02201, 617-635-3911, SpecialEvents@ci.boston.ma.us, http://www.cityofboston.gov/mayor/spevents/

6. **Seaside Heights, New Jersey:** The Ocean County, New Jersey, Columbus Day Parade and Italian Festival includes an Italian flag-raising ceremony and traditional Italian folk music and dance. Contact Ocean County Columbus Day Parade Committee, Inc., P.O. Box 1492, 500 Christopher Columbus Blvd., Seaside Heights, NJ 08751, 732-477-6507 or 732-914-0351, http://www.ameri-com.com/columbus/

7. **Baltimore, Maryland:** Parade, wreath-laying ceremony, food, and other festivities in Little Italy. Contact Columbus Celebrations, Inc., 410-529-6345, http://www.littleitalymd.com/columbus_day.htm

8. **Tampa, Florida:** Columbus Day Commemoration Ceremonies and Queen Isabella Coronation & Gala Ball since the 1960s. The Ceremonies take

place at the Christopher Columbus Memorial on the Hillsborough River. Contact The Krewe of Columbus, Columbus Celebration of Tampa, Inc., P.O. Box 153091, Tampa, FL 33684-3091, mail@kreweofcolumbus.com, http://www.kreweofcolumbus.com

Web Sites

Library of Congress exhibits:
  American Memory page on Columbus Day at
    http://memory.loc.gov/ammem/today/oct12.html
  "1492: An Ongoing Voyage" at http://www.loc.gov/exhibits/1492/

Ships of Discovery web site, associated with the Corpus Christi Museum of Science and History, offers an online exhibit of Columbus's lost ships at http://www.shipsofdiscovery.org/

Transform Columbus Day Alliance at http://www.transformcolumbusday.org

Sources for Further Reading

Boorstin, Daniel. *The Discoverers*. New York: Vintage Books, 1985.

Dennis, Matthew. *Red, White, and Blue Letter Days: An American Calendar*. Ithaca, N.Y.: Cornell University Press, 2002.

Fernández-Armesto, Felipe. *Columbus*. Oxford: Oxford University Press, 1991.

Haskins, Jim. *Christopher Columbus: Admiral of the Ocean Sea*. New York: Scholastic, 1991. For young adults.

Least Heat-Moon, William. *Columbus in the Americas*. Hoboken, N.J.: John Wiley & Sons, 2002.

Morison, Samuel Eliot. *Admiral of the Ocean Sea: A Life of Christopher Columbus*. 2 vols. Boston: Little, Brown, 1942.

Phillips, William D., Jr., and Carla Rahn Phillips. *The Worlds of Christopher Columbus*. Cambridge: Cambridge University Press, 1992.

Provost, Foster. *Columbus Dictionary*. Detroit: Omnigraphics, 1991.

Election Day and Inauguration Day

Election Day

Date Established by Congress: 1845
Date Observed: The Tuesday after the first Monday in November

Arguably the most important day in the patriotic calendar of the United States, Election Day is when Americans 18 and older can exercise their right to select government leaders and decide on local issues. The U.S. Constitution provided for the election of a president every four years, but did not set a date. In 1792 Congress established the first Wednesday in December as the day on which members of the Electoral College (see below) must vote for president. The same law required states to appoint their electors within 34 days of the first Wednesday in December, thus elections were usually held in November. It was not until 1845 that Congress passed a law setting a uniform election day for the nation. Since November 4, 1845, all Americans have voted for president on the same day.

The date on which Congress chose to hold elections may seem odd in the 21st century, but it made perfect sense to the rural nation in the late 18th century. Most Americans were farmers in those days. By November most would have brought in their crops for the season. In addition, voting in 1800 was not always a simple matter of going to a local school or other community building a few convenient blocks away. For most people, voting meant traveling—sometimes for a whole day or more—in most cases, to the courthouse at their county seat. And for anyone who didn't have a horse, that meant walking.

In the modern United States, some states celebrate Election Day as a holiday, while others do not. What this means in practical terms depends on the state. Most people who work for the state government in these states can get the day off. People in these states who work for private companies generally don't get the day off from work, but in Hawaii, Maryland, New York, and Texas, employees are given up to two hours to vote. West Virginia requires employers to allow up to three hours.

The federal Election Day is a holiday in only ten states:

Delaware	Indiana	Montana
Hawaii	Kentucky	New Jersey
Illinois	Louisiana	West Virginia
	Maryland	

People who don't get time off from work can still find ways to vote, however. Polls in most states open early in the morning and close at 7:00, 8:00, or 9:00 P.M. In addition, any registered voter can also vote via absentee ballot.

Congress selected a Tuesday as Election Day with the traveling factor and the public's religious observances in mind. Since many people would have to travel a full day to reach their polling place, holding elections on a Monday would interfere with people's ability to attend church services on Sunday. Congress also wanted to avoid having elections on the first of November, when much court business was scheduled.

History of Voting Rights

Throughout much of American history, the states set their own rules on voting eligibility. Since the ratification of the Constitution in 1789, all states have to provide for the general election day every four years. But each state could, and did, set its own laws regarding who may vote. As discussed below, a series of amendments to the Constitution added over the last 200 years have guaranteed voting rights to most Americans. All states are required to grant voting rights guaranteed by these amendments.

White Men Who Didn't Own Property

The first Americans allowed to vote were white men who owned property. Although it may seem absurdly restrictive to Americans today, in the late 18th and early 19th century, it was the norm in countries such as Britain to restrict voting to men who owned land.

The reasoning went back to British tradition, which held that men who did not possess property likewise did not possess a sufficient "stake in society" to participate in its governance. Such men were also considered to be untrustworthy participants because they were dependent upon property owners who could manipulate their potential vote.

Massachusetts voters on Election Day, 2004.

On June 20, 1818, Connecticut became the first state in the east to grant the right to vote to white men who did not own property. Disenfranchised white men around the country protested through the first half of the century. State by state, most had won the right to vote by the 1860s.

African Americans

The 14th Amendment of 1868 provided African Americans the rights of full citizenship, including the right to vote. But officials in some Southern states passed laws to make it difficult or impossible for many African Americans to vote. In response, Congress passed the 15th Amendment in 1870, which specifically gave all men the right to vote, regardless of "race, color, or previous condition of servitude." Some white officials, however,

85

particularly in the South, continued to devise legal obstacles to prevent black Americans from voting.

Since many African Americans were poor, some states instituted poll taxes. This meant that if you wanted to vote, you had to pay a tax. The amount of poll taxes differed according to the state. These laws effectively disenfranchised many black voters, and continued for nearly 100 years after the passage of the 14th Amendment. Poll taxes were finally abolished by the 24th Amendment, which became law on January 23, 1964.

From the late 1950s to the early 1960s, Martin Luther King Jr. continued the fight for voting rights for African Americans. In 1965 the Voting Rights Act outlawed literacy tests and other tactics that had prevented African Americans from voting. (*See also* **Martin Luther King Jr. Birthday.**)

Unfortunately, civil rights advocates still report that some people continue to try to intimidate or otherwise discourage African Americans from voting in some parts of the nation. Voter intimidation cases are handled by state and local courts.

Women

Back in 1776 Abigail Adams urged her husband John to "remember the ladies" as his committee worked on writing the Declaration of Independence. Neither he nor the U.S. Constitution did, however, and it was not until passage of the 19th Amendment to the Constitution on June 5, 1919, that American women won the right to vote. The movement for women's voting rights began in the 19th century. Its advocates won victories in individual states before the rest of the nation voted to amend the Constitution and grant voting rights to all women. For example, women were given the vote in Wyoming Territory in 1869 (and retained the right when Wyoming became a state in 1890), in Utah Territory in 1870, and in Idaho in 1896.

Native Americans

Although their residence in America preceded Europeans' by centuries, the U.S. government did not grant citizenship to Native Americans until 1924. That year Congress passed the Snyder Act, which included Native Americans as full citizens. While this ostensibly meant they could vote, some states created laws and rules to prevent that. Some states required Native Americans to pass a literacy test or pay a poll tax before voting.

The Basics of the Presidential Election Process

1. **Campaigns** — candidates for each party campaign to become the party's nominee

2. **Primary Elections and Caucuses** — voting processes within each party that choose the delegates who will go to the national conventions and determine which candidate will run for president for each party

3. **Conventions and Nominations of Candidates** — rallies for party members to formally nominate the party's candidate for president and prepare its political platform

4. **Presidential Debates** — provide a forum for candidates to answer questions about issues

5. **Voting** — eligible citizens cast their ballots for the candidate of their choice

6. **The Electoral College** — electors chosen from each state cast the ballots that will assign the state's electoral votes to a candidate for president; some states divide their electoral votes among the candidates based on the percentage of votes each receives

Native Americans in some locales also faced intimidation. In 1962 New Mexico was the last state to grant Native Americans the right to vote. Because the Voting Rights Act of 1965 prohibits discrimination, it further reinforces Native Americans' rights.

Eighteen to Twenty Year Olds

A strong movement to lower the voting age arose in the late 1960s. The United States was involved in the Vietnam War and thousands served who were ineligible to vote because they were younger than the legal voting age of 21. Young people lobbied Congress with the popular slogan, "Old enough to fight, old enough to vote." On March 23, 1971, Congress passed the law which on July 1 of that year would become the 26th Amendment to the Constitution, lowering the voting age from 21 to 18.

People Who Can't Vote Today

The only Americans excluded from voting today are people under the age of 18, people who are judged mentally incompetent, and some people with felony convictions. Some states have laws that don't allow ex-felons to vote; others allow an ex-felon to vote once a sentence has been served; yet others require a pardon from the governor. Some prisoners and ex-felons have protested these laws. In 2004 the U.S. Supreme Court ruled that convicts in Washington state would be allowed to bring lawsuits challenging their disenfranchisement.

Campaigns and Conventions

Before most Americans had radios and, later, televisions, candidates engaged in "front porch" campaigning. Then, like now, they traveled around the country talking to groups of people in attempts to gain their votes and to raise money for the expensive process. Today, presidential campaigns are arduous year-long races.

In the spring before Election Day some states hold primary elections or caucuses in which citizens vote for the candidate they want their party to nominate to run for the presidency.

By the summer before the election the two major political parties, the Democrats and the Republicans, hold huge meetings to nominate their candidates for presi-

An assortment of campaign buttons from past presidential election campaigns.

dent (*for more on American political parties, see* **Patriotism in the United States**). Conventions wrap up by **Labor Day**, which is the unofficial beginning to the campaign, though in reality it begins months earlier.

Once each party has selected its candidate, debates are scheduled. Traditionally, there are three debates, during which nationally known journalists pose questions to the candidates about issues facing the country and their ideas about dealing with them. Since the race between John F. Kennedy and Richard Nixon in 1960, these have been televised.

Voting Methods

Americans vote for the president of the United States every four years — for example, 1996, 2000, and 2004. Representatives in the U.S. House of Representatives and in state legislatures are elected every even-numbered year. Senators in the U.S. Senate and in state senates are chosen every six years, meaning that every two years, one-third of the senators are up for reelection.

Several voting methods have been used in American elections. The oldest, simplest, and most reliable is the paper ballot on which the voter marks a box for the candidate of choice. The newest, and most controversial, is electronic voting, called direct recording electronic voting systems (DREs). In between are mechanical lever voting machines, optical scanning voting, and punchcards (which caused so much confusion in the 2000 presidential election that the federal government has encouraged states to use other methods). Each precinct decides which method to use.

The Electoral College

The Electoral College is a group of 538 people—this number equals the number of representatives and senators in the U.S. Congress. Anyone can be an elector except for members of Congress and people "holding an Office of Trust or Profit under the United States," generally meaning anyone who holds an elected office or is a federal employee, either civilian or military. The Electoral College is not a permanent group. It exists only during the election period in federal election years.

So, who makes up the Electoral College? In most states, political parties choose the electors every four years. Electors are usually older people who have long been active in their political party and can be relied upon to vote for the candidate their party favors. There can be exceptions, however. The 2004 Electoral College, for example, included two teenagers.

On Election Day voters select a candidate for president on their ballots, but they are actually voting for their state's electors, who in turn are pledged to reflect those votes. On the first Monday after the second Wednesday in December following the election, the members of the Electoral College meet, usually in their respective state capitols, and cast their votes for

Shad Planking

A political campaign tradition in Virginia since 1949, this event is named for the method of slowly smoking shad fish nailed to wooden planks that stand around an open fire. The Wakefield Ruritans host the Shad Planking annually on the third Wednesday in April. It serves as a gathering for citizens and politicians of all persuasions to get together, discuss issues, listen to speeches and music, and eat the spicy shad. Volunteers baste the shad with a secret sauce and serve it with coleslaw and corn bread.

Contact: Wakefield Ruritan Club, Sussex County, Virginia; 804-834-2214; fax: 804-834-3023

president and vice president. This completes the formal electoral process — unless neither candidate receives at least 270 votes from the electors. If that happens, the members of the House of Representatives form state delegations in which each state casts one vote for president. The members of the Senate do the same to vote for the vice president.

The framers of the Constitution designed the Electoral College to give states a fair role in federal elections. The number of electors in a state equals the number of that state's representatives in the House of Representatives plus the two senators each state has in the Senate. By balancing electoral power with a state's population, they hoped to create a situation in which each state had proportional power to elect a president. The Founders also thought that under this system presidential candidates would be less likely to neglect less populated parts of the country. In addition, they believed that this method would decrease opportunities for corrupt practices.

Still, many presidential election seasons end with calls to eliminate the Electoral College and elect the president by a direct popular vote of the people. It would take an amendment to the Constitution to abolish the Electoral College. Two-thirds of Congress would have to vote for it, then three-fourths of the states would have to approve it.

Close Elections

The United States has seen several close elections in its history. In 1800, in the third election in the nation's history, Thomas Jefferson and Aaron Burr — who were Republicans running for president and vice president, respectively — received the same number of electoral votes. Both received more electoral votes than the Federalist Party candidates, President John Adams (running for reelection) and Charles C. Pinckney (running for vice president). At that time, electors did not specify on their ballots which office they intended for which candidate. As laid out in the Constitution's provision for dealing with a tie, the election was eventually settled in the House of Representatives. The majority of representatives were Federalists, who were reluctant to vote for either Republican; they finally selected Jefferson on their 36th vote. Congress resolved any such future ties between candidates and their running mates by adding the 12th Amendment to the Constitution, which mandates that electors "name in their ballots the person voted for as President, and in distinct ballots the person voted for as Vice-President."

"Burying the Tomahawk": Return Day in Delaware

Before the development of a fast-traveling mass media, some voters would either stay in, or return to, their county seat two days after elections to learn the outcome. Georgetown, the county seat of Sussex County, Delaware, has maintained this tradition since the 1790s. Return Day festivities take place every even-numbered year two days after the elections. A parade ferries candidates and others in horse-drawn carriages and antique cars to the courthouse grounds, where the town crier reads the results. Next, officials ceremoniously bury a tomahawk as a symbolic end to partisan political grumbling until the next round of campaigning. The formalities over, attendees settle down to free ox roast sandwiches and live musical entertainment.

The 1876 race between Rutherford B. Hayes and Samuel Tilden was disputed because 20 electoral votes were in doubt. Tilden won the popular vote by nearly 300,000, but fell short of the required number of electoral votes. In the end a special congressional commission gave the disputed votes to Hayes, who retired after serving one term.

The 2000 election saw Al Gore, as the then-current vice president serving as president of the Senate, in the odd position of overseeing vote totals for his opponent George W. Bush.

Americans waited 36 days after that election for an outcome. Several states' votes were so close at the end of election night that they could not declare a winner. Voting recounts went on in New Mexico, Oregon, Wisconsin, Iowa, and Florida. In Florida a legal battle ensued which involved no fewer than six courts including, finally, the U.S. Supreme Court, which in effect stopped all the recounts. When the Supreme Court stopped the Florida recounts, that state's electoral votes went to Bush, giving him the victory. Gore won the popular vote by more than 500,000.

This situation led Congress to pass the Help America Vote Act of 2002. The Act created a new government office, the U.S. Election Assistance Commission, and charged it with establishing minimum election standards for all the states, providing assistance for holding federal elections, and distributing funds to states to replace punchcard voting systems.

Inauguration Day

Date Established by Congress: January 23, 1933
Date Observed: January 20

From the inauguration of George Washington in 1789 to that of Herbert Hoover in 1929, every president was sworn in on March 4. In the earlier years of the nation, before technological developments sped up the communication of election results, it often took months for the vote to be tabulated. By the 1930s, results were available within a day or so after the election. So, on March 2, 1932, Congress passed the 20th Amendment, changing Inauguration Day to January 20. It was ratified on January 23, 1933. Since 1933 each new president has been inaugurated on January 20, unless the 20th falls on a Sunday. In that case, the president is sworn in at a small ceremony and the major festivities are held the next day.

On January 11, 1957, Congress passed a law making Inauguration Day a legal holiday in the metropolitan area of Washington, D.C., including Montgomery and Prince George's counties, Maryland; Arlington and Fairfax counties, Virginia; and the cities of Alexandria and Falls Church, Virginia.

President Calvin Coolidge's inaugural parade on March 4, 1925.

The inauguration is a ceremony held to formally swear in the newly elected president. Traditionally the president, vice president, and their families begin the proceedings with a procession to the Capitol Building. There the president must take the Oath of Office, as written in the Constitution, Article II, Section 1:

> I do solemnly swear (or affirm) that I will faithfully execute the office of President of the United States, and will to the best of my ability, preserve, protect and defend the Constitution of the United States.

Most presidents opt to give this oath while placing a hand on a Bible, sometimes open to a page of their choice.

After the swearing-in, the president gives a speech called an inaugural address. This is followed by a parade through the streets of Washington, D.C. Inaugurations are often less elaborate when a president is elected for a second term.

In the evening formal inaugural balls are held in several locations, and the president and first lady try to appear at all of them.

Here are excerpts from two of the most famous inaugural addresses:

> With malice toward none, with charity for all, with firmness in the right as God gives us to see the right, let us strive on to finish the work we are in, to bind up the nation's wounds, to care for him who shall have borne the battle and for his widow and his orphan, to do all which may achieve and cherish a just and lasting peace among ourselves and with all nations.
> —*from Abraham Lincoln's second inaugural address on March 4, 1865*

> And so, my fellow Americans: ask not what your country can do for you—ask what you can do for your country. My fellow citizens of the world: ask not what America will do for you, but what together we can do for the freedom of man.
> —*from John F. Kennedy's inaugural address on January 20, 1961*

(For an account of festivities surrounding the inauguration of James Madison in 1809, see the Appendix: Sarah Ridg [Schuyler] Recalls George Washington's Birthday and Inauguration Day.)

Legend has it that ghosts appear in the U.S. Capitol Building on the night a president is inaugurated. While the living attend formal balls throughout the District of Columbia, some say the 97 statues in Statuary Hall come to life and dance, even though 91 depict men and only 6 represent women.

Web Sites

Ben's Guide to Government at http://bensguide.gpo.gov/6-8/election/index .html

Commission on Presidential Debates at http://www.debates.org/

Election Reform Information Project at http://www.electionline.org/

Inaugural Committee at http://inaugural.senate.gov/

Library of Congress online exhibits:

"Elections the American Way" at http://memory.loc.gov/learn/features/ election/

" 'I Do Solemnly Swear . . .' Presidential Inaugurations" at http:// memory.loc.gov/ammem/pihtml/pihome.html

Inauguration Day at http://memory.loc.gov/ammem/today/ jan20.html

"Inaugurations . . . From George W. to George W." at http://learning.loc .gov/learn/features/inaug

National Archives records of Electoral Colleges at http://www.archives .gov/federal_register/electoral_college/

Sussex County Return Day, Inc., at http://www.returnday.org/

U.S. Election Assistance Commission at http://www.eac.gov/

U.S. Federal Election Commission at http://www.fec.gov/

"Vote: The Machinery of Democracy," Smithsonian Institution's National Museum of American History online exhibit at http://americanhistory.si .edu/vote/index.html

Sources for Further Reading

Clack, George, ed. *United States Elections 2004.* Washington, D.C.: U.S. Department of State, Bureau of International Information Programs, post-ed online (September 2003) at http://usinfo.state.gov/products/pubs/ election04/parties.htm

Coleman, Kevin J., et al. *Presidential Elections in the United States: A Primer.* (CRS Report for Congress.) Washington, D.C.: Congressional Research Service, Library of Congress, April 17, 2000.

DiClerico, Robert. *Voting in America: A Reference Handbook.* Santa Barbara, Calif.: ABC-CLIO, 2004.

Hewson, Martha S. *The Electoral College.* Philadelphia: Chelsea House, 2002. For young adults.

Kelly, Kate. *Election Day: An American Holiday, an American History.* New York: Facts on File, 1991.

Keyssar, Alexander. *The Right to Vote: The Contested History of Democracy in the United States.* New York: Basic Books, 2000.

Levin, Jerome D. *Presidential Elections, 1789-2000.* Washington, D.C.: CQ Press, 2002.

Misiroglu, Gina. *The Handy Politics Answer Book.* Detroit: Visible Ink Press, 2003.

Roberts, Robert North, and Scott Hammond. *Encyclopedia of Presidential Campaigns, Slogans, Issues, and Platforms.* Westport, Conn.: Greenwood Press, 2004. For young adults.

Shade, William G., and Ballard C. Campbell, eds. *American Presidential Campaigns and Elections.* 3 vols. Armonk, N.Y.: M. E. Sharpe, 2003.

Emancipation Day and Juneteenth

Emancipation Day

Date Observed: January 1

E mancipation Day commemorates the anniversary of President Abraham Lincoln's Emancipation Proclamation, which on January 1, 1863, formally proclaimed that the federal government declared the freedom of all slaves in the Southern slave-holding states. Emancipation Day is not a holiday, though it falls on New Year's Day, which is a federal holiday.

The end of slavery became law on January 31, 1865, when Congress passed the 13th Amendment to the Constitution. It read: "Neither slavery nor involuntary servitude, except as a punishment for crime whereof the party shall have been duly convicted, shall exist within the United States, or any place subject to their jurisdiction." On August 12, 1998, Congress designated February 1 as National Freedom Day to commemorate the day Lincoln signed the amendment into law.

President Abraham Lincoln

Freedom from slavery has been celebrated on various other dates around the country depending on the dates local emancipation laws took effect or when people in different areas heard about the Emancipation Proclamation. Juneteenth, June 19, is the most nationally famous of these other days of freedom. On that day in 1865 news of the Proclamation finally reached African Americans in east Texas (*see section on Juneteenth below*).

Slavery in the British Colonies of North America

Slavery existed throughout much of the world since before the beginning of recorded history, and still does in isolated pockets of the world. Slavery was commonplace in the British colonies in America by the 1650s. Historians aren't certain exactly when the first Africans were owned as slaves in America, however, because many were indentured servants.

It is important to note the difference between indentured servitude and slavery. Many English settlers used indentured servants to work their plantations and farms. Indentured servants were people who sold themselves into service for an agreed-upon time period. People usually resorted to indentured servitude to pay off a debt or because they could find no other way to provide themselves with shelter, food, and clothing.

Indentured servants were not a permanent labor force, because they only worked for a temporary time period. So early colonial planters also tried to enslave American Indians. Many died of diseases transmitted by the European settlers for which they had no immunity. Others found ways to escape. Beginning in the mid-1600s, some of the colonies passed laws making slavery — the owning of a person for life — legal. In 1641 Massachusetts was the first colony to pass such a law. The slave trade grew enormously over the next decades. Between 1680 and 1720 the African slave population increased from 4,000 to 37,000. The first U.S. census in 1790 counted 746,000 African Americans, who comprised 19% of the population; of these, more than 697,000 were slaves.

Slavery was practiced in Africa from ancient times. A person was made a slave through capture during war or during raids for the purpose of gathering people to sell to European slave traders. The British would bring goods to the western coast of Africa to trade for slaves. Then they would sail from Africa to the North American colonies to sell the slaves or to the Caribbean islands or Brazil where large slave auctions were also held. This leg of the journey became known as the Middle Passage. The Africans suffered horrific conditions on these ships. Over four centuries, an estimated one to two million died from disease or starvation; some jumped overboard, rather than live a life of slavery.

Plantation owners increased their personal wealth by using slaves. Most slaves were provided only the very basics of life. Before the Civil War some 350,000 white families (out of 2.1 million) in the South owned

Sojourner Truth (c.1797-1883)

was an African-American former slave who was a stirring spokeswoman for the abolitionist cause. She was also a Christian preacher and advocate of women's rights. Truth was born into slavery with the name Isabella Van Wagener, which was her master's last name. After she was freed, she adopted the name Sojourner Truth, signifying what she felt was her mission: sojourning—that is, traveling—and speaking truth to all she met.

I SELL THE SHADOW TO SUPPORT THE SUBSTANCE

SOJOURNER TRUTH.

slaves, and most slaves in the Southern states worked on cotton plantations. Cotton became a valued crop in the South, particularly after Eli Whitney invented the cotton gin in 1793. The cotton gin increased the efficiency of cotton processing. Picking cotton, however, was difficult and labor intensive, and cotton plantation owners required more workers to maximize their profit.

The slave society in the South was both more violent and oppressive than those in other parts of the world, including Africa. Occasionally, desperate slaves organized rebellions against their owners. One of the most dramatic examples in the United States was the Nat Turner rebellion in Jerusalem, Virginia, in 1831. As a consequence of such uprisings, however, many slave owners became even more restrictive and brutal.

Britain outlawed the slave trade in its colonies in 1807. The nearly 800,000 slaves in Britain's Caribbean colonies were freed by Parliament on July 31, 1834. The August 1st Emancipation Day remains a major holiday in such Caribbean countries as Barbados, Guyana, Jamaica, and Trinidad and Tobago.

Frederick Douglass (c.1817-1895) was an African-American former slave and one of the most famous abolitionists. He escaped slavery as a young man and became a great orator and writer and an advisor to President Lincoln. Douglass published the *North Star*, an antislavery newspaper he named after the sky's night light that guided many fleeing slaves safely to the North via the Underground Railroad. Douglass also served in the Union Army during the Civil War by enlisting and organizing African-American soldiers. After the end of the war, he was appointed to various civil service positions, the last of which was the United States Minister to Haiti.

On January 1, 1808, the United States outlawed the slave trade. This meant that no more slaves could be brought legally to the United States for 20 years. But anyone who was already a slave remained a slave. And smugglers illegally continued the slave trade.

Abolition Movement

From the earliest days of slavery in North America, many Americans felt morally outraged by the institution of slavery. A few colonies outlawed it before they even became independent from Britain, but it wasn't until after the Revolutionary War, after the Constitutional Convention resulted in the creation of the United States of America in 1787, and after the War of 1812 that a grassroots movement took hold and began to flourish.

The first American colonists to outlaw slavery were those in Rhode Island, who, on May 18, 1652, passed a law making the practice illegal. This law was rarely enforced, however, and in 1700, the colony legalized slavery. Between 1652 and 1862, slavery was outlawed in seven colonies or states, as well as in Washington, D.C. In 1712, Pennsylvania colony, encouraged by its Quaker population who long opposed slavery, banned the importing of slaves into the colony. In 1760 South Carolina's legislature voted to outlaw the slave trade, but Britain did not allow the law to take effect. In 1774, Connecticut and Rhode Island outlawed the import of slaves into their colonies.

On April 14, 1775, in Philadelphia, revolutionaries Benjamin Franklin and Benjamin Rush formed the Society for the Relief of Free Negroes Unlawfully Held in Bondage. This was the first antislavery organization in America.

Significant Dates in the Abolition of Slavery

May 18, 1652 — Rhode Island colony outlawed slavery

June 7, 1712 — Pennsylvania Colony banned anyone from bringing slaves into the colony

1760 — the legislature of the South Carolina colony voted to outlaw the slave trade, but Britain overruled it

1774 — Connecticut and Rhode Island banned anyone from bringing slaves into their colonies

July 12, 1777 — Vermont outlawed slavery in its new state constitution

March 1, 1780 — Pennsylvania passed a law providing for the gradual end of slavery

July 8, 1783 — Massachusetts abolished slavery

October 7, 1783 — Virginia freed all slaves who fought in the Continental Army

By December 31, 1783 — no northern state allowed the importing of slaves

March 29, 1799 — the New York legislature passed a law providing for the gradual end of slavery

March 1, 1803 — Ohio became the first state of the Union in which slavery was already prohibited

July 4, 1827 — slavery was abolished in New York

April 16, 1862 — slavery was abolished in the District of Columbia

Harriet Tubman and the Underground Railroad

Harriet Tubman (1823-1913)
nurse, spy and scout

The Underground Railroad was a network of whites and free blacks in the North who helped slaves escape the South. When the Fugitive Slave Law was passed in 1850, the operation spread up into Canada, since the law forced the return of all runaway slaves, so even African Americans who had escaped to the North were no longer safe from being captured and sent back to their owners.

One of the people most famously associated with the Underground Railroad is Harriet Tubman (c. 1820-1913). She was one of many courageous African Americans without whom slaves could not have escaped the South for freedom in the North. Tubman herself escaped from slavery in 1849 on the Underground Railroad. Afterward she made many journeys South and led 60-70 other slaves to freedom.

"I had crossed the line of which I had so long been dreaming. I was free; but there was no one to welcome me to the land of freedom. I was a stranger in a strange land, and my home after all was down in the old cabin quarter, with the old folks, and my brothers and sisters. But to this solemn resolution I came; I was free, and they should be free also; I would make a home for them in the North, and the Lord helping me, I would bring them all there." —Harriet Tubman

The next year Thomas Jefferson, a slave holder himself, included a section in the Declaration of Independence that would ban slavery in the new country based on the principle that "all men are created equal." The Continental Congress removed the passage, however, because the colonies of Georgia and South Carolina would not have signed the Declaration otherwise. During a war with powerful Britain, the majority of Congress decided it was more important to stay united than to press such a heated, controversial issue.

After the Declaration of Independence, the states began their own movements against slavery. On July 12, 1777, Vermont citizens wrote the abolition of slavery into their state constitution. The newly formed state of Pennsylvania passed a law on March 1, 1780, providing for the gradual end of slavery. On July 8, 1783, Massachusetts abolished slavery. On October 7, 1783, Virginia freed all slaves who had served in the Revolutionary War. By December 31, 1783, no northern state allowed the slave trade within its boundaries. In 1799 New York voted to ban slavery by July 4, 1827. On March 1, 1803, Ohio joined the United States as the first state in which slavery had already been prohibited. The District of Columbia abolished slavery on April 16, 1862.

Americans involved in the 19th-century antislavery movement were known as abolitionists. During the 1830s, the abolition movement began to gain national attention. Among the movement's leaders were evangelical Christians who powerfully denounced slavery as a national sin. In 1831 journalist William Lloyd Garrison began publishing a newspaper—*The Liberator*—that proclaimed the abolitionists' purpose throughout the country. It would serve to galvanize those with antislavery sentiments and enrage slavery's defenders. Abolitionists often found themselves under attack by slavery proponents, verbally and physically, foreshadowing the Civil War to come.

Civil War

The Civil War was fought in the United States from 1861 to 1865 between Northern states, called the Union, and Southern states, called the Confederacy. The states had been unified through the Revolutionary War and the crafting of the U.S. Constitution. But the differences between the two regions had been building for years. The agricultural South depended upon the institution of slavery for its economy, while the rapidly industrializing North did not. As more Americans moved west, settled in new territories, and began to organize new states, the issue of the spread of slavery became even more impassioned. By the 1830s, many Northerners believed slavery was an unjust system. Southerners argued that each state should be able to determine for itself whether slavery should be allowed. Congress legislated a series of compromises during the 1850s to try to settle the issue by maintaining a balance between the number of slave states and free states.

After Abraham Lincoln—whose opposition to slavery was well known—was elected to the presidency in November 1860, South Carolina became the first Southern state to leave the Union. In February 1861, six states—South Carolina, Mississippi, Florida, Alabama, Georgia, and Louisiana—left the Union and formed the Confederate States of America, electing Jefferson Davis of Mississippi as their president. When Lincoln was inaugurated on March 4, he expressed his determination to keep the Union together and did not recognize the Southern states' secession (or breaking away from the Union).

On April 12, 1861, war began when Confederate troops attacked and captured Fort Sumter, a federal Army post in Charleston, South Carolina. The major battles of the war were fought in Maryland, Virginia, Tennessee, Georgia, Pennsylvania, Alabama, Kentucky, and Mississippi. The South won many of the battles, particularly during the first years of the war.

The battle at Antietam, Maryland, on September 17, 1862, brought the greatest loss of any one day during the war with more than 22,000 casualties. The Confederate Army retreated, and on September 22, Lincoln issued a preliminary proclamation. This proclamation stated that if the South did not surrender, in 100 days he would sign the Emancipation Proclamation.

Emancipation Proclamation

One hundred days later, on January 1, 1863, Lincoln issued the Emancipation Proclamation. It stated that "all persons held as slaves" within the Confederacy "shall be thenceforward and forever free." (*See the Appendix for the text of the Proclamation and for Bishop H. M. Turner's account of public reaction that day in Washington, D.C.*)

In anticipation, on New Year's Eve 1862, many African Americans in the North gathered in churches to hold vigils while awaiting the dawn of what they hoped and prayed would be a truly new day in America. These were also known as Watch Night services, and to this day many African Americans attend Watch Night services on December 31.

Just before Lincoln signed the document, he said to his friends, "I have never, in my life, felt more certain that I was doing right than I do in signing this paper." At around 8 that evening, the announcement of the signing began traveling over the telegraph lines.

The Emancipation Proclamation did not actually free the slaves—it couldn't really be enforced in the South while the Civil War raged on—but it was, as Frederick Douglass put it, "the first step on the part of the nation in its departure from the thraldom of the ages." From his Brooklyn pulpit abolitionist and minister Henry Ward Beecher hailed the document as giving "liberty a moral recognition."

Northern African Americans held huge celebrations on New Year's Day in 1863 and over the next several days. There were speeches and hymn singing in churches. Outside bells rang, cannons fired, and there were public readings of the Proclamation. At Boston's Music Hall Ralph Waldo Emerson read a poem he'd composed especially for the day to an audience of prominent writers sympathetic to the cause, including Harriet Beecher Stowe, Oliver Wendell Holmes, and Henry Wadsworth Longfellow. The poem was titled "Boston Hymn." One verse began:

> To-day unbind the captive,
> So only are ye unbound.

"I have never, in my life, felt more certain that I was doing right than I do in signing this paper."

— President Lincoln, just before signing the Emancipation Proclamation

In the South, celebrations were generally restricted to those areas under Union control, since the Southern states did not accept laws or proclamations from the North.

Turning Point and War's End

The battle at Gettysburg, Pennsylvania, fought on July 1-3, 1863, resulted in about 50,000 Union and Confederate casualties. This battle marked a turning point in the war, producing losses from which the South would not recover. On November 19, 1863, President Lincoln went to Gettysburg to dedicate what would be a new national cemetery. There he delivered one of the best-known speeches in American history, the Gettysburg Address.

In 1864 Lincoln was reelected as president and began drawing up plans to reunify the nation. The Union Army won more battles, capturing key cities in the South. After Sherman's march to the sea in November and December of 1864, the end of the war was near.

This illustration by Thomas Nast appeared in the January 12, 1867, issue of Harper's Weekly. *It had been a little over a year since Congress passed the 13th Amendment to the Constitution which abolished slavery. Nast questioned whether slavery was really dead by illustrating two events that occurred on December 22, 1866: on the left, an African-American man is sold as punishment for a crime in Annapolis, Maryland; on the right, an African-American man in Raleigh, North Carolina, is whipped as punishment for a crime.*

On April 9, 1865, the war ended, when Confederate General Robert E. Lee surrendered to Union General Ulysses S. Grant.

It is estimated that about 1 million troops fought in the Confederate Army and 2.2 million troops fought for the Union. At the end of the war, the South had lost between 133,000 and 165,000 men, and the North, 360,000 men. One by one, the Southern states reentered the Union. In order to do so, they had to ratify the 13th Amendment to the Constitution, which officially ended slavery in the United States (*see the Appendix for the text of the 13th Amendment*). By the end of 1865, every Southern state, except Texas, ratified the Amendment and reentered the United States. It wasn't until

February 18, 1870, that Texas did so; it reentered the Union on March 30, 1870.

Although slavery was now illegal throughout the nation, Southerners in the Reconstruction era found ways to systematically deny African Americans the freedoms outlined in the 13th Amendment. (*See* **Martin Luther King Jr. Birthday** *for more information about race relations in the South after Reconstruction up through the civil rights movement.*)

Early Freedom Festivals

The first major emancipation festivals in the United States celebrated the end of the Atlantic slave trade on January 1, 1808, and African Caribbeans' emancipation by the British on August 1, 1834. African Americans in large northern cities, such as New York, Boston, and Philadelphia, celebrated January 1 with parades, followed by special religious services that included sermons or speeches delivered in some places by black men.

These festivals were similar to Fourth of July celebrations which, up until the early years of the 19th century, blacks attended along with whites in the North. One element common to **Independence Day** festivities in this period — military musters and cannon fire — was usually missing, though. Militia groups excluded African Americans, who generally could not obtain cannons, cannon balls, and other heavy artillery.

In Boston, from 1808 through the 1820s, emancipation celebrations were held on July 14, rather than on January 1. Various theories attempt to explain why this was so. It could have been a nod to French revolutionaries, since July 14 is Bastille Day. It could have been in response to white Americans who excluded them from Independence Day celebrations. Or it could have had something to do with the fact that the weather in Boston is much more pleasant for parades and other outdoor activities in July than in January.

Emancipation Day Observances

In the first years after the Emancipation Proclamation and the passage of the 13th Amendment, celebrations varied among African Americans in the North and in the South. Northern festivals often incorporated political and educational activities. Southern revelers, however, ever mindful of the segregationist Jim Crow laws enacted by their white neighbors, tended to emphasize more purely festive events, and thus shied away from incorporating civic or political elements into celebrations.

During the early to mid-20th century many festival organizers presented pageants dramatizing African-American history from the glories of old African civilizations through slavery on to emancipation and the civil rights movement.

Parades, speeches, and the singing of appropriate songs — such as "John Brown," "America," and "The Battle Hymn of the Republic" — have been favorite events. Other popular activities are dances and dance contests, barbecues, beauty contests, baseball games and other sports and contests, religious services including hymn singing, scripture readings and sermons, and the reading of the Emancipation Proclamation. Programs also frequently include fashion shows, since it is customary to wear beautiful new clothes for the celebration, signifying how far African Americans have come since the days of slavery.

Just as Independence Day has served as an occasion for protest and for civic and community activity, so have Emancipation Day and other freedom day celebrations, particularly in recent years. Organizers often include voter registration drives and other nonpartisan political activities to further advance African-American civil rights and the struggle against racism. At Birmingham, Alabama's, January 1 Emancipation Day celebration in 1956 organizers formally honored those who boycotted buses during the famous Montgomery bus boycott of the civil rights movement.

Emancipation Day in Washington, D.C., is April 16. On that date in 1862 — months before the national proclamation — Lincoln signed into law a bill passed by Congress that freed all slaves in the District of Columbia. In 2005 the District of Columbia made April 16 a legal public holiday. For years Washingtonians have held parades and other festivities on April 16. These days there is a week-long celebration with a parade, speeches, lectures, worship services, a music festival, a golf tournament, and fireworks.

In the latter part of the 20th century, Emancipation Day was more and more eclipsed by Juneteenth, which is widely observed throughout the nation. Juneteenth events range from solemn church services to all-out galas, such as music festivals and parades.

Juneteenth

Date Observed: June 19

Juneteenth commemorates June 19, 1865, the day Union General Gordon Granger and his troops arrived in Galveston, Texas, and announced that they were there to enforce the Emancipation Proclamation. He publicly read General Order No. 3, which stated:

> The people of Texas are informed that, in accordance with a proclamation from the Executive of the United States, all slaves are free. This involves an absolute equality of personal rights and rights of property between former masters and slaves, and the connection heretofore existing between them becomes that between employer and hired labor. The freedmen are advised to remain quietly at their present homes and work for wages. They are informed that they will not be allowed to collect at military posts and that they will not be supported in idleness either there or elsewhere.

On June 19, members of Galveston Island's Juneteenth Coalition annually reenact the reading of the Emancipation Proclamation on the steps of the Ashton Villa, the site where the first reading took place in 1865.

No one is sure why it took news of the Emancipation Proclamation two and a half years to travel to Texas. One tale has it that an earlier messenger was murdered en route. Other stories accuse either Union troops or slave owners of postponing the announcement so that the slaves would bring in one more year's cotton crop.

The observance of Juneteenth has been marked by controversy. When lawmakers in Texas made it a state holiday in 1979, the bill did not pass overwhelmingly. For one thing, many people were urging that Martin Luther King Jr.'s birthday be considered as the state holiday commemorating freedoms gained by African Americans (*see* **Martin Luther King Jr. Birthday**). For another, some expressed dismay that the state would officially celebrate, as one former state representative put it, the fact "that we were kept ignorant" between January 1, 1863, and June 19, 1865.

Nonetheless, Juneteenth is now more widely observed around the United States than is Emancipation Day.

Juneteenth Observances

Juneteenth celebrations often feature readings of the General Order, music festivals, and picnics. Traditional refreshments are fried chicken, barbecued meats, and red soda pop.

Although Juneteenth celebrations have sprung up around the nation as a result of southern African Americans moving north and west after being freed, many descendants prefer to gather at family reunions in the south. Some festivals also include an event honoring fathers, since Juneteenth falls near, and sometimes on, Father's Day, the third Sunday in June.

A Sampling of Observances

1. **San Francisco, California:** Juneteenth Festival since 1950, offers a parade, carnival, and street festival, featuring food, live entertainment, and arts and crafts displays. Contact San Francisco Juneteenth Committee, African American Art & Culture Complex, 762 Fulton St., 3rd Fl., San Francisco, CA 94102, 415-931-2729; fax: 415-931-3854, sfjuneteenth@sbc global.net, http://www.sfjuneteenth.org

2. **Pomona, California:** Juneteenth Celebration and Job Fair since 1989 features musical performances, food, job fair, and more. Contact Juneteenth

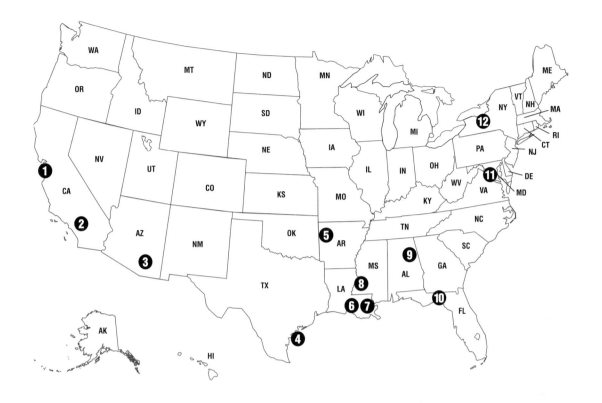

America, Inc., P.O. Box 1356, Ontario, CA 91762, 909-889-8474, jai@juneteenthamerica.us, http://www.juneteenthamerica.us

3. **Tucson, Arizona:** Juneteenth Festival since 1970 features gospel music, BBQ, dance, and sporting events. Contact Tucson Juneteenth Festival Committee, http://www.youthtogether.org/juneteenth/

4. **Galveston, Texas:** Elaborate festivities where Juneteenth began — banquets, picnics, prayer services, parade and march, numerous educational activities, and Gospel by the Sea music festival. For Gospel by the Sea, contact St. Vincent's Episcopal House, 2817 Post Office St., Galveston, TX 77550, 409-763-8521; fax: 409-763-0572, stvhope@stvhope.org, http://www.stvhope.org. For other events, contact Galveston Convention & Visitors Bureau, 2504 Church, Galveston, TX 77550, 866-505-4456 or 409-763-6564, http://www.galveston.com.

5. **Fort Smith, Arkansas:** Freedom and Unity Celebration events include a reenactment of Gen. Granger's arrival, sporting events, pageants, and musical performances. Contact Juneteenth Planning Commission, Inc., P.O. Box 8083, Fort Smith, AR 72901, 479-285-4932, fax: 479-646-0983, http://www.juneteenth-fortsmith.org/

6. **Donaldsonville, Louisiana:** Juneteenth Freedom Festival presents a Gospel Day in the Park, dance, music, food. Festival themes from past years include black cowboys, buffalo soldiers, and Mardi Gras Indians. Contact River Road African-American Museum, P.O. Box 266, 406 Charles St., Donaldsonville, LA 70346, 225-474-5553, http://www .africanamericanmuseum.org

7. **New Orleans, Louisiana:** Juneteenth Jazz Jam & Arts Festival also offers poetry readings, BBQ, and voter registration and education. Contact New Orleans African American Museum of Art, Culture & History, 1418 Governor Nichols St., New Orleans, LA 70116, 504-529-2976, http://www.noaam.org

8. **Natchez, Mississippi:** Juneteenth events feature a fashion show, soul food supper, gospel music, games, picnic, and a Libation Ceremony and Memorial Walk to the site of a former large slave market at Forks of the Road. Contact Juneteenth Committee at 601-445-8878 or 601-445-9781, rhill02@cableone.net

9. **Anniston, Alabama:** Juneteenth Heritage Festival offers musical entertainment, dancing, food, arts & crafts exhibits, a talent contest, and more. Contact Juneteenth Heritage Board of Anniston, P.O. Box 942, Anniston, AL 36202, 256-237-2938 or 256-820-5631, Juneteenthfestival @mail.com, http://www.juneteenthanniston.homestead.com/

10. **Tallahassee, Florida:** May 20th Emancipation Day, marking the date in 1865 when the Emancipation Proclamation was read in Tallahassee. The week-long celebration includes a wreath-laying ceremony, reading of the Proclamation, music, community festival, and other events. Contact The John G. Riley Center/Museum of African American History and Culture, 419 E. Jefferson St., Tallahassee, FL 32301, 850-681-7881, fax: 850-681-7000, staff@rileymuseum.org, http://www .rileymuseum.org

11. **Washington, D.C.:** April 16th Emancipation Day celebration (see description above). Contact The District of Columbia Emancipation Day Foundation, 4101 South Dakota Ave., N.E., Washington, DC 20017, 202-529-4833, http://www.dcemancipation.org

12. **Rochester, New York:** July 5th Emancipation Day celebration, commemorating the state law that freed slaves on July 4, 1827. Festivities include street performances featuring costumed reenactors of historical figures, music, games, and more. Contact The Landmark Society of Western New York, 133 S. Fitzhugh, Rochester, NY 14608, 585-546-7029; fax: 585-546-4788, mail@landmarksociety.org, http://www.landmarksociety.org

Web Sites

"African-American Odyssey" online exhibits of the Library of Congress at http://lcweb2.loc.gov/ammem/aaohtml/

Frederick Douglass Papers at the Library of Congress offers writings of the abolitionist and other documents at http://memory.loc.gov/ammem/doughtml/doughome.html

"From Slavery to Civil Rights: A Timeline of African-American History" at the Library of Congress at http://memory.loc.gov/learn/features/civilrights/flash.html

Harriet Tubman Historical Society at http://www.harriettubman.com

Harriet Tubman Home at http://www.harriettubmanhome.org

"'I Will Be Heard': Abolitionism in America," an online exhibit of Cornell University Library, at http://rmc.library.cornell.edu/abolitionism/

Juneteenth.com offers a database of celebrations held in the U.S. and around the world at http://www.juneteenth.com

National Association of Juneteenth Lineage at http://www.najl.org/

National Underground Railroad Freedom Center at http://www.freedomcenter.org

Public Broadcasting Service (PBS) productions online:

"African American World" at http://www.pbs.org/wnet/aaworld/

"Africans in America" at http://www.pbs.org/wgbh/aia/

Sojourner Truth Memorial Statue Project at http://www.noho.com/sojourner/

Sources for Further Reading

Altman, Linda Jacobs. *Slavery and Abolition in American History*. Berkeley Heights, N.J.: Enslow, 1999. For young adults.

Bentley, Judith. *Harriet Tubman*. New York: Franklin Watts, 1990. For young adults.

Berlin, Ira. *Many Thousands Gone: The First Two Centuries of Slavery in North America*. Cambridge, Mass.: Belknap Press of Harvard University Press, 1998.

Berlin, Ira, Marc Favreau, and Steven F. Miller, eds. *Remembering Slavery: African Americans Talk about Their Personal Experiences of Slavery and Emancipation*. New York: New Press, 1998.

Burnside, Madeleine. *Spirits of the Passage: The Transatlantic Slave Trade in the Seventeenth Century*. New York: Simon & Schuster, 1997.

Clinton, Catherine. *Scholastic Encyclopedia of the Civil War*. New York: Scholastic, 1999. For young adults.

Douglass, Frederick. *Life and Times of Frederick Douglass: His Early Life as a Slave, His Escape from Bondage and His Complete History, Written by Himself*. New York: Bonanza Books, 1962.

Franklin, John Hope. *The Emancipation Proclamation*. Garden City, N.Y.: Doubleday & Company, 1963.

———. *From Slavery to Freedom*. New York: Alfred A. Knopf, 1968.

Genovese, Eugene D. *Roll, Jordan, Roll: The World the Slaves Made*. New York: Pantheon Books, 1974.

Guelzo, Allen C. *Lincoln's Emancipation Proclamation: The End of Slavery in America*. New York: Simon & Schuster, 2004.

Kachun, Mitch. *Festivals of Freedom: Memory and Meaning in African American Emancipation Celebrations, 1808-1915*. Amherst: University of Massachusetts Press, 2003.

Klingaman, William K. *Abraham Lincoln and the Road to Emancipation, 1861-1865.* New York: Viking, 2001.

McFeely, William S. *Frederick Douglass.* New York: W. W. Norton & Company, 1991.

McKissack, Patricia C., and Fredrick L. McKissack. *Days of Jubilee: The End of Slavery in the United States.* New York: Scholastic, 2003. For young adults.

———. *Sojourner Truth: Ain't I a Woman.* New York: Scholastic, 1992. For young adults.

Payne, Charles M., and Adam Green, eds. *Time Longer Than Rope: A Century of African American Activism, 1850-1950.* New York: New York University Press, 2003.

Ripley, C. Peter, ed. *Witness for Freedom: African American Voices on Race, Slavery, and Emancipation.* Chapel Hill: University of North Carolina Press, 1993.

Taylor, Charles A. *Juneteenth: A Celebration of Freedom.* Greensboro, N.C.: Open Hand Publishing, 2002. For young adults.

Temperley, Howard, ed. *After Slavery: Emancipation and Its Discontents.* London: Frank Cass, 2000.

Wiggins, William H., Jr. *O Freedom! Afro-American Emancipation Celebrations.* Knoxville: University of Tennessee Press, 1987.

Wiggins, William H., Jr., and Douglas DeNatale, eds. *Jubilation! African American Celebrations in the Southeast.* [Educator's Guide] Columbia: University of South Carolina Press, 1994.

Flag Day

*Date Established as a Patriotic and National
Observance: August 3, 1949*

Date Observed: June 14

*Resolved, that the Flag of the thirteen United States shall
be thirteen stripes, alternate red and white; that the Union be thirteen
stars, white on a blue field, representing a new constellation.*
— Continental Congress resolution of June 14, 1777

F lag Day is an official patriotic and national observance to celebrate the first flag created to symbolize the new United States. It falls on the anniversary of the day in 1777 that the Continental Congress formally adopted the flag whose design set the precedent for the current flag. In 1877 Congress called for the national observance of Flag Day. On June 14, 1916, President Woodrow Wilson issued a presidential proclamation requesting Americans to observe the day. Congress did not pass a law making Flag Day an official annual patriotic observance, however, until 1949. On June 9, 1966, Congress designated National Flag Week, the week in which June 14 falls, to be a national observance. Today the president of the United States issues a proclamation every year urging Americans to commemorate the flag on Flag Day as well as during National Flag Week.

George Washington said this about the American flag: "We take the stars from heaven, and the red from our Mother Country, separating it by white stripes, thus showing that we have separated from her, and the white stripes shall go down to posterity representing liberty."

History of the Flag

In January 1776 George Washington approved a design for the first flag to represent all the colonies united in the struggle for independence from Britain. The Grand Union Flag had 13 red and white stripes and, instead of stars on a blue field, the red and white crosses of the British flag on a blue field. After the Declaration of Independence in July 1776, the British crosses were replaced with stars (*for more on the Revolution, see* **Independence Day**).

Before the creation of the first official national flag, troops took their own various colonial flags into the early battles of the Revolutionary War. Some from Virginia and Pennsylvania carried the rattlesnake flag bearing the slogan "Don't Tread on Me." Another Pennsylvania flag featured the phrase "Liberty or Death" and a picture of a soldier with a rifle.

Historians are not certain who designed the flag, but some think it was Francis Hopkinson of Pennsylvania, a signer of the Declaration of Independence. Congress did not leave a record of the identities of the designer and creator. But legend has it that a seamstress in Philadelphia named Betsy Ross made the first flag. Ross was the official flagmaker for the Navy in Pennsylvania. The story came from her grandson, William J. Canby. On March 14, 1870, he gave a speech to the Historical Society of Pennsylvania in which he claimed that some years earlier his grandmother told him that George Washington came to her shop and asked her to make the flag.

The Flag Act of 1818 officially established the general design of the flag, but still left room for much variation. The law specified that the flag would have 13 alternating red and white stripes and 13 stars on a blue field and that a star would be added each time a new state joined the Union. The law did not spell out, however, exactly which shades of red and blue should be used nor how the stars should be arranged.

It wasn't until August 21, 1959, that President Dwight D. Eisenhower approved the design guidelines for the current flag in an Executive Order. According to this order, the U.S. flag is to have 13 stripes that represent the original 13 colonies. Seven red stripes alternate with 6 white stripes. The blue field in the upper left is 7 stripes long, and contains 50 white five-pointed stars, one for each state of the Union. The flag has remained the same since the 50th star was added on August 21, 1959, when Hawaii became a state.

Americans have assigned symbolic meanings to the red, white, and blue, but, in fact, there is no official document stipulating these meanings. It was for the Great Seal that Congress approved symbolic meanings for the colors: white for "purity and innocence," red for "valor" and strength, and blue for "vigilance, perseverance, and justice." Tradition has variously con-

Songs for Old Glory

"The Star-Spangled Banner," lyrics written by Francis Scott Key in 1814 (*see* **Patriotism in the United States** *for more about the national anthem*)

"Rally Round the Flag," written by George F. Root in 1862
"Stars and Stripes Forever," written by John Philip Sousa in 1896
"You're a Grand Old Flag," written by George M. Cohan in 1906

The nickname "Old Glory" for the U.S. flag apparently came from one William Driver, a sea captain from Salem, Massachusetts. Different accounts provide varying details, but most historians agree that Driver was given a flag as a gift in the 1820s or 1830s and that he immediately named it "Old Glory." Driver kept the flag with him at sea or on land. He retired to Nashville, Tennessee, in 1837. During the Civil War, after Union soldiers took Nashville in 1862, Driver retrieved his flag from its hiding spot and took it to the capitol building where Union soldiers hoisted it up. In 1922 Driver's descendents presented the flag to the Smithsonian Institution, which preserves it to this day.

sidered the red to represent courage, daring, or defiance, the white liberty or purity, and the blue loyalty, vigilance, or justice (*for more on the Great Seal, see* **Patriotism in the United States**).

Other nations around the world have recognized the U.S. flag as a symbol of liberty, and some countries have designed their flags based on similar elements. The flags of Cuba and Panama are also red, white, and blue. Brazil's flag is green, yellow, blue, and white, but, like the American flag, uses stars to represent the various states that make up the country. El Salvador, Ecuador, and Venezuela also incorporated stars into their national flags. In August 1991, after former Soviet leaders attempted a coup, President-elect Boris Yeltsin climbed onto a tank waving a red, white, and blue banner.

Pledge of Allegiance and the Flag

The Pledge of Allegiance is as follows:

> I pledge allegiance to the flag of the United States of America, and to the republic for which it stands, one nation under God, indivisible, with liberty and justice for all.

Francis Bellamy wrote the Pledge of Allegiance in 1892. Bellamy was a writer for a children's magazine called *The Youth's Companion*. He intended the Pledge to be part of a school program for the 400th anniversary of Columbus's arrival in the New World. The magazine published the Pledge, as well as the rest of the program, in its September 8, 1892, issue. In 1945 Congress made it the official pledge to the flag of the United States. By 2003, 35 states had passed laws that mandate schools to set aside time each day for students to recite the Pledge of Allegiance (*see the Appendix for the text of Bellamy's school program; see also* **Columbus Day**).

It wasn't until 1954, during the Cold War, that Congress voted to add the phrase "under God" to the Pledge. They wanted to highlight a major difference between the United States and the officially atheistic Soviet Union. The Knights of Columbus, a Roman Catholic men's group, led the effort to include the phrase.

The Pledge has been controversial at times in U.S. history. In the early 1940s, for example, during a period of renewed patriotism in America sparked by World War II, the Barnette case drew national attention. It involved two schoolchildren from Minersville, West Virginia, who decided their religious beliefs as Jehovah's Witnesses did not allow them to recite the Pledge of Allegiance and salute the flag. The *West Virginia Board of Education v. Barnette* case went all the way to the U.S. Supreme Court, which ruled in 1943 that to force anyone to recite the Pledge of Allegiance or salute the flag violated his or her First Amendment rights to freedom of speech and expression. Here is a portion of their ruling:

> If there is any fixed star in our constitutional constellation, it is that no official, high or petty, can prescribe what shall be orthodox in politics, nationalism, religion, or other matters of opinion or force citizens to confess by word or act their faith therein. If there are any circumstances which permit an exception, they do not now occur to us.

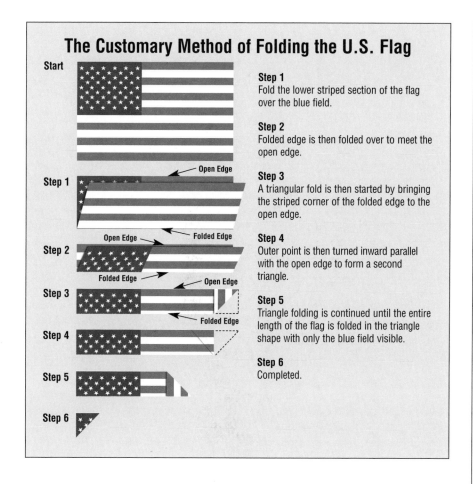

The Customary Method of Folding the U.S. Flag

Start

Step 1
Fold the lower striped section of the flag over the blue field.

Step 2
Folded edge is then folded over to meet the open edge.

Open Edge

Step 1

Step 3
A triangular fold is then started by bringing the striped corner of the folded edge to the open edge.

Open Edge — Folded Edge

Step 2

Folded Edge — Open Edge

Step 4
Outer point is then turned inward parallel with the open edge to form a second triangle.

Step 3

Folded Edge

Step 5
Triangle folding is continued until the entire length of the flag is folded in the triangle shape with only the blue field visible.

Step 4

Step 6
Completed.

Step 5

Step 6

The flag laws and regulations in the U.S. Code of laws do not provide recommendations for how the flag should be folded, but this illustration shows the customary method of folding the U.S. flag.

Flag Etiquette

The U.S. Code of federal laws provides guidelines for the proper handling and use of the American flag. They are listed in the Appendix under "Flag Laws and Regulations."

Observances

On June 14, 1861, residents of Hartford, Connecticut, held the earliest known Flag Day celebration. The Civil War had begun in April, and people in the town organized the event as a show of support for the Union Army.

In 1877 Congress urged the first nationwide observance of Flag Day to commemorate the 100th anniversary of its adoption as the official banner. But Flag Day was still not yet an official annual observance.

As with many other American patriotic days, the adoption of Flag Day as a legally recognized annual day was prompted by an array of political advocates. A few ordinary Americans had been lobbying for such a day since around the turn of the 20th century. The cause was taken up by several organizations over the decades, including the American Legion, the Daughters of the American Revolution (DAR), the Sons of the American Revolution (SAR), the Fraternal Order of the Elks, Chicago schoolteacher and editor of the *American Standard* Bernard J. Cigrand, the American Flag-Day Association, and other grassroots Flag Day associations. In response, President Woodrow Wilson issued his Flag Day proclamation in 1916. Still, many Americans wanted the day to be legally recognized in the official American calendar. In 1949 Congress made Flag Day a permanent patriotic and national observance.

Today, Americans observe Flag Day with flag-raising ceremonies, parades, festivals, and flying the flag at homes, public buildings, and parks. At Fort McHenry National Monument in Baltimore, Maryland (near the location where Francis Scott Key wrote "The Star-Spangled Banner"), more than 3,000 children have formed a living flag on Flag Day each year since 1985. The National Flag Day Foundation organizes that event as well as the Annual Pause for the Pledge of Allegiance.

A Sampling of Observances

1. **Vancouver, Washington:** "Celebrate Freedom" Flag Day Ceremony and Annual Pause for the Pledge at Fort Vancouver. Organized by the Vancouver National Historic Reserve Trust and Partners, General O. O. Howard House, 750 Anderson St., Vancouver, WA 98661, 360-992-1800, fax: 360-992-1810, http://www.vancouverhistoricreserve.org/

2. **Fairfield, Washington:** Locally known as "The Town That Celebrates Flag Day" since 1910, with a parade, fun run, and street dance. Contact Town of Fairfield, P.O. Box 334, Fairfield, WA 99012, 509-283-2414

3. **Appleton, Wisconsin:** Parade since 1950, along with a drum and bugle corps competition. Contact Fox Cities Convention & Visitors Bureau, 3433 W. College Ave., Appleton, WI 54914-3919, 800-2DO-MORE (236-6673) or 920-734-3358; fax: 920-734-1080, tourism@foxcities.org

   The Fox Valley Flag Day Powwow honors veterans. Contact American Indian Center, 128 N. Oneida St., Appleton, WI 54911, 800-482-0030 or 920-968-6363, fax: 920-731-3041, http://www.focol.org/intertribal/

4. **Waubeka, Wisconsin:** Flag ceremony, parade, salute to veterans, and fly-overs. Contact The National Flag Day Foundation, P.O. Box 55, Waubeka, WI 53021-0055, 262-692-9111, http://www.nationalflagday.com

5. **Pittsburgh, Pennsylvania:** Flags Across America Flag Day Celebration with flag raising and speeches at Flag Plaza. Organized by the National Flag Foundation, Flag Plaza, 1275 Bedford Ave., Pittsburgh, PA 15219, 800-615-1776, http://www.americanflags.org

6. **Troy, New York:** Parade, food, and music festival. Contact Flag Day Parade Committee, 518-270-9122

7. **Framingham, Massachusetts:** The town puts on a week of festivities — a parade, concerts, and other activities. Contact Framingham Cele-

bration Committee, Inc., 475 Union Ave., Framingham, MA 01702, 508-620-4834, http://www.geocities.com/flagdayframingham/

8. **Brookline, Massachusetts:** A parade, fun runs, carnival, and more. Contact the Brookline Flag Day Celebrations Committee, 11 Pierce St., Brookline, MA 02445, 617-730-2112, fax: 617-730-2296, http://www .town.brookline.ma.us/FlagDay/Index.html

9. **Baltimore, Maryland:** Ceremonies at Fort McHenry include concerts, speeches, a pause for the Pledge of Allegiance, parade of flags, and the Living Flag. Organized by The National Flag Day Foundation, Inc., P.O. Box 435, Riderwood, MD 21139, 410-563-FLAG (3524) or 410-821-1252, http://www.flagday.org

Web Sites

Flag House & Star-Spangled Banner Museum at http://www.flaghouse .org

Fort McHenry National Monument and Historic Site at http://www.nps .gov/fomc/index.htm

North American Vexillological Association at http://www.nava.org/

Smithsonian Institution's National Museum of American History has an online exhibit about the flag at http://americanhistory.si.edu/ssb/

Sources for Further Reading

Druckman, Nancy. *American Flags: Designs for a Young Nation*. New York: Harry N. Abrams, 2003. For young adults.

Furlong, William Rea, and Byron McCandless. *So Proudly We Hail: The History of the United States Flag*. Washington, D.C.: Smithsonian Institution Press, 1981.

Marling, Karal Ann. *Old Glory: Unfurling History*. Charlestown, Mass.: Bunker Hill Publishing in association with the Library of Congress, 2004.

Our Flag [52-page booklet]. Washington, D.C.: Joint Committee on Printing, U.S. Congress, 2003. Online through the Federal Citizen Information Center at http://www.pueblo.gsa.gov/cic_test/misc/ourflag/title page.htm

Smith, Whitney. *The Flag Book of the United States: The Story of the Stars and Stripes and the Flags of the Fifty States*. Rev. ed. New York: William Morrow & Co., 1975.

Independence Day

Alternate Name: Fourth of July

Date Established as a Federal Holiday: May 13, 1938

Date Observed: July 4

The Second Day of July 1776, will be the most memorable Epocha, in the History of America. I am apt to believe that it will be celebrated, by succeeding Generations, as the great anniversary Festival. It ought to be commemorated, as the Day of Deliverance by solemn Acts of Devotion to God Almighty. It ought to be solemnized with Pomp and Parade, with Shews [shows], Games, Sports, Guns, Bells, Bonfires and Illuminations, from one End of this Continent to the other from this Time forward forever more.

—From a July 3, 1776, letter by future president John Adams
to his wife, Abigail

Americans celebrate the birthday of the United States on Independence Day, also called the Fourth of July. In Philadelphia, Pennsylvania, on July 2, 1776, the Continental Congress voted to become independent from England. For this reason, John Adams believed that July 2 would be the date of the national holiday. But the written final copy of the Declaration of Independence carried the title "In Congress, July 4, 1776" across the top, because that is the date on which the Congress formally approved the document.

Independence Day is the most important patriotic holiday in the United States and is observed throughout the country as well as in the U.S. territories and among Americans overseas. In 1870, Congress passed a law making it a holiday in Washington, D.C. In 1938 Congress made the Fourth a legal public holiday across the nation. In 1975 Congress designated the days from June 14, **Flag Day**, through July 4 as Honor America Days, in hopes of encouraging "public gatherings and activities during that period at which the people of the United States can celebrate and honor their country in an appropriate way."

"All of Us Americans"

By 1776 British people had lived on the North American continent as subjects of the monarch of England since the Jamestown settlement in 1607 in what is now Virginia. They lived in 13 communities, known as colonies, along America's east coast from New Hampshire to Georgia. These communities were called colonies because even though the Atlantic Ocean separated them from England, they were ruled by the monarch and considered part of the British Empire, which referred to these overseas properties as "colonies." From 1727 to 1760 the monarch was King George II. From 1760 to 1820 his grandson George III reigned.

Until the middle of the 18th century, most white people living in America were of British descent, or had come directly from England. They thought of themselves as British subjects living in America, not as "Americans." Before that time, the idea of actually starting a new independent nation was unimaginable. The colonists flew the British flag, read British literature, played British games, sang British songs, and celebrated British holidays. In fact, elaborate celebrations were held in the colonies when King George III took the throne in 1760 as well as for his birthday every year. So, how did the British living in America come to the radical decision to become an independent country?

The creation of the United States was not necessarily inevitable, but there had been seeds planted and ideas in the air. They led to the formation of an entirely new entity in the world: a free and independent republic founded on the belief that all men are created equal.

Looking at the situation from today's vantage point, it is evident that the potential for independence had been developing for some years. The colonies had been acting like self-governing states long before anyone conceived of the need for a declaration of independence. Many towns had elected assemblies of local men who set laws and kept order. In addition, by the 18th century British people — in England and in the colonies — were among the freest peoples in the world. The Revolution of 1688 in England had ush-

> ## American Population in the Late 1700s
>
> In the 1750s, there were about 150,000 Indians living east of the Mississippi River; by 1770, there were more than two million colonists. The 13 original colonies were located in three regions along the eastern coast. The New England colonies included Massachusetts, New Hampshire, Connecticut, and Rhode Island; the middle colonies included New York, New Jersey, Pennsylvania, and Delaware; and the southern colonies included Virginia, Maryland, Georgia, North Carolina, and South Carolina.
>
> **Population according to the first U.S. census in 1790:**
> 3,929,214 (excluding Native Americans and also not counting the Northwest Territories, Spanish Territories, or French Territories)
>   African Americans: 757,208, or 19%
>   Whites: 3,172,006, or 81%
>
> **The white population was made up of immigrants of the following nationalities:**
>
> | | | |
> |---|---|---|
> | English and Welsh: 60.9% | Scotch: 8.3% | French: 1.7% |
> | German: 8.7% | Irish (Ulster): 6.0% | Swedish: 0.7% |
> | | Irish (Free State): 3.7% | Unassigned: 6.6% |
> | | Dutch: 3.4% | |

ered in an era of increased liberty for ordinary British people. They were granted certain civil rights, such as the right to a jury trial, freedom of speech, and the right to elect representatives to the House of Commons, which is part of the British Parliament (the equivalent of the U.S. Congress).

Also spurring the movement toward independence were the growing restrictions on freedoms that King George III and the British Parliament placed on the colonists. The Currency Act of 1751 prohibited the New England colonists from printing their own paper money. In 1761 England decreed that all judges appointed in the colonies must be approved by the King. In 1763 King George III ruled that colonists were not allowed to settle west of the Appalachian mountains, except for an area around the upper Ohio River. In addition, any colonists who had been living in the west were ordered to move back east (many didn't do it). The next year

Benjamin Franklin (1706-1790), writer and printer, statesman and philosopher, scientist and inventor, was a man of countless accomplishments and contributions to the establishment of many social institutions of the new nation. He increased the professionalism of the postal service and helped establish the country's first borrowing library, a hospital, police and fire departments, and the University of Pennsylvania. Franklin signed the Declaration of Independence and, after independence, was a member of the Constitutional Convention. He successfully served as U.S. diplomat to France, where he enlisted that nation's help in the war for independence. Sayings from Franklin's *Poor Richard's Almanac* (1732-57)—such as "A stitch in time saves nine" and "Haste makes waste"—remain familiar in American conversation.

Parliament passed the Sugar Act, which increased the number of indirect taxes, called duties, that colonists had to pay on certain items imported from England. In 1764 another Currency Act prohibited the colonies outside of New England from issuing paper money.

To many colonists, the strongest impetus for revolution was the passage of the Stamp Act. The "stamp" referred to an impression onto paper. Up until this time, many colonists used paper produced in America. Benjamin Franklin, for example, ran a print shop and made his own paper. The Stamp Act, which became law on March 22, 1765, stipulated that only paper produced and sold in England and bearing its official stamp could be used in the colonies for nearly all paper items. It included legal documents, such as wills, mortgages, and licenses, as well as newspapers, almanacs, and other published writings—even playing cards.

Why had Britain imposed the Stamp Act? The country's involvement in the French and Indian War had depleted many of Britain's resources and put the country in debt. The British people at home were already being heavily taxed, so Parliament voted to raise more money by taxing the colonists—something the British government had never directly done before.

The American colonists were outraged at the Stamp Act. Because they had no elected representatives to speak on their behalf in the British Parliament, the colonists deemed it illegal for Parliament to tax them. According to the British constitution, people could not be taxed unless they had elected representatives to Parliament. Even so, some colonies were willing to consider raising money to help out with the mother country's expenses in America. Instead of compromising with the colonists, however, Britain's prime minister George Grenville was determined to impose the tax. A small delegation, including Benjamin Franklin, met with Grenville and attempted to persuade him to consider another course of action. He refused.

One by one, rioters and members of organizations called the Sons of Liberty ousted the British stamp distributors throughout the colonies. In some cases, they threatened them into resigning. According to one historian, "the distributor in Connecticut was threatened with lynching if he didn't"

French and Indian War

From 1689 to 1763, England and France fought a series of wars for the colonial territories in North America. Each country wanted to be more powerful than the other, which in those days meant having the most land. The last war, between 1754 and 1763, is known in the United States as the French and Indian War. At that war's beginning, France possessed land stretching from Quebec to Louisiana, while Spain controlled Florida. England and France both built up relationships with various Indian groups in order to enlist their support. When it was over, England controlled its original colonial holdings as well as all of Canada, the Great Lakes, Florida, and much land east of the Mississippi River. France retained Louisiana, which it then gave to Spain.

resign. On October 7, 1765, representatives from nine colonies met. At this meeting Christopher Gadsden, a delegate from South Carolina, said:

> We should all endeavour to stand upon the broad and common ground of those natural and inherent rights that we all feel and know, as men and as descendants of Englishmen, we have a right to . . . There ought to be no New England men, no New York &c.; known on the continent, but all of us Americans.

Parliament repealed the Stamp Act on March 18, 1766, but more taxes and restrictions were to come. And the combination of Britain's stubborn determination to impose its will on the colonies and the colonists' growing resolve to assert their civil rights was setting a course for revolution.

Dissolving Bonds

By 1769 George Washington speculated that war against the British might become necessary in order to preserve American freedom. And indeed, a series of events from the late 1760s through the 1770s illustrates the escalating tension between Britain and the American colonies.

The Massachusetts Colony, particularly Boston, was the scene of many of these clashes between the British and the colonists. Boston was home to some of the leading radicals behind America's struggle for liberty and self-rule, including John Hancock, Samuel Adams, and Paul Revere. British troops began occupying the city of Boston in the autumn of 1768 to rein in these colonists. The Quartering Act of 1765 had added to the tension by requiring colonists to house and feed the troops. On September 13, 1768, the Boston town council decreed that all residents should equip themselves with weapons. Two weeks later British warships appeared in Boston Harbor.

The Boston Massacre took place a year and a half later, on March 5, 1770. When a raucous group of Bostonians challenged British troops at the Customs House, the soldiers fired into the crowd, killing five people and wounding six. Afterwards, to protect them from the colonists, British troops were stationed on islands in Boston Harbor, rather than on the mainland. Three years later, in 1773, the famous Boston Tea Party played out Boston's resistance against the British tax on tea when a group of men

John Hancock (1737-1793) was president of the Continental Congress and was the first to sign the Declaration of Independence. He is famous for his prominent signature on that document. Hancock served as the governor of Massachusetts from 1780 to 1785, and 1787 to 1793.

Samuel Adams (1722-1803) distinguished himself as one of the most radical of the American revolutionaries. He wrote articles, gave speeches, and generally rallied people against British infringements on colonists' liberties. Sam Adams was a cousin of John Adams, the second president.

Paul Revere (1735-1818) was an active revolutionary who participated in the Boston Tea Party in 1774. But he is best remembered for riding his horse through the night to warn the Massachusetts towns of Lexington and Concord of the impending British invasion of 1775 that started the Revolutionary War. He managed to reach Lexington and warn colonists all along the route, but the British captured Revere before he got to Concord.

dressed as Indians went aboard British ships and threw their loads of tea into Boston Harbor. New York followed suit four months later with its own "tea party."

Patrick Henry (1736-1799) of Virginia was a self-taught lawyer, pamphleteer, and member of the Continental Congress. Americans have found inspiration in his patriotic writings, especially the famous phrase, "Give me liberty, or give me death," with which he concluded a speech to the Virginia legislature in 1775. Henry became governor of Virginia in 1776, served until 1779, and was reelected to serve from 1784 to 1786.

In response, the British government devised the Coercive Acts of 1774 to punish the colonies—especially Boston—for leading the way in what Parliament viewed as treasonous behavior. The Acts closed the Boston port and required its citizens to pay for the tea dumped in the Harbor. Parliament also decreed that the British governor would appoint men to the town council, in place of the colonists' own elected representatives. The governor would also control town meetings and juries. All this would be enforced by the new British governor of Massachusetts, General Thomas Gage, aided by additional British troops.

On April 19, 1775, British soldiers, under orders from Gage, attacked colonial arms and supply houses in Lexington and Concord, Massachusetts. This was "the shot heard round the world." The Revolutionary War began on that day, which Massachusetts residents still commemorate as Patriots' Day. It is also the day of Paul Revere's famous ride to Lexington and Concord.

Meanwhile, other colonists, such as Patrick Henry, Richard Henry Lee, and eventually, the Continental Congress, were working on a more diplomatic approach. They had been writing letters to King George III, calling for the removal of taxes and British troops as well as respect for their civil rights.

By 1775, the colonies were coming together in solidarity and practical action against the British. One by one, they voted to boycott British goods and resist British laws depriving them of their rights. When the first of the Coercive Acts went into effect against the citizens of Boston on June 1, 1774, Virginia held a day of fasting and prayer. As Thomas Jefferson wrote in his autobiography, the purpose of this day was "to implore heaven to avert from us the evils of civil war, to inspire us with firmness in support of our rights, and to turn the hearts of the King & parliament to moderation & justice." As the colonists foresaw the possibility of war with Britain, they considered it to be a civil war, since it would be British soldiers fighting British subjects.

While a feeling of unity was on the rise among the colonies, not everyone wanted to be part of this emerging movement. Many colonists still considered themselves to be British and they also felt allegiance to the King, if no longer to the British government. They wanted to remain part of Britain, but they also didn't want to give up their self-governing way of life. Other colonists continued to be firmly loyal to Britain, in spite of the new taxes and restrictions, and wanted no part of the growing movement against their mother country. According to historian Gordon S. Wood, probably no more than 20% were loyalists to George III.

"The Unanimous Declaration of the Thirteen United States of America"

The movement to unite the colonies began as early as 1754. That year representatives from six colonies met at the Albany Congress in New York, and Benjamin Franklin presented a plan for the colonies to form a union. The union would have a council of officials elected by each colony's assembly, plus a president, whom King George would appoint. Both the King and the colonies turned down this idea. The institution of a centralized government in the colonies was too threatening to the King's power over this part of his empire. And most of the colonies still wanted to be part of Britain.

By the early 1770s Massachusetts declared that the colonies were "distinct States from the mother country." What they meant by this was that, although the colonies continued to consider themselves in alliance with the King, they were no longer under the Parliament's control. This declaration

Thomas Paine (1737-1809)

Proof of the power of the pen, Thomas Paine wrote *Common Sense*, which many historians consider to be the most influential piece of writing of the Revolutionary era. So crucial was Paine to the birth of the independent American nation that John Adams declared that "without the pen of Paine the sword of Washington would have been wielded in vain." Paine came from England to America in 1774, with the encouragement and help of Benjamin Franklin. His major writings, serialized in newspapers over the 1770s-90s, are *Common Sense* (1776), *The Crisis* (1776-83), *The Rights of Man* (1791-92), and *The Age of Reason* (1794-95). Paine served in the army during the Revolutionary War. During that time he wrote an important series of essays called together *The Crisis*. The first essay contains the famous opening sentence: "These are the times that try men's souls."

was in keeping with that colony's radical reputation and caused the other colonies' unease. They were not yet ready to make such a break from England. Moreover, Britain was the world's superpower. In 1760, the British Empire possessed 22 colonies in the Western Hemisphere alone. And it showed no signs of loosening its control over America. If war broke out, how would the colonies ever be able to win against such a power?

The First Continental Congress met between September 5 and October 26, 1774, with representatives from every colony except Georgia. They resolved to ignore the Coercive Acts, collect their own taxes, and form their own militias. Three months after the British attack at Lexington and Concord, the Second Continental Congress sent what is known as the Olive Branch Petition, a letter to the King calling for peace and reconciliation. George III responded on August 23, 1775, with a proclamation that the colonies were in rebellion. He obtained mercenary soldiers from Germany, called Hessians, to help his troops fight the colonists.

But the colonists had yet to draw up a declaration of war. On June 11 the Second Continental Congress appointed a team to write the Declaration: John Adams, Benjamin Franklin, Thomas Jefferson, Roger Sherman, and Robert R. Livingston. The team chose Jefferson to draft the work. In addition to outlining their reasons for war, the Congress hoped the Declaration would show the rest of the world—especially France—that the colonies were serious about becoming independent and thus convince other nations to provide military support.

The Declaration of Independence was actually the last in a string of proposals and declarations written by the colonists and submitted to England throughout the last half of the 18th century. Other resolutions for independence were made by various colonial assemblies, but until July 1776, all maintained at least a thread of connection to the mother country. The Declaration of 1776 made the final break with Britain. It was also the first united expression of all the colonies. For the first time, they all agreed to become independent of Britain.

The Declaration of Independence is an eloquent statement that conveyed the colonists' struggles to live according to their values under Britain's increasing attempts to control them.

Because the Congress wanted the rest of the world, including England, to understand why it was taking such a drastic step, Jefferson wrote that "a decent Respect to the Opinions of Mankind requires that they [Americans] should declare the causes which impel them to the Separation." Those causes were many, and Jefferson spelled them out in the Declaration. He compiled a list of 27 specific ways in which Britain violated the colonists' civil rights and liberties. In this way, Jefferson set a precedent for the U.S. relationship to the world—one in which America explained its stance and hoped to rally others to its cause.

Jefferson also included an item which did not make it into the final draft. He condemned George III for continuing the slave trade, even though the

> *"Resolved, that these United Colonies are, and of right ought to be, free and independent States, that they are absolved from all allegiance to the British Crown, and that all political connection between them and the State of Great Britain is, and ought to be, totally dissolved."*
>
> —a motion Richard Henry Lee of Virginia proposed to the Second Continental Congress on June 7, 1776

John Adams was born on October 30, 1735, and died on the Fourth of July, 1826. He was a member of the Continental Congress and worked hard to bring the colonies together in agreeing to become independent. He also assisted in editing the Declaration of Independence and played a key role as a diplomat. Adams became the first vice president of the United States in 1789. In 1796 he was elected the second president of the United States.

Thomas Jefferson was born on April 13, 1743, in Virginia, and also died on the Fourth of July, 1826. In addition to writing the Declaration of Independence, Jefferson was a farmer, writer, philosopher, architect, member of the Continental Congress, and third president of the United States.

American colonies also participated in the trade. The colonies of Georgia and South Carolina, however, refused to sign the Declaration if that passage was not removed. During a war with powerful Britain, the majority of Congress decided it was more important to stay united than to press such a heated, controversial issue.

The copy of the Declaration that appeared in newspapers as early as July 8, 1776, contained only the printed names of John Hancock and the Secretary of Congress, Charles Thomson. The image of the Declaration of Independence familiar today, with all the signatures, was not printed and circulated until after Congress voted to do so on January 18, 1777. (*See the Appendix for the text of the Declaration.*)

In an interesting note, the only members who didn't sign were John Dickinson of Pennsylvania, who still wanted to reconcile with England, and Robert R. Livingston of New York, even though he was part of the team that produced the document, because he thought it was "premature."

"The Birthday of a New World"

As noted above, the Revolutionary War began on April 19, 1775, with the British attacks on Lexington and Concord, Massachusetts. At that point, the Continental Congress appointed George Washington to organize and lead an army to defend American independence. Battles were fought in every colony, as well as eastern Canada, as Americans sought to prevent or turn away British troop invasions. Some of the heaviest fighting took place in New Jersey and South Carolina. The first major American victory occurred in October 1777, in Saratoga, New York, where American soldiers forced the surrender of British General John Burgoyne's army. This event marked a turning point in the war and caused France to enter the war as an American ally. The addition of French troops played a critical role in winning later battles and, ultimately, the war, which ended on October 19, 1781, when British General Charles Cornwallis, with 8,000 soldiers, surrendered to more than 16,000 American and French troops at Yorktown, Virginia. It is estimated that more than 4,000 American troops died in battles, and an additional 21,000 died as a result of disease, starvation, and other causes.

So, even though Britain was the most powerful nation in the world at that time, it was, in the end, too weak to suppress the colonists. At just about every policy turn, British administrators seemed unaware of how committed the colonists were to establishing their independence. They were also unwilling to consider ways to deal politically with the colonists' complaints. Finally, they refused to accommodate the colonists' view of themselves as Englishmen with constitutional rights.

The members of the Second Continental Congress signed the Declaration according to their state. The three signatures on the far left column are those of the delegates from Georgia. The next column to the right contains the signatures of the delegates from North Carolina and South Carolina. The third column: the signature of John Hancock in the center of the page, as befitting the president of Congress, followed by signatures of delegates from Maryland and Virginia. The fourth column: Pennsylvania and Delaware. The fifth column: New York and New Jersey. And the sixth column: New Hampshire, Massachusetts, Rhode Island, and Connecticut.

The Treaty of Paris formally ended the war on September 3, 1783, and the world recognized the new independent alliance of the former colonies. The establishment of the new confederacy marked the beginning of a new kind of human society. It made possible a world in which people could be governed not by a succession of members from a royal family, or group of families, but by representatives elected by themselves. Tom Paine called it "the birthday of a new world."

Although the new nation did not at once achieve all the ideals suggested by the Declaration of Independence — namely, the end of slavery as well as full rights to all citizens — it did create a framework for a society that would have the potential to accomplish those aims. (*See* **Election Day** *for more information about voting rights throughout America's history and* **Emancipation Day** *for information about the end of slavery.*)

History of Celebrations

In some ways Americans have continued to mark the Fourth of July much as John Adams imagined in the first year of independence (see quote at the beginning of this entry). Parades, concerts, gunshots, fireworks, sports, and games have remained hallmarks of the day. Throughout U.S. history, however, there has been a lot more to the celebration of America's most important national holiday than picnics and fireworks.

The Spirit of '76

Over the span of several weeks in July 1776, Americans found out about the Declaration of Independence by word of mouth, newspapers, and public readings. Congress printed and distributed copies of the Declaration of Independence throughout the states so that all the colonists would be aware of it. They also were eager to see how the other colonists would react to the document. With no telephones, TVs, or emails to spread the word in an instant, the celebration of the first Independence Day actually stretched out over some weeks. For example, it took several days for the mail to travel the 300 miles from Philadelphia to Boston. People in Georgia didn't find out until August of 1776.

The first Independence Day observances in 1776 consisted largely of public readings of the Declaration. In many places the reading was welcomed by the ringing of bells and the shooting of cannons and muskets. The Declaration of Independence's first appearance in public print was in the July 6 edition of the *Pennsylvania Evening Post*. It was printed in the *Maryland Gazetteer* on July 11 and the *New Hampshire Gazette* on July 20.

Even in Philadelphia, the home of the Declaration, the celebration wasn't organized until July 8. On that day a member of Congress's Committee of Safety, Colonel John Nixon, stood on a balcony of the Pennsylvania State House and read the Declaration of Independence to a crowd below.

PULLING DOWN THE STATUE OF GEORGE III. BY THE "SONS OF FREEDOM."

This engraving by John C. McRae shows the "Sons of Freedom" pulling down the statue of George III in New York City in 1776. The engraving was created in the 1870s and was based on a painting by 19th-century artist Johannes A. Oertel.

They responded with cheers. Gunfire rang out and bells chimed for hours. On July 9 General George Washington had the Declaration read to his men in New York City. Washington carried his copy of the document with him all during the Revolutionary War. He also used it to boost the troops' morale.

Setting the standard for independence celebrations for centuries to come, one of the first things people did upon learning the news was to destroy anything that stood for the old regime. In Boston and Philadelphia people gathered British emblems and the King's coat of arms and built bonfires to burn them. In New York City a statue of King George III was pulled down. Revelers broke the statue into pieces and delivered it all to Litchfield, Connecticut. A few women there melted the pieces down and made about 42,000 bullets for the army.

Meanwhile, many other people participated in the less rowdy activity of illuminating their homes and businesses by putting candles in their windows.

Early Fourths

In the early years of the new union, Americans observed the Fourth of July as a country at war. Soldiers' observances were minimal at best. For those Americans spared the sacrifice of the battlefield, Independence Day usually consisted of bell ringing, gun and cannon fire salutes, militia musters, speeches, and dinners and barbecues, followed by toast making and fireworks. The number 13 played a central role in the early years of the holiday. Thirteen-gun salutes and the making of 13 toasts at dinners paid tribute to the new union of 13 states.

In 1777, the city of Philadelphia took a break from war to mark the first anniversary of the Declaration of Independence. On the Delaware River Navy ships fired 13-gun salutes. Members of Congress dined at the posh City Tavern. Two Hessian military bands fighting with the British had been captured at the Battle of Trenton the previous December. One band was enlisted to provide music for the occasion. Throughout the day town bells rang and guns were shot. Later in the day, American troops from North Carolina appeared in town as they traveled to join the main army. They paused in their journey to parade for members of Congress. After dark, fireworks dazzled Philadelphians assembled in the commons, and candle illuminations appeared in many windows around town. In fact, people in Philadelphia who didn't illuminate the windows in their houses risked having them broken. They included people who remained loyal to the King, as well as Quakers, whose religious beliefs opposed such activities.

> *The number 13 played a central role in the early years of the holiday. Thirteen-gun salutes and the making of 13 toasts at dinners paid tribute to the new union of 13 states.*

Musters, Speeches, and Parades

In the first years of the nation, after bells broke the dawn on the Fourth of July, the first order of the day was often a military muster. Members of the local militia would assemble in a central location in town, such as a park or commons. Carrying their weapons and wearing their uniforms (if they had them), the men would parade for spectators and go through military drills. Musters waned in popularity some years after the end of the Revolutionary War, but military parades remained common. War veterans took an honored place in such parades.

After the parades and musters, local dignitaries would give speeches, either at an outdoor site or at a public hall. During the war, these events were largely attended by revolutionaries and had the character of political rallies. By the time independence was won, however, more and more ordinary people showed up for the ceremonies.

Dinners and Toasts

In the late 1700s and early 1800s it was customary to have large, and sometimes quite formal, dinner parties on Independence Day. Though some dinners took place inside elegant eating establishments, hotels, and taverns, many people preferred to dine outside in a pleasant setting. Indoors or out, these meals tended to be large affairs, attended by dozens of people, and, in some cases, hundreds. They were frequently scheduled for mid-afternoon in order to follow the military parades, speeches, readings, and other civic-minded activities of the early part of the day.

Popular foods served on the Fourth during this era included barbecued meat, turtle soup, and ice cream. Turtle soup was a favorite delicacy which some inns and other food-serving businesses offered only on the Fourth of July. Ice cream seems to have been most available for purchase in the new states during the holiday.

No Independence Day dinner was complete without offering and drinking toasts. These were mini-speeches of sorts prepared ahead of time. They served to promote feelings of national pride and unity. Often, thirteen toasts were offered, one for each new state. Some typical toasts:

> to "the Free, Independent and Sovereign States of America"
> to "Prosperity, Freedom and Independency"
> to "General Washington"
> to "the Continental Army"
> to "the Fourth of July 1776"

After leading citizens delivered the formal toasts, other men in attendance could offer impromptu toasts.

Where were the women? Until about the mid-19th century, women were generally excluded from Independence Day dinners. Actually, given the rowdy nature of some of these celebrations, many probably preferred to stay home. The role of women at celebrations would increase in decades to come, mainly at their insistence. As a result, the character of these dinners would become more moderate.

Musical concerts were popular on early Fourths, as they remain today. They typically featured songs of the day but usually concluded with a patriotic piece, such as "Hail Columbia" or "The President's March." Mock battles and theatrical performances depicting Revolutionary events and other patriotic themes were presented as well.

"Hail Columbia"

One verse from "Hail Columbia" (lyrics by Joseph Hopkinson, 1798) to the tune of "The President's March" (by Philip Phile, 1793):

> Immortal Patriots rise once more
> Defend your rights—defend your shore
> Let no rude foe with impious hand
> Let no rude foe with impious hand
> Invade the shrine where sacred lies
> Of toil and blood the well earned prize
> While offering peace sincere and just
> In heav'n we place a manly trust
> That truth and justice may prevail
> And ev'ry scheme of bondage fail

Among the Troops

During the Revolutionary War soldiers usually got a chance to mark Independence Day, even those who were prisoners of war. Commanding officers often allowed the troops extra rations of liquor in order to propose toasts. Bells rang, if any were on hand, but gunfire salutes were more common.

In 1781, American soldiers held prisoner at Graves End in Long Island, New York, celebrated the Fourth by drinking thirteen toasts, including, not surprisingly, one for "a Speedy Releasment to the Allied Prisoners." The British sent other American POWs to Mill Prison near Plymouth, England. In 1778 soldiers there made American flags and fastened them to their hats for the day.

Constitution Controversy

The new United States faced a whole new set of problems after the Revolutionary War was won. Most urgently, now that they had decided and won the right to govern themselves as a union of states, how would they do it?

INDEPENDENCE HALL, PHILADELPHIA 1776.

The Second Continental Congress, which signed the Declaration of Independence, met in this building, the Pennsylvania State House, later known as Independence Hall. Eleven years later, the U.S. Constitution was written and signed here.

Opinion broke down into two major groups: the Federalists and the anti-Federalists. The dispute was over how much power the national government should have over the states. Federalists advocated a strong central government, with the individual states also maintaining some authority. Anti-Federalists disagreed, believing that states' rights should dominate. They worried that if the national government had too much power, it would become like the monarchy they had just ousted. (*More on this at* **Citizenship Day**).

In 1788 Federalists in Philadelphia furthered their cause by making the Fourth of July celebration a tribute to the Constitution. They staged a "Grand Federal Procession," the largest parade in the United States up to that time. The message they wanted to convey was that the Constitution was as American as the Fourth of July. Use of the word "union" (as well as "federal") and the motifs of inclusion and equality at the July 4, 1788, spectacle was intended to rally supporters and convince doubters of the benefits of unity under a federal government.

The 19th Century: New Country, New Century

The United States grew in many ways over the 19th century. Its boundaries expanded as European settlers forged westward and new states joined the Union. Through railroads and telegraphs, technology advanced. Through the bloody Civil War, African Americans gained certain civil rights and the Union was preserved. By the end of the century, the inclusion of women as full American citizens was not far over the horizon. Neither was America's increasing status as a major power in the world. All of these changes and transformations can be seen in Americans' celebrations of Independence Day throughout the century.

Early in the 19th century Americans continued to celebrate the holiday with gunfire, readings and speeches at public gatherings, food, and toasts. And women continued to bow out of most of the events until about mid-century. Those who lived in the south and the frontier areas, however, frequently attended the military spectacles and dinners, though they usually retreated as the men started toasting.

> *"What, to the American slave, is your 4th of July? I answer; a day that reveals to him, more than all other days in the year, the gross injustice and cruelty to which he is the constant victim."*
> —Frederick Douglass, July 5, 1852

Elaborate and large public dinners remained popular until the Civil War. Various political parties and patriotic associations often hosted these affairs, which tended to include lavish spreads of food: barbecued meats, pickles, clam soup, turtle soup, seasonal vegetables and fruit (especially strawberries), breads, cakes, pies, lemonade, limeade, ales, and ice cream made with various fruits.

As the century wore on, the formal celebratory style in which Americans had marked the Fourth since independence gradually developed into observances much like those of the late 20th century. The racial and political divisions in American society before the Civil War were mirrored in the smaller parties and family picnics. Many in the South did not celebrate Independence Day for years after the War. In addition, those celebrations that did occur took on new elements and new activities. No longer could an observer travel to any major town in the United States and expect to see the same sequence of military muster, parade, oratory, and elegant dinner for tens, or hundreds.

Celebrating Progress on the Fourth

From the early years of the 19th century, the excitement generated by new technology mingled with feelings of patriotism on the independence holiday. Beginning a trend that would extend into the 21st century, the Fourth of July often marked technological advances and constructions of important buildings and transportation systems.

Some notable examples of Fourth of July events celebrating technology:

National monuments

- In 1848 construction of the Washington Monument in Washington, D.C., began. President James Polk attended the ceremony in which the cornerstone was laid.
- In 1851 President Fillmore helped lay the cornerstone of the new front for the Capitol Building.

Railroad

- In 1828 construction of the Baltimore and Ohio Railroad began in Baltimore, Maryland.

Ships

- In 1815 officials tried out a new steamship equipped with cannons in New York Harbor.
- In 1818 the steamboat *United States* was first launched from Baltimore, Maryland.

Canals

- In 1817 ground was broken for the construction of the Erie Canal. The completion of the Erie Canal would provide one of the major routes for the settlement of the West.

Cars

- In 1899 the first cars appeared in an Independence Day party in Dyersville, Iowa. They were called "horseless carriages" then.

Frontier Fourths

Explorers Meriwether Lewis and William Clark were among the first people to observe the Fourth of July in the West—west, that is, of the Mississippi River. In 1804, their pioneering party paused at what they dubbed Fourth of July 1804 Creek, near what is now the Kansas-Missouri border.

Here is an excerpt from Clark's journal entry for that day:

> Ushered in the day by a discharge of one shot from our bow piece, proceeded on, passed the mouth of a bayou leading from a large lake on the S.S., which has the appearance of being once the bend of the river, and reaches parallel for several miles. We came to on the L.S. to refresh ourselves [the abbreviation "S.S." stands for "starboard," or the right-hand side when one is facing forward on a ship. "L.S." means "larboard," or left-hand side]. *Joseph Fields* got bitten by a snake, and was quickly doctored with bark by *Captain Lewis.*
>
> We passed a creek twelve yards wide, on the L.S., coming out of an extensive prairie reaching within two hundred yards of the river. As this creek has no name, and this being the Fourth of July, the day of the Independence of the United States, we called it *"Fourth of July 1804 Creek."* We dined on corn. *Captain Lewis* walked on shore above this creek and discovered a high mound from the top of which he had an extensive view. Three paths came together at the mound. We saw great numbers of goslings today which were nearly grown. The lake is clear and contains great quantities of fish and geese and goslings. This induced me to call it *Gosling Lake.* A small creek and several springs run into the lake on the east side from the hills. The land on that side is very good.
>
> —Captain Clark, 4 July 1804
> From *Journals of Lewis and Clark*, Chapter 1 (1893)

The next year, the expedition party celebrated with a campfire meal of buffalo meat, bacon, beans, and the last of their whiskey supply. One man played his fiddle and the others danced into the night until a thunderstorm hit.

Over the rest of the 19th century and into the 20th, thousands followed Lewis and Clark and brought the independence holiday with them. As they did so, they claimed the ever-receding frontier land as America and expanded the idea of American identity to the West. (*See the Appendix for two eyewitness accounts of Fourth of July celebrations in Oregon from the 1860s and 1870s.)*

America Turns 50

The 50th anniversary of the Declaration of Independence in 1826 was marked by a "strange and very striking coincidence," as President John Quincy Adams put it—the deaths of two Founding Fathers and former presidents, John Adams and Thomas Jefferson. President Adams, son of John, had invited both men, as well as other surviving signers of the Declaration, to be honorees at a gala jubilee celebration in the nation's capital. Most were too frail or ill to attend. But John Adams did contribute a toast to be proposed at the feast held in his town of Quincy, Massachusetts. It read: "I give you INDEPENDENCE FOREVER."

American naturalist and writer Henry David Thoreau (1817-1862) embarked on a solitary and meditative adventure on the Fourth of July, 1845. He wrote about it in his book Walden.

Other cities also planned celebrations that gave prominent roles to residents who had participated in the Revolution or the declaring of independence. In Newark, New Jersey, and Providence, Rhode Island, Revolutionary War veterans rode in parades. In Worcester, Massachusetts, and Newport, Rhode Island, the men who read the Declaration of Independence out loud to the public for the first time in 1776 recited it again. When famous revolutionary personalities could not participate, their artifacts could stand in, as in Arlington, Virginia. There people held a celebration under the very tent that had sheltered George Washington in camp in 1775.

In its first 50 years the nation had grown to 24 states and several frontier territories.

Liberty for Some

In the years leading up to the Civil War, the Fourth of July held a very different message for some. For slaves and abolitionists, the day highlighted the disparity between what the Declaration of Independence proclaimed and the fact of slavery in America. The celebration of liberty has always been at the heart of the Fourth of July. To earlier white Americans, liberty meant freedom from British rule. Others saw the broader meaning of liberty. To them, the United States was not truly a free country as long as black people were owned as slaves.

In protest, some black Americans waited until July 5 to celebrate. There was also a practical consideration: black Americans who appeared at public celebrations risked attack by racist whites who could not abide integrated observances. The hypocrisy of the Declaration of Independence's assertion that "all men are created equal" was not the only reason many black Americans shunned the Fourth. In the South, July 4 was often a day on which slave markets were held. Thus, not only were black Americans painfully reminded of their exclusion from freedom, but also on that day slaves might be sold to other owners and separated from their loved ones.

To many African Americans a truer Independence Day was August 1. On that day in 1834 England abolished slavery throughout its colonies, freeing 800,000 slaves in the British West Indies. Freedom for American slaves would not come until the 13th Amendment to the Constitution was ratified in 1865 (see **Emancipation Day**). Until then, some Americans—black and white—found ways to use the Fourth of July holiday to call for universal freedom for all Americans.

One of these was Frederick Douglass, a former slave, a great orator, and an advisor to President Lincoln. On July 5, 1852, he gave a speech at a meeting of the Rochester, New York, Ladies' Anti-Slavery Society. Titled "What to the Slave Is the Fourth of July?" Douglass's speech hammered home, in no uncertain terms, how America had been sacrificing her ideals at the altar of slavery:

> What, to the American slave, is your 4th of July? I answer; a day that reveals to him, more than all other days in the year, the gross injustice and cruelty to which he is the constant victim. To him, your celebration is a sham; your boasted liberty, an unholy license; your national greatness, swelling vanity; your sounds of rejoicing are empty and heartless; your denunciations of tyrants, brass fronted impudence; your shouts of liberty and equality, hollow mockery; your prayers and hymns, your sermons and thanksgivings, with all your religious parade, and solemnity, are to him, mere bombast, fraud, deception, impiety, and hypocrisy—a thin veil to cover up crimes which would disgrace a nation of savages. There is not a nation on the earth guilty of practices, more shocking and bloody, than are the people of these United States, at this very hour.

Fourth of July Celebration, or, Southern ideas of Liberty—July 4, '40.

This 1840 engraving by William K. Rhinehart offers an abolitionist commentary on slavery in the South and the ideals of American liberty.

Like the revolutionary movement during the previous century, the abolitionist movement fell far short of attracting a majority of Americans, even in the North, where many Americans felt slavery was wrong. But it was large enough, and it was active. Independence Day presented a perfect opportunity for abolitionists to organize events to further their cause. Many such events took place from as early as the 1790s. Antislavery societies from Massachusetts to New Jersey and from Pennsylvania to Ohio held meetings and heard speeches encouraging the abolitionists' struggle.

In 1817 New York passed a law decreeing that by July 4, 1827, all slaves would be freed. Thousands of African Americans celebrated that Fourth with special church services, a musical parade through the streets of New York City, readings of the new law as well as the Declaration of Independence, speeches, and dinners.

The 1820s also saw the rise of a controversial organization that aimed to move black Americans to a colony in Africa. The American Colonization Society, whose members were both white and black, formed in 1816 and used the Fourth of July to further its goal. The Society had purchased the land that become the African country of Liberia, which was founded and colonized by freed American slaves in the 1820s. Approximately 15,000 former slaves emigrated to Liberia over the course of three decades.

In the meantime, Southerners, whose economy depended on slavery, countered with their own events on the Fourth. Plantation owners generally gave slaves the Fourth of July off, or the nearest weekend. Some slave-owners made provision for barbecues and for slaves to visit family and friends from other plantations.

Civil War Fourths

The states had been unified through the Revolutionary War, the crafting of the U.S. Constitution, and the War of 1812. But the differences between the two regions came to the fore by the 1820s. The agricultural South depended upon the institution of slavery, while the rapidly industrializing North did not. As more Americans moved west, settled in new territories, and began to organize new states, Northerners and Southerners generally disagreed on whether slavery should be allowed in the new territories and states. By the 1830s, many Northerners believed slavery was an unjust system. Southerners argued that each state should be able to determine for itself whether slavery would be allowed. Congress worked on a series of compromises during the 1850s to maintain a balance between the number of slave states and free states.

On July 4, 1859, former Senator Robert Barnwell Rhett gave a speech in Grahamsville, South Carolina, in which he advocated that the Southern states break away and form their own nation independent from the Union. From December 1860, just after Abraham Lincoln was elected president, until June 1861, 11 Southern states—first South Carolina, then Mississippi, Florida, Alabama, Georgia, Louisiana, Texas, Arkansas, North Carolina, Virginia, and Tennessee—did just that, forming the Confederate States of America (also called the Confederacy). On July 4, 1861, Congress met and authorized war. On that day, although the war had begun a few months before, some Northern and Southern soldiers summoned enough of a unified spirit that when Union warships off Charleston, South Carolina, shot off a salute, Confederate soldiers at Forts Sumter and Moultrie fired a salute in response.

On July 4, 1863, after more than two years of civil war, two military victories appeared to turn the tide and foreshadow the end of the war. The Battle of Gettysburg, Pennsylvania, ended on July 3, when the Union decisively stopped the Confederate invasion. On the Fourth, Union forces under General Ulysses S. Grant captured the city of Vicksburg, Mississippi, with the surrender of more than 29,000 Confederate troops.

In 1863 cities throughout the North celebrated not only the anticipated end of the war, but also the first Independence Day after President Lincoln signed the Emancipation Proclamation. In the South, on the other hand, it would be decades, in some places, before there were public Fourth of July observances. There was no civic celebration in Richmond, Virginia, until 1872. No official Fourth of July observance occurred in South Carolina until the town of Cheraw began celebrating in 1891. And it wasn't until 1901 that Jackson, Mississippi, residents again heard a public reading of the Declaration of Independence.

Bilingual Fourths

Since its founding, the United States has been a beacon to people around the world, a nation in which opportunity, the freedom to pursue life, liberty and happiness, was available to all. Stories about this "land of golden opportunity" spread back to Europe and, eventually, around the world. From 1820 to 1996, more than 70 million people came to the United States, causing one of the largest mass movements of people in recorded history.

Most immigrants in the 19th century were from Europe. Until late in the century, the majority of these were from Germany and Ireland. German immigrants in Indianapolis attracted the ire of longtime residents when they paraded on the Fourth of July in 1852, which fell on a Sunday that year. To a large number of Protestant citizens, it was sacrilegious to engage in such activity on a Sunday; on those years in which the Fourth fell on a Sunday, they celebrated the next day.

Most immigrants were eager to celebrate Independence Day. For many, it was truly a new, and quite personal, independence day. They came to America seeking religious independence as well as job opportunities, and

Fireworks

Fireworks have been part of the Fourth of July since the first observance in 1777, when they were better known as "skyrockets." Historians generally agree that fireworks were invented in China around the 9th century C.E. Firecrackers were first made with gunpowder, which is also thought to have been invented in China around the same time. The technology reached western Europe sometime in the 13th or 14th century. By the 15th century Europeans set off fireworks for all kinds of festivals and special gatherings. Gunpowder is still a primary ingredient in fireworks made today. Other chemicals create the beautiful colors and designs, as well as noises.

Fireworks provide spectacular thrills, but they can also be dangerous. Thousands of people are injured each year, either by using fireworks improperly or by using illegal fireworks. People involved in the Progressive movement of the early years of the 20th century led "Safe and Sane" campaigns to warn about the hazards of fireworks. In those days it was common for people, usually men and boys, to set off fireworks themselves, and many were injured as a result. Progressive reformers also urged local and state lawmakers to ban the sale of private fireworks and to instead organize professional community displays.

After the terrorist attacks in 2001, a North Carolina family decided that something new and special should be added to the observance of the national holiday, something that would pull Americans together and help revive their spirits. They contacted fireworks industry representatives, their congressman, and President George W. Bush with the idea. For the Fourth of July 2002, fireworks organizers in some 40 states included the American Tribute in their displays. The American Tribute is a salute using the national colors. It begins with silence. Then there is one burst of red shot into the sky. When the sky clears, there's a burst of white. Then after the sky clears again, there's a burst of blue. It is a simple display intended to inspire Americans to reflect on the meaning of the holiday. Some displays open with the American Tribute, while others use it as the finale.

generally found them. Not everyone had mastered the English language by the time they arrived, however. Thus, there are records of Fourth of July celebrations in which the Declaration of Independence was publicly read in a European language in addition to being read in English. For example, the Declaration was read in German in Indianapolis in the mid-1850s as well as in Freeport, Illinois, and Chicago, Illinois, in 1876. It was read in Spanish on July 4, 1868, in Santa Fe, New Mexico, and in Swedish in Moorhead, Minnesota, in 1883.

Centennial Celebrations

The centennial anniversary of independence in 1876 fell during a time when the Civil War was still an open wound for many Americans. Thus, for a number of years, Decoration Day—the holiday now observed as **Memorial Day**—took preeminence over the Fourth of July as a time of national commemoration.

Still, many Americans took the anniversary as an opportunity to strive for reconciliation and a renewed sense of national unity. America's 100th birthday party began on New Year's Eve, 1875. In Philadelphia, a crowd rang in the centennial new year outside Independence Hall. At midnight the city was full of noise from bells, fireworks, gunshots, and a band playing "The Star-Spangled Banner."

The biggest event in the nation in 1876 was the International Centennial Exhibition held in Philadelphia. It opened in May and continued through the rest of the year. The latter part of the century began the age of the great world's fairs, and this was the second to take place on American soil.

Millions of Americans and people from around the world visited the International Centennial Exhibition. Thirty-seven countries contributed exhibits, and several even constructed their own display buildings. Visitors could admire an Egyptian temple, Chinese ivory pieces, and silver from Mexico. They could listen to live musical performances and ride a railroad from one end of the complex to another. More than 250 buildings contained the fruits of human effort and progress up to that time. One huge building was dedicated to machinery. Machinery Hall housed 14 acres worth of the latest and best machines of every kind. The enormous Corliss steam engine was one of the highlights of the entire exhibition.

Cities around the nation held special Fourth of July celebrations in honor of the centennial. Some marked the event in a personal way as well: 11 couples wedded a new phase in their lives with the nation's history when they got married in Washington, D.C. A New York couple named their baby, born on the third, American Centenniel Maloney.

Native American Observances

The territorial growth of the United States came at a tremendous cost to Native Americans. White settlers, backed by the government and the military, forced thousands from their lands or killed them, either directly by violence or indirectly by exposing them to new diseases against which they had no immunity. Those who were left struggled to maintain their way of life amid unprecedented challenges. The Indian Removal Act of 1830 forced some Indian tribes, such as the Cherokee, into western lands so that white settlers could move in. By the end of the 19th century many Indians were living on reservations that were administered by the U.S. government.

By and large, the Fourth of July celebrated white independence and freedom of movement at the expense of Native Americans'. Still, some Native American groups have observed the Fourth. This has largely been because legal holidays were the only days on which white officials allowed large ceremonial gatherings. Thus, for some Indians, the Fourth of July, as well as other American holidays, became a more or less acceptable day on which to hold important religious ceremonies.

In the late 1890s, Kiowa Indians in Oklahoma began scheduling the sacred Feather Dance—a variation of the Ghost Dance practiced by many Plains Indians—for July Fourth and Christmas. Meanwhile, the federal Indian Affairs Office had prohibited the Ghost Dance and similar dances. Therefore, some Indians incorporated unmistakable signs of American patriotism and Christianity into the ceremony, such as the display of American flags and prayers addressed to God. In this way, they were successful in holding onto some traditions while the Indian Affairs Office sought to mold them to the ways of white Americans. By the early years of the 20th century, however, Indian Affairs officials threatened to deprive those who observed the Native American dance ceremonies of the payments they were to receive for giving up their lands if they participated. By the 1920s, the formerly grand and open Feather Dance ceremonies had gone underground as private events.

"The Freedom Song"

Johnny was a Cherokee cowboy
Long braids hangin' from his hat
He wrangled up on the Little S Ranch
Rode with my Uncle Jack.
He sat like a shadow in the saddle,
Wrote poetry with his rope,
He had a light hand for the horses,
and a smile for us little folk.

Johnny and Jack come a-callin'
took my brothers, my sisters, and I
To the Hale County picnic,
Ought-seven, the Fourth of July.
They had a big tent and a little brass
   band,
Box lunches on the lawn.
When they raised Old Glory to the top
   of the pole,
We all sang the freedom song.

Chorus:
Oh say can you see?
Johnny why aren't you singin'?
Oh say can you see?
Johnny is there something wrong?
Oh say can you see?
Johnny where are you goin'?
Johnny why don't you stay
and help us sing the freedom song?

The men all whipped their hats off,
Hollered and whooped it up.
But Johnny just stood there, silent,
with a hurt and angry look.
Then his face grew soft and he kneeled
   right down
and he sounded plumb wore out,
when he said, "Little pardner, it's not
   my freedom
That they're singin' about."

Chorus.

He mounted his horse in a couple of
   strides
and I watched as he rode away,
across the plains of the land of the free
'til he vanished in the home of the
   brave.
Since then, I've sung the freedom song
a thousand times or more,
and, every time, I wonder just whose
   freedom
it is that we're singin' for?

Chorus.

"The Freedom Song," music and lyrics by Andy Wilkinson. © 1996 Cain't Quit Music, BMI.

The situation was much the same for Crow Indians in the late 19th and early 20th centuries. They held religious dance ceremonials on the Fourth of July, **Memorial Day**, **Washington's Birthday**, Easter, and Christmas because those were occasions on which white Indian Affairs officers allowed them.

Similarly, in 1912 the U.S. government lifted its prohibition against large gatherings among the Mescalero Apaches with two conditions: they could only hold such reunions once a year and they had to occur on the Fourth of July. So tribal elders decided to hold the Apache Girls' Puberty Ceremonial, an important coming-of-age ritual, over the July holiday. It still takes place on the Reservation's mesa landscape in south central New Mexico, over four days and nights. Since the 1980s there has also been a parade which is scheduled for the Fourth.

Suffragette Movement and the Fourth

The movement for fuller civil rights for women began in the mid-19th century and was known as the suffragette movement. Members of the movement were called "suffragettes" or "suffragists." ("Suffrage" means the right to vote.) At that time, women were denied full citizenship rights (especially the right to vote), property rights, and opportunities to pursue education and careers.

Until the middle of the 19th century, women generally were not included in formal ceremonies held on Independence Day. Some did attend the parades and banquets or meals, though. Even when women took part in parades, however, their role was as a symbol of the nation. This was a reflection of a society in which women were largely considered to be the property of their husbands or fathers. Women were not allowed to vote or go to college. They were expected to marry young, have children, and let their husbands rule the home, and the nation.

In 1848 a few women began changing all that, when Susan B. Anthony, Lucy Stone, Elizabeth Cady Stanton, and others proclaimed their own declaration of independence. The Declaration of Sentiments of 1848 was modeled after the Declaration of Independence. The first three paragraphs are identical except for a few key changes. The Declaration of Sentiments held "these truths to be self-evident: that all men and women are created equal." It then provided a list of specific injustices against women, including the denial of full citizenship, property rights, and educational and professional opportunities.

Unfortunately, neither Anthony nor Stanton lived to see the passage of the 19th Amendment to the Constitution in 1920, which gave women the right to vote. But their work galvanized a national movement for equal rights for women. Suffragettes often scheduled meetings for the Fourth of July in order to highlight the unfulfilled potential of the Declaration of Independence. For example, on July 4, 1876, Susan B. Anthony took the stage and read the Declaration of Rights for Women at the Centennial Exhibition in Philadelphia. Organizers had previously denied her request to address an audience, but that didn't stop her. Anthony's appearance at this highly publicized major event helped bring more national attention and respect to the movement.

The 20th Century and Current Celebrations

Celebrating New Technology and New Frontiers

Americans have continued to mark new inventions and accomplishments on Independence Day. Here are some notable examples from the 20th and 21st centuries:

Telegraph communications
- In 1903 President Theodore Roosevelt sent the first telegraphed message from the United States to the Philippines, using the newly completed Pacific Submarine Cable. He sent the telegram to Governor (and, later, president of the United States) William H. Taft in Manila.

Transatlantic air flight
- On May 21, 1927, Charles A. Lindbergh was the first person to fly alone, nonstop, from New York to Paris. In Sea Gate, New York, citizens named a park for him on July 4 that year.
- The same year, Commander Richard E. Byrd, along with a crew, made a transatlantic flight as well. On July 4, 1927, his accomplishment was noted at a ceremony in Paris.

Television
- On July 4, 1947, Americans watched the first televised broadcast of Fourth of July ceremonies in Washington, D.C.

Space
- On July 4, 1982, the space shuttle Columbia landed at Edwards Air Force Base in California. The shuttle's astronauts were met by President

Ronald Reagan, who gave a patriotic speech in their honor. Ten years later, Americans watched astronauts aboard the space shuttle display the flag and wish the country a "Happy Birthday."

- On July 4, 1997, the Pathfinder landed on Mars and sent photographs of the planet's landscape back to Earth.

- On July 4, 2001, astronauts at the International Space Station orbiting Earth offered the greeting, "We give thanks to our ancestors . . . to all Americans, Happy Independence Day."

Wartime Fourths

World War I

The American armed forces looked very different in the early years of the 20th century. For one thing, few women served. For another, the standing force was smaller— 643,800 troops (before the draft) compared to more than one million men and women in the early 21st century. There were no aircraft carriers because there were few fighter jets. Yet President Woodrow Wilson sent American troops to help America's oldest ally in the world, France, protect itself from Germany's invading forces in World War I (1914-18). Most

> ### Marie Joseph Paul Marquis de Lafayette (1757-1834)
>
> Lafayette was a charming, handsome French nobleman who came to the colonies in 1777 to fight with the Americans against the British. At 20 he already had significant military experience. George Washington welcomed Lafayette's offer to assist the Continental Army— without a salary—and they became great admirers of each other. For his service in the Revolution and the key role he played in the British surrender at Yorktown, Lafayette is considered both an American and a French hero.

Americans did not want to get involved in the European war. Neither did President Wilson. He held off entering the war until April 2, 1917, by which time German U-boats had been attacking American ships in the Atlantic Ocean for more than two years.

In May 1917 Congress voted to draft men into military service. The first troops arrived in France on June 24. On July 4 General John J. Pershing marched his soldiers to Paris to help revive the spirits of the war-weary citizens. As they paraded down the city streets ablaze in red, white, and blue bunting, Parisians decked the troops with flowers. Their destination was the Pipcus cemetery, where the Marquis de Lafayette is buried. Numerous dignitaries gave speeches to celebrate the American support and rally the crowd. One speaker was Colonel Charles E. Stanton, an assistant to General Pershing. His speech concluded with a line that would become a mantra among American troops: "What we have of blood and treasure are yours. In the presence of the illustrious dead, we pledge our hearts and our honor in carrying the war to a successful conclusion. Lafayette, we are here!"

World War I officially ended on November 11, 1918. On July 4, 1919, a huge victory parade in New York City celebrated the United States' role in helping to win back freedom for its allies in Europe. (*See also* **Veterans Day.**)

> *"December 7, 1941 — a date which will live in infamy — the United States of America was . . . attacked."*
> — President Roosevelt's speech to Congress on December 8, 1941

World War II

The Japanese bombing of Pearl Harbor on December 7, 1941, brought the United States into World War II (1939-45). From 1942 to 1945, the Fourth of July was observed by a nation at war. Since the Japanese attacked the naval base in Hawaii, many feared an attack on the mainland. There were a few attacks on the shores of the continental United States, but none nearly as devastating as Pearl Harbor. For example, on February 23, 1942, a Japanese sub bombed an oil refinery on the California coast near Santa Barbara. In response, President Franklin D. Roosevelt created the Office of Civil Defense. This office worked to ensure that communities had air raid sirens to warn of attacks. There were also blackouts along the West and East Coasts, since these areas were most vulnerable to attacks from sea, and Fourth of July fireworks during the war were cancelled.

Observances tended to be somber, and purposeful. On July 4, 1942, for example, 200 young men enlisted in the military in front of the Liberty Bell in Philadelphia. On the same day in New York City, a special "Eternal Light" ceremony was held, in which the Allied nations' flags were formed in a V shape (for victory), amid the sound of air raid sirens at noon throughout the city.

Overseas, U.S. troops marked the day in battle. On July 4, 1944, a month after the D-Day Allied invasion of Normandy, France, U.S. General Omar Bradley orchestrated a massive attack on German targets, ordering every artillery piece on the front to fire exactly at noon (*see also* **National Pearl Harbor Remembrance Day**).

Vietnam War

Americans were deeply divided on United States involvement in the Vietnam War, and antiwar protests were common from the late 1960s until the early 1970s. In 1968 large demonstrations disrupted Fourth of July ceremonies in Philadelphia, Pennsylvania, and Minneapolis, Minnesota. On July 4, 1970, supporters of the Nixon administration, led by the Reverend Billy Graham, staged "Honor America Day" in Washington, D.C.

Iraq War

After the terrorist attacks of September 11, 2001, Americans observed Independence Day with renewed fervor (*see also* **Patriot Day**). After President George W. Bush ordered an invasion of more than 100,000 troops into Iraq in the spring of 2003, American soldiers once again were stationed in a war zone. On July 4, 2003, some soldiers stationed in the city of Tikrit found themselves eating hot dogs, listening to music, and swimming in a luxurious pool at the Republican Palace once occupied by ousted Iraqi dictator Saddam Hussein.

Back home, Americans honored their friends and family members serving in Iraq with special ceremonies. On July 4, 2003, five thousand antiwar protesters in Philadelphia called for the troops' return home.

Bicentennial Celebrations

The nation celebrated its 200th birthday in 1976. As the anniversary approached, however, the nation had yet to heal from the traumatic 1960s, which saw the assassinations of President John F. Kennedy, Martin Luther King Jr., and Attorney General Robert F. Kennedy; violent race riots; and a war that divided the people (*see also* **Martin Luther King Jr. Birthday**). In addition, President Richard M. Nixon resigned in 1974 in the wake of the Watergate scandal.

A National Park Service ranger reenacts the first public reading of the Declaration of Independence at Independence Hall in Philadelphia. Colonel John Nixon read the new Declaration to the public for the first time on July 8, 1776.

Hot Dogs

From New York City to Los Angeles, one of the most popular foods associated with the Fourth of July is the hot dog. Almost 60% of Americans report that they barbecue on the holiday. Some surveys indicate that more people prefer barbecued chicken over hot dogs for their holiday picnics. Still, Americans eat about 150 million hot dogs on the Fourth of July—that's one hot dog for about every two people in the nation. And there is something uniquely American about the hot dog. After all, hot dogs, not chickens, were sent to American soldiers in Bosnia for the Fourth in 1996. The project was codenamed "Operation Weinerlift." In 2003, after capturing Saddam Hussein's palace in Baghdad, occupying soldiers were treated to a hot dog meal on the holiday.

Hot dogs are descended from German sausages. German immigrants in the 19th century brought over their tradition of eating sausages—called "frankfurters" or "wieners"—with bread. ("Frankfurters" derives from Frankfurt, a city in Germany. The nickname "wieners" comes from Wien, the German spelling of Vienna, the capital city of Austria.) But the name used in the United States for the popular finger food is distinctly American. Several legends purport to explain the origin of the name "hot dog," but the truth is a bit elusive. What is known is that some German newcomers went into business selling sausages from pushcarts on city streets. One, Charles Feltman, was a baker who is credited with opening the first sausage and roll stand in New York's Coney Island in 1871. In those days, hot dogs were called "dachshund sausages." Dachshund is the name of a breed of long, skinny dogs. Whether it was the resemblance of the food to the dog or perhaps jokes about what the food was made from, by the 1890s references to "hot dogs" as the name of the food had found their way into print. The sausage in a roll made a splash in Chicago at the 1893 Columbian Exposition, where thousands of Americans tried and loved the unusual new sandwich. One vendor working the fair was Oscar Mayer.

There's nothing pretentious about hot dogs, which may be part of their appeal. They can be dressed up quite a bit, though. Just what they're wearing may depend on where in the United States one looks. New York hot dogs are relatively modest affairs generally served with mustard and onion sauce or sauerkraut. Chicago is famous for its elaborate hot dogs, buried under onions, tomatoes, mustard, relish, pickles, hot peppers, and celery salt on poppy seed buns. Other parts of the country favor the Coney Dog, a hot dog smothered in hamburger-based chili sauce, onions, and optional cheese.

One of the most impressive events held in celebration of the Bicentennial was Operation Sail. Thanks to ship devotee and author Frank O. Braynard, America's Cup holder Emil Mossbacher Jr., and a small group of people, ships from all over the world converged on New York Harbor to sail past the Statue of Liberty. The fireworks display in Washington, D.C., included laser beams spelling out "1776-1976, Happy Birthday USA." And all over the country people rang church and town bells at 2:00 P.M. Eastern Standard Time to commemorate the time of day the Continental Congress voted for the Declaration of Independence.

Fifers march in the annual Fourth of July parade in Pittsfield, Massachusetts.

Festivals and Ceremonies on the Fourth

In the early 21st century, Americans continue the traditional celebrations of the Fourth of July. Communities and families gather for food and festivities, in public and private displays of patriotism. These include parades, picnics, fireworks, and concerts featuring patriotic favorites like "Yankee Doodle," "The Stars and Stripes Forever," "God Bless America," and "The Star-Spangled Banner" (*for more on "The Star-Spangled Banner," see "The National Anthem" in* **Patriotism in the United States**).

The Fourth of July in 2002 was far different from the holiday a year before, arriving nearly ten months after the September 11 attacks (*see* **Patriot Day**). Not since the 1976 bicentennial holiday had there been such widespread public observance of Independence Day. The usual private gathering of family and friends in backyards for barbecues in which the country's birthday may have been hardly remarked was exchanged for a tremendous outpouring of patriotic display and sentiment. More and more, Americans sought out each other for larger community events to observe the Fourth, though smaller celebrations of family and friends continue as well.

A Sampling of Observances

1. **Seattle, Washington:** Hundreds become American citizens at an annual naturalization ceremony. Other Seattle events include a Wooden Boat Festival, concerts, games, contests, and fireworks. Contact Ethnic Heritage Council for naturalization ceremony at 305 Harrison St., Ste. 304, Seattle, WA 98109, 206-443-1410, fax: 206-443-1408, contactus@ethnicheritagecouncil.org, http://www.ethnicheritagecouncil.org/; for Wooden Boat Festival: Center for Wooden Boats, 1010 Valley St., Seattle, WA 98109-4468, 206-382-2628, fax: 206-382-2699, cwb@cwb.org, http://www.cwb.org; for other events: Ivar's, Inc., 1001 Alaskan Way, Pier 54, Seattle, WA 98104, 206-587-6500, http://www.ivars.net

2. **Portland, Oregon:** Waterfront Blues Festival brings in the Fourth, along with films, workshops, and fireworks. Proceeds benefit the Oregon Food Bank. Contact Oregon Food Bank, P.O. Box 55370, Portland, OR 97238-5370, 503-973-FEST (3378) or 503-282-0555, postoffice@oregonfoodbank.org, http://www.waterfrontbluesfest.com

3. **San Francisco, California:** The city marks the Fourth with the Fillmore Street Jazz Festival, fireworks on the water, the "Red, White and True Blue 4th of July" aboard the USS Hornet World War II aircraft carrier across the Bay, and more. Contact the jazz festival at info@fillmorejazzfestival.com, http://fillmorestreetjazzfest.com; for fireworks information: Pier 39, San Francisco, CA 94133, 415-705-5500, info@pier39.com,

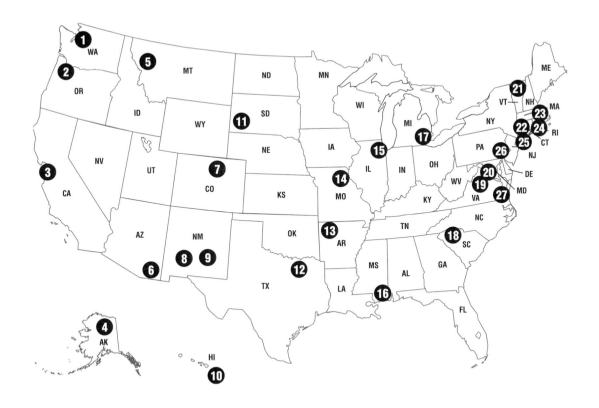

http://www.pier39.com; USS Hornet celebration: USS Hornet Museum, P.O. Box 460, Pier 3, Alameda Point, Alameda, CA 94501, 510-521-8448, fax: 510-521-8327, info@uss-hornet.org, http://www.uss-hornet.org/; San Francisco Visitor Information Center, 900 Market St., San Francisco, CA 94103-2804, 415-391-2000, TDD: 415-392-0328, fax: 415-362-7323, http://www.sfvisitor.org/

4. **Fairbanks, Alaska:** A parade, flyover, and other activities at Pioneer Park. Contact Pioneer Park, P.O. Box 71267, Fairbanks, AK 99707-1267, 907-459-1087 or 907-459-1095

Midnight Sun Intertribal Powwow welcomes the public to dances, parades, music, honoring of veterans, and more. Contact 907-456-2245 or 907-488-2436, info@midnightsunpowwow.org, http://www.midnight sunpowwow.org

5. **Arlee, Montana:** The Flathead (Salish and Kootenai) Nations 4th of July Celebration, first held in 1899, includes parades, dances, drumming, honoring of veterans, and games. Contact 406-726-3215 (powwow), 406-726-3167 (parade)

6. **Bisbee, Arizona:** This old mining town celebrates the Fourth with a parade and fireworks as well as mucking and hard rock drilling contests, coaster races, and music. Contact Bisbee Chamber of Commerce and Visitor Center, P.O. Box BA, Bisbee, AZ 85603, 866-2BISBEE (224-7233) or 520-432-5421, chamber@bisbeezrizona.com, http://www.bisbee arizona.com/ (chamber) or http://www.cityofbisbee.com

7. **Greeley, Colorado:** Rocky Mountain Stampede (formerly Greeley Independence Stampede) features pro rodeo, concerts, parades, and fireworks. Contact Rocky Mountain Stampede, 600 N. 14 Ave., Greeley, CO 80631, 800-982-BULL (2855) or 970-356-2855, http://rockymoun tainstampede.com

8. **Mescalero, New Mexico:** Mescalero Apache Ceremonial & Rodeo also features a parade, dances, and games. Contact Mescalero Apache Tribe, P.O. Box 227, Mescalero, NM 88340, 505-464-4494

9. **Roswell, New Mexico:** Roswell UFO Festival offers concerts, lectures, alien air force convoys, close encounters night parade, and fireworks. Contact Roswell UFO Festival, 505-625-8607, http://www.roswellufo .us/

10. **Kohala Coast, Hawaii Island, Hawaii:** The Fourth is also Turtle Independence Day, when staff members of Mauna Lani resort release grown wild green turtles into the ocean after raising them in the resort's ponds. Live entertainment, games, and food round out the turtle parade to the shore and ceremonial sendoff. Contact Mauna Lani Bay Hotel and Bungalows, 68-1400 Mauna Lani Dr., Kohala Coast, HI 96743-9796, 866-877-6982 or 808-885-6622, http://www.maunalani.com and much about the turtles at the Mauna Lani Culture Department's web site at http://www.maunalaniculture.org/

11. **Mount Rushmore, South Dakota:** Fireworks illuminate Mount Rushmore as the highlight of the Independence celebration, which also offers music, military flyovers, and a flag-folding ceremony. Contact

Mount Rushmore National Memorial, 13000 Hwy. 24, Bldg. 31, Ste. 1, Keystone, SD 57751-0268, 605-574-3171 (recorded message) or 605-574-2523, fax: 605-574-2307, http://www.nps.gov/moru/

12. **Garland, Texas:** The Star Spangled Fourth includes concerts, a multi-cultural art and dance festival, tribute to veterans, sand art, and more. Contact Star Spangled Fourth, City of Garland, 200 N. Fifth St., Garland, TX 75040, 972-205-2000, http://www.starspangledfourth.com/starspangledfourth/

13. **Springdale, Arkansas:** Since 1944, site of the Rodeo of the Ozarks: parade, rodeo, and fireworks. See http://www.parsonsstadium.com/

14. **Hannibal, Missouri:** National Tom Sawyer Days celebrates the Fourth and one of America's best-loved characters with fence-painting and frog-jumping contests, a parade, fireworks, and other activities. Contact Hannibal Jaycees, P.O. Box 484, Hannibal, MO 63401, http://www.hannibaljaycees.org

15. **Chicago, Illinois:** Taste of Chicago features food from more than 70 area restaurants, concerts, and fireworks. Contact Mayor's Office of Special Events, 121 N. LaSalle St., Rm. 703, Chicago, IL 60602, 312-744-3315, fax: 312-744-8523, TTY: 312-744-2964, http://egov.cityofchicago.org/ (click "City Departments," then "Special Events")

16. **Gulfport, Mississippi:** Deep Sea Fishing Rodeo, carnival, crab festival, fireworks, and more. Contact Mississippi Deep Sea Fishing Rodeo, Inc., P.O. Box 1289, Gulfport, MS 39502-1289, 228-863-2713, http://www.fishrodeo.com/ and Mississippi Gulf Coast Convention & Visitors Bureau, P.O. Box 6128, Gulfport, MS 39506-6128, 800-237-9493 or 228-896-6699, tourism@gulfcoast.org, http://www.gulfcoast.org

17. **Detroit, Michigan:** Americans and Canadians on both sides of the Detroit River mingle to celebrate their respective national holidays — the Fourth and Canada Day, celebrated on July 1. The International Freedom Festival offers concerts, food, fireworks on the River, and more. Contact The Parade Company, 9500 Mt. Elliott, Studio A, Detroit, MI 48211, 313-923-7400, fax: 313-923-2920, http://www.theparade.org/freedomfest/index.shtml

18. **Cowpens, South Carolina:** Colonial-style celebration, with music, living history, and fireworks at the site of an important Revolutionary War victory in 1781. Contact Cowpens National Battlefield, P.O. Box 308, Chesnee, SC 29323, 864-461-2828, fax: 864-461-7795, http://www.nps .gov/cowp/

19. **Charlottesville, Virginia:** Immigrants become new citizens every Fourth at Monticello, Thomas Jefferson's home, at an outdoor naturalization ceremony with music and speeches. Contact Thomas Jefferson Foundation, P.O. Box 316, Charlottesville, VA 22902, 434-984-9800 (recorded information), 434-984-9822 (public affairs), 434-984-9822 (TDD), http:// www.monticello.org

20. **Washington, D.C.:** The nation's capital celebrates with a parade, Capitol Fourth Concert, the Smithsonian Folklife Festival, the reading of the Declaration of Independence at the National Archives, and fireworks on the Mall. Contact July 4th Parade, 1424 Kingston Ave., Alexandria, VA 22303, 800-215-6405, fax: 703-354-3109, info@july4th parade.com, http://www.july4thparade.com; for the Capitol Fourth, see http://www.pbs.org/capitolfourth/index.html; Smithsonian Folklife Festival, 750 9th St., N.W., Washington, DC 20560-0953 (mailing address: P.O. Box 37012, Victor Bldg., Ste. 4100, MRC 953, Washington, DC 20013-7012), 202-275-1150, fax: 202-275-1119, folklife-info@si.edu, http://www.folklife.si.edu/index.html; National Archives, 700 Pennsylvania Ave., Washington, DC 20408, 866-272-6272 or 866-325-7208, http://www.archives.gov (search "national archives 4th of july"); for the fireworks, contact National Mall, 900 Ohio Dr., S.W., Washington, DC 20024, 202-426-6841 or 202-485-9880, http://www.nps.gov/nama/ events/events.htm

21. **Moscow, Vermont:** "World's shortest 4th of July parade." Contact Stowe Area Association, P.O. Box 1320, 51 Main St., Stowe, VT 05672, 877-GOSTOWE (467-8693) or 802-253-7321, fax: 802-253-6628, askus@ gostowe.com, http://www.gostowe.com

22. **Bridgeport, Connecticut:** The Barnum Festival celebrates the Fourth and circus master P. T. Barnum, born July 5, 1810, with parades, concerts, and fireworks. Contact Barnum Festival, 1070 Main St., Bridgeport, CT 06604, 866-867-8495 or 203-367-8485, http://www.barnum festival.com/

23. **Boston, Massachusetts:** The birthplace of the Revolution celebrates with Harborfest's hundreds of events and activities, including a public reading of the Declaration of Independence, fife and drum corps, and Chowderfest. Contact Boston Harborfest, 45 School St., Boston, MA 02108, 617-227-1528, fax: 617-227-1886, festival@bostonharborfest.com, http://www.bostonharborfest.com

    And the grand finale: Boston Pops concert and fireworks on the Esplanade. Contact Boston's Fourth of July Foundation, Inc., 222 Berkeley St., 14th Fl., Boston, MA 02116-3763, 888-4th-POPS (484-7677) or 617-267-2400, http://www.july4th.org

24. **Bristol, Rhode Island:** Parade, fireworks, concerts, and lots of activities in the "oldest continuous celebration of its kind in the U.S." Celebration dates to 1785. Contact the Bristol Fourth of July Committee, P.O. Box 561, Bristol, RI 02809-0561, 401-253-0445, http://www.july4thbristolri.com/home.html

25. **New York, New York:** Macy's annual fireworks on the East River. Contact Macy's Fireworks Hotline 212-494-4495.

    Nathan's Famous hot dog eating contest; young men from Japan have won every year from 1997 to 2004 (except in 1999). Contact Nathan's Famous Executive Offices, 1400 Old Country Rd., Westbury, NY 11590, 516-338-8500, fax: 516-338-7220, http://www.nathansfamous.com/nathans/

26. **Philadelphia, Pennsylvania:** A public reading of the Declaration of Independence at Independence Hall, site of the signing of the Declaration, as well as a week of events including a parade, concerts, and fireworks. Contact Welcome America, Inc., 215-683-2200, http://www.americasbirthday.com

27. **Yorktown, Virginia:** Parade, fireworks, readings of the Declaration of Independence, concerts, and more on the site of the final battle of the Revolutionary War. Contact Yorktown Fourth of July Celebration Committee, Inc., P.O. Box 444, Yorktown, VA 23690, 757-890-3500, fax: 757-890-3509, parksandrec@yorkcounty.gov, http://www.yorkcounty.gov/fourth/

Web Sites

American Museum of Natural History online exhibit on American hot dogs at http://www.amnh.org/exhibitions/baseball/hotdogs/

American Pyrotechnics Association provides a directory of state laws on fireworks at http://www.americanpyro.com

Centennial Exhibition Digital Collection through the Free Library of Philadelphia at http://libwww.library.phila.gov/CenCol/

Fourth of July Celebrations Database, compiled by James R. Heintze of American University, at http://gurukul.american.edu/heintze/fourth.htm

Library of Congress American Memory online exhibit on July 4th at http://memory.loc.gov/ammem/today/jul04.html

Library of Congress online exhibit, "Drafting the Documents," at http://www.loc.gov/exhibits/declara/declara2.html

National Council on Fireworks Safety at http://www.fireworksafety.com/

National Hot Dog and Sausage Council provides lots of information about hot dogs at http://www.hot-dog.org/

"An Outline of American History" by Howard Cincotta, United States Information Agency, May 1994, at http://usinfo.state.gov/usa/infousa/facts/history/toc.htm

U.S. National Archives and Records Administration's online exhibit on the Declaration of Independence at http://www.archives.gov/national_archives _experience/charters.html

Sources for Further Reading

Appelbaum, Diana Karter. *The Glorious Fourth: An American Holiday, an American History.* New York: Facts on File, 1989.

Bober, Natalie S. *Countdown to Independence: A Revolution of Ideas in England and Her American Colonies: 1760-1776.* New York: Atheneum, 2001. For young adults.

Dennis, Matthew. *Red, White, and Blue Letter Days: An American Calendar.* Ithaca, N.Y.: Cornell University Press, 2002.

Fleming, Thomas. *Liberty! The American Revolution.* New York: Viking, 1997. Companion to PBS series; online exhibit at http://www.pbs.org/ktca/liberty/

Foner, Philip S., ed. *We, the Other People: Alternative Declarations of Independence by Labor Groups, Farmers, Woman's Rights Advocates, Socialists, and Blacks, 1829-1975.* Urbana: University of Illinois Press, 1976.

Freedman, Russell. *Give Me Liberty: The Story of the Declaration of Independence.* New York: Holiday House, 2000. For young adults.

Gerber, Scott Douglas, ed. *The Declaration of Independence: Origins and Impact.* Washington, D.C.: CQ Press, 2002.

Hoig, Stan. *It's the Fourth of July.* New York: Cobblehill Books, 1995. For young adults.

Library of Congress Symposia on the American Revolution. *The Impact of the American Revolution Abroad.* Papers presented at the fourth symposium, May 8 and 9, 1975. Washington, D.C.: Library of Congress, 1976.

Litwicki, Ellen M. *America's Public Holidays, 1865-1920.* Washington, D.C.: Smithsonian Institution Press, 2000.

Maier, Pauline. *American Scripture: Making the Declaration of Independence.* New York: Knopf, 1997.

———. *From Resistance to Revolution: Colonial Radicals and the Development of American Opposition to Britain, 1765-1776.* New York: Alfred A. Knopf, 1972.

Middlekauff, Robert. *The Oxford History of the United States.* Vol. 2, *The Glorious Cause: The American Revolution, 1763-1789.* New York: Oxford University Press, 1982.

Morgan, Edmund S. *The Birth of the Republic, 1763-89.* 3rd ed. Chicago: University of Chicago Press, 1992.

Newman, Simon P. *Parades and the Politics of the Street: Festive Culture in the Early American Republic.* Philadelphia: University of Pennsylvania Press, 1997.

Sweet, Leonard I. "The Fourth of July and Black Americans in the Nineteenth Century." *Journal of Negro History* 61, 3 (July 1976): 256-75.

Travers, Len. *Celebrating the Fourth: Independence Day and the Rites of Nationalism in the Early Republic.* Amherst: University of Massachusetts Press, 1997.

Warren, Charles. "Fourth of July Myths." *William and Mary Quarterly 2,* 3 (July 1945): 237-72.

Wills, Garry. *Inventing America: Jefferson's Declaration of Independence.* New York: Doubleday & Company, 1978.

Wood, Gordon S. *The American Revolution: A History.* New York: Modern Library, 2002.

———. *The Radicalism of the American Revolution.* New York: Vintage Books, 1992.

Labor Day

Date Established as a Federal Holiday: June 28, 1894

Date Observed: First Monday in September

L abor Day is a federal holiday created to honor working people and the accomplishments of the labor movement. The holiday commemorates the first mass observance of working Americans, which took place in New York City on September 5, 1882. On June 28, 1894, Congress made Labor Day a legal public holiday.

Overview of American Labor History

From the late 1860s to about 1900, the United States was transformed from a mostly agricultural nation to one in which most Americans worked in factories and mines. The American labor movement developed during this period.

By the early 20th century, industry owners like Andrew Carnegie and John D. Rockefeller had amassed enormous wealth due, in part, to the meager wages they paid and the excessive hours of work they demanded of their employees. Americans who worked for many of the nation's largest industries worked 10-14 hours a day, usually six days a week. In 1890, factory workers earned an average of 20 cents an hour and worked an average of 60 hours per week. Wages were so low in proportion to living expenses that women, as well as men, had to work. These conditions also forced children as young as six years old into workplaces.

Labor movement leaders argued that Americans who worked so many hours had little time to become well-informed, responsible citizens. Some also cited St. Augustine's rule for daily monastic life: eight hours for work, eight hours for rest, and eight hours for recreation.

This photograph was taken at the Citizens' Glass Company in Evansville, Indiana, in 1908. Children working in glass factories earned, on average, less than $3 a week in 1910. About half worked 10 hours a day.

Americans working skilled trades in large cities had begun joining together in unions as early as the 1790s. These early unions were usually temporary groups that formed to accomplish a specific purpose and then dissolved. With the rise of industry and the accompanying difficulties for workers in the later 19th century, people organized into more permanent unions in order to better their work situations and standard of living.

Over the last 100 years, American labor unions and working people have struggled to improve working conditions and compensation. Between 1890 and 1923—when the first major American company, U.S. Steel, agreed to reduce its work day to eight hours—there were more than 26,000 strikes nationwide that called attention to the plight of the workers and demanded more equitable treatment on the job.

In 1916 Congress passed the Keating-Owen Child Labor Act, which prohibited the interstate sale of any product made by children under 16 who had been made to work more than eight hours a day or six days a week. Eventual modifications to this law further restricted the employment of children under the age of 16.

In 1938 the Fair Labor Standards Act set a minimum wage and maximum 44-hour work week, but this law, too, applied only to companies involved in interstate commerce.

Finally, in 1962 the Work Hours Act required all employers to pay time-and-a-half for work done after 8 hours a day or 40 hours a week.

Unions also fought for health insurance, workers compensation in case of injury on the job, and increased workplace safety measures. Americans' membership in labor unions peaked in the 1950s and 1960s, and so did their salaries and benefits. Since then, however, the actual value of most people's wages has declined and continues to do so.

Origins of Labor Day

The first nationally recognized Labor Day was organized by the Central Labor Union in New York City on September 5, 1882. (It had predecessors, however: workers in Pittsburgh, Pennsylvania, marched in a labor parade in June 1882, and on August 23, 1882, unions in Rhode Island staged a parade to Rocky Point for a picnic.) It was scheduled for a date in early September in order to take advantage of pleasant weather as well as provide an occasion to fall in the four-month gap between **Independence Day** and **Thanksgiving**. The question of who first proposed the New York event remains unsettled. Earlier histories credit Peter J. McGuire, secretary of the Brotherhood of Carpenters and Joiners, with the idea. But recent accounts suggest the notion could have come from Matthew Maguire, a machinist who was secretary of the Central Labor Union in 1882.

The Union organized a mass public event with two aims: to demonstrate a strong challenge to industries' labor practices and to unite workers from diverse ethnic, political, and religious backgrounds. Organizers thus chose a two-part observance: a parade to demonstrate and a picnic to unite.

It is estimated that 10,000-20,000 people took the day off work (losing a day's wages) and showed up on Tuesday, September 5, 1882, to march in

"Solidarity Forever" by Ralph Chaplin (1915)

When the union's inspiration through
the workers' blood shall run
There can be no power greater anywhere
beneath the sun
Yet what force on earth is weaker than
the feeble strength of one?
For the Union makes us strong.

Chorus:
Solidarity forever, solidarity forever,
Solidarity forever
For the Union makes us strong.

Is there aught we hold in common with
the greedy parasite
Who would lash us into serfdom and
would crush us with his might?
Is there anything left to us but to
organize and fight?
For the Union makes us strong.

Chorus

It is we who ploughed the prairies, built
the cities where they trade,
Dug the mines and built the workshops,
endless miles of railroad laid.
Now we stand outcast and starving 'mid
the wonders we have made
But the Union makes us strong.

Chorus

All the world that's owned by idle
drones is ours and ours alone
We have laid the wide foundations,
built it skyward stone by stone
It is ours, not to slave in, but to
master and to own
While the Union makes us strong.

Chorus

They have taken untold millions that
they never toiled to earn
But without our brain and muscle
not a single wheel can turn
We can break their haughty power,
gain our freedom when we learn
That the Union makes us strong.

Chorus

In our hands is placed a power greater
than their hoarded gold,
Greater than the might of armies
magnified a thousandfold.
We can bring to birth a new world
from the ashes of the old
For the Union makes us strong.

Chorus

In 1915 writer and union organizer Ralph Chaplin wrote these lyrics that continue to rally Americans struggling for more justice on the job. It is sung to the tune of the "Battle Hymn of the Republic," which earlier was the tune of "John Brown's Body."

the parade from City Hall to Union Square. The marchers wore uniforms and carried tools used in their respective trades. After the parade, thousands gathered in Elm Park for picnics, speeches, concerts, and fireworks.

By the late 1880s labor celebrations were being held regularly in hundreds of industrial cities, including Baltimore, Boston, Chicago, Detroit, and Newark. Some of these were scheduled for May 1, however, to coincide with the European observance of labor on May Day. The May 1 date was favored by more militant or socialist groups. The Federation of Organized Trades and Labor Unions, for example, organized a general strike parade in Chicago in 1886 to demand an eight-hour workday. (This event culminated in the riot at Haymarket Square on May 4, 1886, when the explosion of a bomb escalated a confrontation between police and protesters and resulted in the deaths of seven policemen.) The rival May Day trend continued until the turn of the 20th century, when its radical associations with international socialism and communism turned popular favor decisively toward the American-born September holiday.

On February 21, 1887, Oregon was the first state to designate Labor Day a legal holiday (it was observed on the first Saturday in June until 1893, when the state legislature changed the date to the first Monday in September). Connecticut, Pennsylvania, and Nebraska also designated official state holidays for Labor Day by 1890. By the time Congress made Labor Day a federal holiday in 1894, more than 20 states had also declared a Labor Day holiday.

Congress's action was prompted by the Pullman strike in 1894. Pullman, Illinois, near Chicago, was a "company town." The Pullman Palace Car Company appointed the town's government and owned all the businesses, including the newspaper, schools, library, and churches. Workers struck on May 11, 1894, because the Pullman Company reduced their wages without also reducing their housing cost and lowering store prices. They contacted the American Railway Union, led by Eugene V. Debs, who organized a boycott of all Pullman railroad cars. By late June, union members all over the Chicago area had stopped railroad traffic. President Grover Cleveland broke the strike and boycott with troops, but the resulting violence, public sympathy for the workers, and the fact that 1894 was an election year, led Congress to quickly create Labor Day (*see the Appendix for primary sources relating to the Pullman Strike*).

Labor Day was the nation's first "Monday holiday" that established an annual three-day weekend. (Until 1971, all the other legal U.S. holidays fell on established dates each year, such as **Washington's Birthday** on February 22 and **Independence Day** on July 4.) Since the turn of the 20th century, businesses and civic organizations have joined labor unions in creating special events for the holiday weekend to take advantage of Americans' additional leisure time, including festivals unrelated to labor themes, sporting events, inexpensive getaways, special movies, and other entertainments.

Observances

Today, Labor Day is marked in numerous cities with parades, picnics, rallies, and special worship services. Many events are sponsored by local union organizations.

Some festivals commemorate local labor struggles, such as the Bread and Roses Festival in Lawrence, Massachusetts. On January 12, 1912, mill

Workers Memorial Day

Since 1989 the AFL-CIO has promoted April 28 as Workers Memorial Day to honor those who lost their lives or were injured on the job. On that day in 1971 the Occupational Safety and Health Administration came into being under the U.S. Department of Labor. According to the National Institute for Occupational Safety and Health, more than 50,000 Americans die each year from injuries or diseases relating to their jobs.

Monuments, statues, plaques, and other memorials dedicated to workers who died or sustained injuries in the course of performing their work exist in many cities around the United States. Some are sites for annual Workers Memorial Day observances, such as a candlelight vigil in Lafayette, Indiana, and ceremonies in Gary, Indiana; Baltimore, Maryland; Hauppauge, New York; and La Crosse, Wisconsin.

workers struck because the mills reduced wages when a new state law reduced weekly work hours. After two months, the strike caused President William Taft to initiate investigations into working conditions around the country. The strike is celebrated each year with musical and dance performances, poetry, drama, readings, tours, and historical exhibits.

LaborFest in San Francisco is scheduled in July, rather than around Labor Day, in order to celebrate the citywide general strike in that city in 1934 — the first general strike to take place in the United States. Workers in various jobs throughout the city walked out in support of 12,000 striking longshoremen. Today LaborFest is a month-long festival with dozens of musical, dramatic, and educational events.

The giant likeness of Walter Reuther, president of the United Automobile Workers from 1946 to 1970, mingles with the crowd at the Detroit LaborFest in 1998.

A Sampling of Observances

1. **San Francisco, California:** Each July LaborFest commemorates the anniversary of the general strike of July 1934. Events include film showings, dramatic performances, concerts, and tours. Contact LaborFest, P.O. Box 40983, San Francisco, CA 94140, 415-642-8066, fax: 415-695-1369, laborfest@laborfest.net, http://www.laborfest.net

2. **St. Paul, Minnesota:** Labor Day Extravaganza at Harriet Island features musical and dance performances, speakers, exhibits, car show, and games. Contact St. Paul Area Trades and Labor Assembly, 411 Main St., Rm. 202, St. Paul, MN 55102-1032, 651-222-3787, fax: 651-2903-1989, assembly@mtn.org, http://www.stpaulunions.org/

3. **Janesville, Wisconsin:** Three-day Labor Fest includes concerts and games; parade on Labor Day. Contact Labor Fest, Inc., 1605 Center

Ave., Janesville, WI 53546-2819, 608-755-5120, ext. 122, http://www
.laborfest.org

4. **Decatur, Illinois:** Labor Day parade, rally, and evening pops concert. Contact Decatur Convention and Visitors Bureau, 202 E. North St., Decatur, IL 62523, 800-331-4479 or 217-423-7000; fax: 217-423-7455, tourism@decaturcvb.com, http://www.decaturcvb.com

5. **Detroit, Michigan:** Downtown parade and LaborFest featuring musical entertainment, exhibits, speakers, and picnic. Contact LaborFest, 313-961-0800, dlabornews@aol.com, http://www.laborfestdetroit.org

6. **Lawrence, Massachusetts:** Since 1984, the Bread and Roses Festival has celebrated the historic mill strike of 1912. Events include concerts, food festival, tours, and reenactments. Contact Bread and Roses Heritage Committee, 978-794-1655, breadandroses99@hotmail.com, http://www
.breadandroses.net

Web Sites

AFL-CIO (American Federation of Labor-Congress of Industrial Organizations) web site provides information about Labor Day and Workers Memorial Day, at http://laborday.aflcio.org/aboutunions/laborday/ and http://www.aflcio.org/yourjobeconomy/safety/memorial/

American Labor Museum, Haledon, New Jersey, at http://www.geocities
.com/labormuseum/

Labor Hall of Fame at the U.S. Department of Labor at http://www.dol
.gov/oasam/programs/laborhall/about.htm

Library of Congress offers online exhibits related to Labor Day at http://
memory.loc.gov/ammem/today/sep05.html

Walter P. Reuther Library of Wayne State University in Detroit, Michigan, offers online exhibits on the history of the labor movement at http://www
.reuther.wayne.edu/

Sources for Further Reading

Bartoletti, Susan Campbell. *Kids on Strike!* Boston: Houghton Mifflin, 1999. For young adults.

Colman, Penny. *Strike! The Bitter Struggle of American Workers from Colonial Times to the Present.* Brookfield, Conn.: Millbrook Press, 1995. For young adults.

Dennis, Matthew. *Red, White, and Blue Letter Days: An American Calendar.* Ithaca, N.Y.: Cornell University Press, 2002.

Dubofsky, Melvyn, and Foster Rhea Dulles. *Labor in America: A History.* 6th ed. Wheeling, Ill.: Harlan Davidson, 1999.

Dubofsky, Melvyn, and Warren Van Tine, eds. *Labor Leaders in America.* Urbana: University of Illinois Press, 1987.

Litwicki, Ellen M. *America's Public Holidays, 1865-1920.* Washington, D.C.: Smithsonian Institution Press, 2000.

Meltzer, Milton. *Bread—and Roses; The Struggle of American Labor, 1865-1915.* New York: Knopf, 1967.

Nicholson, Philip Yale. *Labor's Story in the United States.* Philadelphia: Temple University Press, 2004.

Riis, Jacob. *How the Other Half Lives: Studies among the Tenements of New York.* New York: C. Scribner's Sons, 1890.

Martin Luther King Jr. Birthday

Date Established as a Federal Holiday: November 2, 1983

Date Observed: Third Monday in January

The arc of history is long, but it bends toward justice.
— Martin Luther King Jr.

The birthday of Martin Luther King Jr. became the newest American federal holiday in 1983. It commemorates the life and contributions of Martin Luther King Jr., the great civil rights leader of the 1950s and 1960s. The holiday is scheduled on the third Monday in January to fall near his birthday (January 15).

Life of Martin Luther King Jr.

Martin Luther King Jr. was born on January 15, 1929, in Atlanta, Georgia. His father, Martin Luther King Sr., was a pastor at Ebenezer Baptist Church in Atlanta, and his mother, Alberta Christine, was a homemaker. He had an older sister, Christine, and a younger brother, Alfred Daniel Williams.

King was an outstanding student and skipped the ninth and twelfth grades of high school; he entered Morehouse College in Atlanta when he was 15. There King majored in sociology and graduated in 1948. He earned a degree in theology from Crozer Theological Seminary in 1951, then, in 1955, a Ph.D. from Boston College. King's ambition was to be a pastor for a church, like his father. In 1954, the congregation of the Dexter Avenue Baptist Church in Montgomery, Alabama, called King to be its pastor. He served there until 1960, when he moved back to Atlanta and shared the church leadership with his father at Ebenezer Baptist Church. He remained co-pastor at Ebenezer until his death.

King married Coretta Scott on June 18, 1953. They had two daughters and two sons: Yolanda Denise (b. 1955), Martin Luther III (b. 1957), Dexter Scott (b. 1961), and Bernice Albertine (b. 1963).

In 1964, after ten years devoted to the cause of civil rights for African Americans, King was awarded the Nobel Peace Prize. He traveled to Europe that autumn to accept the prize in Oslo, Norway. The Nobel Committee bestows the Peace Prize to individuals it considers to have made the most important contributions to the goal of world peace. In his speech presenting the award to King, Nobel Chairman Gunnar Jahn said, "He is the first person in the Western world to have shown us that a struggle can be waged without violence. He is the first to make the message of brotherly love a reality in the course of his struggle, and he has brought this message to all men, to all nations and races."

Like Mohandas Gandhi (1869-1948) of India, one of his spiritual predecessors, King strove to create positive social change using nonviolent methods. He was arrested 30 times and spent many days in jail for resisting racist laws. After leading the struggle to win landmark victories for racial justice in America, he began to turn his attention toward other social issues, such as opposing the Vietnam War and advocating economic justice for working Americans. King's last efforts were in Memphis, where he went to support sanitation workers who were on strike for better wages and working conditions. There, on April 4, 1968, James Earl Ray fatally shot King. Ray was arrested, convicted, and sentenced to 99 years in state prison.

King was just 39 years old at the time of his death. He was buried in Atlanta on April 9, which President Lyndon B. Johnson declared a national day of mourning. King's tomb is in Freedom Plaza in Atlanta, which was designated a National Historic Site in 1980.

The Segregated South

The United States, especially the American South, was a very different place before Martin Luther King Jr. and the civil rights movement. On January 31, 1865, Congress ended slavery when it passed the 13th Amendment to the Constitution, and many white Southerners were angry. Not only had they depended on slave labor to achieve their standard of living, many white people believed that black people were inferior to them and did not perceive black people as fully human. (*See also* **Emancipation Day**.)

In the South, white society put up barriers between the two peoples and created a segregated culture. Southern whites did everything they could to

Who Was Jim Crow?

Laws aimed at preventing black people from voting, as well as laws enforcing segregation practices, were known as Jim Crow laws. "Jim Crow" was not a real person, but a character in white minstrel shows. A white man would darken his face with charcoal or some other substance. This was a performance intended to degrade black people, and black men in particular. It was popular among white people who attended these shows. The character was probably invented by Thomas "Daddy" Rice, a minstrel performer around the 1830s.

This photograph shows a young girl using the "colored" drinking fountain on the lawn of the county courthouse in Halifax, North Carolina, in April 1938.

limit contact with African Americans and to make sure that any contact they did have took place under conditions in which their supposed superiority was evident to any observer.

"Separate but Equal"

Segregation was legalized by local courts and sanctioned by the U.S. Supreme Court. In 1896 the U.S. Supreme Court ruled in the *Plessy v. Ferguson* case that segregation was legal as long as separate public facilities for blacks and whites were equal. Many facilities for blacks, however, were not equal to those for whites. For example, while most white children attended school in sturdy buildings with plenty of desks, books, and other materials, most black children in the South went to school in dilapidated shacks without heat, electricity, desks, and other basics. In addition, there were only a handful of public high schools in Southern states until later in the 20th century, so many black children never had a chance to receive more than an elementary school education.

As a result, African Americans were continually reminded of how such white people viewed them, right down to the most ordinary situations, such as having to use separate drinking fountains and restrooms, sit in the backs of buses, and go to separate, usually inferior, schools. Moreover, African Americans who didn't follow the segregation laws, even accidentally, could be arrested, attacked, or killed. From the emancipation of slaves in 1865 to the 1960s, white racists killed thousands of black people, under the auspices of radical supremacist groups like the Ku Klux Klan and organized lynch mobs. These heinous crimes often went unpunished. According to one historian, "The best estimate is that between 1880 and 1930, Southern lynch mobs summarily executed, without recourse to legal niceties, 3,320 blacks and 723 whites."

Voting and political involvement are the ways in which people in a democratic society make changes in their common life, but for all practical purposes these avenues were closed to African Americans in the South. Although the 15th Amendment of 1870 guaranteed African American men the same voting rights as white men, white Southerners contrived legal obstacles to prevent blacks from voting. One was the literacy test (which the U.S. Congress did not outlaw until 1975). In states that made passing a literacy test a requirement for voting, it was up to local election officials to decide whether a prospective voter sufficiently understood some random section of the state's constitution before allowing him to vote. Another legal tactic used to exclude black men from voting was the grandfather clause. This kind of law typically said that if a man was allowed to vote in, for example, 1867, his sons and grandsons could vote without having to pass a literacy test or prove ownership of property. Because the U.S. Constitution did not guarantee black men's right to vote until 1870, the grandfather clause served as a loophole to prevent black men from voting. Some Southerners simply intimidated prospective black voters by threatening—or practicing—violence.

> *"I, too, am America."*
> —African-American poet
> Langston Hughes,
> last line of his 1926 poem
> "I, Too, Sing America"

Earlier Steps along the Way

From the early years of the 20th century, many black Americans used their talents to help prepare the ground for the more direct opposition to segregation and oppression of black Americans that came about during the civil rights movement.

On February 12, 1909, sociology professor and writer W. E. B. Du Bois (1868-1963), journalist Ida Wells-Barnett (1862-1931), and other Americans, white and black, formed the NAACP—the National Association for the Advancement of Colored People. The NAACP was the first civil rights organization in the United States. It fought to legally overturn Jim Crow laws, focusing much of its effort on antilynching laws. The organization continues to work for racial justice.

Educator Booker T. Washington (1856-1915) stressed the importance of education and self-improvement through his leadership of the famous Tuskegee Institute in Alabama and his book *Up from Slavery* (1901).

Artistic Protest

African-American artists in various fields created poignant testimonies about being black under what is sometimes called the "American apartheid." Here are just a few examples:

Music
James Weldon Johnson (1871-1938) and his brother J. Rosamond— "Lift Every Voice and Sing" (1899), known as the "Negro National Anthem"

Lead Belly (Huddie Ledbetter, 1885-1949)—"The Bourgeois Blues" (1937)

Billie Holiday (1915-1959)—"Strange Fruit" (1939)

Big Bill Broonzy (1893-1958)—"Black, Brown and White" (1945)

Literature
Paul Lawrence Dunbar (1872-1906)—poem "We Wear the Mask" (1896)

Langston Hughes (1902-1967)—poem "The Negro Speaks of Rivers" (1926)

Richard Wright (1908-1960)—novel *Native Son* (1940)

Ralph Ellison (1914-1994)—novel *Invisible Man* (1952)

A. Philip Randolph (1889-1979) led the March on Washington movement. Thousands of black marchers planned to assemble in Washington, D.C., on July 1, 1941, to protest employment discrimination in the defense industry, which was excluding many African Americans from new jobs. In order to avoid such a huge gathering—which might also provoke a race riot—President Franklin D. Roosevelt signed Executive Order 8802 on June 25, which pronounced that the federal government or the defense industry could not discriminate against anyone based on race, color, national origin, or creed when hiring workers. The Order also created the Fair Employment Practices Committee to investigate reports of hiring discrimination. This was a victory, but Randolph continued to call for nonviolent marches, protests, and boycotts in order to gain the right to vote, abolish discriminatory hiring practices in other industries, and effect desegregation. With the U.S. entrance into World War II, though, black Americans united with the rest of the nation, largely putting their own interests at home on the sidelines, for the moment.

Civil Rights Movement

The civil rights movement, led by Martin Luther King Jr. and others, inspired self-respect and courage to shore up a people who faced a monumental struggle to improve life for themselves and future generations. By the mid-1950s people began to rally behind emerging leaders such as King to call for equal rights and liberties.

The U.S. Supreme Court's landmark decision in *Brown v. Board of Education* provided some momentum. The case involved Oliver Brown—a minister who, in 1950, attempted to enroll his daughter in a segregated public school in Topeka, Kansas—and other African-American parents in Delaware, South Carolina, Virginia, and Washington, D.C., who had attempted the same. Each all-white school refused to admit the children. The parents brought lawsuits against their respective school systems. The state courts ruled against the parents, who in 1952 appealed to the U.S. Supreme Court. On May 17, 1954, the Supreme Court ruled that segregation in public schools was unconstitutional—that the concept of "separate but equal" facilities was against the law.

Civil rights leaders were now eager to extend the promise of *Brown* to all aspects of public life. They embarked on a series of public protests (also known as direct actions). Marches, protests, boycotts, sit-ins, acts of civil

191

disobedience, and vigils are all examples of direct actions employed during the civil rights movement.

One of the best-known examples was the Montgomery, Alabama, bus boycott. The protest was instigated by the December 1, 1955, arrest of Rosa Parks, a black resident who refused to follow the Alabama law that said blacks must sit only in the back of a bus. Three days after her arrest, a group of black Americans in Montgomery called a mass meeting to discuss boycotting the city's buses and selected King to be president of the protest group. He gave his first protest speech at the organizing meeting and stirred the attendees to action. During that winter people walked or carpooled in order to show they were no longer going to be treated as second-class citizens on buses. On June 4, 1956, a U.S. District Court ruled that segregation on city buses was unconstitutional. The case was appealed to the U.S. Supreme Court, which ruled in favor of the lower court on November 13, 1956. The bus boycott was the first successful mass direct action of the civil rights movement and it threw King into the national spotlight.

In February 1960 young black college students in seven states conducted sit-ins at more than 30 lunch counters in the South, where proprietors refused to serve black people. At the Nashville, Tennessee, sit-ins, participants included John Lewis (who was later elected a congressman from Georgia) and Marion Barry (who later became the mayor of Washington, D.C.). The students were arrested on trespassing charges, and this prompted the first civil rights movement march. On the morning of April 19, 1960, someone bombed the house of Z. Alexander Looby, a lawyer who represented the students arrested for the sit-ins and who was also the city's first black councilman. Students gathered when they heard the news. Their destination was city hall. Student leader Diane Nash asked Mayor Ben West whether he believed it was wrong to deny service to black people at lunch counters. Mayor West replied that he did believe it was wrong. The lunch counters at which the students had held sit-ins began serving blacks three weeks later. On October 19, 1960, King participated in a sit-in at two eating areas in a department store in Atlanta. The group was arrested for trespassing, and King went to jail for the first time.

In May 1961, a group of black and white Americans, known as the Freedom Riders, boarded interstate buses in northern states and headed south, testing the ruling on a national level. King met with and encouraged

the Freedom Riders, though he did not participate in any rides. The Riders met with violence in several Alabama cities. But later that year the Interstate Commerce Commission outlawed discrimination and segregation in all interstate buses and stations.

Marching for Justice

In 1963 and 1964, King led two massive demonstrations for civil rights that led to the creation of two important laws. He also met with Presidents John F. Kennedy and Lyndon B. Johnson, who both supported the aims of the civil rights movement.

The historic March on Washington took place on August 28, 1963. The event was designed to urge action on President Kennedy's civil rights legislation (which became the Civil Rights Act of 1964; see below). More than 250,000 Americans, including about 60,000 white supporters, from all over

In one of the most famous photos of the civil rights movement, protesters John R. Salter, Joan Trunpauer, and Annie Moody conduct a sit-in at a lunch counter in Jackson, Mississippi, in 1963.

"We Shall Overcome"

Civil rights activists often relied on the sustenance of music. The signature song associated with the movement was "We Shall Overcome." Zilphia Horton, Frank Hamilton, Guy Carawan, and Pete Seeger wrote new words and adapted the music to an older tune and published the song in 1960. President Lyndon Johnson quoted from the song during a speech he gave asking Congress to pass the Voting Rights Act of 1965. Here are the lyrics:

We shall overcome, we shall overcome,
We shall overcome some day,
Oh, deep in my heart I do believe
We shall overcome some day.

We'll walk hand in hand, we'll walk hand
    in hand,
We'll walk hand in hand some day,
Oh, deep in my heart I do believe
We shall overcome some day.

We are not afraid, we are not afraid,
We are not afraid today,
Oh, deep in my heart I do believe
We shall overcome some day.

We shall stand together, we shall stand
    together,
We shall stand together—now,
Oh, deep in my heart I do believe
We shall overcome some day.

The truth will make us free, the truth will
    make us free,
The truth will make us free some day,
Oh, deep in my heart I do believe
We shall overcome some day.

The Lord will see us through, the Lord
    will see us through,
The Lord will see us through some day,
Oh, deep in my heart I do believe
We shall overcome some day.

We shall be like Him, we shall be like Him,
We shall be like Him some day,
Oh, deep in my heart I do believe
We shall overcome some day.

We shall live in peace, we shall live in
    peace,
We shall live in peace some day,
Oh, deep in my heart I do believe
We shall overcome some day.

The whole wide world around, the whole
    wide world around,
The whole wide world around some day,
Oh, deep in my heart I do believe
We shall overcome some day.

We shall overcome, we shall overcome,
We shall overcome some day,
Oh, deep in my heart I do believe
We shall overcome some day.

the United States filled the Washington Mall. Never before in the United States had so many people peacefully gathered in one place to call for equality, job opportunities, and justice for all. Popular musicians lent their talents to the event: Bob Dylan, Mahalia Jackson, Joan Baez, Josh White, Odetta, and Peter, Paul and Mary.

All had come to hear King, who stood at the Lincoln Memorial and delivered one of the most renowned speeches in American history. He inspired the crowd with his words of encouragement and his powerful dream of a peacefully integrated America. (*See the Appendix for the full text of the speech.*)

After Kennedy was assassinated in November 1963, Johnson became president and successfully oversaw the passage of new civil rights legislation through Congress. He signed the Civil Rights Act of 1964 into law on July 2 and then offered King his pen as they shook hands. The Civil

On July 2, 1964, President Lyndon B. Johnson signed the Civil Rights Act of 1964 into law. Afterward, he turned around to shake hands with King and offer his pen.

195

Rights Act outlawed discrimination in any public place under the domain of interstate commerce and discrimination in hiring on the basis of race or gender.

In the spring of 1965 King helped organize and rally activists in Alabama who planned a march from Selma to Montgomery, the state capital, to call for voting rights. They began on Sunday, March 7, but police teargassed and beat marchers before they finished crossing the Edmund Pettus Bridge that leads out of Selma toward Montgomery. That day became known as "Bloody Sunday." A U.S. District Court judge, Frank M. Johnson, later ruled that the demonstrators had a legal right to march to Montgomery. The march began again on Sunday, March 21. This time President Johnson called in National Guard and Army troops, FBI agents, and federal marshals to protect the marchers. King and other leaders headed 4,000 people for the 54-mile trip. By the time they reached Montgomery, five days later, the crowd had grown to 25,000.

On August 6, 1965, Johnson signed into law the Voting Rights Act. The Voting Rights Act outlawed literacy tests and provided for federal observers at polling places to ensure fair voting practices.

> *"All Americans should be indignant when one American is denied the right to vote. The loss of that right to a single citizen undermines the freedom of every citizen."*
>
> —President Lyndon B. Johnson at a press conference on February 4, 1965

Nonviolent Resistance

King led the civil rights movement using strategies of nonviolent resistance and direct action. Nonviolent resistance and direct action as modern methods for creating positive social change can be traced to an essay written by American writer Henry David Thoreau in 1849. His "Civil Disobedience" inspired Mohandas Gandhi, who in turn inspired King.

In the early to mid-20th century Gandhi used these methods to lead the Indian people in resisting Britain's unjust rule in India. Gandhi called his strategy *satyagraha*, a Hindi word meaning "insistence on the truth by means of nonviolence." The world watched in awe as they pressured Britain—long the most powerful nation in the world—to leave their country, largely through nonviolent actions. As a result, India became an independent democratic country in 1947.

On September 6, 1957, Elizabeth Eckford was one of the first nine African-American students to attend Central High School in Little Rock, Arkansas, by order of a federal court.

In the early years of the 20th century African-American civil rights activists met with Indian activists to learn about nonviolent techniques. Their quest would bear fruit just a few decades later. Rev. Glenn Smiley, James Lawson, and Bayard Rustin taught King the fine points of nonviolent philosophy and strategies. Lawson had studied nonviolence in India, where he served as a Methodist missionary in the early 1950s. This helped inspire King to travel to India himself to meet with veterans of that country's independence struggle.

Nonviolent resistance proved to be incredibly powerful in many potentially explosive situations during the struggle for civil rights. Nonviolent resistance does not mean backing down or retreating from a fight. On the contrary, it takes a tremendous amount of courage and strength of will. As

King wrote in his *Letter from Birmingham Jail*, "This is not a method for cowards."

Nonviolent resistance means, for example, that when a white police officer beat a black man for refusing to leave a protest area, the black man would not hit back, or yell back, or give any resistance whatsoever. By not participating in the fight, the nonviolent resister holds his ground peacefully and thus communicates with his whole person that any violence that happens around him, or to him, ends with him. He "breaks the chain of hate," in King's words. As King said, "Returning violence with violence only multiplies violence."

In addition, by not participating in the violence, such resisters presented to the world painfully clear images of the ugliness of hatred and racial injustice. They also earned the respect and admiration of many watching from the sidelines. A crucial long-term goal of this strategy, again in King's words, is that "nonviolent resistance does not seek to defeat or humiliate the opponent, but to win his friendship and understanding. . . . The aftermath of nonviolence is the creation of the beloved community, while the aftermath of violence is tragic bitterness."

Though King urged nonviolence in working for changes in society, he was often the target of violence. His home was bombed twice. On September 20, 1958, he was stabbed in the chest by a black woman who was later committed to a facility for the criminally insane. He received hate mail and death threats. It is a tragic irony that the man who championed nonviolence would himself become the victim of the hatred and violence he sought to overcome. Yet when King lost his life to an assassin's bullet on April 4, 1968, it did not still his message or accomplishments.

Legacy

Perhaps the most concrete legacy of King's life and work was the passage of the Civil Rights Act of 1964 and the Voting Rights Act of 1965. King also left a successful model of using nonviolent resistance and direct action to make society more fair and just.

The United States was indeed a different place before Martin Luther King Jr. It has been a better place because of his example and because of the thousands of Americans who followed him.

Creation of the Martin Luther King Jr. Birthday Holiday

The first proposal to create a federal holiday to commemorate King's message and accomplishments was introduced by U.S. Representative John Conyers Jr. of Detroit, just four days after King was assassinated. From that time until the legal establishment of the holiday in 1983, controversy and debate surrounded the issue.

Throughout the 1970s and 1980s many African Americans lobbied Congress for a national holiday in King's honor. They held marches and rallies in Washington, D.C., and elsewhere, and organized petition drives that gathered signatures from millions of Americans who agreed there should be a holiday for King. They met resistance from other Americans who raised two objections. For one thing, opponents to the holiday argued that it would cost the federal government $18 million to give its employees the day off with pay. The second objection claimed that other Americans who made noteworthy contributions to the nation were not similarly honored with a federal holiday.

> *"Returning violence for violence only multiplies violence, adding deeper darkness to a night already devoid of stars. Darkness cannot drive out darkness, only light can do that. Hate cannot drive out hate, only love can do that."*
>
> —Martin Luther King Jr., in his book *Where Do We Go from Here: Chaos or Community?*

Many states declared King's birthday a holiday while the national effort continued. Illinois was the first state to make the King holiday state law in 1973. In 1974 Massachusetts and Connecticut passed similar state laws. By 1989, 44 states had passed laws designating a Martin Luther King Jr. holiday. In the early 1990s, the debate in Arizona, one of the remaining six states without the holiday, gained nationwide attention. In 1990 Arizona residents narrowly voted down initiatives to create the King holiday. In response, advocates of the holiday moved to boycott Arizona tourist attractions, and the National Football League removed Phoenix from consideration as a site for the 1993 Super Bowl. Their efforts paid off when, in 1992, Arizonans officially voted to celebrate the King holiday.

On November 2, 1983, the U.S. Congress passed the holiday bill, after heated debates, including one in which Senator Jesse Helms of North

Carolina baselessly accused King of being a communist. President Ronald Reagan signed the holiday bill into law on November 3, 1983. Martin Luther King Jr. Day was first observed as a federal holiday in 1986.

Some Americans argued against a national holiday for King, believing that it was only for African Americans. But proponents argued that all Americans have been enriched by the civil rights movement King led. By confronting white racism, the civil rights movement encouraged those with racist attitudes to see the humanity in all people. As abolitionist Frederick Douglass said in 1883, "No man can put a chain about the ankle of his fellow man without at last finding the other end fastened about his own neck."

Some southern states have incorporated the observance into a joint holiday commemorating Confederate leaders Robert E. Lee and Stonewall Jackson as well as King. In this way the holiday would, oddly, take note of those who opposed the abolition of slavery as well as one who championed African-American freedom and civil rights. Virginia had this joint holiday from 1989 until 2001, when the state approved a separate holiday for King.

At the conclusion of one of his sermons, known as "The Drum Major Instinct," King talked about what he wanted people to say about him after he died: "I'd like someone to mention that day that Martin Luther King Jr. tried to give his life serving others."

Observances

As is the case with other federal holidays, the president of the United States issues a proclamation every year calling on Americans to observe Martin Luther King Jr.'s life and achievements with appropriate ceremonies and activities.

Ebenezer Baptist Church, where King served as pastor, hosts an annual service which includes tributes to King by notable national leaders.

Churches, schools, universities, and other organizations around the country organize special programs. Many event organizers emphasize community service and volunteerism as the most appropriate ways in which to remember and honor King. Other observances around the nation feature memorial religious services, marches and parades, speeches, and concerts.

Related Observances

March—Thousands gather for the Bridge Crossing Jubilee, which commemorates the 1965 march from Selma to Montgomery. It begins the first weekend in March, near the anniversary of "Bloody Sunday," with a special church service and ceremony in Selma, followed by a reenactment of the five-day march to Montgomery and a rally at the state capitol.

April 4—Ebenezer Baptist Church holds a Day of Remembrance in commemoration of King's death.

A Sampling of Observances

1. **Sacramento, California:** MLK Community Celebration features a march; job, health, and education fairs; children's events; entertainment; and more. Contact Martin Luther King Jr. Celebration Committee, 916-479-1918, info@mlksacramento.org, http://www.mlksacramento.org

2. **San Antonio, Texas:** Annual march and commemoration, including speakers and awards for distinguished service, attended by tens of thousands. Contact City of San Antonio Martin Luther King Jr. Commission, 210-207-2098, http://www.sanantonio.gov/mlk

3. **Ann Arbor, Michigan:** The University of Michigan hosts an annual month-long symposium in honor of Martin Luther King Jr. each January with guest speakers, concerts, and other events. Contact the Office of Academic Multicultural Initiatives, 3009 Student Activities Bldg., Ann Arbor, MI 48109-1316, 734-936-1055, fax: 734-764-3595, mlkteam@umich.edu, http://www.mlksymposium.umich.edu

4. **Albany, New York:** Memorial service with music and speeches followed by a march to the King Monument where there is a wreath-laying ceremony. Contact MLK Observance, NYS Office of General Services, Office of Special Events, Empire State Pl., Concourse Rm. 130, Albany, NY 12242, 518-486-9866, fax: 518-473-0058, http://www.nyking.org/

5. **Boston, Massachusetts:** Community breakfast begins a day of concerts and other events around the city. Contact Mayor's Office, 617-734-6109, mayor@ci.boston.ma.us

6. **Philadelphia, Pennsylvania:** Tens of thousands participate in hundreds of volunteer activities. Contact Greater Philadelphia Martin Luther King

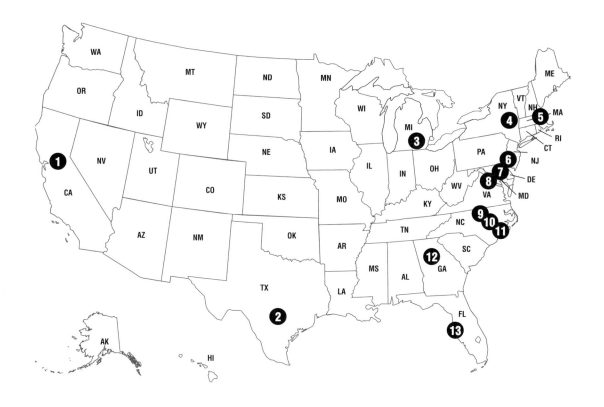

Day of Service, United Way of Southeastern PA, 7 Benjamin Franklin Parkway, Philadelphia, PA 19103, 215-665-2475, fax: 215-665-2531, http://www.mlkdayofservice.org

7. **Baltimore, Maryland:** Annual Martin Luther King Jr. Birthday Celebration Parade. Contact Baltimore Office of Promotion & the Arts, 7 E. Redwood St., Ste. 500, Baltimore, MD 21202, 410-752-8632, fax: 410-385-0361, http://www.bop.org

8. **Washington, D.C.:** Observance features a wreath-laying ceremony, interfaith services, prayer breakfasts, gospel music concert, anti-crime rally and march, and other events. Contact The District of Columbia Martin Luther King Jr. Holiday Commission, 202-727-6306, http://os.dc.gov

9. **Durham, North Carolina:** Annual parade and gospel concert. Contact Another COLEY Event, P.O. Box 361, Durham, NC 27702, 919-680-0840, fax: 919-544-9854, acoleyevent@msn.com

10. **Cary, North Carolina:** Annual events "keeping the dream alive" include a unity march, ecumenical service, musical performances, art, speakers, and more. Contact Cary Parks, Recreation and Cultural Resources, 919-460-4963, http://townofcary.org/mlk/

11. **Raleigh, North Carolina:** Interfaith prayer breakfast, youth concert, memorial march, and wreath-laying at the statue of King. Contact The Wake-Raleigh Martin Luther King Celebration Committee, P.O. Box 28696, Raleigh, NC 27611, 919-832-3193 or 919-834-6264, fax: 919-833-0723, http://www.king-raleigh.org

12. **Atlanta, Georgia:** Annual service at Ebenezer Baptist Church and programs at the King Center for Nonviolent Social Change, 449 Auburn Ave., Atlanta, GA 30312, 404-526-8900, http://www.thekingcenter.org

13. **St. Petersburg, Florida:** Martin Luther King Jr. Drum Major for Justice Parade and Festival of Bands draws about 100,000. Contact Southern Christian Leadership Conference, 3235 16th Ave. S., St. Petersburg, FL 33712, 727-327-0085

Web Sites

Civil Rights Movement Veterans web site at http://www.crmvet.org/

Library of Congress American Memory exhibit on King at http://memory .loc.gov/ammem/today/jan15.html

Martin Luther King Jr. Center for Nonviolent Social Change at http:// www.thekingcenter.org

Martin Luther King Jr. Day of Service, a web site sponsored by the Corporation for National & Community Service and USA Freedom Corps, at http://www.mlkday.org

Martin Luther King Jr. National Historic Site at http://www.nps.gov/ malu/

Martin Luther King Jr. Papers Project at Stanford University publishes King's writings and speeches at http://www.stanford.edu/group/King/

National Archives has a small online exhibit on the Civil Rights Act of 1964 at http://www.archives.gov/exhibit_hall/treasures_of_congress/page_24.html

National Association for the Advancement of Colored People official web site at http://www.naacp.org/

National Civil Rights Museum at http://www.civilrightsmuseum.org/

National Park Service offers pages on historic sites of the civil rights movement at http://www.cr.nps.gov/nr/travel/civilrights/

"The Rise and Fall of Jim Crow," companion web site to the 2002 PBS series, at http://www.pbs.org/wnet/jimcrow/ and http://www.jimcrowhistory.org/home.htm

Voices of Civil Rights, oral history on a web site sponsored by the American Association of Retired Persons, the Library of Congress, and the Leadership Conference on Civil Rights at http://www.voicesofcivilrights.org

"Will the Circle Be Unbroken?" A site produced by the Southern Regional Council that offers an audio history of the civil rights movement in five southern communities at http://unbrokencircle.org/

Sources for Further Reading

Branch, Taylor. *Parting the Waters: America in the King Years, 1954-63.* New York: Simon & Schuster, 1988.

———. *Pillar of Fire: America in the King Years, 1963-65.* New York: Simon & Schuster, 1998.

Carson, Clayborne, et al., eds. *The Eyes on the Prize Civil Rights Reader.* New York: Penguin Books, 1991.

Fairclough, Adam. *Better Day Coming: Blacks and Equality, 1890-2000.* New York: Viking, 2001.

Halberstam, David. *The Children.* New York: Random House, 1998.

Haskins, Jim. *I Have a Dream: The Life and Words of Martin Luther King, Jr.* Brookfield, Conn.: Millbrook Press, 1992. For young adults.

King, Coretta Scott. *My Life with Martin Luther King.* Rev. ed. New York: H. Holt, 1993.

Levine, Ellen, ed. *Freedom's Children: Young Civil Rights Activists Tell Their Stories.* New York: Putnam, 1993. For young adults.

McKissack, Patricia C. *Martin Luther King, Jr.: A Man to Remember.* Chicago: Children's Press, 1984. For young adults.

Meltzer, Milton. *There Comes a Time: The Struggle for Civil Rights.* New York: Random House, 2001. For young adults.

Oates, Stephen B. *Let the Trumpet Sound: The Life of Martin Luther King, Jr.* New York: Mentor, 1982.

Payne, Charles M., and Adam Green, eds. *Time Longer Than Rope: A Century of African-American Activism, 1850-1950.* New York: New York University Press, 2003.

Watley, William D. *Roots of Resistance: The Nonviolent Ethic of Martin Luther King, Jr.* Valley Forge, Pa.: Judson Press, 1985.

Williams, Juan. *Eyes on the Prize: America's Civil Rights Years, 1954-1965.* Introduction by Julian Bond. New York: Viking, 1987. Companion volume to PBS series.

Writings by Martin Luther King Jr.

Letter from Birmingham City Jail. Philadelphia: American Friends Service Committee, May 1963.

The Measure of a Man. Philadelphia: Pilgrim Press, 1959. Meditations.

Strength to Love. New York: Harper & Row, 1963. A collection of 15 sermons.

Stride Toward Freedom. New York: Harper & Row, 1958. Account of the Montgomery bus boycott.

The Trumpet of Conscience. New York: Harper & Row, 1968. Five talks given as the Massey Lectures series over the Canadian Broadcasting Corporation in 1967.

Where Do We Go from Here: Chaos or Community? New York: Harper & Row, 1967. Discussion of war, poverty, and the struggle for racial equality.

Why We Can't Wait. New York: Harper & Row, 1964. Analysis and description of the civil rights movement.

TO
Louis P. Goullaud Esq.

O'er graves of the loved ones

PLANT BEAUTIFUL FLOWERS

SONG AND CHORUS   POETRY AND MUSIC

BY

JOHN. P. ORDWAY. M.D.

BOSTON.

Published by OLIVER DITSON & CO. 277 Washington St

PHILADA.   CINN.   NEW YORK   BOSTON.   CHICAGO.
LEE & WALKER.   JOHN CHURCH & CO.   C.H. DITSON & CO.   J.C. HAYNES & CO.   LYON & HEALY.

J.H.Bufford's Lith. 490 Wash.º St. Boston.

Memorial Day

Date Established as a Federal Holiday: May 13, 1938

Date Observed: Last Monday in May

Memorial Day is a federal holiday created to remember those who have died in the military service of the nation. It was originally called Decoration Day, because the primary activity associated with the observance was, and is, decorating the graves of fallen soldiers. Decoration Day observances began during the Civil War. By 1890 every state in the North, as well as the District of Columbia, had passed legislation making Decoration Day or Memorial Day a legal holiday on May 30 or May 31. On May 13, 1938, Congress passed a law making Memorial Day, May 30, a legal public holiday. The Monday Holiday Law of June 28, 1968, took effect in 1971, changing the observance date of Memorial Day to the last Monday in May.

In 1996 Congress instituted the White House Commission on Remembrance to promote Memorial Day activities, encourage Americans to participate in a National Moment of Remembrance, and educate children about the meaning of Memorial Day. In addition, on December 28, 2000, Congress passed a law designating 3:00 P.M. (local time) on Memorial Day as the National Moment of Remembrance.

History of Memorial Day

People around the world have decorated graves of fallen warriors and loved ones since ancient times. The American Memorial Day dates from the Civil War, which began in 1861 and ended in 1865. The war was fought between the Union of Northern states, which sought to abolish slavery throughout the United States, and the Confederacy of Southern states, which aimed to preserve states' rights to allow slavery. Many battles were

Opposite page: A grave-decorating scene on the cover of sheet music for the 1868 song "O'er Graves of the Loved Ones Plant Beautiful Flowers" by John P. Ordway.

207

fought in the Southern states, though one of the most decisive, the Battle of Gettysburg, took place in Pennsylvania. Of the more than 2.3 million Union soldiers, more than 360,000 were killed. About 1 million soldiers fought in the Confederacy, and between 133,000 and 165,000 died. It is the bloodiest war in the nation's history. (*For more on* slavery and the Civil War, *see* **Emancipation Day**.)

The sheer devastation of the war demanded recognition and response. According to most accounts, women began decorating graves during the war, and some decorated the graves of both Union and Confederate soldiers. The *New York Tribune* hailed women in Columbus, Mississippi, for performing this "healing touch for the nation."

Historians are uncertain exactly where and when the first Civil War-era grave-decorating observance occurred. Several towns claim to be the site of the earliest Memorial Day observance: Boalsburg, Pennsylvania (which claimed its first observance took place in 1864), Vicksburg, Mississippi (claiming April 1865), Winchester, Virginia (claiming May 1865), Columbus, Mississippi, and Carbondale, Illinois (each claiming April 1866), and Waterloo, New York (claiming May 5, 1866). The Waterloo commemoration was formally recognized by Congress and President Lyndon Johnson in 1966 as the official birthplace of Memorial Day.

Confederate Memorial Days

Some southern states observe their own memorial day holidays to honor fallen Confederate soldiers. Alabama, Georgia, and Mississippi have legal state holidays designating the fourth, or last, Monday in April as Confederate Memorial Day. Their holidays commemorate Confederate General Joseph E. Johnston's formal surrender to Union General William T. Sherman near Greensboro, North Carolina, on April 26, 1865. South Carolina's Memorial Day is May 10 to observe the death anniversary of Confederate General Thomas J. "Stonewall" Jackson. In Texas Confederate Heroes Day is January 19, the birthday of Confederate General Robert E. Lee. In Tennessee June 3, Jefferson Davis's birthday, is a special observance.

In September 1867 a poem published in the *Atlantic Monthly*, "The Blue and the Gray" by Francis Miles Finch, drew a verbal portrait of decorated graves of both Union soldiers — who wore blue uniforms — and Confederate soldiers — who wore gray. The poem's popularity helped spread the custom of grave decorating in the years after the war.

The first official observance of Memorial Day can be traced back to a General Order issued by Union General John A. Logan. On May 5, 1868, he sent this order to all posts of the Grand Army of the Republic:

> The thirtieth day of May, 1868, is designated for the purpose of strewing with flowers or otherwise decorating the graves of comrades who died in defense of their country during the late rebellion, and whose bodies now lie in almost every city, village and hamlet churchyard in the land. In this observance no form of ceremony is prescribed, but posts and comrades will in their own way arrange such fitting services and testimonials of respect as circumstances may permit.
>
> It is the purpose of the commander-in-chief to inaugurate this observance with the hope that it will be kept up from year to year while a survivor of the war remains to honor the memory of his departed comrades. He earnestly desires the public press to call attention to this order and lend its friendly aid in bringing it to the notice of comrades in all parts of the country in time for simultaneous compliance therewith.
>
> Department commanders will use every effort to make this order effective.

General Logan reportedly got the idea from his wife. Earlier that spring she and a few friends had traveled to Virginia and visited Confederate battlefields and graveyards. Moved by Southern women's practice of decorating their soldiers' graves, Mrs. Logan urged her husband to formalize the custom in the North.

For years after the Civil War, particularly in the South, Americans observed Memorial Day much more widely than the Fourth of July. The ideas surrounding **Independence Day** aggravated too many open wounds, but both sides could share in mourning the Civil War dead. (*See the Appendix for two accounts of Memorial Day observances in Washington, D.C., in the late 19th century.*)

Although Memorial Day originally commemorated those who died in the Civil War, after World War I, the holiday honored Americans who died in all wars.

Red Poppies

Red poppies grow wild in fields in France and Belgium where many battles of World War I were fought. After the war soldiers carried memories of the arresting sight of the beautiful flowers sharing the land with their fallen comrades. This vision is perhaps most poignantly rendered by Canadian Colonel John McCrae's poem "In Flanders Fields," written in 1915, three years before he was killed in the war.

In Flanders Fields

In Flanders fields the poppies blow
Between the crosses, row on row,
    That mark our place; and in the sky
    The larks, still bravely singing, fly
Scarce heard amid the guns below.

We are the Dead. Short days ago
We lived, felt dawn, saw sunset glow,
    Loved and were loved, and now we lie
        In Flanders fields.

Take up our quarrel with the foe:
To you from failing hands we throw
    The torch; be yours to hold it high.
    If ye break faith with us who die
We shall not sleep, though poppies grow
        In Flanders fields.

Soon after World War I a few women — including Anna Guerin in France, and Moina Michael and Mary Hanecy in the United States — who were deeply affected by McCrae's poem, headed efforts to sell poppies to raise funds for families in war-torn regions. Today disabled and unemployed veterans make the millions of paper poppies sold by the Veterans of Foreign Wars and American Legion Auxiliary each year around Memorial Day.

Fallen Americans

Revolutionary War (1775-83): 4,435

War of 1812 (1812-15): 2,260

Indian Wars (about 1817-98): 1,000

Mexican War (1846-48): 13,283

Civil War (1861-65): at least 497,832 (Union: 364,511;
Confederate: 133,321-164,820)

Spanish-American War (1898-1902): 2,446

World War I (1917-18): 116,516 (422 were women***)

World War II (1941-45): 405,399 (470 were women***)

Korean War (1950-53): 54,246* (16 were women***)

Vietnam War (1964-75): 58,209* (8 were women)

Persian Gulf War (1990-91): 382 (13 were women)

War in Afghanistan/Operation Enduring Freedom (2001-):
193** (at least 6 were women)

War in Iraq/Operation Iraqi Freedom (2003-): 1,712** (at least 33
were women)

* According to the Department of Defense, numbers continue to be
added to these totals.

** Department of Defense totals as of June 16, 2005

***Figures from Women in Military Service for America Memorial
Foundation, Inc.; research is ongoing and statistics are incomplete.

Observances

Americans observe Memorial Day in both public and private ways. Many decorate the graves of departed loved ones, whether they served in the armed forces or not. Towns and cities around the country also hold ceremonies for Memorial Day that often include prayers, speeches, and the singing of the national anthem and the playing of "Taps." (*For more on "Taps," see* **Veterans Day**.)

Washington, D.C., is the location of the most elaborate observances during the weekend of Memorial Day. On the evening before the holiday the National Symphony Orchestra pays musical tribute at the National Memorial Day Concert on the West Lawn of the U.S. Capitol Building.

The Tomb of the Unknown Soldiers

On Memorial Day, 1993, President Bill Clinton participated in the wreath-laying ceremony at the Tomb of the Unknown Soldiers at Arlington National Cemetery in Arlington, Virginia.

Three unknown soldiers rest in the Tomb at Arlington National Cemetery. The first unidentified soldier to be buried at Arlington died in World War I. His remains were interred on November 11, 1921. On Memorial Day, 1958, remains of an unknown soldier who fought in World War II and another who fought in Korea were also buried there. The remains of a Vietnam War soldier were buried at the Tomb in 1984. DNA testing later identified the Vietnam War veteran, and his family was able to claim his remains.

The Tomb is inscribed: "Here rests in honored glory an American soldier known but to God." Specially selected sentinels from the Army's Third Infantry maintain constant guard at the Tomb.

Before the ceremonies, members of the Old Guard of the Third U.S. Infantry—the Army's official ceremonial unit—take part in a tradition known as "Flags-in." They place more than 280,000 American flags at each grave site at Arlington National Cemetery and at the U.S. Soldier's and Airmen's Home National Cemetery. Old Guard soldiers stand guard over both cemeteries the entire weekend.

Memorial Day begins with the National Memorial Day Parade. Active military, veterans, bands, and others march down Independence Avenue. During the afternoon numerous wreath-layings and memorial services are held at monuments honoring the armed forces: the Tomb of the Unknowns at Arlington National Cemetery, the U.S. Navy Memorial, the Vietnam Veterans Memorial, the Women in Military for America Memorial, and at Logan Circle Park, named after John A. Logan, the Union Army General who ordered the first official observance of Memorial Day (see above). In addition, the U.S. Army Band performs a concert for the ceremony at Arlington, and the U.S. Navy Band plays at the Navy Memorial.

The National Moment of Remembrance from 3:00 P.M. to 3:01 P.M. honors the fallen as buglers play "Taps" at various monuments and government buildings.

A Sampling of Observances

1. **Austin, Texas:** America's Triathlon and Memorial Day Remembrance Celebration combines triathletic events with special observance ceremony and concert. Contact America's Triathlon, info@americastriathlon.com, http://www.americastriathlon.com

2. **Columbia, Missouri:** Salute to Veterans Memorial Day Weekend Celebration includes an air show, visiting veterans, a parade, and special ceremonies with speakers, wreath laying, 21-gun salute, and "Taps." Contact Salute to Veterans Corporation, 573-443-2651, airshow@salute.org, http://www.salute.org

3. **Nelsonville, Ohio:** Ohio Valley Honoring All Veterans Memorial Day Powwow since 1980. Other offerings include crafts and food. Contact Hocking College, 3301 Hocking Pkwy., Nelsonville, OH 45764-9704, 740-753-3591

4. **Waterloo, New York:** In 1966 Congress and President Lyndon B. Johnson officially recognized this village as the "Birthplace of Memorial Day." Since 1866 Waterloo has commemorated Memorial Day. Events

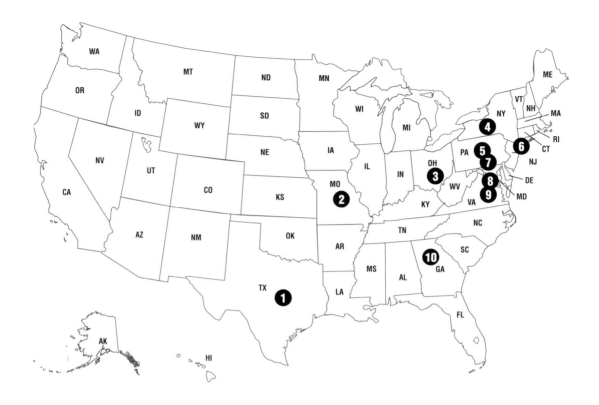

feature marches to cemetery memorial services with wreath layings, speakers, gun salutes, and "Taps." Other activities include a parade, fireworks, musical entertainment, living history demonstrations, and more. Contact Village Office, 41 W. Main St., Waterloo, NY 13165, 315-539-9131, http://www.waterloony.com/

5. **Boalsburg, Pennsylvania:** This village also asserts "Birthplace of Memorial Day" status, claiming annual observances since 1864. Events include a walk to the cemetery for special services, reenactments, a parade, and speeches. Contact Centre County Visitors Bureau, 814-231-1400, http://www.boalsburgcentral.com and also see Boal Mansion Museum, P.O. Box 116, Boalsburg, PA 16827-0116, 814-466-6210, office@boalmuseum.com, http://www.boalmuseum.com/memorialday04.village.htm

6. **New York, New York:** U.S. Navy and Marines participate in Fleet Week, which includes Memorial Day services and parades. For more information, see http://www.fleetweek.navy.mil

7. **Gettysburg, Pennsylvania:** A parade through town leads to the Gettysburg National Cemetery where a ceremony, including prayers, speeches, and wreath laying, concludes with children strewing flowers on the graves. Contact Gettysburg National Military Park, 97 Taneytown Rd., Gettysburg, PA 17235-2804, 717-334-1124, fax: 717-334-1891, http:// www.nps.gov/gett/

8. **Washington, D.C.:** The Taste of DC food and music festival accompanies the national observances described above. For parade information, contact Music Celebrations International, info@musiccelebrations.com, http://www.musiccelebrations.com

    For Taste of DC, contact 202-789-7002, http://www.tasteofdc.org/

    For information on other events, contact National Capitol Parks-East, 1900 Anacostia Dr., S.E., Washington, DC 20020-6722, 202-690-5185, fax: 202-690-0862, http://www.nps.gov/nace/ or Washington, DC, Convention and Tourism Corporation, 901 7th St., N.W., 4th Fl., Washington, DC 20001-3719, 800-422-8644 or 202-789-7000; fax: 202-789-7037, http://www.washington.org

9. **Fredericksburg, Virginia**: Luminaria observance features the placement of 15,300 candles at gravesites honoring as many fallen soldiers. The nighttime commemoration also includes the playing of "Taps" and a walking tour at the site of one of the deadliest Civil War battles. Contact Fredericksburg National Cemetery, 120 Chatham Ln., Fredericksburg, VA 22405-2508, 540-373-6122, fax: 540-371-1907, http:// www.nps.gov/frsp/luminari.htm

10. **Roswell, Georgia:** The Roswell Remembers Memorial Day observance includes special ceremonies and speakers, followed by community picnic and music. Contact the Roswell Memorial Day Committee, 617 Atlanta St., Roswell, GA 30075, 770-640-3253 or 800-776-7935, fax: 770-640-3252, rcvb@mindspring.com, http://www.roswellmemorialday.com

Memorials

African-American Civil War Memorial at http://www.nps.gov/afam/index.htm

Arlington National Cemetery at http://www.arlingtoncemetery.org

Korean War Veterans Memorial at http://www.nps.gov/kowa/index.htm

National Park Service administers many more memorials commemorating Civil War and other war veterans. See http://www.nps.gov for more information.

Vietnam Veterans Memorial at http://www.nps.gov/vive/index.htm

Women in Military Service for America Memorial at http://www.womens memorial.org/ and http://www.nps.gov/gwmp/wimsa.htm

World War II Memorial at http://wwiimemorial.com and http://www.nps .gov/nwwm/

Other Web Sites

American Legion Auxiliary provides information about its poppy program at http://www.legion-aux.org/

Library of Congress presents a timeline and photographs of the Civil War at http://memory.loc.gov/ammem/cwphtml/cwphome.html

Smithsonian Institution has an online exhibit on Civil War images and artifacts at http://www.civilwar.si.edu/home.html

Veterans of Foreign Wars gives information about the Buddy Poppy program at http://www.vfw.org

White House Commission on Remembrance, established by Congress in 1996, promotes Memorial Day observances and the National Moment of Remembrance at http://www.remember.gov

Sources for Further Reading

Blight, David W. *Race and Reunion: The Civil War in American Memory.* Cambridge, Mass.: Harvard University Press, 2001.

Clinton, Catherine. *Scholastic Encyclopedia of the Civil War.* New York: Scholastic, 1999. For young adults.

Dennis, Matthew. *Red, White, and Blue Letter Days: An American Calendar.* Ithaca, N.Y.: Cornell University Press, 2002.

Heidler, David S., and Jeanne T. Heidler, eds. *Encyclopedia of the American Civil War: A Political, Social, and Military History.* 5 vols. Santa Barbara, Calif.: ABC-CLIO, 2000.

Litwicki, Ellen M. *America's Public Holidays, 1865-1920.* Washington, D.C.: Smithsonian Institution Press, 2000.

McPherson, James M. *Battle Cry of Freedom: The Civil War Era.* New York: Oxford University Press, 1988.

Piehler, G. Kurt. *Remembering War the American Way.* Washington, D.C.: Smithsonian Institution Press, 1995.

Ward, Geoffrey C. *The Civil War: An Illustrated History.* New York: Alfred A. Knopf, 1990.

USS ARIZONA BB·39

National Pearl Harbor Remembrance Day

Date Established as a Patriotic and National Observance:
August 23, 1994

Date Observed: December 7

On December 7, 1941, Japan attacked the U.S. naval base at Pearl Harbor on the Hawaiian island of Oahu, shocking Americans and marking the entrance of the United States into World War II. In 1994 Congress passed a bill designating December 7 as National Pearl Harbor Remembrance Day. It is not a federal holiday, but every year the president issues a proclamation calling for appropriate ceremonies and for flags to fly at half-staff.

Attack on Pearl Harbor

The attack on Pearl Harbor began on Sunday at 7:55 A.M., Hawaiian time. Within minutes the Navy's commanding officer at the base sent an urgent radiogram to all ships around Hawaii: "AIRRAID ON PEARL HARBOR X THIS IS NO DRILL."

The Japanese air raids devastated the American naval base on Oahu. Nearly all the ships of the U.S. Pacific fleet were anchored off the shore, and most were damaged or destroyed. In addition, more than 150 planes were destroyed. The battleship USS *Arizona* sank, entombing 1,777 sailors and Marines on board. In sum, the attack claimed more than 3,000 casualties— 2,403 killed and 1,178 injured. American civilian deaths numbered 68.

The next day President Franklin D. Roosevelt addressed Congress to ask for a declaration of war against Japan. His opening words are part of the

Visitors drop orchid petals into the water over the sunken USS Arizona in tribute to the fallen crew members who rest below.

This marble memorial was built over the sunken USS Arizona and dedicated in 1962.

American memory: "Yesterday, December 7, 1941—a date which will live in infamy—the United States of America was suddenly and deliberately attacked by naval and air forces of the Empire of Japan." (*See Appendix for text of entire speech.*) Congress immediately declared war.

In response, Japan and its allies, Germany and Italy, declared war on the United States.

On the home front, preparation for war began. Men and women joined the armed services, and President Roosevelt ordered an investigative commission to determine how the U.S. military was taken unawares and what, if any, responsibility rested with commanders. As a result of the inquiry, the Army and Navy commanders in charge in Hawaii were relieved of their positions.

World War II

Between 1939 and 1945, World War II was fought in Europe, north Africa, the Middle East, Asia, and many Pacific islands. The conflict pitted the Allies—led by Britain and the United States—against the Axis, led by

Germany, Italy, and Japan. A combination of events during the 1930s led to the war, including the rise of militaristic dictatorships in Germany, Italy, and Japan; unresolved problems stemming from World War I; and the spread of the Great Depression. In 1933 Adolf Hitler's Nazi Party came to power in Germany, which had been defeated in World War I. Hitler advocated an aggressive, racist program to restore Germany as a major world power and solve its economic problems. He encouraged Germans to view themselves as a superior race and began creating concentration camps in 1933 for the ultimate purpose of exterminating European Jews and others whom he hated.

In May 1939 Hitler entered an alliance with Benito Mussolini, the fascist dictator of Italy, who also sought to take control of countries in eastern Europe and north Africa. This agreement led to the formation of what became known as the Axis powers.

World War II started when Germany invaded Poland on September 1, 1939. By 1940 Germany had invaded Austria, part of Czechoslovakia, Denmark, Norway, Belgium, Luxembourg, the Netherlands, and France. Later that year Germany began an air attack against Britain to prepare for an invasion.

In September 1940, Japan joined the Axis alliance. Japan was ruled by military leaders who sought to dominate east Asia and the Pacific. The United States opposed these plans, and Japan attacked Pearl Harbor, Malaya, and the Philippines. As a result of the attack, the United States entered World War II. Though the U.S. government had been assisting Britain and France by providing arms and financial help, most Americans were opposed to direct involvement in the war. Pearl Harbor changed all that, and Americans enlisted by the thousands.

When Germany invaded the Soviet Union in June 1941, Stalin joined the Allies. On January 1, 1942, the Allies—France, Britain, the United States, and the Soviet Union—signed a formal pact called the United Nations Declaration, which later lent its name to the international organization founded after the war. With this they pledged their commitment to defeat the Axis together.

Allied forces fought many battles in the Pacific, the Soviet Union, Europe, north Africa, and Sicily. The Allies next determined to liberate Europe and began an air campaign in preparation for an invasion of Normandy, France.

The invasion, known as D-Day, took place on June 6, 1944. Allied troops fought major battles which led to the defeat of the German army in France, Belgium, and, finally, Germany.

The war ended in Europe on May 7, 1945, when Germany surrendered. Japan surrendered on August 14, 1945, after the United States dropped the devastating atomic bombs on the Japanese cities of Hiroshima and Nagasaki. It is estimated that 17-25 million troops on both sides were killed. About 400,000 were Americans. There is no certain count of how many civilians died, but estimates indicated that more than 30 million civilian lives were lost; in addition, some 6 million Jews perished in the Nazi concentration camps.

Observances

Each year on December 7 ceremonies around the nation commemorate the lives lost at Pearl Harbor. At the USS Arizona Memorial the annual program features a moment of silence, veteran and survivor speakers, a wreath laying, patriotic music, a 21-gun salute, and a naval parade. In 1991 a 50th anniversary commemoration took place over four days at Pearl Harbor.

A Sampling of Observances

1. **Mount Diablo, California:** A ceremonial lighting of a beacon atop the mountain at dusk every December 7 remembers the fallen of Pearl Harbor. Contact Mount Diablo State Park, 96 Mitchell Canyon Rd., Clayton, CA 94517, 925-837-2525, http://www.parks.ca.gov/default.asp ?page_id=517

2. **Pearl Harbor, Hawaii:** See description above. Contact USS Arizona Memorial, 1 Arizona Memorial Pl., Honolulu, HI 96818, 808-422-0561, fax: 808-483-8608, http://www.nps.gov/usar/

3. **Fredericksburg, Texas:** The National Museum of the Pacific War at the Admiral Nimitz State Historic Site hosts an annual commemoration that includes guest speakers and special recognition of troops on active duty and their families. Contact National Museum of the Pacific War, 340 E. Main St., Fredericksburg, TX 78624, 830-997-4379; fax: 830-997-8220, http://www.nimitz-museum.org/

4. **LaPorte, Texas:** Ceremony aboard the Battleship *Texas*. Contact Battleship Texas State Historic Site, 3523 Highway 134, LaPorte, TX 77571, 281-479-2431, http://www.tpwd.state.tx.us/park/battlesh/

5. **Chicago, Illinois:** Chicago remembers Pearl Harbor at Navy Pier with the reading of names of Chicago natives who died in the attack, tolling of bells, "Taps," a 21-gun salute, the tossing of a wreath into the lake, and the playing of the "Navy Hymn." Contact Mayor's Office of Special Events, 121 N. LaSalle St., Rm. 703, Chicago, IL 60602, 312-744-3315; fax: 312-744-8523; TTY: 312-744-2964, moseinquiry@cityofchicago.org, http://egov.cityofchicago.org/ (click on "City Departments," then scroll to and click "Special Events")

6. **Fall River, Massachusetts:** Ceremony aboard the Battleship *Massachusetts* that includes tossing a wreath into the sea. The *Massachusetts* houses an exhibit and memorials on Pearl Harbor. Contact Battleship Cove, Five Water St., P.O. Box 11, Fall River, MA 02722-0111, 508-678-1100; fax: 508-674-5596, battleship@battleshipcove.org, http://www .battleshipcove.org

7. **Washington, D.C.:** Wreath laying at the Lone Sailor Statue at the U.S. Navy Memorial. Contact U.S. Navy Memorial Foundation & Naval Heritage Center, 701 Pennsylvania Ave., N.W., Ste. 123, Washington,

DC 20004-2608, 202-737-2300, ext. 768 (Events Hotline), http://www
.lonesailor.org/

8. **Morgantown, West Virginia:** Since the 1970s VFW Post 548 and West
Virginia University ROTCs have paraded to Ogleby Plaza, to the bell
and mast from the USS *West Virginia*, a battleship that sank in the
attack. The ceremony includes a 21-gun salute, the playing of "Taps,"
the dedication of a wreath, and guest speakers. Contact VFW Post #548,
494 Spruce St., Morgantown, WV 26505, 304-292-9352.

Web Sites

"After the Day of Infamy: 'Man on the Street' Interviews Following the Attack on Pearl Harbor," an online presentation of the American Folklife Cen-

ter, Library of Congress at http://memory.loc.gov/ammem/afcphhtml/afc phhome.htm

Arizona Memorial Museum Association at http://arizonamemorial.org/

Library of Congress online exhibit at http://memory.loc.gov/ammem/today/ dec07.html

National D-Day Museum in New Orleans provides information about Pearl Harbor and World War II at http://www.ddaymuseum.org

National Japanese American Memorial Foundation at http://www.njamf .com/

Pearl Harbor Survivors Association at http://www.pearlharborsurvivorson line.org/

U.S. Naval Historical Center offers information and images of the attack on Pearl Harbor at http://www.history.navy.mil/photos/events/wwii-pac/ pearlhbr/pearlhbr.htm

USS Arizona Memorial at http://www.nps.gov/usar/

Sources for Further Reading

Prange, Gordon W. *At Dawn We Slept: The Untold Story of Pearl Harbor.* New York: McGraw-Hill, 1981.

———. *Pearl Harbor: The Verdict of History.* New York: McGraw-Hill, 1986.

Rice, Earle, Jr. *The Bombing of Pearl Harbor.* San Diego: Lucent Books, 2001. For young adults.

Rosenberg, Emily S. *A Date Which Will Live: Pearl Harbor in American Memory.* Durham, N.C.: Duke University Press, 2003.

Streissguth, Thomas, ed. *The Attack on Pearl Harbor.* San Diego: Greenhaven Press, 2002.

Taylor, Theodore. *Air-Raid-Pearl-Harbor! The Story of December 7, 1941.* San Diego: Harcourt Brace Jovanovich, 1991. For young adults.

Patriot Day

Alternate Names: 9/11, September 11

**Date Established as a Patriotic and National Observance:
December 18, 2001**

Date Observed: September 11

O n September 11, 2001, the U.S. mainland sustained the worst attack since the British set fire to Washington, D.C., during the War of 1812. For the first time, civilians—not military personnel, as at Pearl Harbor—were the targets (*see also* **National Pearl Harbor Remembrance Day**). More than 2,700 people died in the attacks, which took place in New York City, Washington, D.C., and aboard a plane that crashed in Shanksville, Pennsylvania.

The Tribute in Light shines from the World Trade Center site each year from sundown September 11 until daybreak on the 12th.

Since that tragic day Americans have marked the anniversary with solemn commemoration. This day is not an official federal holiday, but it is observed by many Americans. The U.S. Congress voted for a resolution on December 18, 2001, requesting that the president issue a proclamation each year designating September 11 as Patriot Day. (Patriot Day should not be confused with Patriots' Day, a state holiday in Massachusetts and Maine that marks the battle of Lexington and Concord; *see* **Independence Day**.) Each year since then the president has called for appropriate observances, including flying the flag at half-staff and observing a moment of silence beginning at 8:46 A.M. (all times here and below are Eastern Daylight Time).

The Attacks

At 7:59 A.M. American Airlines Flight 11 left Boston's Logan International Airport, bound for Los Angeles, California. At 8:46 A.M. the plane flew into the North Tower of the World Trade Center in New York City. Most initial news reports considered it an accident. However, at 9:03 A.M., United Airlines Flight 175, also from Logan and bound for Los Angeles, crashed into the South Tower of the World Trade Center. At 10:05 A.M. the South Tower of the World Trade Center collapsed. At 10:28 A.M. the North Tower fell. The United States was under attack, and it appeared that the planes had been hijacked.

At 9:37 A.M. American Airlines Flight 77, which had taken off from Dulles International Airport in Washington, D.C., for Los Angeles, crashed into the Pentagon Building near Washington, D.C. A fourth airplane, United Airlines Flight 93, took off at 8:42 A.M. from Newark, New Jersey, Liberty International Airport, bound for San Francisco, California. But the flight veered from its course and began heading toward Washington, D.C. Later investigations indicated that the hijackers aboard that plane planned to strike the White House or the Capitol Building. The 37 passengers on the flight—who had learned of the other hijackings after talking to family members and friends via cell phone—saved many lives by aborting the hijackers' plans and causing the plane to crash in a field in Shanksville, Pennsylvania, at 10:03 that morning.

Al Qaeda

It soon became clear that the al Qaeda terrorist group perpetrated the attacks. Before 9/11, as the day is now widely known, most Americans had not heard of the group, but its leader, Osama bin Laden, had been calling for attacks against Americans since 1992.

Al Qaeda, which means "the base," came into being during the war in Afghanistan (1979-89) between the former Soviet Union and rebel Muslims within Afghanistan, which was then under Soviet rule. When the Soviet Army invaded Afghanistan in December 1979, thousands of outraged Muslim men from around the world descended on the country to help oust the Soviets. One of them was 23-year-old Osama bin Laden. The U.S. provided assistance to help the *mujaheddin*—the young Muslim fighters—against the Soviet troops. Over the course of the war bin Laden built bases inside Afghanistan to train these volunteers to fight the Soviets. That war ended when the Soviet Union withdrew its troops in 1989.

In August 1990, Iraqi leader Saddam Hussein invaded Kuwait. In December 1990 the United Nations authorized its member nations to use all necessary means to restore peace and security in Kuwait, if Hussein did not leave by January 15, 1991. Hussein ignored the U.N. resolution, and on January 18, 1991, the United States led a 32-nation coalition to liberate Kuwait from Hussein's forces. By February 28, 1991, the coalition successfully ousted Iraqi forces from Kuwait. The United States left forces in Saudi Arabia to guard against further incursions by Hussein or others.

Angered at the presence of American troops on Saudi soil, bin Laden headed back to Afghanistan to run his training camps in 1991. He considered the presence of non-Muslim troops in Islam's holiest land an offense to the Muslim religion.

Bin Laden issued a declaration of war against the United States in 1996. Certain foreign policies of the U.S. government—in particular, support for the government of the Saudi royal family and the maintenance of a military base in Saudi Arabia—were among his reasons. Bin Laden's declaration included a call to kill any Americans, civilian and military.

Since 1992 al Qaeda is known or suspected to have attacked several U.S. targets. These include:

- On December 29, 1992, bin Laden associates bombed a hotel in Aden, Yemen, where U.S. soldiers often stayed.

- On February 26, 1993, al Qaeda associate Ramzi Yousef placed a bomb in the parking garage under the World Trade Center towers in New York. Six people were killed and over 1,000 were wounded.

- On June 25, 1996, al Qaeda is suspected of playing a role in the bombing of the Khobar Towers in Dhahran, Saudi Arabia, which killed 19 Americans.

- On August 7, 1998, al Qaeda members drove trucks rigged with bombs into the U.S. Embassy in Nairobi, Kenya, and the U.S. Embassy in Dar es Salaam, Tanzania.

- On December 14, 1999, an alert border guard foiled an attempted millennium attack on Los Angeles International Airport when explosives were found in the car of Ahmed Ressam, an al Qaeda operative who'd trained in Afghanistan.

- On October 12, 2000, al Qaeda operatives bombed the USS *Cole* off the coast of Yemen, killing 17 crew members.

Aftermath

American society underwent many changes after September 11. Some were immediate and short-term, such as the grounding of all airplanes for several days. Others were more permanent, such as the creation of a five-color coded alert system; unprecedented security checks for boarding airplanes, attending major events, and entering landmarks and important buildings; and efforts to improve intelligence about plots for more attacks.

On September 20, 2001, President George W. Bush addressed Congress, declaring war on terror and announcing the creation of the Office of Homeland Security, which later became the Cabinet-level Department of Homeland Security (*see the Appendix for the text of the speech*).

On October 26, 2001, Congress passed the Patriot Act, which allows various government agencies to share intelligence information, provides terrorism victims with financial aid, and numerous other provisions. The same month, the U.S. began attacks on Afghanistan.

"I Saw the Buildings"

I saw the buildings fall from the sky,
I saw the people, I watched them die,
I saw it all on the morning news,
And I saw what hate will do —
I saw brave men risk their lives,
I saw brave men, I watched them die,
There in the darkness of that afternoon,
Oh, I saw what brave men do —

Chorus:
But the stars come out at night,
and the moon it shines so bright,
And the mystery holds, which no one knows,
And our hopes and dreams sustain us.

Some lyrics from "I Saw the Buildings," music and lyrics by James Talley. © 2002 Hardhit Songs, ASCAP.

Rebuilding and Memorials

Workers struggled for months to clean the rubble from Ground Zero, as the site of the World Trade Center became popularly known. Many felt that new structures should be built on the site. In 2003, planning began for a new tower on the site. Called the Freedom Tower, it will reach 1,776 feet into the air as a structural symbol of the year of the nation's birth. When completed, the Freedom Tower will also be the tallest building in the world. On July 4, 2004, New York state and city officials ceremoniously laid the cornerstone for the new skyscraper.

The Pentagon was repaired by February 2003. The U.S. Army Corp of Engineers sponsored a design competition for a memorial to honor the 184 people lost at the Pentagon. This memorial will be a park containing 184 "memorial units." Each unit consists of a stainless steel cantilevered bench on which is inscribed the name of an individual victim. Below each bench is a reflecting pool that glows at night.

Organizers for the Shanksville, Pennsylvania, memorial began a competition to select the best memorial for the site. It will include the words "A common field one day, a field of honor forever."

Hundreds of other memorials have been created and dedicated throughout the nation. In addition, pieces of steel from the ruins of the World Trade Center have traveled to provide memorials in such cities as Albuquerque, New Mexico; Jacksonville, Florida; Lafayette, Louisiana; Scottsdale, Arizona; Sherman Oaks, California; Salem, Virginia; and Oak Ridge, Tennessee. The U.S. Navy has named three new warships in honor of the victims—USS *New York*, USS *Arlington*, and USS *Somerset*.

The U.S. Forestry Service sponsors the Living Memorial Project to encourage communities to plant tree groves as memorials to the victims of 9/11. Americans have initiated various public art projects and healing fields as well.

A drawing of the planned memorial to be built on the Pentagon grounds to commemorate the 184 people who lost their lives there on September 11, 2001.

Participants hold a flag at sunrise as part of the memorial ceremony for the passengers of United Airlines Flight 93 in Shanksville, Pennsylvania, on September 11, 2004.

Participants hold a flag at sunrise as part of the memorial ceremony for the passengers of United Airlines Flight 93 in Shanksville, Pennsylvania, on September 11, 2004.

Observances

At the World Trade Center site in New York City, an annual ceremony begins with a moment of silence at 8:46 A.M., the time American Airlines Flight 11 crashed into the North Tower. The reading of victims' names is the central part of the observance. In 2002, relatives and public figures read the names of those who died in the Trade Center attack. In 2003 children read the names of their mothers and fathers. In 2004 parents and grandparents read the names of their children and grandchildren. At 9:03 A.M., the time Flight 175 crashed into the South Tower, 10:05 A.M., the time the South Tower collapsed, and at 10:28 A.M., when the North Tower collapsed, the readers stop for moments of silence.

Some attendees bring flowers to drop into two reflecting pools or memorabilia to place at the site. Later, the Tribute in Light, a light display that echoes the design of the Twin Towers, shines from sundown September 11 until daybreak on the 12th.

Near Washington, D.C., an annual wreath-laying ceremony at Arlington National Cemetery remembers the victims at the Pentagon. There is also a private ceremony at the Pentagon itself for the families, friends, and co-workers of those lost. A moment of silence is observed at 9:37 A.M., when American Airlines Flight 77 crashed into the Pentagon.

At the field outside Shanksville, Pennsylvania, where United Airlines Flight 93 crashed, an annual service of remembrance includes the tolling of bells, a wreath laying, and the reading of the names of the passengers and crew.

Many Americans around the country mark the day by tolling bells and observing moments of silence. State capitols and fire houses hold special ceremonies. Many gather at local memorials in their towns and cities. Countries around the world also observe special ceremonies for the victims, including their own citizens who were lost in the attacks. Services are held among troops in Afghanistan and Iraq.

A Sampling of Observances

1. **New York, New York:** Contact Office of the Mayor, City Hall, New York, NY 10007, 212-639-9675, fax: 212-788-2460, http://www.nyc.gov

2. **Shanksville, Pennsylvania:** Contact Flight 93 National Memorial, National Park Service, 109 W. Main St., Ste. 104, Somerset, PA 15501-2035, 814-443-4557; fax: 814-443-2180, http://www.nps.gov/flni/

3. **Arlington, Virginia:** Contact Arlington National Cemetery, Arlington, VA 22211, 703-607-8000, http://www.arlingtoncemetery.org

Web Sites

Flight 93 National Memorial at http://www.nps.gov/flni/

Living Memorials Project at http://www.livingmemorialsproject.net/

Lower Manhattan Development Corporation provides information about planning at the World Trade Center site at http://www.renewnyc.com

National Healing Field Foundation at http://healingfield.org

Pentagon Memorial Project at http://memorial.pentagon.mil

"September 11: Bearing Witness to History," an online exhibit of the Smithsonian Institution's National Museum of American History at http://americanhistory.si.edu/september11/

"September 11, 2001, Documentary Project," an American Memory collection of the Library of Congress holds drawings, interviews, and accounts of reactions at http://memory.loc.gov/ammem/collections/911_archive/

Sources for Further Reading

Bergen, Peter L. *Holy War, Inc.: Inside the Secret World of Osama bin Laden.* New York: Free Press, 2001.

Calhoun, Craig, Paul Price, and Ashley Timmer, eds. *Understanding September 11.* New York: New Press, 2002.

Clarke, Richard A. *Against All Enemies: Inside America's War on Terror.* New York: Free Press, 2004.

Coll, Steve. *Ghost Wars: The Secret History of the CIA, Afghanistan, and bin Laden, from the Soviet Invasion to September 10, 2001.* New York: Penguin, 2004.

Frank, Mitch. *Understanding September 11th: Answering Questions about the Attacks on America.* New York: Viking, 2002. For young adults.

Gulevich, Tanya. *Understanding Islam and Muslim Traditions: An Introduction to the Religious Practices, Celebrations, Festivals, Observances, Beliefs, Folklore, Customs, and Calendar System of the World's Muslim Communities, Including an Overview of Islamic History and Geography.* Detroit: Omnigraphics, 2004. For young adults.

The 9/11 Commission Report: Final Report of the National Commission on Terrorist Attacks Upon the United States. Authorized ed. New York: W. W. Norton & Company, 2004.

Thanksgiving

Date Established as a Federal Holiday: December 26, 1941

Date Observed: Fourth Thursday in November

Thanksgiving is a federal holiday set aside for expressing gratitude for the material and spiritual blessings bestowed on the United States. The holiday commemorates the feast of thanksgiving the Pilgrims held in the fall of 1621. Thanksgiving is observed on the fourth Thursday in November, a time of year that follows the annual harvest. On December 26, 1941, Congress passed a law designating Thanksgiving as a legal public holiday.

The Tom Turkey float in the annual Macy's Thanksgiving Day Parade in New York City.

People all over the world have held special harvest feasts of thanksgiving since ancient times. In October the Romans celebrated the Cerealia, in honor of Ceres, goddess of the harvest. In October or November the Greeks celebrated the Thesmophoria, in honor of the harvest goddess Demeter. Europeans who came to America were accustomed to political and religious leaders proclaiming days of fasting and prayer for both fortunate and dire circumstances. Early colonists carried the tradition across the Atlantic Ocean to the New World.

Early Spanish Thanksgivings in America

The first Thanksgiving is popularly associated with the Pilgrims at Plymouth Plantation in 1621. Some historians believe, however, that that celebration was not the first Thanksgiving in America. They point south for the first such occasion.

Various groups of explorers and colonists celebrated thanksgiving in America 100 years before the Pilgrims arrived. There is historical evidence that parties led by Juan Ponce de León in 1513 and 1521 and Hernando de

Soto in 1529 gave thanks for reaching land after their voyages with special prayers or masses.

The first thanksgivings that included the basic elements we associate with the Pilgrim Thanksgiving—prayers of gratitude and a feast—took place on September 8, 1565, and April 1598.

According to a Florida historian, on September 8, 1565, about 800 Spanish colonists, led by Pedro Menéndez de Avilés, celebrated the first thanksgiving mass and feast in St. Augustine, Florida. They reportedly included Seloy Indians in their celebration. The meal would have consisted of whatever the Spanish had brought from their ship, stew and wine perhaps, as well as any contributions from the Seloy, which could have included venison, tortoise, squash, beans, and turkey.

In April 1598 explorer Juan de Oñate and 400 colonists are said to have celebrated thanksgiving in New Mexico with a mass and meal featuring goat, corn, fish, berries, and cactus. Every April Texans and New Mexicans mark the Oñate Thanksgiving with a festival and reenactment.

Early English Thanksgivings in America

Historians also have identified a few thanksgiving observances among English colonists that predate the more well known celebration of the Pilgrims at Plymouth. Rev. Richard Seymour's account of the "voyage to Sagadahoc" tells of a thanksgiving service that took place on the coast of Maine on August 9, 1607.

Another English settlement, founded by John Woodleaf, observed a thanksgiving day at Berkeley Hundred colony in Virginia. These colonists held a service on December 4, 1619, and planned to keep the day as an annual holy day. But Indians destroyed the colony in the spring of 1622.

The first permanent English settlement in America was at Jamestown, Virginia. One hundred four colonists landed on May 14, 1607. More came over the next years, but after the winter of 1609-10, only 60 settlers were left; the others had died of starvation and diseases. In the spring of 1610 English ships laden with food and other supplies were greeted with a thanksgiving prayer service.

The Pilgrims

The Pilgrims set sail for America on the *Mayflower* in September 1620 and reached Cape Cod in Massachusetts on November 11, 1620. Before leaving the ship, 41 men signed what eventually became known as the Mayflower Compact (*see the Appendix for the text of the Mayflower Compact*). This was a pledge to each other to live together as a "civil body politic" under mutually agreed upon laws. They named their colony Plymouth.

The Pilgrims were members of a Christian group called the Puritans. Before the Protestant Reformation that began in the 16th century, there was only one official English religion—the Church of England. All other religions were banned; anyone practicing another faith faced persecution. The Puritans left England to find a new home where they could practice their religion freely.

The Puritans shunned the lively Harvest Home Festival and other holidays of their mother country. They accepted only three kinds of holy days: Sundays, days of fasting, and days of thanksgiving. All were somber and prayerful occasions. Yet the event Americans commemorate as "the first Thanksgiving" didn't really fall into any of these three categories. It was truly a new celebration in the New World.

The first winter the Pilgrims faced in their new land was extremely hard: 55 of the 102 colonists perished. Luckily, they were befriended by a Pawtuxet Indian, Tisquantum, who showed the settlers the best fishing and hunting sites and gave them tips about planting corn and squash. The Pilgrims called him Squanto. In addition to helping the Pilgrims produce enough food to survive, Squanto mediated between the Plymouth colony's leader, Governor William Bradford, and the powerful Wampanoag tribe and was instrumental in producing the treaty with Chief Massasoit that made for their peaceful coexistence.

After that difficult first year, the autumn of 1621 brought in a bountiful harvest, for which the Puritans were heartily grateful. Massasoit and some 90 other Wampanoags joined them for three days of eating, games, dances (by the Indians), and relaxation. The Wampanoags contributed five deer,

> *"For three days we entertained and feasted, and [the Indians] went out and killed five Deere which they brought to the Plantacion and bestowed on our Governour, and upon the Captaine, and others."*
>
> —Pilgrim Edward Winslow, 1621

239

The Pilgrims set sail for America on the Mayflower *in September 1620 and reached Cape Cod in Massachusetts on November 11, 1620.*

while Pilgrim women prepared fowl, pumpkins, and corn. Historians do not know exactly when the celebration occurred, but guess it was sometime between September and November. Whatever the actual date, its significance was passed down through the generations, and it is considered the first Thanksgiving in America.

One Pilgrim, Edward Winslow, left this account of the events in a letter to a friend in England, George Morton, dated December 11, 1621:

> Our harvest being gotten in, our Governour sent foure men fowling, so that we might after a more special manner rejoyce together, after we had gathered the fruit of our labours; they foure in one day killed as much fowle, as with a little helpe beside, served the Company almost a weeke, at which time amongst other Recreations we excercised our Armes, many of the Indians coming amongst us, and amonst the rest their greatest King Massassoyt, with some ninetie men, whom for three days we entertained and feasted, and they went out and killed five Deere which they brought to the Plantacion and bestowed on our Governour, and upon the Captaine, and others.

Creation of the Thanksgiving Holiday

From the earliest European settlements to the Revolutionary era and beyond, Americans designated numerous days of thanksgiving for occasions ranging from good harvests to victories. As the first president, George Washington issued the first national proclamation in 1789 giving thanks for the peaceful formation of the United States government. But it was not until the mid-1800s that the nation had one specific and annual Thanksgiving holiday to share in common.

Much of the credit for the establishment of the Thanksgiving holiday goes to Sarah Josepha Hale, who began her campaign to create the holiday in 1827. Hale edited a popular women's magazine, *Lady's Book*, and regularly penned editorials that elaborated on the potential benefits to the nation of setting aside a national day of giving thanks.

Almost 40 years later, during the Civil War, Hale wrote President Abraham Lincoln a letter asking him to proclaim a national day of thanksgiving. (*See the Appendix for the text of the letter.*) On October 3, 1863, Lincoln issued a proclamation inviting citizens to observe the last Thursday of November as "a Day of Thanksgiving and Praise to our beneficient Father who dwelleth in the heavens." National celebrations remained on that date for nearly 80 years.

In 1939, President Franklin D. Roosevelt, struggling to lead the nation out of the Great Depression, gave in to retailers' requests to move up the date of Thanksgiving in order to lengthen the Christmas shopping season. That year Thanksgiving was observed on the third Thursday of November, amid much controversy.

In December 1941 the U.S. Congress made Thanksgiving an annual federal holiday and moved it back to the fourth Thursday in November, where it has remained.

And why is Thanksgiving on a Thursday? The answer seems to lie somewhere in a mixture of 18th-century custom and the process of elimination. First of all, it had to be on a weekday because Sunday was reserved for the Sabbath, and many people spent Saturdays making arrangements for Sunday. It could not be a Friday because that was a Roman Catholic fasting day. Some northeastern colonists were somewhat accustomed to following the old "fish day" rules of Queen Elizabeth I (1533-1603), who forbade people to eat meat on Wednesdays, Fridays, and Saturdays in order to bolster the fishing industry. Finally, in Massachusetts, Thursday was a popular market day and "lecture day," on which ministers gave sermons.

The Dinner

Most of the foods associated with Thanksgiving dinner are native to North America, and to New England in particular. Wild turkey, squash, corn, cranberries, and pumpkins were all available to the Pilgrims. The traditional menu, also including mashed potatoes and stuffing, was fairly standard by the middle of the 19th century. The majority of Americans, who lived in rural areas before the 20th century, usually hunted their own turkeys for Thanksgiving dinner. By the 1940s, however, the growing poultry industry combined with the greater numbers of Americans living in cities to establish the storebought turkey as the meal's centerpiece.

Some modern regional and cultural variations on the customary meal include the following:

- In Louisiana, a Cajun Thanksgiving dinner has usually featured pork. Turkey is also prepared, though instead of being roasted, some choose to deep-fry it and blacken it with spices.

Cornucopia

The cornucopia, featured in many traditional Thanksgiving decorations, is the horn of plenty, filled to overflowing with fruits and vegetables of the harvest. It has been a symbol of abundance and fertility for millennia. In Roman mythology, the *Cornu Copiae* came from a river god, Achelous, who, in battle with Heracles, became a bull and lost one of his horns. Female water spirits known as *naiads* retrieved the horn and filled it with fruits and flowers. In the Greek version of the myth, the horn came from Amalthea, a goat nymph who had nursed Zeus. According to both myths, the horn of plenty is perpetually full of the earth's bounty.

- In Hawaii, dinner can include a turkey stuffed with dressing made of rice, Chinese sausage, and black-eyed peas baked in a huge underground oven called an *imu*.

- Some feasters in the South favor turducken—a turkey stuffed with a chicken, which is stuffed with a duck.

Football and Other Games

Games and sports have been part of Thanksgiving celebrations since the footraces and other games played at Plymouth in 1621. Hunting, bicycle races, and baseball games have all been part of the festivities. But football is the game associated with Thanksgiving today. In the later decades of the 19th century, the Young Men's Christian Association (YMCA) advocated the importance of physical fitness in the building of moral character and helped create an association between sports and such values as self-control, motivation, and steadfastness. In the 1880s attending community football games became a popular Thanksgiving Day diversion in several cities around the nation. By the 1920s high school, college, and professional games were played on Thanksgiving. Later, as many Americans acquired radios, then televisions, college and professional football games were brought into the home, to be enjoyed among family and friends after Thanksgiving dinner.

A perennial children's favorite Thanksgiving game is wishbone snapping. Each person grasps one end of the turkey wishbone and pulls until it snaps. Whoever has the larger piece will have good luck. Some historians trace the game of breaking the wishbone back to ancient Rome. It was an established game in England when the Pilgrims sailed. It also may be the origin of the expression "to get a lucky break."

Hospitality, Charity, Social Concern

The making of charitable gestures has been a Thanksgiving tradition since at least the 18th century. The custom spread over the 19th century, in part through the encouragement of popular magazines such as *Lady's Book*, *Ladies' Home Journal*, and *Harper's*. Well-off Americans organized feasts for less-fortunate people in poor houses, hospitals, orphanages, and prisons. In Massachusetts governors often pardoned selected prisoners on Thanksgiving Day.

Today the feast-giving continues around the nation and often extends through the Christmas holidays. People also participate in blood drives and other efforts to help those in need.

Observances

Most Americans observe Thanksgiving at home with family and friends. This is the holiday for which more Americans travel to be with loved ones than any other.

Turkey Pardon

Since Harry S. Truman began the custom in 1947, the president of the United States has pardoned a turkey on Thanksgiving Day. Each year the National Turkey Federation selects one turkey, plus an alternate turkey, to be flown to the White House for the pardoning ceremony. Both turkeys live out the rest of their natural lives at Kidwell Farm in Herndon, Virginia.

Thanksgiving Day parades possibly evolved as orderly versions of the Fantastical rampages that began during the 1780s in Pennsylvania and New York City. The Fantasticals consisted of groups of young men who dressed in costumes, some in women's clothes, drank to excess, and roamed the streets, often going door to door and making demands of residents.

Not only did the Fantasticals appear on Thanksgiving, but on **Washington's Birthday**, **Independence Day**, and over the New Year's holiday as well. By the 19th century more and more people were fed up with the Fantasticals' holiday disorder. As a result, some organized themselves into parades, which the general public found much more tolerable, even entertaining. Apparently, the Fantasticals last paraded on Thanksgiving around 1910. But their modern descendants stage Philadelphia's Mummers Parade every New Year's Day.

Parades in large cities typically include a range of elaborate floats, balloons depicting popular characters, celebrity grand marshals, marching bands, and Santa Claus to open the Christmas season. These days the major parades are sponsored by large department stores to launch the Christmas shopping season. The first was Gimbel's in Philadelphia, which began in 1921. The J. L. Hudson Company inaugurated the Detroit parade in 1923, which continues today as America's Thanksgiving Day Parade. In 1924, Macy's started holding its parade in New York City.

A Sampling of Observances

1. **Chicago, Illinois:** State Street Thanksgiving Parade on Thanksgiving morning. Contact Chicago Festivals Association, 111 N. State St., 11th Fl., Chicago, IL 60602, 312-781-5681, fax: 312-781-5407, http://www.chicagofestivals.org/

2. **Detroit, Michigan:** America's Thanksgiving Parade takes place on Woodward Avenue on Thanksgiving morning. The Turkey Trot fun run takes place earlier in the morning. Contact The Parade Company, 9500 Mt. Elliott, Studio A, Detroit, MI 48211, 313-923-7400, fax: 313-923-2920, http://www.theparade.org/parade/index.shtml

3. **Plymouth, Massachusetts:** The celebration includes a parade through Plymouth Common and clam chowder festival on the Saturday before Thanksgiving. Contact Plymouth Rock Foundation, 800-532-1621 or 508-746-1818, info@usathanksgiving.com, http://www.usathanksgiving.com/

4. **New York, New York:** Macy's Thanksgiving Day Parade on Thanksgiving morning. Parade hotline: 212-494-4495

5. **Baltimore, Maryland:** The annual Thanksgiving Parade is held the Saturday before Thanksgiving. Contact Baltimore Office of Promotion & the

Arts, 7 E. Redwood St., Ste. 500, Baltimore, MD 21202, 1-877-Baltimore (225-8466) or 410-752-8632, fax: 410-385-0361, http://www.bop.org

Web Sites

Jamestown-Yorktown Foundation gives information about the Jamestown settlement at http://www.historyisfun.org

Library of Congress provides a Thanksgiving Timeline at http://memory .loc.gov/learn/features/thanks/thanks.html

Macy's web site provides information about the parade each year by October or early November at http://www.macys.com

Plimoth Plantation living history museum offers plentiful information about the Pilgrims who settled in Plymouth at http://www.plimoth.org

Sources for Further Reading

Appelbaum, Diana Karter. *Thanksgiving: An American Holiday, an American History*. New York: Facts on File, 1984.

Bradford, William. *Of Plymouth Plantation, 1620-1647*. Edited by Samuel Eliot Morison. New York: Knopf, 1952.

Dennis, Matthew. *Red, White, and Blue Letter Days: An American Calendar*. Ithaca, N.Y.: Cornell University Press, 2002.

Dickson, Paul. *The Book of Thanksgiving*. New York: Perigee/Berkley, 1995.

Doherty, Kieran. *William Bradford: Rock of Plymouth*. Brookfield, Conn.: Twenty-First Century Books, 1999. For young adults.

Grace, Catherine O'Neill, and Margaret M. Bruchac with Plimoth Plantation. *1621: A New Look at Thanksgiving*. Washington, D.C.: National Geographic Society, 2001. For young adults.

Linton, Ralph, and Adele Linton. *We Gather Together: The Story of Thanksgiving*. 1949. Reprint, Detroit: Omnigraphics, 1990.

Pleck, Elizabeth. "The Making of the Domestic Occasion: The History of Thanksgiving in the United States." *Journal of Social History* 32 (summer 1999): 773-89.

Siskind, Janet. "The Invention of Thanksgiving: A Ritual of American Nationality." *Critique of Anthropology* 12 (1992): 167-91.

Thompson, Sue Ellen, ed. *Holiday Symbols and Customs*. 3rd ed. Detroit: Omnigraphics, 2003.

Wills, Anne Blue. "Pilgrims and Progress: How Magazines Made Thanksgiving." *Church History* 72, 1 (March 2003): 138-58.

Winslow, Edward. Letter to George Morton, December 11, 1621. In *Mourt's Relation, or Journal of the Plantation at Plymouth*, edited by D. B. Heath. New York: Corinth Books, 1963.

Veterans Day

*Date Established as a Federal Holiday: May 13, 1938,
as Armistice Day; June 1, 1954, as Veterans Day*

Date Observed: November 11

*To us in America the reflections of Armistice Day will be filled
with solemn pride in the heroism of those who died in the country's
service and with gratitude for the victory, both because of the thing
from which it has freed us and because of the opportunity it has
given America to show her sympathy with peace and justice in the
councils of nations.*

—President Woodrow Wilson, speaking at the first Armistice Day
observance on November 11, 1919

Veterans Day is a national public holiday set aside to honor those who
have served in the armed forces. The holiday falls on the anniversary
of the end of World War I. It originally commemorated the armistice,
or peace agreement, signed on November 11, 1918, at 11 A.M. Thus, the day
was called Armistice Day, and still is in France and Belgium. In the United
States, Armistice Day was renamed Veterans Day in 1954. In Canada,
Australia, and Great Britain it is known as Remembrance Day. Since 2001
the Congress and the president have also designated the week in which
Veterans Day falls as National Veterans Awareness Week, calling on
Americans to hold and attend educational events to better acquaint them
with the history and contributions of the nation's veterans.

History

Historians consider World War I to have been the first modern war. It was
the first widescale war in which the combatants used new weaponry, such

This scene in Detroit, Michigan, on November 11, 1918, mirrored those in other cities around the nation, when Americans learned World War I was over.

as tanks and poison gas. It was so devastating that people called it "the war to end all wars," or the "Great War." Many thought that the horrors of World War I would prevent nations from ever again resorting to armed conflict. And many throughout the world believed that the peace secured after such a war should never be forgotten and should be commemorated with a holiday.

In the 1920s, however, some Americans argued that the nation already had a holiday to honor veterans — **Memorial Day**. But Memorial Day remembers soldiers who have died in wars. The new holiday was intended to be an occasion upon which Americans thanked those who served in the Great War and survived their service.

By 1926, 27 states had made November 11 a legal holiday honoring the service of World War I veterans. The U.S. Congress passed a resolution on

Veterans Numbers:

- America has produced 48 million veterans since 1776
- 24.7 million veterans are living; 1.6 million are women (as of August and September 2004)

Americans Who Have Served:

- Revolutionary War* (1775-81): 217,000
- War of 1812 (1812-15): 286,730
- Indian Wars (about 1817-98): 106,000
- Mexican War (1846-48): 78,718
- Civil War (1861-65): Union: 2,213,363 Confederate: 1,050,000
- Spanish-American War (1898-1902): 306,760; 1,500 were women
- World War I (1917-18): 4,734,991; 33,000 were women
- World War II (1941-45): 16,112,566; 400,000 women served during this era
- Korean War (1950-53): 5,720,000; 50,000 women served during this era
- Vietnam War (1964-75): 9,200,000 served during this era; 3,403,000 were deployed to Southeast Asia, including 7,000 women
- Persian Gulf War (1990-91): 2,322,332 served during this era; 694,550 were deployed to the Gulf, including 41,000 women
- War in Afghanistan/Operation Enduring Freedom (2001-) and War in Iraq/Operation Iraqi Freedom (2003-): 1,428,383 have served during this era; 185,329 have been deployed to Iraq and Afghanistan (as of September 30, 2004); more than 30,000 are women (as of March 1, 2004)

* Statistics on the numbers of women who served in wars from the Revolution until the Spanish-American War are unavailable.

Statistics for servicewomen are from the Women in Military Service for America Memorial Foundation, Inc.; other totals are from the U.S. Department of Veterans Affairs.

June 4, 1926, asking the president to proclaim November 11 to be a national day of observance every year. It was to be known as Armistice Day and was to honor veterans of World War I. Congress made Armistice Day a legal federal holiday on May 13, 1938.

The next year World War II broke out in Europe. The United States entered the war after the bombing of Pearl Harbor in 1941, and U.S. troops fought until the surrender of the Axis powers in August 1945 (*see* **National Pearl Harbor Remembrance Day**). In 1950 North Korea, allied with the former Soviet Union, invaded South Korea, which was allied with the United States. American troops fought to turn back the invasion until 1953. So, by the early 1950s there were thousands of recent veterans who had served in war, but technically were not acknowledged by the Armistice Day holiday.

The First Veterans Day

A relative of one veteran believed the holiday should be changed to include all veterans. Alvin J. King of Emporia, Kansas, lost his nephew, John Cooper, during World War II. On November 11, 1953, the city of Emporia held what is believed to be the first All Veterans Day observance in the United States. King asked his congressman, Edward J. Rees, to work to legally change the holiday so that it honored all veterans of all wars. Rees did, and on June 1, 1954, President Dwight D. Eisenhower signed the bill that renamed the day Veterans Day. On October 8 President Eisenhower, who had served in both World Wars, issued a proclamation that stated, in part:

> Now, Therefore, I, Dwight D. Eisenhower, President of the United States of America, do hereby call upon all of our citizens to observe Thursday, November 11, 1954, as Veterans Day. On that day let us solemnly remember the sacrifices of all those who fought so valiantly, on the seas, in the air, and on foreign shores, to preserve our heritage of freedom, and let us reconsecrate ourselves to the task of promoting an enduring peace so that their efforts shall not have been in vain.

Veterans Day is one of the two patriotic American holidays observed on the same date each year. (The other is **Independence Day**.) With the exception of **Thanksgiving**, the other patriotic holidays have become Monday holidays—assigned to the nearest Monday in order to provide a three-day weekend. But that has not always been the case. In 1968 Congress passed

Alvin J. King (second from left), Kansas Representative Edward J. Rees (third from left), and President Dwight D. Eisenhower at the signing of the Veterans Day law on June 1, 1954.

the Uniform Holidays Bill, which stated that all holidays—except New Year's Day, Thanksgiving, and Christmas—occur on a Monday near the original holiday date. Many Americans, including veterans organizations, protested the change and argued against moving the observance date of Veterans Day. They believed that the date of this holiday was too important to be changed. In 1975 Congress reversed its decision, and since 1978 (when the new law became effective), Veterans Day has been observed nationwide on November 11.

Related Anniversaries and Days of Observance

In addition to Veterans Day, which honors all veterans, other days observe the sacrifices of particular groups of veterans.

July 27—National Korean War Veterans Armistice Day: Commemorates the July 27, 1953, signing of the armistice ending the Korean War. On that day in 2003 veterans observed the 50th anniversary of the end of the war with special ceremonies at the Korean War Veterans Memorial in Washington, D.C. The U.S. Postal Service issued a commemorative stamp that day as well.

August 7—Purple Heart Day: Commemorates the establishment of the Badge of Military Merit, or Purple Heart, by George Washington on August 7, 1782. Washington originally intended the Badge to be awarded to soldiers who showed distinguished action in battle. After the Revolutionary War, the Badge was not awarded again until the U.S. War Department (now the Department of Defense) revived it in 1932. Since that time the Badge has been reserved for those who have suffered wounds or death in battle.

September 19—National POW/MIA Recognition Day: This day was first observed in 1979 to remember soldiers who were taken prisoners of war and soldiers missing in action in all wars. More than 88,000 Americans remain missing in action in wars going back to World War II. The Department of Defense has a Prisoner of War/Missing Personnel Affairs office that works to find and identify missing soldiers around the world. Each year a ceremony is held in Washington, D.C., as well as others elsewhere around the country. A special flag honors these soldiers with the slogan "You Are Not Forgotten."

Last Sunday in September—Gold Star Mothers' Day: In 1936 Congress designated and President Franklin D. Roosevelt proclaimed this to be a day to honor mothers of veterans who died in service.

November 11—Vietnam Veterans Memorial Anniversary: The Vietnam Veterans Memorial in Washington, D.C., was dedicated on November 13, 1982. However, the anniversary of the dedication is observed on Veterans Day with a wreath-laying ceremony, speakers, and color guard.

(*See also* **Armed Forces Day**.)

The National Observance

Each year the president of the United States issues a Veterans Day proclamation. This is a brief statement summarizing the origins of Veterans Day. The Veterans Day proclamation concludes with the president urging all Americans to acknowledge U.S. veterans with appropriate public ceremonies and private prayers. The president also calls upon local, state, and federal officials to display the flag.

Noncitizen Soldiers

In recent years there have been efforts to speed the process by which non-U.S.-born members of the armed forces can become citizens. As of 2004, there were more than 37,000 noncitizen soldiers on active duty. And, until a Colombian man took action, these soldiers were not American citizens — even after giving their lives for the United States. Thanks to Jorge Rincon, Congress passed a law granting automatic citizenship to any soldier killed while serving.

How did someone from the South American country of Colombia influence an American law?

Rincon moved his family to the United States in 1989. His son Diego joined the Army after the attacks on September 11, 2001 (*see* **Patriot Day**). Diego was deployed to Iraq and was killed near Najaf by a suicide bomber on March 29, 2003. He was 19 years old.

Jorge Rincon, keenly feeling his son's longtime desire to be an American citizen, asked his U.S. senator, Zell Miller, to help expedite the process so his son could be buried as an American citizen. Senator Miller did that and more. He and his fellow senator from Georgia, Saxby Chambliss, introduced a bill that would automatically grant U.S. citizenship to any foreign-born soldier who died in action after September 11, 2001. Congress passed the bill into law on November 12, 2003.

Earlier in 2003 Senator Barbara Boxer of California, Representative Martin Frost of Texas, and other congressional representatives had introduced legislation that would make it easier and less expensive for foreign-born soldiers to become U.S. citizens after two years of faithful and honorable service in the American armed forces. Amendments to the Immigration and Nationality Act in 2004 made soldiers eligible for citizenship after one year of service or sooner. It also waived application fees and provided for soldiers serving overseas to go through the naturalization process at the nearest U.S. embassy, rather than having to complete the process in the United States. (*See also* **Citizenship Day**.)

The national ceremony at the amphitheater at the Tomb of the Unknowns (also known as the Tomb of the Unknown Soldiers) at Arlington National Cemetery is a solemn, moving event. Thousands of invited guests gather at the amphitheater, including government officials, members of the U.S. Congress, and heads of veterans programs and organizations. Traditionally, the observance begins at 11 A.M. with two minutes of silence. Then there is the singing of "The Star-Spangled Banner." The president or vice president of the United States lays a wreath at the Tomb and gives a speech. A bugler plays "Taps." The Army Band plays the "National Emblem March" as soldiers and veterans from the Army, Navy, Air Force, Marines, Coast Guard, and various service organizations, such as AMVETS and the American Legion, parade their flags.

A religious leader offers prayers for all veterans. Attendees recite the Pledge of Allegiance. The master of ceremonies introduces heads of veterans and service organizations seated on the podium. To conclude the ceremony, the flags are marched out once more as the band again plays the "National Emblem March."

"Taps"

"Taps" is the famous standard bugle call played at soldiers' funerals and special military occasions, such as Veterans Day and Memorial Day. The tune's soul-stirring quality is produced by the arrangement of only 24 musical notes.

There are several touching, if apocryphal, stories about the origin of "Taps." According to one tale, the melody was discovered during the Civil War at Harrison's Landing, Virginia, in July 1862. A Union Army captain named Robert Ellicombe found the music in the pocket of a dead Confederate soldier on the battlefield, who turned out to be his son. As the father buried the son, he arranged to have a bugler play the tune at the funeral, and thus the tradition was born.

The actual story agrees with the legend as far as time, place and the involvement of a Union officer go, but is not quite so poetic. The actual story, as best can be determined, has to do with a nightly military custom and a Union Army general with an ear for music.

According to Army tactics manuals of the time, a bugle call was played each night to summon soldiers to put out camp fires and head for bed. The call used in the Union Army was a French bugle call, "L'Extinction des feux." In English the name translates to "Extinguish Lights" and was also known as "Lights Out."

In July 1862 Union General Daniel Adams Butterfield was resting his troops after the Seven Days' battle with Robert E. Lee's Confederate troops at Harrison's Landing, Virginia. Apparently weary of the standard bugle call, Butterfield made some changes to the music in his head and, because he could not write musical notes, asked an aide to write them down. Then he brought in the brigade's bugler, Oliver W. Norton, to play the new version. After some tinkering, they produced the call known today as "Taps." That night and thereafter the new call was used in Butterfield's brigade and spread to other brigades, even Confederate ones.

And the name? According to Webster's Third New International Dictionary, "taps" was probably adapted from an old Dutch word, *taptoe*, which meant "to tap shut," or shut the tap of a keg. "Taptoe" evolved into the English word "tattoo." The word "tattoo" is still used to refer to a nighttime bugle or drum call played before "Taps" each evening to signal soldiers to quarters.

Observances

Many towns and cities around the country hold local observances, which may include a moment of silence, parades, speeches, wreath layings at cemeteries or monuments, and other ceremonies. Numerous churches, as well, hold special services and recognize veterans in attendance. Many Native American groups hold pow-wows honoring veterans at various times during the year.

Popular Taps Lyrics

Numerous sets of lyrics have been written to accompany "Taps." Two of the most popular are:

Day is done, gone the sun,
From the hills, from the lake, from the sky.
All is well, safely rest,
God is nigh.

Thanks and praise, for our days,
'Neath the sun, 'neath the stars, 'neath the sky,
As we go, this we know,
God is nigh.

Among the most notable Veterans Day ceremonies are those held in the city of Emporia, Kansas. As noted above, Emporians held the first All Veterans Day observance in 1953, one year before it became an official federal holiday. Congress formally recognized Emporia as the "Founding City of the Veterans Day Holiday" in a joint resolution approved by both the House of Representatives and the Senate on October 31, 2003.

A scene from the 2004 Veterans Day Parade in Houston, Texas.

A Sampling of Observances

1. **Auburn, Washington:** Wreath-laying ceremony, parade, luncheon, marching band competition, and other activities. Contact City of Auburn, 253-931-3043, http://www.auburn.govoffice.com/

2. **Albany, Oregon:** Described as "the largest Veteran's Day parade west of the Mississippi," it is a little over a mile long. Contact Veterans Commemoration Association, P.O. Box 2027, Lebanon, OR 97355, 541-367-8323, vetsparade@hotmail.com

3. **Long Beach, California:** Parade to the Long Beach Vietnam Veterans Memorial, followed by a concert and ceremony. Contact the Long Beach Veterans Day Parade, 333 W. Ocean Blvd., 14th Fl., Long Beach,

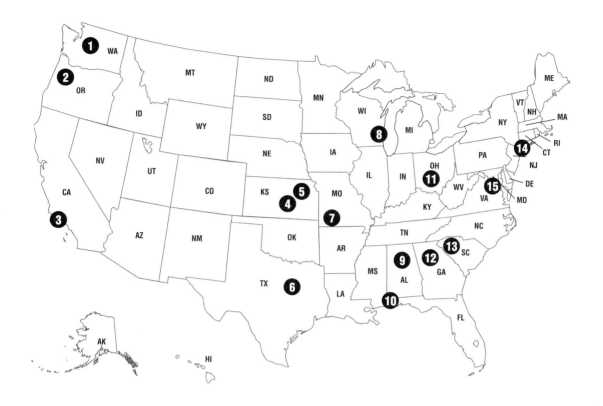

CA 90802, 562-570-6137; fax: 562-570-6659, http://www.veteransday parade.com

4. **Emporia, Kansas**: Veterans Remembrance program and Passing the Torch Ceremony in the "Founding City of the Veterans Day Holiday." Contact Emporia Area Chamber of Commerce and Convention & Visitors Bureau, 719 Commercial, P.O. Box 703, Emporia, KS 66801, 800-279-3730 or 620-342-1803; fax: 620-342-3223, visitors@emporiaks chamber.org, http://www.emporiakschamber.org/

5. **Topeka, Kansas:** Annual Veterans Pow Wow on the Washburn University campus honors veterans with dancing, drumming, and special ceremonies. Contact Awi Akta District of the Northern Cherokee Nation of the Old Louisiana Territory, http://awiakta.org or Washburn University Multicultural Affairs, Morgan Hall, Rm. 110, Topeka, KS 66621, 785-231-1010, ext. 1622

6. **Houston, Texas:** Annual Houston Salutes American Heroes Veterans Day parade. Contact Mayor's Office of Special Events, City Hall, 901 Bagby, 4th Fl., Houston, TX 77002, 713-437-6893, http://www.houston specialevents.org

7. **Branson, Missouri:** Veterans Homecoming is a week-long salute to veterans with more than 60 special events including a parade, concerts and musical shows, golf tournament, banquet, ceremonies, and more. Contact Branson Veterans Task Force, 4460 N. Gretna Rd., Branson, MO 65616-7202, 417-337-8387, fax: 417-334-7894, info@bransonveterans .com, http://www.bransonveterans.com

8. **Milwaukee, Wisconsin:** Winners of the middle-school-age essay contest — based on interviews with veterans — ride in the parade. Contact Veterans Day Parade of Milwaukee, Inc., P.O. Box 684, Milwaukee, WI 53201-0684, 414-453-8753, http://www.veteransdayparade-milw.org/

9. **Birmingham, Alabama:** Observance includes a parade, drill competition, memorial service, a world peace luncheon, and a dinner honoring the chosen outstanding veteran of the year. Contact National Veterans Day in Birmingham, P.O. Box 642, Birmingham, AL 35201, 205-325-1432, info@nationalveteransday.org, http://www.nationalveteransday .org

10. **Mobile, Alabama:** Annual Freedom Foundation celebration includes a parade, luncheon honoring patriots of the year, and a concert by the Mobile Symphonic Pops at the USS Alabama Battleship Memorial Park. Contact Mobile Bay Area Veterans Day Commission, Inc., P.O. Box 2187, Mobile, AL 36652-2187

11. **Columbus, Ohio:** Music, a memorial service, speeches, and a parade round out this observance. Contact the Military Veterans Education Foundation, 250 W. Broad St., Columbus, OH 43215 or City of Columbus, Dept. of Veterans Affairs, Mayor's Office, 90 W. Broad St., Columbus, OH 43215, 614-645-6504; fax: 614-724-0222, http://mayor.ci .columbus.oh.us/Veterans/Index.htm

12. **Atlanta, Georgia:** Downtown parade and ball. Contact Georgia Veterans Day Parade Association of Atlanta, Inc., http://www.gavetsday parade.org/

13. **Columbia, South Carolina:** Parade and celebrations. Contact Columbia Action Council, 722 Blanding St., Columbia, SC 29201, 803-343-8750; fax: 803-343-8747, CAC@ColumbiaSC.net, http://www.columbia actioncouncil.org

14. **New York, New York:** Ceremony and wreath laying at the Eternal Light Monument, followed by the annual parade on Fifth Ave. Contact United War Veterans Council of New York County, Inc., 346 Broadway, Rm. 807, New York, NY 10013-3990, 212-693-1476

15. **Arlington, Virginia:** National ceremony at Arlington National Cemetery. Contact Arlington National Cemetery, Arlington, VA 22211, 703-607-8000, http://www.arlingtoncemetery.org/

U.S. Marines in Military Aircraft Group 42, a unit from the naval air station in Atlanta, Georgia, march in the 2004 Veterans Day Parade in Atlanta.

Web Sites

Arlington National Cemetery at http://www.arlingtoncemetery.org/

Library of Congress American Memory exhibit on Veterans Day at http://memory.loc.gov/ammem/today/nov11.html

U.S. Army Institute of Heraldry provides information about decorations for distinguished service at http://www.tioh.hqda.pentagon.mil/

U.S. Citizenship and Immigration Services gives information for military personnel interested in applying for citizenship at http://uscis.gov

U.S. Department of Veterans Affairs Nationwide Gravesite Locator at http://www.cem.va.gov

U.S. Department of Veterans Affairs Veterans Day page at http://www.appc1.va.gov/vetsday/

Veterans History Project at the Library of Congress collects memories from veterans about their experiences at http://www.loc.gov/folklife/vets/

National Veterans and War Memorials

Korean War Veterans Memorial, Washington, D.C.: http://www.nps.gov/kowa/index.htm

Spirit of Freedom African-American Civil War Memorial, Washington, D.C.: http://www.nps.gov/afam/home.htm

Vietnam Veterans Memorial, Washington, D.C.: http://www.nps.gov/vive/index.htm

Vietnam Women's Memorial, Washington, D.C.: http://www.nps.gov/vive/index.htm

Women in Military Service for America Memorial, Washington, D.C.: http://www.nps.gov/gwmp/wimsa.htm (also http://www.womensmemorial.org/)

World War II Memorial, Washington, D.C.: http://www.nps.gov/nwwm/index.htm (also http://wwiimemorial.com)

Some Veterans Organizations Include:

American Ex-Prisoners of War: http://www.axpow.org/

American Legion: http://www.legion.org/

AMVETS: http://www.amvets.org/

Blinded Veterans Association: http://www.bva.org/

Disabled American Veterans: http://www.dav.org/

Gulf War Veteran Resource Pages: http://www.gulfweb.org/

Iraq War Veterans Organization: http://www.iraqwarveterans.org/

Korean War Veterans Association: http://www.kwva.org/

Military Order of the Purple Heart: http://www.purpleheart.org/

Paralyzed Veterans of America: http://www.pva.org/

Veterans for Peace: http://www.veteransforpeace.org/

Veterans of Foreign Wars of the United States: http://www.vfw.org/

Veterans of the Vietnam War: http://www.vvnw.org/

Vietnam Veterans of America: http://www.vva.org/

Women's Army Corps Veterans Association: http://www.armywomen.org/

Organizations of Families of Servicemembers Include:

American Gold Star Mothers (mothers who have lost a son or daughter serving in the armed forces): http://www.goldstarmoms.com/

Blue Star Mothers (mothers of servicemen and women): http://www.bluestarmoms.org/

Gold Star Wives of America (widows of men who died serving in the armed forces): http://www.goldstarwives.org/

National League of POW/MIA Families: http://www.pow-miafamilies.org/

Sources for Further Reading

Dennis, Matthew. *Red, White, and Blue Letter Days: An American Calendar*. Ithaca, N.Y.: Cornell University Press, 2002.

English, June A., and Thomas D. Jones. *Scholastic Encyclopedia of the United States at War*. New York: Scholastic, 1998. For young adults.

Kindsvatter, Peter S. *American Soldiers: Ground Combat in the World Wars, Korea, and Vietnam*. Lawrence: University Press of Kansas, 2003.

Litwicki, Ellen M. *America's Public Holidays, 1865-1920*. Washington, D.C.: Smithsonian Institution Press, 2000.

Norton, Bruce H., ed. *Encyclopedia of American War Heroes*. New York: Facts on File, 2002.

Piehler, G. Kurt. *Remembering War the American Way*. Washington, D.C.: Smithsonian Institution Press, 1995.

Washington's Birthday

Alternate Name: Presidents' Day
Date Established as a Federal Holiday: May 13, 1938
Date Observed: Third Monday in February

George Washington's Birthday, February 22, first became a holiday on January 31, 1879, in the District of Columbia. In 1885, the law was amended to provide the holiday for federal government employees in all the states. Congress established Washington's Birthday as a federal holiday on May 13, 1938. On June 28, 1968, Congress passed the Uniform Monday Holiday Bill, which moved Washington's Birthday to the third Monday in February. That law became effective on January 1, 1971.

Holiday Name Confusion

The holiday observed on the third Monday in February has become popularly known as Presidents' Day, but, in fact, U.S. law officially designates the holiday as Washington's Birthday. How did Americans come to call the third Monday in February "Presidents Day"?

George Washington, the first president of the United States

Part of the mix-up may stem from legislative debate in Congress in 1968. That year, Representative Robert McClory of Illinois sponsored the bill that would become the Uniform Monday Holiday Law, passed by Congress on June 28, 1968. McClory advocated not only the rescheduling of most federal holidays to Monday dates, but also the renaming of the Washington's Birthday holiday to "Presidents' Day." In this way, he hoped to have the holiday also officially honor President Abraham Lincoln, who spent much of his life in McClory's state of Illinois. The majority of

Congress did not agree, however, and retained the holiday to commemorate Washington.

The Uniform Monday Holiday Law became effective in 1971 and created many three-day weekends on the American calendar. Within a decade, businesses and advertisers had developed marketing campaigns to encourage Americans to shop during these long weekends. For the February holiday, advertisers promoted "Presidents Day" sales, hoping to extend the shopping period to include Lincoln's birthday on February 12 through Washington's birthday on the third Monday of the month.

Adding to the confusion is the fact that some states—including Connecticut, Illinois, Indiana, Missouri, and New Jersey—have separate official holidays for Lincoln (around February 12) and Washington (on the third Monday in February). Other states—including California, Georgia, Michigan, and Texas—have a holiday on the third Monday in February, but call it "Presidents' Day," "President's Day," or "Presidents Day." Calendars, too, are inconsistent. Some show all three holidays in February.

So, by the 1990s, many Americans thought the holiday was intended to honor Lincoln and Washington, or even all presidents.

The First U.S. President: George Washington

George Washington was born on February 22, 1732, in Westmoreland County, Virginia. He worked a few years as a surveyor with his half-brother, marking boundaries in western Virginia. Then he began the military career that would eventually lead him to the highest office in the new nation he helped to create. Congress selected Washington to command the Continental Army during the Revolutionary War, and he led the states to victory for independence from Britain without accepting a salary.

"Observe good faith and justice toward all nations. Cultivate peace and harmony with all."
—George Washington in his farewell address in 1797

When the Constitutional Convention created the federal government of the United States with the Constitution, the delegates wanted Washington to be the first president. Washington was famously reluctant, however, expressing uncertainty about whether he was capable. He knew that not only would he be the first holder of executive power, but that his decisions and conduct would shape the nature of the office

"Hail to the Chief"

The president's ceremonial entrance song comes from an early 19th-century dramatic musical, *The Lady of the Lake*. The play is based on Sir Walter Scott's poem of the same name. Scott was one of the most popular writers in the United States in the early 1800s. One of the play's songs was called "the boat song" in Scott's poem and "Hail to the Chief" in the play.

The song gained great popularity when the play began to be performed in American cities. It premiered in Philadelphia in 1812. Three years later the song, transformed into a march, was performed for George Washington's birthday celebration in Boston. In the 1840s First Lady Julia Tyler asked the Marine Band to play "Hail to the Chief" for her husband's official appearances, and it has been the president's ceremonial theme song ever since.

for future presidents. Yet such was the character of the man that the framers had no doubt that Washington would preside over the nation with integrity and honor. He was the only president to have been unanimously elected by the Electoral College (*see* **Election Day** *for more on the Electoral College*).

A war hero and a statesman, Washington was revered by leaders across the political spectrum, from Federalists, who advocated a strong central government, to Anti-Federalists, who believed a strong central government threatened states' rights. They saw in Washington a judicious leader, ever mindful of the importance of setting the right course for the new nation.

The country could not have asked for a finer first president. He was careful in the exercise of executive power, aware of the tyranny they had fought to overthrow. And even though he could have been reelected as long as he wished, it was Washington who chose to step down after two terms, setting a precedent that lasted into the mid-20th century.

The Presidents

1. George Washington (1732-1799) 1789-97   F
2. John Adams (1735-1826) ....1797-1801 F
3. Thomas Jefferson (1743-1826) 1801-9   D-R
4. James Madison (1751-1836) 1809-17   D-R
5. James Monroe (1758-1831) 1817-25   D-R
6. John Quincy Adams (1767-1848) 1825-29   D-R
7. Andrew Jackson (1767-1845) 1829-37   D
8. Martin Van Buren (1782-1862) 1837-41   D
9. William Henry Harrison (1773-1841) 1841   W
10. John Tyler (1790-1862) 1841-45   W
11. James Knox Polk (1795-1849) 1845-49   D
12. Zachary Taylor (1784-1850) 1849-50   W
13. Millard Fillmore (1800-1874) 1850-53   W
14. Franklin Pierce (1804-1869) 1853-57   D
15. James Buchanan (1791-1868) 1857-61   D
16. Abraham Lincoln (1809-1865) 1861-65   R
17. Andrew Johnson (1808-1875) 1865-69   D
18. Ulysses Simpson Grant (1822-1885)...............1869-77   R
19. Rutherford Birchard Hayes (1822-1893) 1877-81   R
20. James Abram Garfield (1831-1881) 1881   R
21. Chester Alan Arthur (1829-1886) 1881-85   R
22. Grover Cleveland (1837-1908)..........................1885-89   D

About the Presidency

In 1787 the members of the Constitutional Convention created the office of the presidency in defining the position in the United States Constitution. According to the Constitution, in order to be eligible to run for president, a person must be a natural-born citizen, at least 35 years old, and a resident of the United States for 14 years.

The Constitution describes the president's duties as: commander-in-chief of the armed forces, chief executive and administrator of the U.S. government, and chief diplomat and head of state in dealings with other nations. The pres-

23. Benjamin Harrison (1833-1901)	1889-93	R
24. Grover Cleveland	1893-97	D
25. William McKinley (1843-1901)	1897-1901	R
26. Theodore Roosevelt (1858-1919)	1901-9	R
27. William Howard Taft (1857-1930)	1909-13	R
28. Woodrow Wilson (1856-1924)	1913-21	D
29. Warren Gamaliel Harding (1865-1923)	1921-23	R
30. Calvin Coolidge (1872-1933)	1923-29	R
31. Herbert Clark Hoover (1874-1964)	1929-33	R
32. Franklin Delano Roosevelt (1882-1945)	1933-45	D
33. Harry S. Truman (1884-1972)	1945-53	D
34. Dwight David Eisenhower (1890-1969)	1953-61	R
35. John Fitzgerald Kennedy (1917-1963)	1961-63	D
36. Lyndon Baines Johnson (1908-1973)	1963-69	D
37. Richard Milhous Nixon (1913-1994)	1969-74	R
38. Gerald Rudolph Ford (b. 1913)	1974-77	R
39. James Earl Carter (b. 1924)	1977-81	D
40. Ronald Wilson Reagan (1911-2004)	1981-89	R
41. George Herbert Walker Bush (b. 1924)	1989-93	R
42. William Jefferson Clinton (b. 1946)	1993-2001	D
43. George Walker Bush (b. 1946)	2001-	R

Political party:

F = Federalist	D-R = Democratic-Republican
D = Democratic	W = Whig R = Republican

ident is also expected to develop policies; suggest, sign, or veto legislation; appoint individuals to federal offices; and be a popular leader of the American people. In addition, the president is the leader of the political party to which he or she belongs. Above all, as the presidential oath states, the president must protect and uphold the Constitution and other U.S. laws.

Observances

Americans have celebrated George Washington's birthday since the days of his earliest service to the Revolutionary cause. His troops at Valley Forge

Abraham Lincoln

Abraham Lincoln was born in a log cabin in Hardin County, Kentucky, on February 12, 1809. His parents were uneducated farmers, and Lincoln educated himself, spending more time working on the family farm than going to school. As a young man he held various jobs until he discovered a love for politics and the law. In 1834 Lincoln was elected to the Illinois House of Representatives, beginning a political and legal career. In 1860 he was elected president of a bitterly divided nation that would soon erupt into civil war over the issue of whether slavery could be expanded into the new western territories.

"I am loath to close. We are not enemies, but friends. We must not be enemies. Though passion may have strained it must not break our bonds of affection. The mystic chords of memory, stretching from every battlefield and patriot grave to every living heart and hearthstone all over this broad land, will yet swell the chorus of the Union, when again touched, as surely they will be, by the better angels of our nature."

—conclusion of Abraham Lincoln's First Inaugural Address, March 4, 1861

Lincoln was passionate in his belief that slavery was wrong and should no longer exist in the United States. His election to the presidency caused the Southern states to leave the Union and fed hope among abolitionists who strove to end slavery. In 1863 Lincoln issued his Emancipation Proclamation which formally announced his intention to free slaves. (*See also* **Emancipation Day**.) It is for the abolition of slavery and his heartfelt struggle to preserve the Union that Lincoln has been remembered and honored.

On Good Friday, April 14, 1865—six days after Confederate General Robert E. Lee surrendered at Appomattox Court House, Virginia, which ended the Civil War—Lincoln was assassinated by John Wilkes Booth in Ford's Theater in Washington, D.C. A funeral train carried Lincoln's body through the country for two weeks. Crowds gathered at every station to mourn and pay tribute to the slain president.

observed his birthday in 1778. Community celebrations were held the next year in Williamsburg, Virginia, and Milton, Connecticut. In the early years of the United States' nationhood, the importance and widespread observance of Washington's birthday was rivaled only by **Independence Day**. People celebrated with militia musters, parades, and elegant banquets with dancing, musical entertainment, and toasts in his home state of Virginia, as well as in Philadelphia, New York, and other cities (*for a description of an 1809 celebration in Alexandria, Virginia, see the Appendix: Sarah Ridg [Schuyler] Recalls President George Washington's Birthday and Inauguration Day*).

Today the largest celebrations of Washington's birthday take place in his native state of Virginia and in Laredo, Texas (see descriptions below). The Washington Benevolent Society, established in 1801 in Alexandria, Virginia, continues to celebrate with one of the biggest birthday parties for the first president of the United States. Because Americans popularly know the holiday as Presidents' Day and because some states honor Abraham Lincoln with an official holiday, celebrations for Lincoln occur as well.

A Sampling of Observances

1. **Laredo, Texas:** More than 30 events mark Washington's birthday on the Texas-Mexico border, including colonial parades and pageants, concerts, and fireworks. The celebration dates back to 1898. Contact Washington's Birthday Celebration Association, 1819 E. Hillside Rd., Laredo, TX 78041, 956-722-0589, fax: 956-722-5528, wbca@wbcalaredo.org, http://www.wbcalaredo.org/

2. **Lincoln, Illinois:** Several celebrations in the city include a procession to the site of one of Lincoln's former law offices, a party at another former law office, and games and children's activities at the Logan County Courthouse. Contact Lincoln-Logan County Chamber of Commerce, 303 S. Kickapoo St., Lincoln, IL 62656, 217-735-2385, chamber@lincolnillinois.com

3. **Springfield, Illinois:** Annual pilgrimage to Lincoln's tomb for wreath-laying ceremonies. Contact American Legion Post 32, 505 American Legion Ave., Springfield, IL 62701, 217-523-3415, amleg32@warpnet.net, http://members.warpnet.net/amleg32/

4. **Hodgenville, Kentucky:** Lincoln Days Celebration over the second weekend in October features a parade, games, and railsplitting and look-alike contests. Contact Lincoln Days Celebration, Inc., 58 Lincoln Sq., P.O. Box 176, Hodgenville, KY 42748.

5. **Washington, D.C.:** Wreath-laying service at the Lincoln Memorial on February 12, includes patriotic music and a reading of the Gettysburg Address. Contact Lincoln Memorial, 900 Ohio Dr., S.W., Washington DC 20024, 202-426-6841, http://www.nps.gov/linc/index.htm

6. **Alexandria, Virginia:** A gala Birthnight Ball complete with revelers in colonial costume and a nationally known speaker, a colonial parade, wreath-laying ceremonies, and more in the city billed as Washington's hometown. Contact George Washington Birthday Celebration Committee, 1108 Jefferson St., Alexandria, VA 22314, 703-991-4474, gwbcc@ email.com, http://www.washingtonbirthday.net/

7. **Mount Vernon, Virginia:** Wreath-laying ceremony, military musters, and patriotic music at Washington's home and burial site. Contact Mount Vernon Ladies' Association, 3200 Mount Vernon Memorial Hwy., P.O. Box 110, Mount Vernon, VA 22121, 703-780-2000, info@ mountvernon.org, http://www.mountvernon.org

Web Sites

Abraham Lincoln Bicentennial Commission was charged by the U.S. government to plan events for the 200th anniversary of Lincoln's birth in 2009 at http://www.lincolnbicentennial.gov

Library of Congress offers presidential images and documents online:

Abraham Lincoln Papers at http://memory.loc.gov/ammem/alhtml/mal home.html

American Memory page on Abraham Lincoln at http://memory.loc .gov/ammem/today/mar04.html

American Memory page on George Washington at http://memory.loc .gov/ammem/today/feb22.html

George Washington Papers at http://lcweb2.loc.gov/ammem/gwhtml/ gwhome.html

"I Hear America Singing—Patriotic Melodies" online exhibit has a page on "Hail to the Chief" at http://lcweb2.loc.gov/cocoon/ihas/html/ patriotic/patriotic-home.html

Portraits of the Presidents and First Ladies from 1789 at http://memory .loc.gov/ammem/odmdhtml/preshome.html

National Archives web site offers links to the presidential libraries at http:// www.archives.gov/presidential_libraries/index.html

National Park Service provides information about many historic sites related to Washington and Lincoln, including:

Lincoln Memorial at http://www.nps.gov/linc/index.htm

Washington Monument at http://www.nps.gov/wash/index.htm

Public Broadcasting Service has an online companion to the 2000 series "The American President" at http://www.pbs.org/wnet/amerpres/

Smithsonian Institution's National Museum of American History has an online exhibit "The American Presidency: A Glorious Burden" at http://americanhistory.si.edu/presidency/

Sources for Further Reading

Arbelbide, C. L. "By George, IT IS Washington's Birthday." *Prologue* 36, 4 (winter 2004). Online at http://www.archives.gov/publications/prologue/2004/winter/gw_birthday_1.html

Dennis, Matthew. *Red, White, and Blue Letter Days: An American Calendar*. Ithaca, N.Y.: Cornell University Press, 2002.

Donald, David Herbert. *Lincoln*. New York: Simon & Schuster, 1995.

Ellis, Joseph J. *His Excellency: George Washington*. New York: Alfred A. Knopf, 2004.

Flexner, James Thomas. *Washington, the Indispensable Man*. Boston: Little, Brown, 1974.

Marrin, Albert. *George Washington and the Founding of a Nation*. New York: Dutton Children's Books, 2001. For young adults.

Oates, Stephen B. *With Malice toward None: The Life of Abraham Lincoln*. New York: Harper & Row, 1977.

Rubel, David. *The Scholastic Encyclopedia of the Presidents and Their Times*. 3rd ed. New York: Scholastic, 2001. For young adults.

Schwartz, Barry. *George Washington: The Making of an American Symbol*. New York: Free Press, 1987.

Appendix:
Primary Sources

Excerpts from the Journal of Christopher Columbus (1492)

Related Holiday: Columbus Day

Christopher Columbus first reached land in the New World on October 12, 1492, on an island in the Bahamas. This excerpt from his journal contains a description of the landfall, an event commemorated each year on Columbus Day. His journal (known as the diario, or diary) was preserved by Bartolomé de Las Casas, a priest and friend of the explorer, who copied or paraphrased Columbus's notes in his Historia de las Indias *(written 1527-63). When paraphrasing the journal, Las Casas refers to Columbus as "the Admiral." For another primary source related to Columbus Day, see "A Columbus Day Program by Francis Bellamy (1892)."*

The land was first seen by a sailor called Rodrigo de Triana. But the Admiral, at ten o'clock at night [October 11] . . . saw a light, though it was so indistinct that he did not dare to affirm that it was land. . . . It was like a small wax candle that was being hoisted and raised, which would seem to few to be an indication of land. The Admiral however was quite convinced of the proximity of land. . . .

Two hours after midnight the land appeared, about two leagues off. They lowered all the sails, leaving only a storm square sail . . . and lay to until Friday when they reached a small island of the Lucayos, called Guanahani by the natives. They soon saw people naked, and the Admiral went on shore in the armed boat, also Martin Alonso Pinzon and Vincente Anes, his brother, who was commander of the *Niña*. . . .

As soon as they had landed they saw trees of a brilliant green abundance of water and fruits of various kinds. The Admiral called the two captains and the rest who had come on shore . . . as witnesses to certify that he in the presence of them all, was taking, as he in fact took possession of said island for the King and Queen his masters, making the declarations that were required. Soon after a large crowd of natives congregated there.

Source: Colbert, David, ed. *Eyewitness to America: 500 Years of America in the Words of Those Who Saw It Happen.* New York: Pantheon Books, 1997. From Hakluyt, Richard. *The Principal Navigations, Voyages, Traffiques, and Discoveries of the English Nation.* Edinburgh: E. & G. Goldsmid, 1889.

The Mayflower Compact (1620)

Related Holiday: Thanksgiving

The document below, known as the Mayflower Compact, was written and signed by English colonists, popularly known as Pilgrims, who were aboard the Mayflower. *They wrote the Mayflower Compact on November 11, 1620, about one year before they celebrated their first Thanksgiving. The Compact is a brief pledge among the colonists to govern themselves; it was the first English document in America that created a government by majority rule. The original document was lost, but the earliest version printed, in* Mourt's Relation *in 1622, included the signatures of each male head of household in Plymouth Colony. This transcript retains the spelling and punctuation of the document as it appeared in the source below. For another primary source related to Thanksgiving, see "A Letter from Sarah Josepha Hale to President Abraham Lincoln about the Creation of Thanksgiving (1863)."*

Agreement Between the Settlers at New Plymouth: 1620

IN THE NAME OF GOD, AMEN. We, whose names are underwritten, the Loyal Subjects of our dread Sovereign Lord King *James*, by the Grace of God, of *Great Britain*, *France*, and *Ireland*, King, *Defender of the Faith*, &c. Having undertaken for the Glory of God, and Advancement of the Christian Faith, and the Honour of our King and Country, a Voyage to plant the first Colony in the northern Parts of *Virginia*; Do by these Presents, solemnly and mutually, in the Presence of God and one another, covenant and combine ourselves together into a civil Body Politick, for our better Ordering and Preservation, and Furtherance of the Ends aforesaid: And by Virtue hereof do enact, constitute, and frame, such just and equal Laws, Ordinances, Acts, Constitutions, and Officers, from time to time, as shall be thought most meet and convenient for the general Good of the Colony; unto which we promise all due Submission and Obedience. IN WITNESS whereof we have hereunto subscribed our names at *Cape-Cod* the eleventh of November, in the Reign of our Sovereign Lord King *James*, of *England*, *France*, and *Ireland*, the eighteenth, and of *Scotland* the fifty-fourth, *Anno Domini*; 1620.

Mr. John Carver,	Isaac Allerton,	Francis Eaton,
Mr. William Bradford,	Myles Standish,	James Chilton,
Mr Edward Winslow,	John Alden,	John Craxton,
Mr. William Brewster.	John Turner,	John Billington,

Joses Fletcher,
John Goodman,
Mr. Samuel Fuller,
Mr. Christopher Martin,
Mr. William Mullins,
Mr. William White,
Mr. Richard Warren,
John Howland,
Mr. Steven Hopkins,
Digery Priest,

Thomas Williams,
Gilbert Winslow,
Edmund Margesson,
Peter Brown,
Richard Britteridge
George Soule,
Edward Tilly,
John Tilly,
Francis Cooke,
Thomas Rogers,

Thomas Tinker,
John Ridgdale
Edward Fuller,
Richard Clark,
Richard Gardiner,
Mr. John Allerton,
Thomas English,
Edward Doten,
Edward Liester.

Source: Thorpe, Francis Newton, ed. *The Federal and State Constitutions, Colonial Charters, and Other Organic Laws of the States, Territories, and Colonies Now or Heretofore Forming the United States of America.* Compiled and edited under the Act of Congress of June 30, 1906. Washington, D.C.: Government Printing Office, 1909.

The Declaration of Independence (1776)

Related Holiday: Independence Day

On July 4, 1776, the Continental Congress approved the Declaration of Independence, which articulated why the colonists determined to become independent of Britain. The transcript below retains the original spelling and punctuation of the signed document. For another primary source related to Independence Day, see "Fourth of July Celebrations in Oregon (1867, 1870s)."

IN CONGRESS, July 4, 1776.

The unanimous Declaration of the thirteen united States of America,

When in the Course of human events, it becomes necessary for one people to dissolve the political bands which have connected them with another, and to assume among the powers of the earth, the separate and equal station to which the Laws of Nature and of Nature's God entitle them, a decent respect to the opinions of mankind requires that they should declare the causes which impel them to the separation.

We hold these truths to be self-evident, that all men are created equal, that they are endowed by their Creator with certain unalienable Rights, that among these are Life, Liberty and the pursuit of Happiness.—That to secure these rights, Governments are instituted among Men, deriving their just powers from the consent of the governed,—That whenever any Form of Government becomes destructive of these ends, it is the Right of the People to alter or to abolish it, and to institute new Government, laying its foundation on such principles and organizing its powers in such form, as to them shall seem most likely to effect their Safety and Happiness. Prudence, indeed, will dictate that Governments long established should not be changed for light and transient causes; and accordingly all experience hath shewn, that mankind are more disposed to suffer, while evils are sufferable, than to right themselves by abolishing the forms to which they are accustomed. But when a long train of abuses and usurpations, pursuing invariably the same Object evinces a design to reduce them under absolute Despotism, it is their right, it is their duty, to throw off such Government, and to provide new Guards for their future security.—Such has been the patient sufferance of these Colonies; and such is now the necessity which constrains them to alter their former Systems of Government. The history of the present King of Great Britain is a history of repeated injuries and usurpations, all having in direct object the establishment of an absolute Tyranny over these States. To prove this, let Facts be submitted to a candid world.

He has refused his Assent to Laws, the most wholesome and necessary for the public good.

He has forbidden his Governors to pass Laws of immediate and pressing importance, unless suspended in their operation till his Assent should be obtained; and when so suspended, he has utterly neglected to attend to them.

He has refused to pass other Laws for the accommodation of large districts of people, unless those people would relinquish the right of Representation in the Legislature, a right inestimable to them and formidable to tyrants only.

He has called together legislative bodies at places unusual, uncomfortable, and distant from the depository of their public Records, for the sole purpose of fatiguing them into compliance with his measures.

He has dissolved Representative Houses repeatedly, for opposing with manly firmness his invasions on the rights of the people.

He has refused for a long time, after such dissolutions, to cause others to be elected; whereby the Legislative powers, incapable of Annihilation, have returned to the People at large for their exercise; the State remaining in the mean time exposed to all the dangers of invasion from without, and convulsions within.

He has endeavoured to prevent the population of these States; for that purpose obstructing the Laws for Naturalization of Foreigners; refusing to pass others to encourage their migrations hither, and raising the conditions of new Appropriations of Lands.

He has obstructed the Administration of Justice, by refusing his Assent to Laws for establishing Judiciary powers.

He has made Judges dependent on his Will alone, for the tenure of their offices, and the amount and payment of their salaries.

He has erected a multitude of New Offices, and sent hither swarms of Officers to harrass our people, and eat out their substance.

He has kept among us, in times of peace, Standing Armies without the Consent of our legislatures.

He has affected to render the Military independent of and superior to the Civil power.

He has combined with others to subject us to a jurisdiction foreign to our constitution, and unacknowledged by our laws; giving his Assent to their Acts of pretended Legislation:

For Quartering large bodies of armed troops among us:

For protecting them, by a mock Trial, from punishment for any Murders which they should commit on the Inhabitants of these States:

For cutting off our Trade with all parts of the world:

For imposing Taxes on us without our Consent:

For depriving us in many cases, of the benefits of Trial by Jury:

For transporting us beyond Seas to be tried for pretended offences

For abolishing the free System of English Laws in a neighbouring Province, establishing therein an Arbitrary government, and enlarging its Boundaries so as to render it at once an example and fit instrument for introducing the same absolute rule into these Colonies:

For taking away our Charters, abolishing our most valuable Laws, and altering fundamentally the Forms of our Governments:

For suspending our own Legislatures, and declaring themselves invested with power to legislate for us in all cases whatsoever.

He has abdicated Government here, by declaring us out of his Protection and waging War against us.

He has plundered our seas, ravaged our Coasts, burnt our towns, and destroyed the lives of our people.

He is at this time transporting large Armies of foreign Mercenaries to compleat the works of death, desolation and tyranny, already begun with circumstances of Cruelty & perfidy scarcely paralleled in the most barbarous ages, and totally unworthy the Head of a civilized nation.

He has constrained our fellow Citizens taken Captive on the high Seas to bear Arms against their Country, to become the executioners of their friends and Brethren, or to fall themselves by their Hands.

He has excited domestic insurrections amongst us, and has endeavoured to bring on the inhabitants of our frontiers, the merciless Indian Savages, whose known rule of warfare, is an undistinguished destruction of all ages, sexes and conditions.

In every stage of these Oppressions We have Petitioned for Redress in the most humble terms: Our repeated Petitions have been answered only by repeated injury. A Prince whose character is thus marked by every act which may define a Tyrant, is unfit to be the ruler of a free people.

Nor have We been wanting in attentions to our Brittish brethren. We have warned them from time to time of attempts by their legislature to extend an unwarrantable jurisdiction over us. We have reminded them of the circumstances of our emigration and settlement here. We have appealed to their native justice and magnanimity, and we have conjured them by the ties of our common kindred to disavow these usurpations, which, would inevitably interrupt our connections and correspondence. They too have been deaf to the voice of justice and of consanguinity. We must, therefore, acquiesce in the necessity, which denounces our Separation, and hold them, as we hold the rest of mankind, Enemies in War, in Peace Friends.

We, therefore, the Representatives of the united States of America, in General Congress, Assembled, appealing to the Supreme Judge of the world for the rectitude of our intentions, do, in the Name, and by Authority of the good People of these Colonies, solemnly publish and declare, That these United Colonies are, and of Right ought to be Free and Independent States; that they are Absolved from all Allegiance to the British Crown, and that all political connection between them and the State of Great Britain, is and ought to be totally dissolved; and that as Free and Independent States, they have full Power to levy War, conclude Peace, contract

Alliances, establish Commerce, and to do all other Acts and Things which Independent States may of right do. And for the support of this Declaration, with a firm reliance on the protection of divine Providence, we mutually pledge to each other our Lives, our Fortunes and our sacred Honor.

The 56 signatures on the Declaration appear in the positions indicated:

Column 1
Georgia:
   Button Gwinnett
   Lyman Hall
   George Walton

Column 2
North Carolina:
   William Hooper
   Joseph Hewes
   John Penn
South Carolina:
   Edward Rutledge
   Thomas Heyward, Jr.
   Thomas Lynch, Jr.
   Arthur Middleton

Column 3
Massachusetts:
   John Hancock
Maryland:
   Samuel Chase
   William Paca
   Thomas Stone
   Charles Carroll of
      Carrollton

Virginia:
   George Wythe
   Richard Henry Lee
   Thomas Jefferson
   Benjamin Harrison
   Thomas Nelson, Jr.
   Francis Lightfoot Lee
   Carter Braxton

Column 4
Pennsylvania:
   Robert Morris
   Benjamin Rush
   Benjamin Franklin
   John Morton
   George Clymer
   James Smith
   George Taylor
   James Wilson
   George Ross
Delaware:
   Caesar Rodney
   George Read
   Thomas McKean

Column 5
New York:
   William Floyd
   Philip Livingston

   Francis Lewis
   Lewis Morris
New Jersey:
   Richard Stockton
   John Witherspoon
   Francis Hopkinson
   John Hart
   Abraham Clark

Column 6
New Hampshire:
   Josiah Bartlett
   William Whipple
Massachusetts:
   Samuel Adams
   John Adams
   Robert Treat Paine
   Elbridge Gerry
Rhode Island:
   Stephen Hopkins
   William Ellery
Connecticut:
   Roger Sherman
   Samuel Huntington
   William Williams
   Oliver Wolcott
New Hampshire:
   Matthew Thornton

Source: The Declaration of Independence. From the U.S. National Archives and Records Administration, 1776. http://www.ourdocuments.gov/doc.php?flash=true&doc=2.

The Constitution of the United States (1787), The Bill of Rights (1791), and Amendments to the Constitution (1795-1992)

Related Holiday: Citizenship Day

The U.S. Constitution was approved and signed by members of the Constitutional Convention on September 17, 1787. The Constitution established the federal government of the United States and delineated its laws. The Bill of Rights contains the first ten amendments to the Constitution, which were approved on December 15, 1791. From February 7, 1795 to May 7, 1992, seventeen additional amendments were made to the Constitution. The transcript below, which includes the Constitution and the subsequent amendments, retains the spelling and punctuation of the original documents.

The Constitution of the United States

Preamble

We the People of the United States, in Order to form a more perfect Union, establish Justice, insure domestic Tranquility, provide for the common defense, promote the general Welfare, and secure the Blessings of Liberty to ourselves and our Posterity, do ordain and establish this Constitution for the United States of America.

Article. I.

Section. 1.

All legislative Powers herein granted shall be vested in a Congress of the United States, which shall consist of a Senate and House of Representatives.

Section. 2.

The House of Representatives shall be composed of Members chosen every second Year by the People of the several States, and the Electors in each State shall have the Qualifications requisite for Electors of the most numerous Branch of the State Legislature.

No Person shall be a Representative who shall not have attained to the Age of twenty five Years, and been seven Years a Citizen of the United States, and who shall not, when elected, be an Inhabitant of that State in which he shall be chosen.

Representatives and direct Taxes shall be apportioned among the several States which may be included within this Union, according to their respective Numbers, which shall be determined by adding to the whole Number of free Persons, including those bound to Service for a Term of Years, and excluding Indians not taxed, three fifths of all other Persons. The actual Enumeration shall be made within three Years after the first Meeting of the Congress of the United States, and within every subsequent Term of ten Years, in such Manner as they shall by Law direct. The Number of Representatives shall not exceed one for every thirty Thousand, but each State shall have at Least one Representative; and until such enumeration shall be made, the State of New Hampshire shall be entitled to chuse three, Massachusetts eight, Rhode-Island and Providence Plantations one, Connecticut five, New-York six, New Jersey four, Pennsylvania eight, Delaware one, Maryland six, Virginia ten, North Carolina five, South Carolina five, and Georgia three.

When vacancies happen in the Representation from any State, the Executive Authority thereof shall issue Writs of Election to fill such Vacancies.

The House of Representatives shall chuse their Speaker and other Officers; and shall have the sole Power of Impeachment.

Section. 3.

The Senate of the United States shall be composed of two Senators from each State, chosen by the Legislature thereof for six Years; and each Senator shall have one Vote.

Immediately after they shall be assembled in Consequence of the first Election, they shall be divided as equally as may be into three Classes. The Seats of the Senators of the first Class shall be vacated at the Expiration of the second Year, of the second Class at the Expiration of the fourth Year, and of the third Class at the Expiration of the sixth Year, so that one third may be chosen every second Year; and if Vacancies happen by Resignation, or otherwise, during the Recess of the Legislature of any State, the Executive thereof may make temporary Appointments until the next Meeting of the Legislature, which shall then fill such Vacancies.

No Person shall be a Senator who shall not have attained to the Age of thirty Years, and been nine Years a Citizen of the United States, and who shall not, when elected, be an Inhabitant of that State for which he shall be chosen.

The Vice President of the United States shall be President of the Senate, but shall have no Vote, unless they be equally divided.

The Senate shall chuse their other Officers, and also a President pro tempore, in the Absence of the Vice President, or when he shall exercise the Office of President of the United States.

The Senate shall have the sole Power to try all Impeachments. When sitting for that Purpose, they shall be on Oath or Affirmation. When the President of the United States is tried, the Chief Justice shall preside: And no Person shall be convicted without the Concurrence of two thirds of the Members present.

Judgment in Cases of Impeachment shall not extend further than to removal from Office, and disqualification to hold and enjoy any Office of honor, Trust or Profit under the United States: but the Party convicted shall nevertheless be liable and subject to Indictment, Trial, Judgment and Punishment, according to Law.

Section. 4.

The Times, Places and Manner of holding Elections for Senators and Representatives, shall be prescribed in each State by the Legislature thereof; but the Congress may at any time by Law make or alter such Regulations, except as to the Places of chusing Senators.

The Congress shall assemble at least once in every Year, and such Meeting shall be on the first Monday in December, unless they shall by Law appoint a different Day.

Section. 5.

Each House shall be the Judge of the Elections, Returns and Qualifications of its own Members, and a Majority of each shall constitute a Quorum to do Business; but a smaller Number may adjourn from day to day, and may be authorized to compel the Attendance of absent Members, in such Manner, and under such Penalties as each House may provide.

Each House may determine the Rules of its Proceedings, punish its Members for disorderly Behaviour, and, with the Concurrence of two thirds, expel a Member.

Each House shall keep a Journal of its Proceedings, and from time to time publish the same, excepting such Parts as may in their Judgment require Secrecy; and the Yeas and Nays of the Members of either House on any question shall, at the Desire of one fifth of those Present, be entered on the Journal.

Neither House, during the Session of Congress, shall, without the Consent of the other, adjourn for more than three days, nor to any other Place than that in which the two Houses shall be sitting.

Section. 6.

The Senators and Representatives shall receive a Compensation for their Services, to be ascertained by Law, and paid out of the Treasury of the United States. They shall in all Cases, except Treason, Felony and Breach of the Peace, be privileged from Arrest during their Attendance at the Session of their respective Houses, and in going to and returning from the same; and for any Speech or Debate in either House, they shall not be questioned in any other Place.

No Senator or Representative shall, during the Time for which he was elected, be appointed to any civil Office under the Authority of the United States, which shall have been created, or the Emoluments whereof shall have been encreased during such time; and no Person holding any Office under the United States, shall be a Member of either House during his Continuance in Office.

Section. 7.

All Bills for raising Revenue shall originate in the House of Representatives; but the Senate may propose or concur with Amendments as on other Bills.

Every Bill which shall have passed the House of Representatives and the Senate, shall, before it become a Law, be presented to the President of the United States: If he approve he shall sign it, but if not he shall return it, with his Objections to that House in which it shall have originated, who shall enter the Objections at large on their Journal, and proceed to reconsider it. If after such Reconsideration two thirds of that House shall agree to pass the Bill, it shall be sent, together with the Objections, to the other House, by which it shall likewise be reconsidered, and if approved by two thirds of that House, it shall become a Law. But in all such Cases the Votes of both Houses shall be determined by yeas and Nays, and the Names of the Persons voting for and against the Bill shall be entered on the Journal of each House respectively. If any Bill shall not be returned by the President within ten Days (Sundays excepted) after it shall have been presented to him, the Same shall be a Law, in like Manner as if he had signed it, unless the Congress by their Adjournment prevent its Return, in which Case it shall not be a Law.

Every Order, Resolution, or Vote to which the Concurrence of the Senate and House of Representatives may be necessary (except on a question of Adjournment) shall be presented to the President of the United States; and before the Same shall take Effect, shall be approved by him, or being disapproved by him, shall be repassed by two thirds of the Senate and House of Representatives, according to the Rules and Limitations prescribed in the Case of a Bill.

Section. 8.

The Congress shall have Power To lay and collect Taxes, Duties, Imposts and Excises, to pay the Debts and provide for the common Defence and general Welfare of the United States; but all Duties, Imposts and Excises shall be uniform throughout the United States;

To borrow Money on the credit of the United States;

To regulate Commerce with foreign Nations, and among the several States, and with the Indian Tribes;

To establish an uniform Rule of Naturalization, and uniform Laws on the subject of Bankruptcies throughout the United States;

To coin Money, regulate the Value thereof, and of foreign Coin, and fix the Standard of Weights and Measures;

To provide for the Punishment of counterfeiting the Securities and current Coin of the United States;

To establish Post Offices and post Roads;

To promote the Progress of Science and useful Arts, by securing for limited Times to Authors and Inventors the exclusive Right to their respective Writings and Discoveries;

To constitute Tribunals inferior to the supreme Court;

To define and punish Piracies and Felonies committed on the high Seas, and Offences against the Law of Nations;

To declare War, grant Letters of Marque and Reprisal, and make Rules concerning Captures on Land and Water;

To raise and support Armies, but no Appropriation of Money to that Use shall be for a longer Term than two Years;

To provide and maintain a Navy;

To make Rules for the Government and Regulation of the land and naval Forces;

To provide for calling forth the Militia to execute the Laws of the Union, suppress Insurrections and repel Invasions;

To provide for organizing, arming, and disciplining, the Militia, and for governing such Part of them as may be employed in the Service of the United States, reserving to the States respectively, the Appointment of the Officers, and the Authority of training the Militia according to the discipline prescribed by Congress;

To exercise exclusive Legislation in all Cases whatsoever, over such District (not exceeding ten Miles square) as may, by Cession of particular States, and the Acceptance of Congress, become the Seat of the Government of the United States, and to exercise like Authority over all Places purchased by the Consent of the Legislature of the State in which the Same shall be, for the Erection of Forts, Magazines, Arsenals, dock-Yards, and other needful Buildings;—And

To make all Laws which shall be necessary and proper for carrying into Execution the foregoing Powers, and all other Powers vested by this Constitution in the Government of the United States, or in any Department or Officer thereof.

Section. 9.

The Migration or Importation of such Persons as any of the States now existing shall think proper to admit, shall not be prohibited by the Congress prior to the Year one thousand eight hundred and eight, but a Tax or duty may be imposed on such Importation, not exceeding ten dollars for each Person.

The Privilege of the Writ of Habeas Corpus shall not be suspended, unless when in Cases of Rebellion or Invasion the public Safety may require it.

No Bill of Attainder or ex post facto Law shall be passed.

No Capitation, or other direct, Tax shall be laid, unless in Proportion to the Census or enumeration herein before directed to be taken.

No Tax or Duty shall be laid on Articles exported from any State.

No Preference shall be given by any Regulation of Commerce or Revenue to the Ports of one State over those of another; nor shall Vessels bound to, or from, one State, be obliged to enter, clear, or pay Duties in another.

No Money shall be drawn from the Treasury, but in Consequence of Appropriations made by Law; and a regular Statement and Account of the Receipts and Expenditures of all public Money shall be published from time to time.

No Title of Nobility shall be granted by the United States: And no Person holding any Office of Profit or Trust under them, shall, without the Consent of the Congress, accept of any present, Emolument, Office, or Title, of any kind whatever, from any King, Prince, or foreign State.

Section. 10.

No State shall enter into any Treaty, Alliance, or Confederation; grant Letters of Marque and Reprisal; coin Money; emit Bills of Credit; make any Thing but gold and silver Coin a Tender in Payment of Debts; pass any Bill of Attainder, ex post facto Law, or Law impairing the Obligation of Contracts, or grant any Title of Nobility.

No State shall, without the Consent of the Congress, lay any Imposts or Duties on Imports or Exports, except what may be absolutely necessary for executing it's inspection Laws: and the net Produce of all Duties and Imposts, laid by any State on Imports or Exports, shall be for the Use of the Treasury of the United States; and all such Laws shall be subject to the Revision and Controul of the Congress.

No State shall, without the Consent of Congress, lay any Duty of Tonnage, keep Troops, or Ships of War in time of Peace, enter into any Agreement or Compact with another State, or with a foreign Power, or engage in War, unless actually invaded, or in such imminent Danger as will not admit of delay.

Article. II.

Section. 1.

The executive Power shall be vested in a President of the United States of America. He shall hold his Office during the Term of four Years, and, together with the Vice President, chosen for the same Term, be elected, as follows:

Each State shall appoint, in such Manner as the Legislature thereof may direct, a Number of Electors, equal to the whole Number of Senators and Representatives to which the State may be entitled in the Congress: but no Senator or Representative, or Person holding an Office of Trust or Profit under the United States, shall be appointed an Elector.

The Electors shall meet in their respective States, and vote by Ballot for two Persons, of whom one at least shall not be an Inhabitant of the same State with themselves. And they shall make a List of all the Persons voted for, and of the Number of Votes for each; which List they shall sign and certify, and transmit sealed to the Seat of the Government of the United States, directed to the President of the Senate. The President of the Senate shall, in the Presence of the Senate and House of Representatives, open all the Certificates, and the Votes shall then be counted. The Person having the greatest Number of Votes shall be the President, if such Number be a Majority of the whole Number of Electors appointed; and if there be more than one who have such Majority, and have an equal Number of Votes, then the House of Representatives shall immediately chuse by Ballot one of them for President; and if no Person have a Majority, then from the five highest on the List the said House shall in like Manner chuse the President. But in chusing the President, the Votes shall be taken by States, the Representation from each State having one Vote; A quorum for this purpose shall consist of a Member or Members from two thirds of the States, and a Majority of all the States shall be necessary to a Choice. In every Case, after the Choice of the President, the Person having the greatest Number of Votes of the Electors shall be the Vice President. But if there should remain two or more who have equal Votes, the Senate shall chuse from them by Ballot the Vice President.

The Congress may determine the Time of chusing the Electors, and the Day on which they shall give their Votes; which Day shall be the same throughout the United States.

No Person except a natural born Citizen, or a Citizen of the United States, at the time of the Adoption of this Constitution, shall be eligible to the Office of President; neither shall any Person be eligible to that Office who shall not have attained to the Age of thirty five Years, and been fourteen Years a Resident within the United States.

In Case of the Removal of the President from Office, or of his Death, Resignation, or Inability to discharge the Powers and Duties of the said Office, the Same shall devolve on the Vice President, and the Congress may by Law provide for the Case of Removal, Death, Resignation or Inability, both of the President and Vice President, declaring what Officer shall then act as President, and such Officer shall act accordingly, until the Disability be removed, or a President shall be elected.

The President shall, at stated Times, receive for his Services, a Compensation, which shall neither be increased nor diminished during the Period for which he shall have been elected, and he shall not receive within that Period any other Emolument from the United States, or any of them.

Before he enter on the Execution of his Office, he shall take the following Oath or Affirmation: — "I do solemnly swear (or affirm) that I will faithfully execute the Office of President of the United States, and will to the best of my Ability, preserve, protect and defend the Constitution of the United States."

Section. 2.

The President shall be Commander in Chief of the Army and Navy of the United States, and of the Militia of the several States, when called into the actual Service of the United States; he may require the Opinion, in writing, of the principal Officer in each of the executive Departments, upon any Subject relating to the Duties of their respective Offices, and he shall have Power to grant Reprieves and Pardons for Offences against the United States, except in Cases of Impeachment.

He shall have Power, by and with the Advice and Consent of the Senate, to make Treaties, provided two thirds of the Senators present concur; and he shall nominate, and by and with the Advice and Consent of the Senate, shall appoint Ambassadors, other public Ministers and Consuls, Judges of the supreme Court, and all other Officers of the United States, whose Appointments are not herein otherwise provided for, and which shall be established by Law: but the Congress may by Law vest the Appointment of such inferior Officers, as they think proper, in the President alone, in the Courts of Law, or in the Heads of Departments.

The President shall have Power to fill up all Vacancies that may happen during the Recess of the Senate, by granting Commissions which shall expire at the End of their next Session.

Section. 3.

He shall from time to time give to the Congress Information of the State of the Union, and recommend to their Consideration such Measures as he shall judge necessary and expedient; he may, on extraordinary Occasions, convene both Houses, or either of them, and in Case of Disagreement between them, with Respect to the Time of Adjournment, he may adjourn them to such Time as he shall think proper; he shall receive Ambassadors and other public Ministers; he shall take Care that the Laws be faithfully executed, and shall Commission all the Officers of the United States.

Section. 4.

The President, Vice President and all civil Officers of the United States, shall be removed from Office on Impeachment for, and Conviction of, Treason, Bribery, or other high Crimes and Misdemeanors.

Article III.

Section. 1.

The judicial Power of the United States shall be vested in one supreme Court, and in such inferior Courts as the Congress may from time to time ordain and establish. The Judges, both of the supreme and inferior Courts, shall hold their Offices during good Behaviour, and shall, at stated Times, receive for their Services a Compensation, which shall not be diminished during their Continuance in Office.

Section. 2.

The judicial Power shall extend to all Cases, in Law and Equity, arising under this Constitution, the Laws of the United States, and Treaties made, or which shall be made, under their Authority;—to all Cases affecting Ambassadors, other public Ministers and Consuls;—to all Cases of admiralty and maritime Jurisdiction;—to Controversies to which the United States shall be a Party;—to Controversies between two or more States;—between a State and Citizens of another State;—between Citizens of different States;—between Citizens of the same State claiming Lands under Grants of different States, and between a State, or the Citizens thereof, and foreign States, Citizens or Subjects.

In all Cases affecting Ambassadors, other public Ministers and Consuls, and those in which a State shall be Party, the supreme Court shall have original Jurisdiction. In all the other Cases before mentioned, the supreme Court shall have appellate Jurisdiction, both as to Law and Fact, with such Exceptions, and under such Regulations as the Congress shall make.

The Trial of all Crimes, except in Cases of Impeachment, shall be by Jury; and such Trial shall be held in the State where the said Crimes shall have been committed; but when not committed within any State, the Trial shall be at such Place or Places as the Congress may by Law have directed.

Section. 3.

Treason against the United States, shall consist only in levying War against them, or in adhering to their Enemies, giving them Aid and Comfort. No Person shall be convicted of Treason unless on the Testimony of two Witnesses to the same overt Act, or on Confession in open Court.

The Congress shall have Power to declare the Punishment of Treason, but no Attainder of Treason shall work Corruption of Blood, or Forfeiture except during the Life of the Person attainted.

Article. IV.

Section. 1.

Full Faith and Credit shall be given in each State to the public Acts, Records, and judicial Proceedings of every other State. And the Congress may by general Laws prescribe the Manner in which such Acts, Records and Proceedings shall be proved, and the Effect thereof.

Section. 2.

The Citizens of each State shall be entitled to all Privileges and Immunities of Citizens in the several States.

A Person charged in any State with Treason, Felony, or other Crime, who shall flee from Justice, and be found in another State, shall on Demand of the executive Authority of the State from which he fled, be delivered up, to be removed to the State having Jurisdiction of the Crime.

No Person held to Service or Labour in one State, under the Laws thereof, escaping into another, shall, in Consequence of any Law or Regulation therein, be discharged from such Service or Labour, but shall be delivered up on Claim of the Party to whom such Service or Labour may be due.

Section. 3.

New States may be admitted by the Congress into this Union; but no new State shall be formed or erected within the Jurisdiction of any other State; nor any State be formed by the Junction of two or more States, or Parts of States, without the Consent of the Legislatures of the States concerned as well as of the Congress.

The Congress shall have Power to dispose of and make all needful Rules and Regulations respecting the Territory or other Property belonging to the United States; and nothing in this Constitution shall be so construed as to Prejudice any Claims of the United States, or of any particular State.

Section. 4.

The United States shall guarantee to every State in this Union a Republican Form of Government, and shall protect each of them against Invasion; and on Application of the Legislature, or of the Executive (when the Legislature cannot be convened), against domestic Violence.

Article. V.

The Congress, whenever two thirds of both Houses shall deem it necessary, shall propose Amendments to this Constitution, or, on the Application of the Legislatures of two thirds of the several States, shall call a Convention for proposing Amendments, which, in either Case, shall be valid to all Intents and Purposes, as Part of this Constitution, when ratified by the Legislatures of three fourths of the several States, or by Conventions in three fourths thereof, as the one or the other Mode of Ratification may be proposed by the Congress; Provided that no Amendment which may be made prior to the Year One thousand eight hundred and eight shall in any Manner affect the first and fourth Clauses in the Ninth Section of the first Article; and that no State, without its Consent, shall be deprived of its equal Suffrage in the Senate.

Article. VI.

All Debts contracted and Engagements entered into, before the Adoption of this Constitution, shall be as valid against the United States under this Constitution, as under the Confederation.

This Constitution, and the Laws of the United States which shall be made in Pursuance thereof; and all Treaties made, or which shall be made, under the Authority of the United States, shall be the supreme Law of the Land; and the Judges in every State shall be bound thereby, any Thing in the Constitution or Laws of any State to the Contrary notwithstanding.

The Senators and Representatives before mentioned, and the Members of the several State Legislatures, and all executive and judicial Officers, both of the United States and of the several States, shall be bound by Oath or Affirmation, to support this Constitution; but no religious Test shall ever be required as a Qualification to any Office or public Trust under the United States.

Article. VII.

The Ratification of the Conventions of nine States, shall be sufficient for the Establishment of this Constitution between the States so ratifying the Same.

The Word, "the," being interlined between the seventh and eighth Lines of the first Page, the Word "Thirty" being partly written on an Erazure in the fifteenth Line of the first Page, The Words "is tried" being interlined between the thirty second and thirty third Lines of the first Page and the Word "the" being interlined between the forty third and forty fourth Lines of the second Page.

Attest William Jackson Secretary

Done in Convention by the Unanimous Consent of the States present the Seventeenth Day of September in the Year of our Lord one thousand seven hundred and Eighty seven and of the Independence of the United States of America the Twelfth In witness whereof We have hereunto subscribed our Names,

G°. Washington
Presidt and deputy from Virginia

Delaware
Geo: Read
Gunning Bedford jun
John Dickinson
Richard Bassett
Jaco: Broom

Maryland
James McHenry
Dan of St Thos. Jenifer
Danl. Carroll

Virginia
John Blair
James Madison Jr.

North Carolina
Wm. Blount
Richd. Dobbs Spaight
Hu Williamson

South Carolina
J. Rutledge
Charles Cotesworth Pinckney
Charles Pinckney
Pierce Butler

Georgia
William Few
Abr Baldwin

New Hampshire
John Langdon
Nicholas Gilman

Massachusetts
Nathaniel Gorham
Rufus King

Connecticut
Wm. Saml. Johnson
Roger Sherman

New York
Alexander Hamilton

New Jersey
Wil: Livingston
David Brearley
Wm. Paterson
Jona: Dayton

Pennsylvania
B Franklin
Thomas Mifflin
Robt. Morris
Geo. Clymer
Thos. FitzSimons
Jared Ingersoll
James Wilson
Gouv Morris

The Bill of Rights (1791)

The Bill of Rights: A Transcription

Note: The following text is a transcription of the first ten amendments to the Constitution in their original form. These amendments were ratified December 15, 1791, and form what is known as the "Bill of Rights."

The Preamble to The Bill of Rights

Congress of the United States
begun and held at the City of New-York, on
Wednesday the fourth of March, one thousand seven hundred and eighty nine.

THE Conventions of a number of the States, having at the time of their adopting the Constitution, expressed a desire, in order to prevent misconstruction or abuse of its powers, that further declaratory and restrictive clauses should be added: And as extending the ground of public confidence in the Government, will best ensure the beneficent ends of its institution.

RESOLVED by the Senate and House of Representatives of the United States of America, in Congress assembled, two thirds of both Houses concurring, that the following Articles be proposed to the Legislatures of the several States, as amendments to the Constitution of the United States, all, or any of which Articles, when ratified by three fourths of the said Legislatures, to be valid to all intents and purposes, as part of the said Constitution; viz.

ARTICLES in addition to, and Amendment of the Constitution of the United States of America, proposed by Congress, and ratified by the Legislatures of the several States, pursuant to the fifth Article of the original Constitution.

Amendment I

Congress shall make no law respecting an establishment of religion, or prohibiting the free exercise thereof; or abridging the freedom of speech, or of the press; or the right of the people peaceably to assemble, and to petition the Government for a redress of grievances.

Amendment II

A well regulated Militia, being necessary to the security of a free State, the right of the people to keep and bear Arms, shall not be infringed.

Amendment III

No Soldier shall, in time of peace be quartered in any house, without the consent of the Owner, nor in time of war, but in a manner to be prescribed by law.

Amendment IV

The right of the people to be secure in their persons, houses, papers, and effects, against unreasonable searches and seizures, shall not be violated, and no Warrants shall issue, but upon probable cause, supported by Oath or affirmation, and particularly describing the place to be searched, and the persons or things to be seized.

Amendment V

No person shall be held to answer for a capital, or otherwise infamous crime, unless on a presentment or indictment of a Grand Jury, except in cases arising in the land or naval forces, or in the Militia, when in actual service in time of War or public danger; nor shall any person be subject for the same offence to be twice put in jeopardy of life or limb; nor shall be compelled in any criminal case to be a witness against himself, nor be deprived of life, liberty, or property, without due process of law; nor shall private property be taken for public use, without just compensation.

Amendment VI

In all criminal prosecutions, the accused shall enjoy the right to a speedy and public trial, by an impartial jury of the State and district wherein the crime shall have been committed, which district shall have been previously ascertained by law, and to be informed of the nature and cause of the accusation; to be confronted with the witnesses against him; to have compulsory process for obtaining witnesses in his favor, and to have the Assistance of Counsel for his defence.

Amendment VII

In Suits at common law, where the value in controversy shall exceed twenty dollars, the right of trial by jury shall be preserved, and no fact tried by a jury, shall be otherwise re-examined in any Court of the United States, than according to the rules of the common law.

Amendment VIII

Excessive bail shall not be required, nor excessive fines imposed, nor cruel and unusual punishments inflicted.

Amendment IX

The enumeration in the Constitution, of certain rights, shall not be construed to deny or disparage others retained by the people.

Amendment X

The powers not delegated to the United States by the Constitution, nor prohibited by it to the States, are reserved to the States respectively, or to the people.

Amendments to the Constitution (1795-1992)

Amendment XI

Passed by Congress March 4, 1794. Ratified February 7, 1795.

Note: Article III, section 2, of the Constitution was modified by amendment 11.

The Judicial power of the United States shall not be construed to extend to any suit in law or equity, commenced or prosecuted against one of the United States by Citizens of another State, or by Citizens or Subjects of any Foreign State.

Amendment XII

Passed by Congress December 9, 1803. Ratified June 15, 1804.

Note: A portion of Article II, section 1 of the Constitution was superseded by the 12th amendment.

The Electors shall meet in their respective states and vote by ballot for President and Vice-President, one of whom, at least, shall not be an inhabitant of the same state with themselves; they shall name in their ballots the person voted for as President, and in distinct ballots the person voted for as Vice-President, and they shall make distinct lists of all persons voted for as President, and of all persons voted for as Vice-President, and of the number of votes for each, which lists they shall sign and certify, and transmit sealed to the seat of the government of the United States, directed to the President of the Senate; —the President of the Senate shall, in the presence of the Senate and House of Representatives, open all the certificates and the votes shall then be counted;—The person having the greatest number of votes for President, shall be the President, if such number be a majority of the whole number of Electors appointed; and if no person have such majority, then from the persons having the highest numbers not exceeding three on the list of those voted for as President, the House of Representatives shall choose immediately, by ballot, the President. But in choosing the President, the votes shall be taken by states, the representation from each state having one vote; a quorum for this purpose shall consist of a member or members from two-thirds of the states, and a majority of all the states shall be necessary to a choice. [And if the House of Representatives shall not choose a President whenever the right of choice shall devolve upon them, before the fourth day of March next following, then the Vice-President shall act as President, as in case of the death or other constitutional disability of the President. —]* The person having the greatest number of votes as Vice-President, shall be the Vice-President, if such number be a majority of the whole number of Electors appointed, and if no person have a majority, then from the two highest numbers on the list, the Senate shall choose the Vice-President; a quorum for the purpose shall consist of two-thirds of the whole number of Senators, and a majority of the whole number shall be necessary to a choice. But no person constitutionally ineligible to the office of President shall be eligible to that of Vice-President of the United States.

*Superseded by section 3 of the 20th amendment.

Amendment XIII

Passed by Congress January 31, 1865. Ratified December 6, 1865.

Note: A portion of Article IV, section 2, of the Constitution was superseded by the 13th amendment.

Section 1.

Neither slavery nor involuntary servitude, except as a punishment for crime whereof the party shall have been duly convicted, shall exist within the United States, or any place subject to their jurisdiction.

Section 2.

Congress shall have power to enforce this article by appropriate legislation.

Amendment XIV

Passed by Congress June 13, 1866. Ratified July 9, 1868.

Note: Article I, section 2, of the Constitution was modified by section 2 of the 14th amendment.

Section 1.

All persons born or naturalized in the United States, and subject to the jurisdiction thereof, are citizens of the United States and of the State wherein they reside. No State shall make or enforce any law which shall abridge the privileges or immunities of citizens of the United States; nor shall any State deprive any person of life, liberty, or property, without due process of law; nor deny to any person within its jurisdiction the equal protection of the laws.

Section 2.

Representatives shall be apportioned among the several States according to their respective numbers, counting the whole number of persons in each State, excluding Indians not taxed. But when the right to vote at any election for the choice of electors for President and Vice-President of the United States, Representatives in Congress, the Executive and Judicial officers of a State, or the members of the Legislature thereof, is denied to any of the male inhabitants of such State, being twenty-one years of age,* and citizens of the United States, or in any way abridged, except for participation in rebellion, or other crime, the basis of representation therein shall be reduced in the proportion which the number of such male citizens shall bear to the whole number of male citizens twenty-one years of age in such State.

Section 3.

No person shall be a Senator or Representative in Congress, or elector of President and Vice-President, or hold any office, civil or military, under the United States, or under any State, who, having previously taken an oath, as a member of Congress, or as an officer of the United States, or as a member of any State legislature, or as an executive or judicial officer of any State, to support the Constitution of the United States, shall have engaged in insurrection or rebellion against the same, or given aid or comfort to the enemies thereof. But Congress may by a vote of two-thirds of each House, remove such disability.

Section 4.

The validity of the public debt of the United States, authorized by law, including debts incurred for payment of pensions and bounties for services in suppressing insurrection or rebellion, shall not be questioned. But neither the United States nor any State shall assume or pay any debt or obligation incurred in aid of insurrection or rebellion against the United States, or any claim for the loss or emancipation of any slave; but all such debts, obligations and claims shall be held illegal and void.

Section 5.

The Congress shall have the power to enforce, by appropriate legislation, the provisions of this article.

Changed by section 1 of the 26th amendment.

300

Amendment XV

Passed by Congress February 26, 1869. Ratified February 3, 1870.

Section 1.

The right of citizens of the United States to vote shall not be denied or abridged by the United States or by any State on account of race, color, or previous condition of servitude—

Section 2.

The Congress shall have the power to enforce this article by appropriate legislation.

Amendment XVI

Passed by Congress July 2, 1909. Ratified February 3, 1913.

Note: Article I, section 9, of the Constitution was modified by amendment 16.

The Congress shall have power to lay and collect taxes on incomes, from whatever source derived, without apportionment among the several States, and without regard to any census or enumeration.

Amendment XVII

Passed by Congress May 13, 1912. Ratified April 8, 1913.

Note: Article I, section 3, of the Constitution was modified by the 17th amendment.

The Senate of the United States shall be composed of two Senators from each State, elected by the people thereof, for six years; and each Senator shall have one vote. The electors in each State shall have the qualifications requisite for electors of the most numerous branch of the State legislatures.

When vacancies happen in the representation of any State in the Senate, the executive authority of such State shall issue writs of election to fill such vacancies: *Provided*, That the legislature of any State may empower the executive thereof to make temporary appointments until the people fill the vacancies by election as the legislature may direct.

This amendment shall not be so construed as to affect the election or term of any Senator chosen before it becomes valid as part of the Constitution.

Amendment XVIII

Passed by Congress December 18, 1917. Ratified January 16, 1919. Repealed by amendment 21.

Section 1.

After one year from the ratification of this article the manufacture, sale, or transportation of intoxicating liquors within, the importation thereof into, or the exportation thereof from the United States and all territory subject to the jurisdiction thereof for beverage purposes is hereby prohibited.

Section 2.

The Congress and the several States shall have concurrent power to enforce this article by appropriate legislation.

Section 3.

This article shall be inoperative unless it shall have been ratified as an amendment to the Constitution by the legislatures of the several States, as provided in the Constitution, within seven years from the date of the submission hereof to the States by the Congress.

Amendment XIX

Passed by Congress June 4, 1919. Ratified August 18, 1920.

The right of citizens of the United States to vote shall not be denied or abridged by the United States or by any State on account of sex.

Congress shall have power to enforce this article by appropriate legislation.

Amendment XX

Passed by Congress March 2, 1932. Ratified January 23, 1933.

Note: Article I, section 4, of the Constitution was modified by section 2 of this amendment. In addition, a portion of the 12th amendment was superseded by section 3.

Section 1.

The terms of the President and the Vice President shall end at noon on the 20th day of January, and the terms of Senators and Representatives at noon on the 3d day of January, of the years in which such terms would have ended if this article had not been ratified; and the terms of their successors shall then begin.

Section 2.

The Congress shall assemble at least once in every year, and such meeting shall begin at noon on the 3d day of January, unless they shall by law appoint a different day.

Section 3.

If, at the time fixed for the beginning of the term of the President, the President elect shall have died, the Vice President elect shall become President. If a President shall not have been chosen before the time fixed for the beginning of his term, or if the President elect shall have failed to qualify, then the Vice President elect shall act as President until a President shall have qualified; and the Congress may by law provide for the case wherein neither a President elect nor a Vice President shall have qualified, declaring who shall then act as President, or the manner in which one who is to act shall be selected, and such person shall act accordingly until a President or Vice President shall have qualified.

Section 4.

The Congress may by law provide for the case of the death of any of the persons from whom the House of Representatives may choose a President whenever the right of choice shall have devolved upon them, and for the case of the death of any of the persons from whom the Senate may choose a Vice President whenever the right of choice shall have devolved upon them.

Section 5.

Sections 1 and 2 shall take effect on the 15th day of October following the ratification of this article.

Section 6.

This article shall be inoperative unless it shall have been ratified as an amendment to the Constitution by the legislatures of three-fourths of the several States within seven years from the date of its submission.

Amendment XXI

Passed by Congress February 20, 1933. Ratified December 5, 1933.

Section 1.

The eighteenth article of amendment to the Constitution of the United States is hereby repealed.

Section 2.

The transportation or importation into any State, Territory, or Possession of the United States for delivery or use therein of intoxicating liquors, in violation of the laws thereof, is hereby prohibited.

Section 3.

This article shall be inoperative unless it shall have been ratified as an amendment to the Constitution by conventions in the several States, as provided in the Constitution, within seven years from the date of the submission hereof to the States by the Congress.

Amendment XXII

Passed by Congress March 21, 1947. Ratified February 27, 1951.

Section 1.

No person shall be elected to the office of the President more than twice, and no person who has held the office of President, or acted as President, for more than two years of a term to which some other person was elected President shall be elected to the office of President more than once. But this Article shall not apply to any person holding the office of President when this Article was proposed by Congress, and shall not prevent any person who may be holding the office of President, or acting as President, during the term within which this Article becomes operative from holding the office of President or acting as President during the remainder of such term.

Section 2.

This article shall be inoperative unless it shall have been ratified as an amendment to the Constitution by the legislatures of three-fourths of the several States within seven years from the date of its submission to the States by the Congress.

Amendment XXIII

Passed by Congress June 16, 1960. Ratified March 29, 1961.

Section 1.

The District constituting the seat of Government of the United States shall appoint in such manner as Congress may direct:

A number of electors of President and Vice President equal to the whole number of Senators and Representatives in Congress to which the District would be entitled if it were a State, but in no event more than the least populous State; they shall be in addition to those appointed by the States, but they shall be considered, for the purposes of the election of President and Vice President, to be electors appointed by a State; and they shall meet in the District and perform such duties as provided by the twelfth article of amendment.

Section 2.

The Congress shall have power to enforce this article by appropriate legislation.

Amendment XXIV

Passed by Congress August 27, 1962. Ratified January 23, 1964.

Section 1.

The right of citizens of the United States to vote in any primary or other election for President or Vice President, for electors for President or Vice President, or for Senator or Representative in Congress, shall not be denied or abridged by the United States or any State by reason of failure to pay poll tax or other tax.

Section 2.

The Congress shall have power to enforce this article by appropriate legislation.

Amendment XXV

Passed by Congress July 6, 1965. Ratified February 10, 1967.

Note: Article II, section 1, of the Constitution was affected by the 25th amendment.

Section 1.

In case of the removal of the President from office or of his death or resignation, the Vice President shall become President.

Section 2.

Whenever there is a vacancy in the office of the Vice President, the President shall nominate a Vice President who shall take office upon confirmation by a majority vote of both Houses of Congress.

Section 3.

Whenever the President transmits to the President pro tempore of the Senate and the Speaker of the House of Representatives his written declaration that he is unable to discharge the powers and duties of his office, and until he transmits to them a written declaration to the contrary, such powers and duties shall be discharged by the Vice President as Acting President.

Section 4.

Whenever the Vice President and a majority of either the principal officers of the executive departments or of such other body as Congress may by law provide, transmit to the President pro tempore of the Senate and the Speaker of the House of Representatives their written declaration that the President is unable to discharge the powers and duties of his office, the Vice President shall immediately assume the powers and duties of the office as Acting President.

Thereafter, when the President transmits to the President pro tempore of the Senate and the Speaker of the House of Representatives his written declaration that no inability exists, he shall resume the powers and duties of his office unless the Vice President and a majority of either the principal officers of the executive department or of such other body as Congress may by law provide, transmit within four days to the President pro tempore of the Senate and the Speaker of the House of Representatives their written declaration that the President is unable to discharge the powers and duties of his office. Thereupon Congress shall decide the issue, assembling within forty-eight hours for that purpose if not in session. If the Congress, within twenty-one days after receipt of the latter written declaration, or, if Congress is not in session, within twenty-one days after Congress is required to assemble, determines by two-thirds vote of both Houses that the President is unable to discharge the powers and duties of his office, the Vice President shall continue to discharge the same as Acting President; otherwise, the President shall resume the powers and duties of his office.

Amendment XXVI

Passed by Congress March 23, 1971. Ratified July 1, 1971.

Note: Amendment 14, section 2, of the Constitution was modified by section 1 of the 26th amendment.

Section 1.

The right of citizens of the United States, who are eighteen years of age or older, to vote shall not be denied or abridged by the United States or by any State on account of age.

Section 2.

The Congress shall have power to enforce this article by appropriate legislation.

Amendment XXVII

Originally proposed Sept. 25, 1789. Ratified May 7, 1992.

No law, varying the compensation for the services of the Senators and Representatives, shall take effect, until an election of representatives shall have intervened.

Source: The Constitution of the United States, 1787; The Bill of Rights, 1791; and Amendments to the Constitution, 1795-1992. From the U.S. National Archives and Records Administration. http://www.archives.gov/national _archives_experience/charters/constitution.html.

Sarah Ridg [Schuyler] Recalls President George Washington's Birthday and Inauguration Day (1809)

Related Holidays: Election Day and Inauguration Day, Washington's Birthday (Presidents' Day)

This document includes a portion of the diary of Sarah Ridg [Schuyler] of Burlington, New Jersey. In 1809 she traveled to Alexandria, Virginia, and Washington, D.C. In the following excerpt, she describes her experiences at festivities in Alexandria for George Washington's Birthday on February 22, 1809, and in the nation's capital for the inauguration of James Madison, the fourth U.S. president, on March 4, 1809. The transcript below retains Ridg's original spelling and punctuation.

February 22. — This is the memorable day that gave birth to our illustrious patriot, General George Washington. We went to church in the morning and heard an excellent sermon preached by Dr. Muir. We had also some good music. Mrs. Nat C. who came down in the packet this morning accompanied us. She did not stay to the ball, but returned to Washington immediately after dinner. Nancy Riddle sent to request us to go with herself and her mama this evening. . . . . A great number had assembled when we arrived at Caton's ,* and the room was only partially lighted, which surprised us very much. At one end of the room was a curtain hung from the ceiling to the floor; in a few moments this was raised and an elegant painting representing the Tomb of Washington was presented to our view. A great number of lights were behind the curtain. When that was removed the room had a very elegant appearance. Mrs. Young, one of the managers, carried around a basket of laurel; we each took a sprig. Washington March was played, we all moved in procession and threw the laurel before the shrine of Washington. The set dances took up a great part of the evening. I had Mr. M. for my partner, and was obliged to refuse a great favorite, W. T., in consequence of my engagements, which provoked me very much. There were a number of very splendid dresses. Mrs. Fowler was the bell of the ball. Mrs. Judge Washington had enough gold fringe about her to have distributed among us all a sufficient quantity. We were led down to supper at twelve o'clock. The table was decorated more handsomely than any I ever saw, and afforded every delicacy. The whole house was illuminated, several of us went out into the street and looked at it, and were very much pleased with the beautiful appearance.

[* *Ridg may well be referring to an establishment better known as Gadsby's Tavern and City Hotel, which has hosted the George Washington Birthnight Ball since 1787. In 1808, manager John Gadsby turned the operation over to one William Caton.*]

February 28.—In the afternoon Julia and I went up King Street to make some purchases for the ball in Washington, which we are in expectation of attending on the fourth of March. We sewed and played backgammon all evening.

March 2.—We set out for Washington this afternoon, going on board the packet at half-past three. We had a fair wind and performed our voyage in an hour. Mr. and Mrs. Cocke met us near the landing and we all walked to the house together. Commodore Decatur* came in after tea, and we spent the evening playing loo.

[Original footnote: Stephen Decatur, the "Bayard of the Seas," tho' at this time only thirty years old, had been two years a Commodore and was already justly famous throughout the Nation on account of his gallant exploit—the burning of the *Philadelphia* in the Harbor of Tripoli *[during the Tripolitan War of 1801-5]*, which the great *[British naval admiral Horatio]* Nelson had pronounced "the most bold and daring act of the age."]

March 3.—Mrs. C., Julia and I walked down to Mr. Craven's store soon after breakfast to purchase a white carcenet dress for Nancy. In the afternoon we all walked to the Capitol. The House was so crowded it was with difficulty we got seats. Mr. Randolph made a very eloquent speech. It was the first time either Julia or I had heard him speak. Mr. Nelson and several others spoke also.

March 4.—Saturday. A federal salute from Fort Warburton and from the Navy Yard was the harbinger of this day's dawn. At an early hour the volunteer corps, cavalry and infantry, were in uniform and under arms. Pennsylvania Avenue was overspread with persons of every description. Carriages, horse and foot, all were hastening to the Capitol. But large and capacious as the passages, lobbies, galleries, chambers and Hall of the south wing of the Capitol are, the concourse of people was so immense that at least ten thousand persons must have been compelled to remain outside of the building. We went early and had a pleasant situation. At eleven o'clock the members of the Senate assembled in the House of Representatives. The Hon. John Melledge, Esq., took the chair; Ex-President of the United States on the right, foreign ministers and suites on the left, Judges of the Supreme Court in front; heads of departments on the right of the President of the Senate; Members of the House of Representatives on the floor; other public characters as propriety and convenience dictated. Ladies were in the seats usually occupied by the Representatives.

Mr. *[Thomas]* Jefferson repaired to the Capitol about twelve o'clock. Mr. Madison left his own house in F Street in his carriage, accompanied by Mr. Coles, the ex-President's private Secretary, and escorted by two troops of cavalry, one belonging to Georgetown and the other to the city. Mr. Madison was dressed in an entire suit of American manufacture, made of cloth of merino wool, presented by Colonel Humphrey and Chancellor Livingston. He entered the Hall supported by the Secretary of the Navy. The Attorney-General, the Secretary of the Treasury and Mr. Coles, and was ushered in by a Senatorial Committee. Mr. Melledge left the chair, conducted Mr. Madison to it and seated himself upon the right. Mr. Madison appeared very much embarrased. He rose from his seat and delivered his inaugural speech, after which he took the oath of office, which was administered to him by Chief Justice Marshall. Two rounds of minute guns were fired at the conclusion of the ceremony: and, as the President withdrew from the Capitol, nine companies of Infantry belonging to the District, which were in complete uniform and made a very military appearance, were drawn up to receive the President, who passed them in review, entered his carriage and proceeded under the escort of the cavalry, to his dwelling, which was crowded with ladies and gentlemen—among others Mr. Jefferson.

Abundance of refreshments were spread before us. Mrs. Madison appeared as though she had attained the summit of her happiness. She was much extolled for her beauty and elegance of manners, but I did not view her with so much admiration—probably it was want of taste. I was pleased with her neatness of attire. The day terminated with a brilliant ball at Long's Hotel. Mr. Jefferson was there. Mr. and Mrs. Madison were also present; so were the French and English Ministers and other diplomatic characters. They were solicited by special invitation. Upwards of four hundred persons graced the scene.

Source: Ridg, Sarah. "Washington in 1809—A Pen-Picture. Diary of Sarah Ridg [Schuyler], January 3 – November 2, 1809." From the Library of Congress Manuscript Division, 1809. http://memory.loc.gov/ammem/pihtml/pihome .html.

A Letter from Sarah Josepha Hale to President Abraham Lincoln about the Creation of Thanksgiving (1863)

Related Holiday: Thanksgiving

Sarah Josepha Hale was the editor of a popular women's magazine, Lady's Book, *who had advocated a national Thanksgiving holiday since 1827. On September 28, 1863, she wrote this letter to President Abraham Lincoln. In response, on October 3, 1863, Lincoln issued a presidential proclamation designating the last Thursday of November "a Day of Thanksgiving and Praise to our beneficient Father who dwelleth in the heavens." For another primary source related to Thanksgiving, see "The Mayflower Compact (1620)."*

Private

Philadelphia, Sept. 28th 1863.

Sir.—

Permit me, as Editress of the "Lady's Book", to request a few minutes of your precious time, while laying before you a subject of deep interest to myself and—as I trust—even to the President of our Republic, of some importance. This subject is to have the <u>day of our annual Thanksgiving made a National and fixed Union Festival.</u>

You may have observed that, for some years past, there has been an increasing interest felt in our land to have the Thanksgiving held on the same day, in all the States; it now needs National recognition and authoritive <u>fixation</u>, only, to become permanently, an American custom and institution.

Enclosed are three papers (being printed these are easily read) which will make the idea and its progress clear and show also the popularity of the plan.

For the last fifteen years I have set forth this idea in the "Lady's Book", and placed the papers before the Governors of all the States and Territories—also I have sent these to our Ministers abroad, and our Missionaries to the heathen—and commanders in the Navy. From the recipients I have received, uniformly the most kind approval. Two of these letters, one from Governor (now General) Banks and one from Governor Morgan [Nathaniel P. Banks and Edwin

D. Morgan] are enclosed; both gentlemen as you will see, have nobly aided to bring about the desired Thanksgiving Union.

But I find there are obstacles not possible to be overcome without legislative aid—that each State should, by statute, make it obligatory on the Governor to appoint the last Thursday of November, annually, as Thanksgiving Day;—or, as this way would require years to be realized, it has ocurred to me that a proclamation from the President of the United States would be the best, surest and most fitting method of National appointment.

I have written to my friend, Hon. Wm. H. Seward, and requested him to confer with President Lincoln on this subject As the President of the United States has the power of appointments for the District of Columbia and the Territories; also for the Army and Navy and all American citizens abroad who claim protection from the U. S. Flag—could he not, with right as well as duty, issue his proclamation for a Day of National Thanksgiving for all the above classes of persons? And would it not be fitting and patriotic for him to appeal to the Governors of all the States, inviting and commending these to unite in issuing proclamations for the last Thursday in November as the Day of Thanksgiving for the people of each State? Thus the great Union Festival of America would be established.

Now the purpose of this letter is to entreat President Lincoln to put forth his Proclamation, appointing the last Thursday in November (which falls this year on the 26th) as the National Thanksgiving for all those classes of people who are under the National Government particularly, and commending this Union Thanksgiving to each State Executive: thus, by the noble example and action of the President of the United States, the permanency and unity of our Great American Festival of Thanksgiving would be forever secured.

An immediate proclamation would be necessary, so as to reach all the States in season for State appointments, also to anticipate the early appointments by Governors.

Excuse the liberty I have taken

With profound respect
Yrs truly
Sarah Josepha Hale,
Editress of the "Ladys Book"

Source: Hale, Sarah Josepha. Letter to Abraham Lincoln. Transcribed and annotated by the Lincoln Studies Center, Knox College, Galesburg, Illinois. From the Abraham Lincoln Papers at the Library of Congress, 1863. http://memory.loc.gov/ammem/alhtml/malhome.html.

The Emancipation Proclamation (1863) and the 13th Amendment (1865)

Related Holiday: Emancipation Day and Juneteenth

The following includes two documents: the Emancipation Proclamation and the 13th Amendment to the U.S. Constitution. President Abraham Lincoln issued the Emancipation Proclamation on January 1, 1863, declaring freedom for all slaves in Southern states. The end of slavery became law on January 31, 1865, when Congress passed the 13th Amendment to the U.S. Constitution. For another primary source related to Emancipation Day, see "Bishop H.M. Turner Recalls the Issuance of the Emancipation Proclamation (1863)."

By the President of the United States of America: A Proclamation.

Whereas, on the twenty-second day of September, in the year of our Lord one thousand eight hundred and sixty-two, a proclamation was issued by the President of the United States, containing, among other things, the following, to wit:

"That on the first day of January, in the year of our Lord one thousand eight hundred and sixty-three, all persons held as slaves within any State or designated part of a State, the people whereof shall then be in rebellion against the United States, shall be then, thenceforward, and forever free; and the Executive Government of the United States, including the military and naval authority thereof, will recognize and maintain the freedom of such persons, and will do no act or acts to repress such persons, or any of them, in any efforts they may make for their actual freedom.

"That the Executive will, on the first day of January aforesaid, by proclamation, designate the States and parts of States, if any, in which the people thereof, respectively, shall then be in rebellion against the United States; and the fact that any State, or the people thereof, shall on that day be, in good faith, represented in the Congress of the United States by members chosen thereto at elections wherein a majority of the qualified voters of such State shall have participated, shall, in the absence of strong countervailing testimony, be deemed conclusive evidence that such State, and the people thereof, are not then in rebellion against the United States."

Now, therefore I, Abraham Lincoln, President of the United States, by virtue of the power in me vested as Commander-in-Chief, of the Army and Navy of the United States in time of actual armed rebellion against the authority and government of the United States, and as a fit and necessary war measure for suppressing said rebellion, do, on this first day of January, in the year of our Lord one thousand eight hundred and sixty-three, and in accordance with my purpose so to do publicly proclaimed for the full period of one hundred days, from the day first above mentioned, order and designate as the States and parts of States wherein the people thereof respectively, are this day in rebellion against the United States, the following, to wit:

Arkansas, Texas, Louisiana, (except the Parishes of St. Bernard, Plaquemines, Jefferson, St. John, St. Charles, St. James Ascension, Assumption, Terrebonne, Lafourche, St. Mary, St. Martin, and Orleans, including the City of New Orleans) Mississippi, Alabama, Florida, Georgia, South Carolina, North Carolina, and Virginia, (except the forty-eight counties designated as West Virginia, and also the counties of Berkley, Accomac, Northampton, Elizabeth City, York, Princess Ann, and Norfolk, including the cities of Norfolk and Portsmouth[)], and which excepted parts, are for the present, left precisely as if this proclamation were not issued.

And by virtue of the power, and for the purpose aforesaid, I do order and declare that all persons held as slaves within said designated States, and parts of States, are, and henceforward shall be free; and that the Executive government of the United States, including the military and naval authorities thereof, will recognize and maintain the freedom of said persons.

And I hereby enjoin upon the people so declared to be free to abstain from all violence, unless in necessary self-defence; and I recommend to them that, in all cases when allowed, they labor faithfully for reasonable wages.

And I further declare and make known, that such persons of suitable condition, will be received into the armed service of the United States to garrison forts, positions, stations, and other places, and to man vessels of all sorts in said service.

And upon this act, sincerely believed to be an act of justice, warranted by the Constitution, upon military necessity, I invoke the considerate judgment of mankind, and the gracious favor of Almighty God.

In witness whereof, I have hereunto set my hand and caused the seal of the United States to be affixed.

Done at the City of Washington, this first day of January, in the year of our Lord one thousand eight hundred and sixty three, and of the Independence of the United States of America the eighty-seventh.

By the President: ABRAHAM LINCOLN
WILLIAM H. SEWARD, Secretary of State.

The 13th Amendment to the Constitution

Amendment XIII

Section 1.

Neither slavery nor involuntary servitude, except as a punishment for crime whereof the party shall have been duly convicted, shall exist within the United States, or any place subject to their jurisdiction.

Section 2.

Congress shall have power to enforce this article by appropriate legislation.

Passed by Congress January 31, 1865. Ratified December 6, 1865.

Note: A portion of Article IV, section 2, of the Constitution was superseded by the 13th amendment.

Sources:

Excerpt 1: The Emancipation Proclamation. From the U.S. National Archives and Records Administration, 1863. http://www.ourdocuments.gov/doc.php?doc=34.

Excerpt 2: The 13th Amendment to the U.S. Constitution. From the U.S. National Archives and Records Administration, 1865. http://www.ourdocuments.gov/doc.php?doc=40.

Bishop H. M. Turner Recalls the Issuance of the Emancipation Proclamation (1863)

Related Holiday: Emancipation Day and Juneteenth

This excerpt from an article about Emancipation Day offers an eyewitness account of the response in Washington, D.C., on January 1, 1863, when Abraham Lincoln issued the Emancipation Proclamation. The writer, Bishop H. M. Turner, was the pastor at Israel Church at the time. Bishop Turner composed his reminiscences of that day in the following article, published for the occasion of the 50th anniversary of the Proclamation. For another primary source related to Emancipation Day, see "The Emancipation Proclamation (1863) and the 13th Amendment (1865)."

Reminiscences Of The Proclamation Of Emancipation

By Bishop H. M. Turner, D. D., D.C. L.

We are now upon the verge of the fiftieth anniversary, since the Immortal Abraham Lincoln, then President of the United States, by the grace of God hurled against the institution of American slavery the thunderbolt which had been smelted in the furnace of fair play, justice and eternal equity.

Well do I remember the circumstances and incidents connected with my surroundings and experience on that occasion. . . .

The Civil War between the states was then in full blast, and the seeming odds were at that time in favor of the Confederate forces, or to use a familiar term, "the rebel army." The agitation of enlisting colored soldiers was engaging public attention. Israel Church was only a couple of hundred yards from the United States Capitol, where mighty speeches were being made in the United States Congress in favor of enlisting colored men in the Union army. On several occasions I could be found in the galleries of the United States House of Representatives, listening attentively to such great men as Lovejoy, Henry Winter Davis, of Maryland; Kelley, of Philadelphia, and in the gallery of the Senate of the United States, while such men as Charles Sumner, of Boston; Wade, of Ohio; Wilson, of Massachusetts; Bishop Simpson, of the Methodist Episcopal Church, and others of great distinction and eloquence, either spoke or preached to the vast throng of listeners.

In 1862, on the 22d day of September, Mr. Lincoln issued a proclamation that in a hundred days, unless the rebel army disbanded, and the several Southern states resumed their relation to the general government, he would declare the slaves in all the states free with a few local exceptions. The newspapers of the country were prolific and unsparing in their laudations of Mr. Lincoln. Every orator after reviewing in their richest eloquence, concluded their speeches and orations by saying, "God save Abraham Lincoln," or "God bless our President." Mass-meetings were held in Baltimore, Philadelphia, New York, Boston, Cincinnati, Cleveland, St. Louis, San Francisco and hundreds of minor towns, and such a time I never expect to witness on earth in the future. I may witness such a time again in heaven, but not in the flesh.

In the great Union Cooper Hall in New York City, a colored man leaped and jumped with so much agility when the proclamation was read that he drew the attention of every man and woman, till Mr. Lincoln's proclamation was scarcely listened to. New songs were sung and new poems were composed, and the people shouted to such an extent that horses became frightened, and many ran away and smashed carriages into kindling wood. Whites and blacks realized no racial discriminations. On the first day of January, 1863, odd and unique conditions attended every mass-meeting, and the papers of the following day were not able to give them in anything like detail. Long before sunset Israel Church and its yard were crowded with people. The writer was vociferously cheered in every direction he went because in a sermon I tried to deliver I had said that Richmond, the headquarters of the Southern Confederacy, would never fall till black men led the army against this great slave-mart, nor did it fall and succumb to the general government till black men went in first. This was only a popular prediction, and delivered under a general excitement, but strange to say, it was fully realized.

Seeing such a multitude of people in and around my church, I hurriedly went up to the office of the first paper in which the proclamation of freedom could be printed, known as the "Evening Star," and squeezed myself through the dense crowd that was waiting for the paper. The first sheet run off with the proclamation in it was grabbed for by three of us, but some active young man got possession of it and fled. The next sheet was grabbed for by several, and was torn into tatters. The third sheet from the press was grabbed for by several, but I succeeded in procuring so much of it as contained the proclamation, and off I went for life and death. Down Pennsylvania Ave. I ran as for my life, and when the people saw me coming with the paper in my hand they raised a shouting cheer that was almost deafening. As many as could get around me lifted me to a great platform, and I started to read the proclamation. I had run the best end of a mile, I was out of breath, and could not read. Mr. Hinton, to whom I handed the paper, read it with great force and clearness. While he was reading every kind of demonstration and gesticulation was going on. Men squealed, women fainted, dogs barked, white and colored people shook hands, songs were sung, and by this time cannons began to fire at the navy-yard, and follow in the wake of the roar that had for some time been going on behind the

White House. Every face had a smile, and even the dumb animals seemed to realize that some extraordinary event had taken place. Great processions of colored and white men marched to and fro and passed in front of the White House and congratulated President Lincoln on his proclamation. The President came to the window and made responsive bows, and thousands told him, if he would come out of that palace, they would hug him to death. Mr. Lincoln, however, kept at a safe distance from the multitude, who were frenzied to distraction over his proclamation.

I do not know the extent that the excitement in Russia led to, when the humane Emperor proclaimed the freedom of twenty-two million serfs, I think in 1862, but the jubilation that attended the proclamation of freedom by His Excellency Abraham Lincoln, I am sure has never been surpassed, if it has ever been equaled. Nor do I believe it will ever be duplicated again. Rumor said that in several instances the very thought of being set at liberty and having no more auction blocks, no more Negro-traders, no more forced parting of man and wife, no more separation of parents and children, no more horrors of slavery, was so elative and heart gladdening that scores of colored people literally fell dead with joy. It was indeed a time of times, and a half time, nothing like it will ever be seen again in this life. Our entrance into Heaven itself will only form a counterpart. January 1st, 1913, will be fifty years since Mr. Lincoln's proclamation stirred the world and avalanched America with joy, and the first day of next January, 1913, our race should fill every Church, every hall, and every preacher regardless of denomination should deliver a speech on the results of the proclamation.

Source: Turner, Bishop H. M. "Reminiscences of the Proclamation of Emancipation." *African Methodist Episcopal Church Review* (January 1913): 211-14.

Fourth of July Celebrations in Oregon (1867, 1870s)

Related Holiday: Independence Day

These excerpts offer two eyewitness accounts of Independence Day celebrations in Oregon dating from the 1860s and 1870s. These accounts were later recorded by staff members of the Folklore Project, a division of the Federal Writers' Project. This group was part of the Works Projects Administration, a federal program that gave jobs to people who were unemployed during the Great Depression. From 1936 to 1940, staff members of the Folklore Project traveled around the U.S. and interviewed ordinary people about their local and personal histories and traditions. Both people interviewed in these excerpts were born during the 1850s and lived in Oregon in the first decades after Americans began settling the area, and both describe community-wide celebrations of the Fourth of July that were common during the 19th century. For another primary source related to Independence Day, see "The Declaration of Independence (1776)."

In this excerpt, James E. Twadell of Portland, Oregon, shares his memories of the first Independence Day festival in Uniontown, Oregon, in 1867. His memories were recorded in an interview on May 12, 1939.

I was at the first Fourth of July Celebration ever held in the Grande Ronde Valley. That was at Uniontown in 1867, located in the south end of the valley, near the canyon which cuts through the mountain there going to Baker. I saw all this stuff, mind you, but you probably won't believe me, because they never have nothing like it nowadays. They had the celebration in a beautiful grove, where they had erected three tables each three feet wide and a hundred yards long. The stuff was cooked by every one in the valley and brought there, and every one came and ate at no charge, whether he had contributed or not. And when the plates were empty, they were all refilled until everyone had enough. Underneath the tables ever so often was a big candy bucket set, a sort of tub like affair full of candy. And then they had a big parade. Music was furnished by tenor and bass drums and bugles. There were quite a few ex-soldiers there . . . maybe a company of about a hundred in the parade. Of course, it was shortly after the war, and not so many had come then as there were later.

In this excerpt, Nettie Spencer of Portland, Oregon, describes the Independence Day celebration in Corvallis, Oregon, during the 1870s. Her memories were recorded in an interview on December 14-15, 1938.

The big event of the year was the Fourth of July. Everyone in the countryside got together on that day for the only time in the year. The new babies were shown off, and the new brides who would be exhibiting babies next year. Everyone would load their wagons with all the food they could haul and come to town early in the morning. On our first big Fourth at Corvallis mother made two hundred gooseberry pies. You can see what an event it was. There would be floats in the morning and the one that got the girls' eye was the Goddess of Liberty. She was supposed to be the most wholesome and prettiest girl in the countryside — if she wasn't she had friends who thought she was. But the rest of us weren't always in agreement on that. She rode on a hay-rack and wore a white gown. Sometimes the driver wore an Uncle Sam hat and striped pants. All along the sides of the hay-rack were little girls who represented the states of the union. The smallest was always Rhode Island. (All this took place at Corvallis and the people from Albany used to come up river by boat.) Following the float would be the Oregon Agricultural College cadets, and some kind of a band. Sometimes there would be political effigies.

Just before lunch — and we'd always hold lunch up for an hour—some senator or lawyer would speak. These speeches always had one pattern. First the speaker would challenge England to a fight and berate the King and say that he was a skunk. This was known as twisting the lion's tail. Then the next theme was that any one could find freedom and liberty on our shores. The speaker would invite those who were heavy laden in other lands to come to us and find peace. The speeches were pretty fiery and by that time the men who drank got into fights and called each other Englishmen. In the afternoon we had what we called the "plug uglies" — funny floats and clowns who took off on the political subjects of the day. There would be some music and then the families would start gathering together to go home. There were cows waiting to be milked and the stock to be fed and so there was no night life. The Fourth was the day of the year that really counted then. Christmas wasn't much; a Church tree or something, but no one twisted the lion's tail.

Sources:

Excerpt 1: Twadell, James E. "American Life Histories: Manuscripts from the Federal Writers' Project, 1936-1940." Interview with James E. Twadell by Manly M. Banister. From the Library of Congress, 1939. http://memory.loc.gov/ammem/wpaintro/wpahome.html.

Excerpt 2: Spencer, Nettie. "American Life Histories: Manuscripts from the Federal Writers' Project, 1936-1940." Interview with Nettie Spencer by Walker Winslow. From the Library of Congress, 1938. http://memory.loc.gov/ammem/wpaintro/wpahome.html.

Memorial Day Observances in Washington, D.C. (ca. 1870, 1885)

Related Holiday: Memorial Day

These excerpts offer descriptions of Memorial Day observances in Washington, D.C., in the years after the Civil War. The authors' original spelling and punctuation are retained.

In this excerpt from her book Ten Years in Washington, *author and columnist Mary Clemmer Ames discusses two celebrations of Memorial Day around 1870. She contrasts the major ceremony at Arlington National Cemetery with a personal and poignant observance at a smaller cemetery.*

Last Saturday was Memorial Day. With banners and bands, music and speech under the softest of May skies, and in its serenest airs tens of thousands of our soldiers' graves were decorated with flowers. Most lovely was Arlington that day! No words could have been more eloquently fitting than those which were spoken; no music tenderer, nor fuller of precious memories, nor sweeter with suggestions of Heaven, than that sung under those patriarchal trees by fifty orphan children. And no sight could have been more touching than when these soldiers' orphans laid their flower-wreaths down upon ten thousand soldiers' graves. Yet the magnetism of the multitude was there. The tide followed the banners and the bands, the blooming maidens, the eloquent speech.

Miles out Seventh street, beyond Fort Stevens, there is a little cemetery where forty soldiers lie alone, who fell in defence of Washington. One of these was a poor widow's son. She had three; and this was the last that she gave to her country. She, a poor widow, living far in northern Vermont, has never even seen the graves of her three soldier sons, whom she gave up, one by one, as they came to man's estate; and who went forth from her love to return to it living no more.

To this little grave-yard on Seventh street one woman went alone with her children, carrying forty wreaths of May's loveliest flowers, and laid one on every grave. Forty mother's sons slept under the green turf; and one mother, in her large love, remembered and consecrated them all. She chose these because, with more than thirty thousand others in the larger cemeteries to be decorated, she feared the forty, in their isolation, might be forgotten. No others followed her;

and this mother, alone with her children, scattering flowers in the silence of love upon those unremembered graves, some way wears a halo which does not shine about the multitude.

We look on Arlington through softest airs. How beautiful it is! how sad it is! how holy! Again the tender spring grasses have crept over its sixteen thousand graves. The innocents, the violets of the woods, are blooming over the heads of our brave. In the rear of the house a granite obelisk has been raised to the two thousand who sleep in one grave. Four cannon point from its summit, and on its face it bears this inscription: —

> "Beneath this stone repose the bones of two thousand one hundred and eleven unknown soldiers, gathered after the war from the fields of Bull Run, and the route to the Rappahannock. Their ~~bodies~~remains could not be identified, but their names and deaths are recorded in the archives of their country, and its grateful citizens honor them as their noble army of martyrs. May they rest in peace."

The rooms and conservatories of the house are filled with luxurious plants, soon to be set out on the graves of this cemetery. Beauty and silence reign through this domain of the dead. There is a hush in the air, and a hush in the heart, as you walk through it, reading its names, pausing by the graves of its "unknown," thinking of the past. Far as the sight reaches, stretch the long columns of immortal dead. The beauty of their sleeping-place, the reverent care covering it everywhere, tells how dear to the Nation's heart is the dust of its heroes, how sacred the spot where they lie. In this let us not forget the still higher love which we owe them; let us attest it by a deeper devotion to the principles for which they died.

In this excerpt from her book American Court Gossip, *Mrs. E. N. Chapin describes Memorial Day observances in the nation's capital in 1885.*

On the 30th of May, 1885, Decoration Day [Memorial Day] came in a mist and rain and the exercises at the different National cemeteries were solemn, indeed, to the anxious old soldiers of the city. The President, Col. Vilas, Secretaries Endicott and Whitney went to New York to witness the ceremonies of Union Square, and from the published reports seemed to be in sympathy with the occasion.

The exercises on the classic grounds of the Congressional cemetery were opened by the Glee Club, and an oration by Col. McLean, of Indiana, the new Deputy Commissioner of Pensions. Considering, that he was trying to harmonize the apparent incongruity of rebels on top, and lauding their victors for licking them, it was a very excellent speech. He said among other good things, "Providence was with the Union army, and none knew it better than the rebels." The exercises were under the direction of Captain Pipes, a brave soldier, whose empty sleeve told the story of his devotion to his country's call. Another feeble soldier, (who died a few months, afterward,) Captain Richard Middleton was Chairman of the Decorating Committee and with his wife and another lady tramped all the morning through the rain, and they showered roses, never so beautiful as on this May day, covering the green mounds with heaps of smiling flowers. Others helped until the whole cemetery was a flower garden, and not a lonely stretch of marble and solemn pines. At Arlington cemetery, where nearly 16,000 of "our brave boys" lie buried—the graves marked by the little slabs and tiny flags, made a peculiar sight, as the wind lifted their folds of red, white and blue against the marble standing upon the close shaven green of the turf below. . . .

The decoration exercises were mostly under the direction of General S. S. Burdette, late Grand Commander of the G.A.R. *[Grand Army of the Republic],* and his speech of an hour's length was brim full of eloquence and patriotic sentiment. The Memorial stand is a long grassy esplanade, bricked up in front, and then descends backward to the acres of marble, stretching to the stone wall, which encloses the sacred dust.

Over the seats and platform was thrown an immense tent decorated with national flags, and draped with streamers of red, white and blue, although some careful hand had trained sweet scented honeysuckles and ivy all over the unsightly props and braces. Beyond the Arlington enclosure is Fort Meyer —a real fort and signal office. There is a large magazine, guard house, and ammunition in abundance. The sunset gun is heard daily in the city. But we digress and go back to the Decoration programme.

The Orpheus Club, a band of colored men, twelve in number, with remarkably fine voices, gave that pathetic number the "Sleeping Soldier" in such harmony, that there was not a dry eye in the whole assembly, and there were hundreds present, who dared to show, then, their love for the old soldier.

The regular army had no officer present, but Generals Greene B. Raum and Col. Alexander, Fifth Auditor of the Treasury, were on the platform.

The graves of that heroic band of war nurses were decorated by the Washington Association, wherever their fellow laborers had fallen in different parts of the country. Mrs. Helen Speare had lately died at Pittsburg. There was such a call for flowers that Miss Cleveland was appealed to the day before Decoration, asking for a small supply from the White House. The request was gracefully acknowledged by the lady, and the box upon being opened presented a glowing mass of purple passion flowers and pansies, white camelias and roses—white carnations and a soft mass of ferns. A note came with the messenger, which read as follows:

Executive Mansion, Washington, D. C., May 29, 1885.

My Dear Mrs. S—d: I am very happy to contribute toward the basket of flowers which you intend sending for the grave of the army nurse—Mrs. Helen Speare.

Yours very truly, Elizabeth Cleveland.

[Elizabeth Cleveland was President Grover Cleveland's sister; she was the White House hostess until Cleveland married Frances Folsom in 1886.]

Sources:

Excerpt 1: Ames, Mary Clemmer. *Ten Years in Washington. Life and Scenes in the National Capital, as a Woman Sees Them.* Hartford, Conn.: A. D. Worthington & Co., 1873.

Excerpt 2: Chapin, Mrs. E. N. *American Court Gossip; Or, Life at the National Capitol.* Marshalltown, Iowa: Chapin & Hartwell Bros., 1887.

A Columbus Day Program by Francis Bellamy (1892)

Related Holidays: Columbus Day, Flag Day

In 1892, Francis Bellamy was a writer for the magazine The Youth's Companion. *He arranged a school program for the 400th anniversary of the landfall of Christopher Columbus. The program, reprinted below, includes the first appearance of the Pledge of Allegiance, which was also written by Bellamy. One portion of the program later became controversial. In 1942, the salute to the flag that Bellamy suggested was deemed too similar to the Nazi salute and was replaced by the current gesture—placing the right hand over the heart. In the program included below, Bellamy's original spelling and punctuation are retained. For another primary source related to Columbus Day, see "Excerpts from the Journal of Christopher Columbus (1492)"; for another primary source related to Flag Day, see "Flag Laws and Regulations (1942; amended 1998)."*

National School Celebration of Columbus Day: The Official Programme

(Prepared by Executive Committee, Francis Bellamy, Chairman)

The schools should assemble at 9 A.M. in their various rooms. At 9:30 the detail of Veterans is expected to arrive. It is to be met at the entrance of the yard by the Color-Guard of pupils, — escorted with dignity to the building, and presented to the Principal. The Principal then gives the signal, and the several teachers conduct their students to the yard, to beat of drum or other music, and arrange them in a hollow square about the flag, the Veterans and Color-Guard taking places by the flag itself. The Master of Ceremonies then gives the command "Attention!" and begins the exercises by reading the Proclamation.

1. READING OF THE PRESIDENT'S PROCLAMATION—by the Master of Ceremonies

At the close of the reading he announces, "In accordance with this recommendation by the President of the United States, and as a sign of our devotion to our country, let the Flag of the Nation be unfurled above this School."

2. RAISING OF THE FLAG—by the Veterans

As the Flag reaches the top of the staff, the Veterans will lead the assemblage in "Three Cheers for 'Old Glory.' "

3. SALUTE TO THE FLAG—by the Pupils

At a signal from the Principal the pupils, in ordered ranks, hands to the side, face the Flag. Another signal is given; every pupil gives the flag the military salute—right hand lifted, palm downward, to a line with the forehead and close to it. Standing thus, all repeat together, slowly, "I pledge allegiance to my Flag and the Republic for which it stands; one Nation indivisible, with Liberty and Justice for all." At the words, "to my Flag," the right hand is extended gracefully, palm upward, toward the Flag, and remains in this gesture till the end of the affirmation; whereupon all hands immediately drop to the side. Then, still standing, as the instruments strike a chord, all will sing AMERICA—"My Country, 'tis of Thee."

4. ACKNOWLEDGMENT OF GOD—Prayer or Scripture

5. SONG OF COLUMBUS DAY—by Pupils and Audience

Contributed by The Youth's Companion Air: Lyons
Columbia, my land! All hail the glad day
When first to thy strand Hope pointed the way.
Hail him who thro' darkness first followed the Flame
That led where the Mayflower of Liberty came.
Dear Country, the star of the valiant and free!
Thy exiles afar are dreaming of thee.
No fields of the Earth so enchantingly shine,
No air breathes such incense, such music as thine.
Humanity's home! Thy sheltering breast
Give welcome and room to strangers oppress'd.
Pale children of Hunger and Hatred and Wrong
Find life in thy freedom and joy in thy song.
Thy fairest estate the lowly may hold,
Thy poor may grow great, thy feeble grow bold
For worth is the watchword to noble degree,
And manhood is mighty where manhood is free.
O Union of States, and union of souls!
Thy promise awaits, thy future unfolds,
And earth from her twilight is hailing the sun,
That rises where people and rulers are one.
Theron Brown

6. THE ADDRESS

"The Meaning of the Four Centuries" A Declamation of the Special Address prepared for the occasion by The Youth's Companion.

7. THE ODE

"Columbia's Banner," A Reading of the Poem written for the Occasion by Edna Dean Proctor.

Here should follow whatever additional Exercises, Patriotic Recitations, Historic Representations, or Chorals may be desired.

8. ADDRESSES BY CITIZENS, and National Songs.

Source: Bellamy, Francis. *The Youth's Companion* (September 8, 1892): 446-47.

The Pullman Workers' Strike (1894)

Related Holiday: Labor Day

In 1894, workers at the Pullman Palace Car Company in Illinois went on a protracted strike. Their actions led the U.S. Congress to create Labor Day as a federal holiday. The series of excerpts below reflects the hardships suffered by the strikers and the efforts of Illinois Governor John P. Altgeld to resolve the crisis, as he repeatedly wrote to George M. Pullman, president of the Pullman Palace Car Company. U.S. President Grover Cleveland sent troops to break the strike, and the American Railway Union ended the strike on August 3, 1894. The Pullman Company hired many replacement workers and refused to take back workers who had struck unless they signed an agreement stating they would not join a union.

In June 1894, the following statement of the Pullman strikers was presented to the American Railway Union's convention in Chicago to enlist its support.

Mr. President and Brothers of the American Railway Union: We struck at Pullman because we were without hope. We joined the American Railway Union because it gave us a glimmer of hope. Twenty thousand souls, men, women, and little ones, have their eyes turned toward this convention today, straining eagerly through dark despondency for a glimmer of the heaven-sent message you alone can give us on this earth.

In stating to this body our grievances it is hard to tell where to begin. You all must know that the proximate cause of our strike was the discharge of two members of our grievance committee the day after George M. Pullman, himself, and Thomas H. Wickes, his second vice-president, had guaranteed them absolute immunity. The more remote causes are still imminent. Five reductions in wages, in work, and in conditions of employment swept through the shops at Pullman between May and December, 1893. The last was the most severe, amounting to nearly 30 percent, and our rents had not fallen. We owed Pullman $70,000 when we struck May 11. We owe him twice as much today. He does not evict us for two reasons: One, the force of popular sentiment and public opinion; the other because he hopes to starve us out, to break through in the back of the American Railway Union, and to deduct from our miserable wages when we are forced to return to him the last dollar we owe him for the occupancy of his houses.

Rents all over the city in every quarter of its vast extent have fallen, in some cases to one-half. Residences, compared with which ours are hovels, can be had a few miles away at the prices we have been contributing to make a millionaire a billionaire. What we pay $15 for in Pullman is leased for $8 in Roseland; and remember that just as no man or woman of our 4,000 toilers has ever felt the friendly pressure of George M. Pullman's hand, so no man or woman of us all has ever owned or can ever hope to own one inch of George M. Pullman's land. Why, even the very streets are his. . . . He may debar any man . . . from walking in his highways. And those streets; do you know what he has named them? He says after the four great inventors in methods of transportation. And do you know what their names are? Why, Fulton, Stephenson, Watt, and Pullman. . . .

When we went to tell him our grievances he said we were all his "children." Pullman, both the man and the town, is an ulcer on the body politic. He owns the houses, the schoolhouses, and churches of God in the town he gave his once humble name. The revenue he derives from these, the wages he pays out with one hand — the Pullman Palace Car Company, he takes back with the other — the Pullman Land Association. He is able by this to bid under any contract car shop in this country. His competitors in business, to meet this, must reduce the wages of their men. This gives him the excuse to reduce ours to conform to the market. His business rivals must in turn scale down; so must he. And thus the merry war — the dance of skeletons bathed in human tears — goes on, and it will go on, brothers, forever, unless you, the American Railway Union, stop it; end it; crush it out.

Our town is beautiful. In all these thirteen years no word of scandal has arisen against one of our women, young or old. What city of 20,000 persons can show the like? Since our strike, the arrests, which used to average four or five a day, has dwindled down to less than one a week. We are peaceable; we are orderly, and but for the kindly beneficence of kindly-hearted people in and about Chicago we would be starving. We are not desperate today, because we are not hungry, and our wives and children are not begging for bread. But George M. Pullman, who ran away from the public opinion that has arisen against him, like the genie from the bottle in the Arabian Nights, is not feeding us. He is patiently seated beside his millions waiting for what? To see us starve. We have grown better acquainted with the American Railway Union these convention days, and as we have heard sentiments of the noblest philanthropy fall from the lips of our general officers — your officers and ours — we have learned that there is a balm for all our troubles, and that the box containing it is in your hands today only awaiting opening to disseminate its sweet savor of hope.

George M. Pullman, you know, has cut our wages from 30 to 70 percent. George M. Pullman has caused to be paid in the last year the regular quarterly dividend of 2 percent on his stock and an extra slice of 1 1/2 percent, making 9 1/2 percent on $30,000,000 of capital. George M. Pullman, you know, took three contracts on which he lost less than $5,000. Because he loved us? No. Because it was cheaper to lose a little money in his freight car and his coach shops than to let his workingmen go, but that petty loss, more than made up by us from money we needed to clothe our wives and little ones, was his excuse for effecting a gigantic reduction of wages in every department of his great works, of cutting men and boys and girls; with equal zeal, including everyone in the repair shops of the Pullman Palace cars on which such preposterous profits have been made. . . .

We will make you proud of us, brothers, if you will give us the hand we need. Help us make our country better and more wholesome. Pull us out of our slough of despond. Teach arrogant grinders of the faces of the poor that there is still a God in Israel, and if need be a Jehovah—a God of battles. Do this, and on that last great day you will stand, as we hope to stand, before the great white throne "like gentlemen unafraid."

On August 17, 1894, a committee of former Pullman strikers wrote this letter to Governor John P. Altgeld after the company refused to give them back their jobs.

Kensington, Ill.,

August 17, 1894.

To His Excellency, the Governor of the State of Illinois:

We, the people of Pullman, who, by the greed and oppression of George M. Pullman, have been brought to a condition where starvation stares us in the face, do hereby appeal to you for aid in this our hour of need. We have been refused employment and have no means of leaving this vicinity, and our families are starving. Our places have been filled with workmen from all over the United States, brought here by the Pullman Company, and the surplus were turned away to walk the streets and starve also. There are over 1600 families here in destitution and want, and their condition is pitiful. We have exhausted all the means at our command to feed them, and we now make this appeal to you as a last resource. Trusting that God will influence you in our behalf and that you will give this your prompt attention, we remain,

Yours in distress,
THE STARVING CITIZENS OF PULLMAN
F. E. POLLANS,
L. J. NEWELL,
THEO. RODHE,
Committee.

In response to the above letter, Governor Altgeld appealed to George M. Pullman, president of the Pullman Palace Car Company, to rehire the former strikers.

August 19, 1894.

To George M. Pullman, President Pullman Palace Car Co., Chicago:

Sir:—I have received numerous reports to the effect that there is great distress at Pullman. To-day I received a formal appeal as Governor from a committee of the Pullman people for aid. They state that sixteen hundred families including women and children, are starving; that they cannot get work and have not the means to go elsewhere; that your company has brought men from all over the United States to fill their places. Now these people live in your town and were your employees. Some of them worked for your company for many years. They must be people of industry and character or you would not have kept them. Many of them have practically given their lives to you. It is claimed they struck because after years of toil their loaves were so reduced that their children went hungry. Assuming that they were wrong and foolish, they had yet served you long and well and you must feel some interest in them. They do not stand on the same footing with you, so that much must be overlooked. The State of Illinois has not the least desire to meddle in the affairs of your company, but it cannot allow a whole community within its borders to perish of hunger. The local overseer of the poor has been appealed to, but there is a limit to what he can do. I cannot help them very much at present. So unless relief comes from some other source I shall either have to call an extra session of the Legislature to make special appropriations, or else issue an appeal to the humane people of the State to give bread to your recent employees. It seems to me that you would prefer to relieve the situation yourself, especially as it has just cost the State upwards of fifty thousand dollars to protect your property, and both the State and the public have suffered enormous loss and expense on account of disturbances that grew out of trouble between your company and its workmen. I am going to Chicago to-night to make a personal investigation before taking any official action. I will be at my office in the Unity block at 10 A.M. to-morrow, and shall be glad to hear from you if you care to make any reply.

JOHN P. ALTGELD, Governor.

After visiting the former strikers, Governor Altgeld again urged Pullman to remedy their situation.

August 21st, 1894.

Mr. George M. Pullman, President Pullman Car Company, Chicago, Ill.:

Sir: — I have examined the conditions at Pullman yesterday, visited even the kitchens and bedrooms of many of the people. Two representatives of your company were with me and we found the distress as great as it was represented. The men are hungry and the women and children are actually suffering. They have been living on charity for a number of months and it is exhausted. Men who had worked for your company for more than ten years had to apply to the relief society in two weeks after the work stopped.

I learn from your manager that last spring there were 3,260 people on the pay roll; yesterday there were 2,200 at work, but over 600 of these are new men, so that only about 1,600 of the old employees have been taken back, thus leaving over 1600 of the old employees who have not been taken back, a few hundred have left, the remainder have nearly all applied for work, but were told that they were not needed. These are utterly destitute. The relief committee on last Saturday gave out two pounds of oat meal and two pounds of corn meal to each family. But even the relief committee has exhausted its resources.

Something must be done at once. The case differs from instances of destitution found elsewhere, for generally there is somebody in the neighborhood able to give relief; this is not the case at Pullman. Even those who have gone to work are so exhausted that they cannot help their neighbors if they would. I repeat now that it seems to me your company cannot afford to have me appeal to the charity and humanity of the State to save the lives of your old employes. Four-fifths of those people are women and children. No matter what caused this distress, it must be met.

If you will allow me, I will make this suggestion: If you had shut down your works last fall when you say business was poor, you would not have expected to get any rent for your tenements. Now, while a dollar is a large sum to each of these people, all the rent now due you is a comparatively small matter to you. If you would cancel all rent to October 1st, you would be as well off as if you had shut down. This would enable those who are at work to meet their most pressing wants. Then if you cannot give work to all why work some half-time so that all can at least get something to eat for their families. This will give immediate relief to the whole situation. And then by degrees assist as many to go elsewhere as desire to do so, and all to whom you cannot give work. In this way something like a normal condition could be re-established at Pullman before winter and you would not be out any more than you would have been had you shut down a year ago.

I will be at the Unity block for several hours and will be glad to see you if you care to make any reply.

Yours, respectfully,
JOHN P. ALTGELD.

Governor Altgeld wrote this final impassioned communication to Pullman.

Chicago, August 21st, 1894.

George M. Pullman, Esq., President Pullman Palace Car Company, City.

Sir:—I have your answer to my communication of this morning. I see by it that your company refuses to do anything toward relieving the situation at Pullman. It is true that Mr. Wickes offered to take me to Pullman and show me around. I told him that I had no objections to his going, but that I doubted the wisdom of my going under anybody's wing. I was, however, met at the depot by two of your representatives, both able men, who accompanied me everywhere. I took pains to have them present in each case. I also called at your office and got what information they could give me there, so that your company was represented and heard, and no man there questioned either the condition of the extent of the suffering. If you will make the round I made, go into the houses of the people, meet them face to face and talk with them, you will be convinced that none of them had $1,300, or any other some of money only a few weeks ago.

I cannot enter into a discussion with you as to the merits of the controversy between you and your former workmen.

It is not my business to fix the moral responsibility in this case. There are nearly six thousand people suffering for the want of food—they were your employees—four-fifths of them women and children—some of these people have worked for you for more than twelve years. I assumed that even if they were wrong and had been foolish, you would not be willing to see them perish. I also assumed that as the State had just been to a large expense to protect your property you would not want to have the public shoulder the burden of relieving distress in your town.

As you refuse to do anything to relieve suffering in this case, I am compelled to appeal to the humanity of the people of Illinois to do so.

Respectfully yours,
JOHN P. ALTGELD

Sources:

Excerpt 1: Statement of the Pullman Strikers, U.S. Strike Commission. *Report and Testimony on the Chicago Strike of 1894*. Washington, D.C.: Government Printing Office, 1895.

Excerpts 2-5: Altgeld, John. *Live Questions*. Chicago: George S. Bowen and Son, 1899.

President Franklin D. Roosevelt's Speech after the Attack on Pearl Harbor (1941)

Related Holiday: National Pearl Harbor Remembrance Day

On December 7, 1941, the United States suffered a terrible attack that would ultimately lead the nation into World War II. Japanese airplanes and submarines struck the U.S. Pacific Fleet, stationed at a naval base at Pearl Harbor in Hawaii. The attack damaged or destroyed 21 naval vessels and more than 150 aircraft, killed or wounded 3,000 U.S. military personnel, and killed 68 American civilians. The following day, December 8, 1941, President Franklin D. Roosevelt delivered this speech to Congress and the nation, asking Congress to declare war against Japan.

Joint Address to Congress Leading to a Declaration of War Against Japan
December 8, 1941

Mr. Vice President, and Mr. Speaker, and Members of the Senate and House of Representatives:

Yesterday, December 7, 1941—a date which will live in infamy—the United States of America was suddenly and deliberately attacked by naval and air forces of the Empire of Japan.

The United States was at peace with that Nation and, at the solicitation of Japan, was still in conversation with its Government and its Emperor looking toward the maintenance of peace in the Pacific. Indeed, one hour after Japanese air squadrons had commenced bombing in the American Island of Oahu, the Japanese Ambassador to the United States and his colleague delivered to our Secretary of State a formal reply to a recent American message. And while this reply stated that it seemed useless to continue the existing diplomatic negotiations, it contained no threat or hint of war or of armed attack.

It will be recorded that the distance of Hawaii from Japan makes it obvious that the attack was deliberately planned many days or even weeks ago. During the intervening time the Japanese Government has deliberately sought to deceive the United States by false statements and expressions of hope for continued peace.

The attack yesterday on the Hawaiian Islands has caused severe damage to American naval and military forces. I regret to tell you that very many American lives have been lost. In addition American ships have been reported torpedoed on the high seas between San Francisco and Honolulu.

Yesterday the Japanese Government also launched an attack against Malaya.
Last night Japanese forces attacked Hong Kong.
Last night Japanese forces attacked Guam.
Last night Japanese forces attacked the Philippine Islands.
Last night the Japanese attacked Wake Island. And this morning the Japanese attacked Midway Island.

Japan has, therefore, undertaken a surprise offensive extending throughout the Pacific area. The facts of yesterday and today speak for themselves. The people of the United States have already formed their opinions and well understand the implications to the very life and safety of our Nation.

As Commander in Chief of the Army and Navy I have directed that all measures be taken for our defense.

But always will our whole Nation remember the character of the onslaught against us.

No matter how long it may take us to overcome this premeditated invasion, the American people in their righteous might will win through to absolute victory. I believe that I interpret the will of the Congress and of the people when I assert that we will not only defend ourselves to the uttermost but will make it very certain that this form of treachery shall never again endanger us.

Hostilities exist. There is no blinking at the fact that our people, our territory, and our interests are in grave danger.

With confidence in our armed forces—with the unbounding determination of our people—we will gain the inevitable triumph—so help us God.

I ask that the Congress declare that since the unprovoked and dastardly attack by Japan on Sunday, December 7, 1941, a state of war has existed between the United States and the Japanese Empire.

Source: Roosevelt, Franklin D. "Joint Address to Congress Leading to a Declaration of War Against Japan." Transcription from the Franklin D. Roosevelt Presidential Library and Museum. From the U.S. National Archives and Records Administration, 1941. http://www.ourdocuments.gov/doc.php?flash=true&doc=73.

Flag Laws and Regulations (1942; amended 1998)

Related Holiday: Flag Day

The laws relating to the flag of the United States of America are currently found in detail in the United States Code, Title 4, Chapter 1. On June 22, 1942, when President Franklin D. Roosevelt originally approved the laws, popularly known as the Flag Code, they appeared in Title 36 of the U.S. Code of laws. In 1998 Congress moved the Flag Code from Title 36 to Title 4 with some changes.

Title 4 United States Code

§4. Pledge of Allegiance to the Flag; Manner of Delivery

The Pledge of Allegiance to the Flag, "I pledge allegiance to the Flag of the United States of America, and to the Republic for which it stands, one Nation under God, indivisible, with liberty and justice for all.", should be rendered by standing at attention facing the flag with the right hand over the heart. When not in uniform men should remove their headdress with their right hand and hold it at the left shoulder, the hand being over the heart. Persons in uniform should remain silent, face the flag, and render the military salute.

§5. Display and Use of Flag by Civilians; Codification of Rules and Customs; Definition

The following codification of existing rules and customs pertaining to the display and use of the flag of the United States of America is established for the use of such civilians or civilian groups or organizations as may not be required to conform with regulations promulgated by one or more executive departments of the Government of the United States. The flag of the United States for the purpose of this chapter shall be defined according to sections 1 and 2 of this title and Executive Order 10834 issued pursuant thereto.

§6. Time and Occasions for Display

(a) It is the universal custom to display the flag only from sunrise to sunset on buildings and on stationary flagstaffs in the open. However, when a patriotic effect is desired, the flag may be displayed 24 hours a day if properly illuminated during the hours of darkness.

(b) The flag should be hoisted briskly and lowered ceremoniously.

(c) The flag should not be displayed on days when the weather is inclement, except when an all-weather flag is displayed.

(d) The flag should be displayed on all days, especially on New Year's Day, January 1; Inauguration Day, January 20; Martin Luther King Jr.'s birthday, the third Monday in January; Lincoln's Birthday, February 12; Washington's Birthday, third Monday in February; Easter Sunday (variable), Mother's Day, second Sunday in May; Armed Forces Day, third Saturday in May: Memorial Day (half-staff until noon), the last Monday in May; Flag Day, June 14; Independence Day, July 4; Labor Day, first Monday in September; Constitution Day, September 17; Columbus Day, second Monday in October; Navy Day, October 27; Veterans Day, November 11; Thanksgiving Day, fourth Thursday in November; Christmas Day, December 25; and such other days as may be proclaimed by the President of the United States; the birthdays of States (date of admission); and on State holidays.

(e) The flag should be displayed daily on or near the main administration building of every public institution.

(f) The flag should be displayed in or near every polling place on election days.

(g) The flag should be displayed during school days in or near every schoolhouse.

§7. Position and Manner of Display

The flag, when carried in a procession with another flag or flags, should be either on the marching right; that is, the flag's own right, or, if there is a line of other flags, in front of the center of that line.

(a) The flag should not be displayed on a float in a parade except from a staff, or as provided in subsection (i) of this section.

(b) The flag should not be draped over the hood, top, sides, or back of a vehicle or of a railroad train or a boat. When the flag is displayed on a motorcar, the staff shall be fixed firmly to the chassis or clamped to the right fender.

(c) No other flag or pennant should be placed above or, if on the same level, to the right of the flag of the United States of America, except during church services conducted by naval chaplains at sea, when the church pennant may be flown above the flag during church services for the personnel of the Navy. No person shall display the flag of the United Nations or any other national or international flag equal, above, or in a position of superior prominence or honor to, or in place of, the flag of the United States at any place within the United States or any Territory or possession thereof. Provided, That nothing in this section shall make unlawful the continuance of the practice heretofore followed of displaying the flag of the United Nations in a position of superior prominence or honor, and other national flags in positions of equal prominence or honor, with that of the flag of the United States at the headquarters of the United Nations.

(d) The flag of the United States of America, when it is displayed with another flag against a wall from crossed staffs, should be on the right, the flag's own right, and its staff should be in front of the staff of the other flag.

(e) The flag of the United States of America should be at the center and at the highest point of the group when a number of flags of States or localities or pennants of societies are grouped and displayed from staffs.

(f) When flags of States, cities, or localities, or pennants of societies are flown on the same halyard with the flag of the United States, the latter should always be at the peak. When the flags are flown from adjacent staffs, the flag of the United States should be hoisted first and lowered last. No such flag or pennant may be placed above the flag of the United States or to the United States flag's right.

(g) When flags of two or more nations are displayed, they are to be flown from separate staffs of the same height. The flags should be of approximately equal size. International usage forbids the display of the flag of one nation above that of another nation in time of peace.

(h) When the flag of the United States is displayed from a staff projecting horizontally or at an angle from the window sill, balcony, or front of a building, the union of the flag should be placed at the peak of the staff unless the flag is at half-staff.

When the flag is suspended over a sidewalk from a rope extending from a house to a pole at the edge of the sidewalk, the flag should be hoisted out, union first, from the building.

(i) When displayed either horizontally or vertically against a wall, the union should be uppermost and to the flag's own right, that is, to the observer's left. When displayed in a window, the flag should be displayed in the same way, with the union or blue field to the left of the observer in the street.

(j) When the flag is displayed over the middle of the street, it should be suspended vertically with the union to the north in an east and west street or to the east in a north and south street.

(k) When used on a speaker's platform, the flag, if displayed flat, should be displayed above and behind the speaker. When displayed from a staff in a church or public auditorium, the flag of the United States of America should hold the position of superior prominence, in advance of the audience, and in the position of honor at the clergyman's or speaker's right as he faces the audience. Any other flag so displayed should be placed on the left of the clergyman or speaker or to the right of the audience.

(l) The flag should form a distinctive feature of the ceremony of unveiling a statue or monument, but it should never be used as the covering for the statue or monument.

(m) The flag, when flown at half-staff, should be first hoisted to the peak for an instant and then lowered to the half-staff position. The flag should be again raised to the peak before it is lowered for the day. On Memorial Day the flag should be displayed at half-staff until noon only, then raised to the top of the staff. By order of the President, the flag shall be flown at half-staff upon the death of principal figures of the United States Government and the Governor of a State, territory, or possession, as a mark of respect to their memory. In the event of the death of other officials or foreign dignitaries, the flag is to be displayed at half-staff according to Presidential instructions or orders, or in accordance with recognized customs or practices not inconsistent with law. In the event of the death of a present or former official of the government of any State, territory, or possession of the United States, the Governor of that State, territory, or possession may proclaim that the National flag shall be flown at half-staff. The flag shall be flown at half-staff thirty days from the death of the President or a former President; ten days from the day of death of the Vice-President, the Chief Justice or a retired Chief Justice of the United States, or the Speaker of the House of Representatives; from the day of death until interment of an Associate Justice of the Supreme Court, a Secretary of an executive or military department, a former Vice-President, or the Governor of a State, territory, or possession; and on the day of death and the following day for a Member of Congress. The flag shall be flown at half-staff on Peace Officers Memorial Day, unless that day is also Armed Forces Day. As used in this subsection—

   (1) the term "half-staff" means the position of the flag when it is one-half the distance between the top and bottom of the staff;

   (2) the term "executive or military department" means any agency listed under sections 101 and 102 of Title 5, United States Code; and

   (3) the term "Member of Congress" means a Senator, a Representative, a Delegate, or the Resident Commissioner from Puerto Rico.

(n) When the flag is used to cover a casket, it should be so placed that the union is at the head and over the left shoulder. The flag should not be lowered into the grave or allowed to touch the ground.

(o) When the flag is suspended across a corridor or lobby in a building with only one main entrance, it should be suspended vertically with the union of the flag to the observer's left upon entering. If the building has more than one main entrance, the flag should be suspended vertically near the center of the corridor or lobby with the union to the north, when entrances are to the east and west or to the east when entrances are to the north and south. If there are entrances in more than two directions, the union should be to the east.

§8. Respect for the Flag

No disrespect should be shown to the flag of the United States of America; the flag should not be dipped to any person or thing. Regimental colors, State flags, and organization or institutional flags are to be dipped as a mark of honor.

(a) The flag should never be displayed with the union down, except as a signal of dire distress in instances of extreme danger to life or property.

(b) The flag should never touch anything beneath it, such as the ground, the floor, water, or merchandise.

(c) The flag should never be carried flat or horizontally, but always aloft and free.

(d) The flag should never be used as wearing apparel, bedding, or drapery. It should never be festooned, drawn back, nor up, in folds, but always allowed to fall free. Bunting of blue, white, and red, always arranged with the blue above, the white in the middle, and the red below, should be used for covering a speaker's desk, draping the front of the platform, and for decoration in general.

(e) The flag should never be fastened, displayed, used, or stored in such a manner as to permit it to be easily torn, soiled, or damaged in any way.

(f) The flag should never be used as a covering for a ceiling.

(g) The flag should never have placed upon it, nor on any part of it, nor attached to it any mark, insignia, letter, word, figure, design, picture, or drawing of any nature.

(h) The flag should never be used as a receptacle for receiving, holding, carrying, or delivering anything.

(i) The flag should never be used for advertising purposes in any manner whatsoever. It should not be embroidered on such articles as cushions or handkerchiefs and the like, printed or otherwise impressed on paper napkins or boxes or anything that is designed for temporary use and discard. Advertising signs should not be fastened to a staff or halyard from which the flag is flown.

j) No part of the flag should ever be used as a costume or athletic uniform. However, a flag patch may be affixed to the uniform of military personnel, firemen, policemen, and members of patriotic organizations. The flag represents a living country and is itself considered a living thing. Therefore, the lapel flag pin being a replica, should be worn on the left lapel near the heart.

(k) The flag, when it is in such condition that it is no longer a fitting emblem for display, should be destroyed in a dignified way, preferably by burning.

§9. Conduct during Hoisting, Lowering or Passing of Flag

During the ceremony of hoisting or lowering the flag or when the flag is passing in a parade or in review, all persons present except those in uniform should face the flag and stand at attention with the right hand over the heart. Those present in uniform should render the military salute. When not in uniform, men should remove their headdress with their right hand and hold it at the left shoulder, the hand being over the heart. Aliens should stand at attention. The salute to the flag in a moving column should be rendered at the moment the flag passes.

§10. Modification of Rules and Customs by President

Any rule or custom pertaining to the display of the flag of the United States of America, set forth herein, may be altered, modified, or repealed, or additional rules with respect thereto may be prescribed, by the Commander-in-Chief of the Armed Forces of the United States, whenever he deems it to be appropriate or desirable; and any such alteration or additional rule shall be set forth in a proclamation.

Source: The Flag. United States Code, Title 4, Chapter 1. From the U.S Government Printing Office, 1998. http://www.access.gpo.gov/uscode/title4/chapter1_.html.

"I Have a Dream," Address at March on Washington for Jobs and Freedom (1963)

Related Holiday: Martin Luther King Jr. Birthday

In the early 1960s, the civil rights movement in the United States was fighting for equality and civil rights. Several groups together organized a huge march on August 28, 1963, in Washington, D.C. About 250,000 people gathered there, the largest crowd that had ever assembled on the Mall in Washington. Martin Luther King Jr. stood in front of the Lincoln Memorial, in homage to the man who 100 years earlier took the first step toward outlawing slavery in the United States, and delivered his most famous speech, included below. To many listeners, then and today, his moving words articulated the goals of the civil rights movement. For other primary sources related to the Martin Luther King Jr. Birthday, see "U.S. Representative William Lacy Clay Discusses the 40th Anniversary of the 1963 March on Washington (2003)" and "U.S. Representative John Conyers Jr. Reflects on the Significance of Martin Luther King Jr. Day (2004)."

28 August 1963
Washington, D. C.

I am happy to join with you today in what will go down in history as the greatest demonstration for freedom in the history of our nation. [*applause*]

Fivescore years ago, a great American, in whose symbolic shadow we stand today, signed the Emancipation Proclamation. This momentous decree came as a great beacon light of hope to millions of Negro slaves who had been seared in the flames of withering injustice. It came as a joyous daybreak to end the long night of their captivity.

But one hundred years later, the Negro still is not free. [*Audience:*] (*My Lord*) One hundred years later, the life of the Negro is still sadly crippled by the manacles of segregation and the chains of discrimination. One hundred years later, the Negro lives on a lonely island of poverty in the midst of a vast ocean of material prosperity. One hundred years later, (*My Lord*) [*applause*] the Negro is still languished in the corners of American society and finds himself an exile in his own land. And so we've come here today to dramatize a shameful condition.

In a sense we've come to our nation's capital to cash a check. When the architects of our republic wrote the magnificent words of the Constitution and the Declaration of Independence (*Yeah*), they were signing a promissory note to which every American was to fall heir. This note was a promise that all men, yes, black men as well as white men, would be guaranteed the "unalienable Rights of Life, Liberty, and the pursuit of Happiness." It is obvious today that America has defaulted on this promissory note insofar as her citizens of color are concerned. Instead of honoring this sacred obligation, America has given the Negro people a bad check, a check which has come back marked "insufficient funds." [*sustained applause*]

But we refuse to believe that the bank of justice is bankrupt. (*My Lord*) [*applause, laughter*] (*Sure enough*) We refuse to believe that there are insufficient funds in the great vaults of opportunity of this nation. And so we've come to cash this check (*Yes*), a check that will give us upon demand the riches of freedom (*Yes*) and the security of justice. [*Sustained Applause*]

We have also come to this hallowed spot to remind America of the fierce urgency of now. This is no time (*My Lord*) to engage in the luxury of cooling off or to take the tranquilizing drug of gradualism. [*applause*] Now is the time to make real the promises of democracy. (*Now My Lord*) Now is the time (*Now*) to rise from the dark and desolate valley of segregation to the sunlit path of racial justice. Now is the time [*applause*] to lift our nation from the quicksands of racial injustice to the solid rock of brotherhood. Now is the time [*applause*] to make justice a reality for all of God's children.

It would be fatal for the nation to overlook the urgency of the moment. This sweltering summer of the Negro's legitimate discontent will not pass until there is an invigorating autumn of freedom and equality. (*Right*) Nineteen sixty-three is not an end, but a beginning. And those who hope that the Negro needed to blow off steam and will now be content will have a rude awakening if the nation returns to business as usual. [*applause*] There will be neither rest nor tranquility in America until the Negro is granted his citizenship rights. The whirlwinds of revolt will continue to shake the foundations of our nation until the bright day of justice emerges.

But there is something that I must say to my people, who stand on the warm threshold which leads into the palace of justice: in the process of gaining our rightful place, we must not be guilty of wrongful deeds. Let us not seek to satisfy our thirst for freedom by drinking from the cup of bitterness and hatred. (My Lord) [*applause*] We must forever conduct our struggle on the high plane of dignity and discipline. We must not allow our creative protest to degenerate into physical violence. Again and again, we must rise to the majestic heights of meeting physical force with soul force. The marvelous new militancy which has engulfed the Negro community must not lead us to a distrust of all white people, for many of our white brothers, as evidenced by their presence here today, have come to realize that their destiny is tied up with our destiny. [*applause*] And they have come to realize that their freedom is inextricably bound to our freedom. We cannot walk alone.

And as we walk, we must make the pledge that we shall always march ahead. We cannot turn back. There are those who are asking the devotees of civil rights, "When will you be satisfied?" (*Never*)

We can never be satisfied as long as the Negro is the victim of the unspeakable horrors of police brutality. We can never be satisfied [*applause*] as long as our bodies, heavy with the fatigue of travel, cannot gain lodging in the motels of the highways and the hotels of the cities. [*applause*] We cannot be satisfied as long as the Negro's basic mobility is from a smaller ghetto to a larger one. We can never be satisfied as long as our children are stripped of their selfhood and robbed of their dignity by signs stating "for whites only." [*Applause*] We cannot be satisfied as long as a Negro in Mississippi cannot vote and a Negro in New York believes he has nothing for which to vote. (*Yes*) [*applause*] No, no, we are not satisfied and we will not be satisfied until "justice rolls down like waters and righteousness like a mighty stream." [*applause*]

I am not unmindful that some of you have come here out of great trials and tribulations. (*My Lord*) Some of you have come fresh from narrow jail cells. Some of you have come from areas where your quest for freedom left you battered by the storms of persecution (*Yes*) and staggered by the winds of police brutality. You have been the veterans of creative suffering. Continue to work with the faith that unearned suffering is redemptive. Go back to Mississippi (*Yes*), go back to Alabama, go back to South Carolina, go back to Georgia, go back to Louisiana, go back to the slums and ghettos of our northern cities, knowing that somehow this situation can and will be changed. (*Yes*) Let us not wallow in the valley of despair.

[*Applause*]

I say to you today, my friends [*applause*], so even though we face the difficulties of today and tomorrow, I still have a dream. (*Yes*) It is a dream deeply rooted in the American dream.

I have a dream that one day (*Yes*) this nation will rise up and live out the true meaning of its creed: "We hold these truths to be self-evident, that all men are created equal." (*Yes*) [*applause*]

I have a dream that one day on the red hills of Georgia, the sons of former slaves and the sons of former slave owners will be able to sit down together at the table of brotherhood.

I have a dream that one day even the state of Mississippi, a state sweltering with the heat of injustice (*Well*), sweltering with the heat of oppression, will be transformed into an oasis of freedom and justice.

I have a dream (*Well*) [*applause*] that my four little children will one day live in a nation where they will not be judged by the color of their skin but by the content of their character. (*My Lord*) I have a dream today. [*applause*]

I have a dream that one day down in Alabama, with its vicious racists (*Yes*), with its governor having his lips dripping with the words of "interposition" and "nullification" (*Yes*), one day right there in Alabama little black boys and black girls will be able to join hands with little white boys and white girls as sisters and brothers. I have a dream today. [*applause*]

I have a dream that one day "every valley shall be exalted (*Yes*), and every hill and mountain shall be made low, the rough places will be made plain, and the crooked places will be made straight (*Yes*), and the glory of the Lord shall be revealed, and all flesh shall see it together." (*Yes*)

This is our hope. This is the faith that I go back to the South with. (*Yes*) With this faith we will be able to hew out of the mountain of despair a stone of hope. (*Yes*) With this faith we will be able to transform the jangling discords of our nation into a beautiful symphony of brotherhood. (*Talk about it*) With this faith (*My Lord*) we will be able to work together, to pray together, to struggle together, to go to jail together, to stand up for freedom together, knowing that we will be free one day. [*applause*] This will be the day [*applause continues*], this will be the day when all of God's children (*Yes*) will be able to sing with new meaning:

> My country, 'tis of thee (*Yes*), sweet land of liberty, of thee I sing.
> Land where my fathers died, land of the pilgrim's pride (*Yes*),
> From every mountainside, let freedom ring!

> And if America is to be a great nation, this must become true.
> And so let freedom ring (*Yes*) from the prodigious hilltops of New Hampshire.
> Let freedom ring from the mighty mountains of New York.
> Let freedom ring from the heightening Alleghenies of Pennsylvania. (*Yes, All right*)
> Let freedom ring from the snowcapped Rockies of Colorado. (*Well*)
> Let freedom ring from the curvaceous slopes of California. (*Yes*)
> But not only that: Let freedom ring from Stone Mountain of Georgia. (*Yes*)
> Let freedom ring from Lookout Mountain of Tennessee. (*Yes*)
> Let freedom ring from every hill and molehill of Mississippi. (*Yes*) [*Applause*]
> From every mountainside, [*Applause*] let freedom ring. [*applause*]

And when this happens [*Applause continues*], when we allow freedom ring, when we let it ring from every village and every hamlet, from every state and every city (*Yes*), we will be able to speed up that day when all of God's children, black men and white men, Jews and Gentiles, Protestants and Catholics, will be able to join hands and sing in the words of the old Negro spiritual:

> Free at last! (*Yes*) Free at last!
> Thank God Almighty, we are free at last! [*applause*]

Source: King, Martin Luther, Jr. "'I Have a Dream,' Address at March on Washington for Jobs and Freedom." From the Martin Luther King Papers Project, Stanford University, 1963. http://www.stanford.edu/group/King/popular _requests.

President George W. Bush Addresses the Nation after the Attacks of September 11 (2001)

Related Holiday: Patriot Day (September 11)

On September 11, 2001, the United States suffered a horrifying attack. Terrorists hijacked four airplanes, which they used to attack the twin towers of the World Trade Center in New York City as well as the Pentagon near Washington, D.C.; the fourth plane crashed in a field in Pennsylvania when brave and quick-witted passengers were able to thwart the hijackers' plans. On September 20, 2001, President George W. Bush delivered this speech to Congress. Simultaneously addressing the nation and the world, the president declared war on terror and both reassured and gave strength to the American people.

Address to a Joint Session of Congress and the American People

United States Capitol
Washington, D.C.
September 20, 2001

THE PRESIDENT: Mr. Speaker, Mr. President Pro Tempore, members of Congress, and fellow Americans:

In the normal course of events, Presidents come to this chamber to report on the state of the Union. Tonight, no such report is needed. It has already been delivered by the American people. . . .

We have seen the state of our Union in the endurance of rescuers, working past exhaustion. We have seen the unfurling of flags, the lighting of candles, the giving of blood, the saying of prayers—in English, Hebrew, and Arabic. We have seen the decency of a loving and giving people who have made the grief of strangers their own.

My fellow citizens, for the last nine days, the entire world has seen for itself the state of our Union—and it is strong. *(Applause.)*

Tonight we are a country awakened to danger and called to defend freedom. Our grief has turned to anger, and anger to resolution. Whether we bring our enemies to justice, or bring justice to our enemies, justice will be done. *(Applause.)* . . .

On September the 11th, enemies of freedom committed an act of war against our country. Americans have known wars—but for the past 136 years, they have been wars on foreign soil, except for one Sunday in 1941. Americans have known the casualties of war—but not at the center of a great city on a peaceful morning. Americans have known surprise attacks—but never before on thousands of civilians. All of this was brought upon us in a single day—and night fell on a different world, a world where freedom itself is under attack.

Americans have many questions tonight. Americans are asking: Who attacked our country? The evidence we have gathered all points to a collection of loosely affiliated terrorist organizations known as al Qaeda. . . .

This group and its leader—a person named Osama bin Laden—are linked to many other organizations in different countries, including the Egyptian Islamic Jihad and the Islamic Movement of Uzbekistan. There are thousands of these terrorists in more than 60 countries. They are recruited from their own nations and neighborhoods and brought to camps in places like Afghanistan, where they are trained in the tactics of terror. They are sent back to their homes or sent to hide in countries around the world to plot evil and destruction.

The leadership of al Qaeda has great influence in Afghanistan and supports the Taliban regime in controlling most of that country. In Afghanistan, we see al Qaeda's vision for the world.

Afghanistan's people have been brutalized—many are starving and many have fled. Women are not allowed to attend school. You can be jailed for owning a television. Religion can be practiced only as their leaders dictate. A man can be jailed in Afghanistan if his beard is not long enough.

The United States respects the people of Afghanistan—after all, we are currently its largest source of humanitarian aid—but we condemn the Taliban regime. *(Applause.)* It is not only repressing its own people, it is threatening people everywhere by sponsoring and sheltering and supplying terrorists. By aiding and abetting murder, the Taliban regime is committing murder.

And tonight, the United States of America makes the following demands on the Taliban: Deliver to United States authorities all the leaders of al Qaeda who hide in your land. *(Applause.)* Release all foreign nationals, including American citizens, you have unjustly imprisoned. Protect foreign journalists, diplomats and aid workers in your country. Close immediately and permanently every terrorist training camp in Afghanistan, and hand over every terrorist, and every person in their support structure, to appropriate authorities. *(Applause.)* Give the United States full access to terrorist training camps, so we can make sure they are no longer operating.

These demands are not open to negotiation or discussion. *(Applause.)* The Taliban must act, and act immediately. They will hand over the terrorists, or they will share in their fate.

I also want to speak tonight directly to Muslims throughout the world. We respect your faith. It's practiced freely by many millions of Americans, and by millions more in countries that America counts as friends. Its teachings are good and peaceful, and those who commit evil in the name of Allah blaspheme the name of Allah. *(Applause.)* The terrorists are traitors to their own faith, trying, in effect, to hijack Islam itself. The enemy of America is not our many Muslim friends; it is not our many Arab friends. Our enemy is a radical network of terrorists, and every government that supports them. *(Applause.)*

Our war on terror begins with al Qaeda, but it does not end there. It will not end until every terrorist group of global reach has been found, stopped and defeated. *(Applause.)*

Americans are asking, why do they hate us? They hate what we see right here in this chamber — a democratically elected government. Their leaders are self-appointed. They hate our freedoms — our freedom of religion, our freedom of speech, our freedom to vote and assemble and disagree with each other. . . .

This war will not be like the war against Iraq a decade ago, with a decisive liberation of territory and a swift conclusion. It will not look like the air war above Kosovo two years ago, where no ground troops were used and not a single American was lost in combat.

Our response involves far more than instant retaliation and isolated strikes. Americans should not expect one battle, but a lengthy campaign, unlike any other we have ever seen. It may include dramatic strikes, visible on TV, and covert operations, secret even in success. We will starve terrorists of funding, turn them one against another, drive them from place to place, until there is no refuge or no rest. And we will pursue nations that provide aid or safe haven to terrorism. Every nation, in every region, now has a decision to make. Either you are with us, or you are with the terrorists. *(Applause.)* From this day forward, any nation that continues to harbor or support terrorism will be regarded by the United States as a hostile regime.

Our nation has been put on notice: We are not immune from attack. We will take defensive measures against terrorism to protect Americans. Today, dozens of federal departments and agencies, as well as state and local governments, have responsibilities affecting homeland security. These efforts must be coordinated at the highest level. So tonight I announce the creation of a Cabinet-level position reporting directly to me — the Office of Homeland Security. . . .

These measures are essential. But the only way to defeat terrorism as a threat to our way of life is to stop it, eliminate it, and destroy it where it grows. *(Applause.)*

Many will be involved in this effort, from FBI agents to intelligence operatives to the reservists we have called to active duty. All deserve our thanks, and all have our prayers. And tonight, a few miles from the damaged Pentagon, I have a message for our military: Be ready. I've called the Armed Forces to alert, and there is a reason. The hour is coming when America will act, and you will make us proud. *(Applause.)*

This is not, however, just America's fight. And what is at stake is not just America's freedom. This is the world's fight. This is civilization's fight. This is the fight of all who believe in progress and pluralism, tolerance and freedom.

We ask every nation to join us. We will ask, and we will need, the help of police forces, intelligence services, and banking systems around the world. The United States is grateful that many nations and many international organizations have already responded—with sympathy and with support. Nations from Latin America, to Asia, to Africa, to Europe, to the Islamic world. Perhaps the NATO Charter reflects best the attitude of the world: An attack on one is an attack on all.

The civilized world is rallying to America's side. They understand that if this terror goes unpunished, their own cities, their own citizens may be next. Terror, unanswered, can not only bring down buildings, it can threaten the stability of legitimate governments. And you know what—we're not going to allow it. *(Applause.)*

Americans are asking: What is expected of us? I ask you to live your lives, and hug your children. I know many citizens have fears tonight, and I ask you to be calm and resolute, even in the face of a continuing threat.

I ask you to uphold the values of America, and remember why so many have come here. We are in a fight for our principles, and our first responsibility is to live by them. No one should be singled out for unfair treatment or unkind words because of their ethnic background or religious faith. *(Applause.)* . . .

I ask for your patience, with the delays and inconveniences that may accompany tighter security; and for your patience in what will be a long struggle.

I ask your continued participation and confidence in the American economy. Terrorists attacked a symbol of American prosperity. They did not touch its source. America is successful because of the hard work, and creativity, and enterprise of our people. These were the true strengths of our economy before September 11th, and they are our strengths today. *(Applause.)*

And, finally, please continue praying for the victims of terror and their families, for those in uniform, and for our great country. Prayer has comforted us in sorrow, and will help strengthen us for the journey ahead. . . .

After all that has just passed—all the lives taken, and all the possibilities and hopes that died with them—it is natural to wonder if America's future is one of fear. Some speak of an age of terror. I know there are struggles ahead, and dangers to face. But this country will define our times, not be defined by them. As long as the United States of America is determined and strong, this will not be an age of terror; this will be an age of liberty, here and across the world. *(Applause.)*

Great harm has been done to us. We have suffered great loss. And in our grief and anger we have found our mission and our moment. Freedom and fear are at war. The advance of human freedom—the great achievement of our time, and the great hope of every time—now depends on us. Our nation—this generation—will lift a dark threat of violence from our people and our future. We will rally the world to this cause by our efforts, by our courage. We will not tire, we will not falter, and we will not fail. *(Applause.)* . . .

I will not forget this wound to our country or those who inflicted it. I will not yield; I will not rest; I will not relent in waging this struggle for freedom and security for the American people.

The course of this conflict is not known, yet its outcome is certain. Freedom and fear, justice and cruelty, have always been at war, and we know that God is not neutral between them. *(Applause.)*

Fellow citizens, we'll meet violence with patient justice—assured of the rightness of our cause, and confident of the victories to come. In all that lies before us, may God grant us wisdom, and may He watch over the United States of America.

Thank you. *(Applause.)*

Source: Bush, George W. "Address to a Joint Session of Congress and the American People." From the Office of the Press Secretary, The White House, 2001. http://www.whitehouse.gov/news/releases/2001/09/20010920-8.html.

U.S. Representative William Lacy Clay
Discusses the 40th Anniversary of the 1963 March
on Washington (2003)

Related Holiday: Martin Luther King Jr. Birthday

In this speech by U.S. Representative William Lacy Clay of Missouri, he reminds the audience of the importance of Martin Luther King Jr. and the 1963 March on Washington for Jobs and Freedom. On August 25, 2003, three days before the 40th anniversary of the March, Clay delivered the speech to the Arkansas Legislative Black Caucus in Ferndale, Arkansas. For other primary sources related to the Martin Luther King Jr. Birthday, see "'I Have a Dream,' Address at March on Washington for Jobs and Freedom (1963)" and "U.S. Representative John Conyers Jr. Reflects on the Significance of Martin Luther King Jr. Day (2004)."

A Call to Action

Thank you for that introduction.

This is a wonderful event in many ways. Not only is it always a good feeling to see black elected officials come together, also, it is another chance to send a message, another call to action for the young people — those following in our footsteps as future black elected officials.

I believe it is imperative that you understand how we got where we are and the price our mothers and fathers paid to get us here.

As black elected officials in Arkansas, Missouri, Michigan, Illinois, California, Georgia and so many other states in this nation, we must never forget the high price paid for us to serve.

Today, the politics of the 21st Century demands the same diligence, courage and dedication as the politics of the 20th Century. Today, it demands a call to action from the young, much as it has done throughout our history. That history, of our ancestors held in bondage and persecuted as so-called freedmen in a forsaken land is as real as the air we breathe, the food we eat and the love we have for our people.

Certainly, one could begin to argue that America is no longer the forsaken land for people of color. And certainly, others could just as easily argue that we are still a forsaken people.

For black elected officials, these are difficult times. From the elected committeeman and committeewoman in the neighborhoods to the school board members to the halls of city governments, statehouses and even in Congress, black elected officials and black voters are being taken for granted in many ways.

A new attitude of self-disenfranchisement is sweeping the nation.

Disgruntled and disillusioned, some African Americans appear to be stepping back and away from the political process, seeking power in other arenas. I urge the disenchanted to remain steadfast and loyal to the power of the vote. I urge black elected officials to respond to this reversal of fortunes with a new call to action.

In spite of a few political setbacks, the political reality is that black voters and black elected officials remain powerful and often make the difference in elections. Their votes – at the polls and among their elected bodies — still count!

Our fathers and mothers struggled hard to win the right to vote. In winning the right to vote, they gave us the opportunity to be elected to office in greater numbers. That part of our history is a major, major accomplishment. I need only remind you that there are those who have turned their backs on us, as both voters and black elected officials.

As elected officials, we cannot and should not turn our backs on the accomplishments that won us the right to vote and the power to be elected representatives of our people.

But, as I said, there are those who would deny us those victories and tell our children that the almighty dollar is more powerful than the right to vote. The dollar vs. the ballot box? I don't see it as an EITHER / OR situation. Rather, it is a BOTH / AND situation.

We can both celebrate our electoral achievements and at the same time develop our economic prowess.

Let me give a timely, historic example of just how important the right to vote really is.

In their call to action, the heroes and heroines of the civil rights movement issued a call to action on many fronts. There was one such event that would help change American forever. This month, on August 28, marks the 40th Anniversary of the 1963 March on Washington. For those who don't realize the impact that march had on the nation, then let us consider the impact the march had on Congress and the American promise of one person, one vote, and truly representative politics.

In the summer of 1963, I turned 7 years old — one month before the March on Washington.

At that age, the August 28 gathering of some 250,000 people, while impressive, had little political meaning to me. Gathered at the foot of the Lincoln Memorial, the event had greater, historic meaning for my father, William Clay, Sr.

Then, a member of the St. Louis Board of Aldermen and active in the city's civil rights movement, my father worked to organize and get people mobilized to go to Washington to participate in the march. Like so many of his peers, he too answered the call to action. Even so, little did he know how much that day would later impact his life.

Six years later and on the heels of the civil rights and voting rights laws the March on Washington help create, he would be elected to Congress and become a founding member of the esteemed Congressional Black Caucus. Now, this is where most people forget their history. Officially the March on Washington was called the March on Washington for Jobs and Freedom. That's right, The March for Jobs and Freedom.

Few people remember that in addition to Dr. Martin Luther King Jr. and the Southern Christian Leadership Conference, there were five other sponsors of the March on Washington:

A. Philip Randolph of the Brotherhood of Sleeping Car Porters; Roy Wilkins of the NAACP; Whitney Young of the National Urban League, James Farmer of the Congress of Racial Equality (CORE); and John Lewis of the Student Nonviolent Coordinating Committee (SNCC). And fewer still remember all their demands. Called "WHAT WE DEMAND," they asked for:

1) Comprehensive and effective civil rights legislation from the present Congress—without compromise or filibuster—to guarantee all Americans access to all public accommodations, decent housing, adequate and integrated education (and) the right to vote;

2) Withholding of Federal funds from all programs in which discrimination exits;

3) Desegregation of all school districts in 1963

4) Enforcement of the Fourteenth Amendment – reducing Congressional representation of states where citizens are disfranchised.

5) A new Executive Order banning discrimination in all housing supported by federal funds.

6) Authority for the Attorney General to institute injunctive suits when any constitutional right is violated.

7) A massive federal program to train and place all unemployed workers—Negro and white—on meaningful and dignified jobs at decent wages.

8) A national minimum wage act that will give all Americans a decent standard of living. (Government surveys show that anything less than $2.00 an hour fails to do this.)

9) A broadened Fair Labor Standards Act to include all areas of employment which are presently excluded.

10) A federal Fair Employment Practices Act barring discrimination by federal, state, and municipal governments, and by employers, contractors, employment agencies, and trade unions.

So, you see, the quest for voting rights was only a small part of their demands. By and larger, they wanted economic parity more than anything else. Those marchers, many nameless faces in a crowd, answered a call to action and got results.

The immediate impact of the March on Washington was the Civil Rights Act of 1964 that addressed discrimination based on race, color, religion or national origin in colleges and places of employment, public accommodations and gender. That major legislation was followed the next year by the Voting Rights Act of 1965 and soon the election to Congress of a record number of African Americans, including my father.

The run-up to the 1960s Civil Rights Act began long ago and was the result of efforts by our forefathers who answered the call to action.

No, the March on Washington did not happen in a vacuum. As the thousands of people who answered the call to action and made their way to the Lincoln Memorial by "freedom buses" and "freedom trains," they bore witness to the demand for jobs and freedom, traveling through towns scarred by bombs, lynchings, shootings and terror.

In their collective memory were the roar of angry mobs, rapists and crooked racists police officers, judges and elected officials.

Haunted by bosses who denied them work or treated them as chattel if they did hire them; and restaurants who denied them food or fed it to them at the back door, like dogs; or public swimming pools that refused to let a black child cool off in the summer heat; or see the face of a teacher who told them they were ignorant and dumb as a natural course of their birth, and not because the government refused to educate them with the same imperative as they educated white children.

Those people who stood in the summer sun of 1963 and heard King's appeal for a better America, got there by way of bus boycotts in Montgomery, Ala., Freedom Rides for voting rights, fire hoses and Eugene "Bull" Connor's vicious police dogs, tear gas and police clubs in Birmingham. They were veterans of nonviolent sit-ins across the nation, jailed for daring to raise their voice for freedom and justice, terrorized by the 16th Avenue Baptist Church bombing in Birmingham that killed four innocent girls and assassins bullets in Mississippi and other Deep South states.

Still, they answered the call to action.

So powerful was that year, that juncture in history with its massive roll call of events, that within two months after the March on Washington, Congress passed into law a new civil rights bill that would lead to yet another new law, and another and yet another.

We all know that riding side-by-side with our hopes and dreams was the sadness of death and terrorism. Assassins claimed the NAACP's Medgar Evers and later, President John F. Kennedy. Five years later, Dr. King himself fell victim to that constant companion of all great people and movements—hate.

For the most part, the marchers of '63 got what they asked for – new laws to fight racism and new hope for all of America's citizens.

Even today, as some debate the relevance of integration, the Civil Rights Movement or even the power of our vote, all that needs to be done is look into the faces of this nation's children and think of the King's dream, where "the sons of former slaves and the sons of former slave owners" . . . "sit down together at the table of brotherhood . . . (and) live in a nation where they will not be judged by the color of their skin but by the content of their character. . . ."

In 2003, some 40 years after the great March on Washington, we are a little freer, a little more American than our forefathers and a little better off without Jim Crow and second-class citizenship.

As black elected officials, we can gather and hopefully parlay our united votes into laws that help every American.

And for anyone to question the validity of our unity, and our call to action, all they need do is look at our small numbers, look at our struggle to pass just laws and hear our voices as we continue to demand for our people what is fair, what is right, what is just. And if they still doubt, then let them come our way. Or let them answer the call to action in some way. For it is a standing call to action. It has not wavered over time nor been diminished by a few reluctant plums handed out by those who would try to swish us away, to dismiss both us and our constituents.

It is a call to action that once you hear it, you cannot ignore it. And those who act, become the leaders we desperately need.

Do you hear it?

Do you hear our forefathers? Our Martin, our Malcolm, our Du Bois, our Conyers, our Dullums, our Waters, our Elijah Cummings?

Do you hear them calling you to leadership?

I do. And I too, am calling you to join us.

It is your turn. Your people await you.

Source: Clay, William Lacy. "A Call to Action." Speech given August 25, 2003, to the Arkansas Legislative Black Caucus in Ferndale, Arkansas. From the Office of U.S. Representative William Lacy Clay, 2003. http://www.house.gov/clay/sp030825.htm.

U.S. Representative John Conyers Jr. Reflects on the Significance of Martin Luther King Jr. Day (2004)

Related Holiday: Martin Luther King Jr. Birthday

This statement is by U.S. Representative John Conyers Jr. from Michigan, ranking member of the House Judiciary Committee and Dean of the Congressional Black Caucus. Conyers issued these comments on the anniversary of the birth of Martin Luther King Jr. Conyers has had a long history of supporting Dr. King. On April 8, 1968, Conyers was the first U.S. legislator to call for the creation of a federal holiday in King's honor. Conyers continued to issue bills for the holiday until it became federal law in 1983. For other primary sources related to the Martin Luther King Jr. Birthday, see "'I Have a Dream,' Address at March on Washington for Jobs and Freedom (1963)" and "U.S. Representative William Lacy Clay Discusses the 40th Anniversary of the 1963 March on Washington (2003)."

Reflections on the Significance of Martin Luther King Day

On March 12, 1968, I hosted Dr. Martin Luther King Jr. during his visit to Michigan where he gave an address titled "The Other America" at Grosse Pointe High School. In his remarks Dr. King noted:

> "Every city in our country has this kind of dualism, this schizophrenia, split at so many points and so every city ends up being two cities rather than one, there are two Americas."

Dr. King went on to depict the struggles of the jobless America, the undereducated America, the America living in obscene poverty—the hopeless America. Despite the social progress America has seen since 1968, the other America still exists today. Our country has failed the over 40 million uninsured, the 3.5 million homeless, and the millions of school children who are left behind every day.

One of my former constituents, Linda Gruber, recorded Dr. King's speech that day, less than one month before his assassination. Her son John, a school teacher, shares the tape with his students every year to commemorate Martin Luther King Day and discuss his dream of a unified America. Not every American has a recording of one of Dr. King's powerful speeches, but we all have Martin Luther King Day.

This national holiday provides Americans with the opportunity to honor Dr. King and recommit ourselves to continuing his legacy by fighting to bring hope to the hopeless. Dr. King envisioned a Nation and a world without deep race and class divisions—where all people would live, learn and work together equally and harmoniously. King instructed, "Make a career of humanity—and you will make a greater person of yourself, a greater nation of your country, and a finer world to live in."

Source: Conyers, John, Jr. "Reflections on the Significance of Martin Luther King Day." From the Office of U.S. Representative John Conyers Jr., 2004. http://www.house.gov/apps/list/press/mi14_conyers/108_01_19_04.html.

Bibliography

Bibliography

This bibliography lists all sources consulted for *Patriotic Holidays of the United States*.

Abrams, Jim. "Capitol Is One of D.C.'s Favorite Haunts: Tales Abound of Ghostly Sightings from History." *Seattle Times* (October 31, 2003): A7.

Ackerman, Peter, and Christopher Kruegler. *Strategic Nonviolent Conflict: The Dynamics of People Power in the Twentieth Century*. Westport, Conn., and London: Praeger, 1994.

Alden, Jan. "Sagas on the Trail to Vinland." *Americas* [English Edition] 48, 1 (January-February 1996): 6-13.

Altgeld, John. *Live Questions*. Chicago: George S. Bowen and Son, 1899.

Altman, Linda Jacobs. *Slavery and Abolition in American History*. Berkeley Heights, N.J.: Enslow, 1999. For young adults.

Ames, Mary Clemmer. *Ten Years in Washington. Life and Scenes in the National Capital, as a Woman Sees Them*. Hartford, Conn.: A. D. Worthington & Co., 1873.

Appelbaum, Diana Karter. *The Glorious Fourth: An American Holiday, an American History*. New York: Facts on File, 1989.

———. *Thanksgiving: An American Holiday, an American History*. New York: Facts on File, 1984.

Arbelbide, C. L. "By George, IT IS Washington's Birthday." *Prologue* 36, 4 (winter 2004). Online at http://www.archives.gov/publications/prologue/2004/winter/gw_birthday_1.html

Avery, Catherine B., ed. *The New Century Classical Handbook*. New York: Appleton-Century-Crofts, 1962.

Bach, Caleb. "Behind Bountiful Banners: Pursuing a Lifelong Passion, Whitney Smith Has Documented the Origins and Significance of Hundreds of Flags of the Hemisphere." *Americas* [English Edition] 54, 6 (November-December 2002): 38-43.

Bartlett, Merrill L., and Jack Sweetman. *The U.S. Marine Corps: An Illustrated History*. Annapolis, Md.: Naval Institute Press, 2001.

Bartoletti, Susan Campbell. *Kids on Strike!* Boston: Houghton Mifflin, 1999. For young adults.

Bateman, Teresa. *Red, White, Blue, and Uncle Who? The Stories Behind Some of America's Patriotic Symbols*. New York: Holiday House, 2003. For young adults.

Becker, Carl L. *The Declaration of Independence: A Study in the History of Political Ideas*. New York: Harcourt, Brace and Company, 1922.

Bellamy, Francis. *The Youth's Companion* (September 8, 1892): 446-47.

Bentley, Judith. *Harriet Tubman*. New York: Franklin Watts, 1990. For young adults.

Bergen, Peter L. *Holy War, Inc.: Inside the Secret World of Osama bin Laden*. New York: Free Press, 2001.

Berkin, Carol. *A Brilliant Solution: Inventing the American Constitution.* New York: Harcourt Brace & Company, 2002.

Berlin, Ira. *Many Thousands Gone: The First Two Centuries of Slavery in North America.* Cambridge, Mass.: Belknap Press of Harvard University Press, 1998.

Berlin, Ira, Marc Favreau, and Steven F. Miller, eds. *Remembering Slavery: African Americans Talk about Their Personal Experiences of Slavery and Emancipation.* New York: New Press, 1998.

Blight, David W. *Race and Reunion: The Civil War in American Memory.* Cambridge, Mass.: Harvard University Press, 2001.

Bober, Natalie S. *Countdown to Independence: A Revolution of Ideas in England and Her American Colonies: 1760-1776.* New York: Atheneum, 2001. For young adults.

Bodnar, John. *Remaking America: Public Memory, Commemoration, and Patriotism in the Twentieth Century.* Princeton, N.J.: Princeton University Press, 1992.

Bodnar, John, ed. *Bonds of Affection: Americans Define Their Patriotism.* Princeton, N.J.: Princeton University Press, 1996.

Boorstin, Daniel. *The Discoverers.* New York: Vintage Books, 1985.

Bowers, Detine L. "A Place to Stand: African Americans and the First of August Platform." *The Southern Communication Journal* 60, 4 (summer 1995): 348-61.

Boyd, Maurice, ed. *Kiowa Voices: Ceremonial Dance, Ritual and Song.* Fort Worth: Texas Christian University Press, 1981.

Boyne, Walter J. *Beyond the Wild Blue: A History of the United States Air Force, 1947-1997.* New York: St. Martin's Press, 1997.

————. "A Great Tradition in the Making: The United States Air Force." *Aviation Week & Space Technology* 146, 16 (April 16, 1997): 84-139.

Bradford, William. *Of Plymouth Plantation, 1620-1647.* Edited by Samuel Eliot Morison. New York: Knopf, 1952.

Branch, Taylor. *Parting the Waters: America in the King Years, 1954-63.* New York: Simon & Schuster, 1988.

————. *Pillar of Fire: America in the King Years, 1963-65.* New York: Simon & Schuster, 1998.

Brogan, Hugh. *The Penguin History of the USA.* 2nd ed. London: Penguin Books, 1999.

Bronner, Simon J. *Folk Nation: Folklore in the Creation of American Tradition.* Wilmington, Del.: Scholarly Resources, 2002.

Brownstone, David M. *Facts about American Immigration.* New York: H. W. Wilson, 2001.

Burgos, Anthony. "Large Turnout as Navy Honors Its History, Traditions at Sigonella." *Stars and Stripes* (October 20, 2001). Online at http://www.estripes.osd.mil/

Burnside, Madeleine. *Spirits of the Passage: The Transatlantic Slave Trade in the Seventeenth Century.* New York: Simon & Schuster, 1997.

Burstein, Andrew. *America's Jubilee: How in 1826 a Generation Remembered Fifty Years of Independence.* New York: Knopf, 2001.

Calhoun, Craig, Paul Price, and Ashley Timmer, eds. *Understanding September 11.* New York: New Press, 2002.

Canipe, Lee. "Under God and Anti-Communist: How the Pledge of Allegiance Got Religion in Cold-War America." *Journal of Church and State* 45, 2 (spring 2003): 305-23.

Carson, Clayborne, et al., eds. *The Eyes on the Prize Civil Rights Reader*. New York: Penguin Books, 1991.

Cavendish, Richard. "The Birth of Amerigo Vespucci." *History Today* 54, 3 (March 2004): 54.

Chapin, E. N. *American Court Gossip; Or, Life at the National Capitol*. Marshalltown, Iowa: Chapin & Hartwell Bros., 1887.

Christianson, Stephen G., comp. and ed. *The American Book of Days*. 4th ed. New York: H. W. Wilson, 2000.

Chu, Jolene, and Donna P. Couper. "The Flag and Freedom." *Social Education* 67, 6 (October 2003): 327-31.

Clack, George, ed. *United States Elections 2004*. Washington, D.C.: U.S. Department of State, Bureau of International Information Programs, posted online (September 2003) at http://usinfo.state.gov/products/pubs/election04/parties.htm

Clarke, Richard A. *Against All Enemies: Inside America's War on Terror*. New York: Free Press, 2004.

Clinton, Catherine. *Harriet Tubman: The Road to Freedom*. New York: Little, Brown and Company, 2004.

———. *Scholastic Encyclopedia of the Civil War*. New York: Scholastic, 1999. For young adults.

Colbert, David, ed. *Eyewitness to America: 500 Years of America in the Words of Those Who Saw It Happen*. New York: Pantheon Books, 1997.

Coleman, Kevin J., et al. *Presidential Elections in the United States: A Primer*. (CRS Report for Congress.) Washington, D.C.: Congressional Research Service, Library of Congress, April 17, 2000.

Coll, Steve. *Ghost Wars: The Secret History of the CIA, Afghanistan, and bin Laden, from the Soviet Invasion to September 10, 2001*. New York: Penguin, 2004.

Colman, Penny. *Strike! The Bitter Struggle of American Workers from Colonial Times to the Present*. Brookfield, Conn.: Millbrook Press, 1995. For young adults.

Connell, Royal W., and William P. Mack. *Naval Ceremonies, Customs, and Traditions*. 6th ed. Annapolis, Md.: Naval Institute Press, 2004.

Connery, Sam. "One Thousand and One Ways of Saying Uncle." *Smithsonian* 26, 4 (July 1995): 70.

Crosby, Alfred W. *The Columbian Exchange: Biological and Cultural Consequences of 1492*. Westport, Conn.: Greenwood Press, 1972.

Cullen, Jim. *The American Dream: A Short History of an Idea That Shaped a Nation*. Oxford: Oxford University Press, 2003.

Curti, Merle. *The Roots of American Loyalty*. 1946. Reprint, New York: Atheneum, 1968.

Daniels, Roger. *American Immigration: A Student Companion*. Oxford: Oxford University Press, 2001. For young adults.

———. *Coming to America: A History of Immigration and Ethnicity in American Life*. New York: HarperCollins, 1990.

Davis, Susan G. *Parades and Power: Street Theatre in Nineteenth-Century Philadelphia*. Philadelphia: Temple University Press, 1986.

Dennis, Matthew. *Red, White, and Blue Letter Days: An American Calendar*. Ithaca, N.Y.: Cornell University Press, 2002.

Dickson, Paul. *The Book of Thanksgiving*. New York: Perigee/Berkley, 1995.

DiClerico, Robert. *Voting in America: A Reference Handbook*. Santa Barbara, Calif.: ABC-CLIO, 2004.

Doherty, Kieran. *William Bradford: Rock of Plymouth*. Brookfield, Conn.: Twenty-First Century Books, 1999. For young adults.

Donald, David Herbert. *Lincoln*. New York: Simon & Schuster, 1995.

Doubler, Michael D., and John W. Listman, Jr. *The National Guard: An Illustrated History of America's Citizen-Soldiers*. Washington, D.C.: Brassey's, 2003.

Douglass, Frederick. *Life and Times of Frederick Douglass: His Early Life as a Slave, His Escape from Bondage and His Complete History, Written by Himself*. New York: Bonanza Books, 1962.

Dover, E. D. *The Disputed Presidential Election of 2000: A History and Reference Guide*. Westport, Conn.: Greenwood Press, 2003.

Druckman, Nancy. *American Flags: Designs for a Young Nation*. New York: Harry N. Abrams, 2003. For young adults.

Dubofsky, Melvyn, and Foster Rhea Dulles. *Labor in America: A History*. 6th ed. Wheeling, Ill.: Harlan Davidson, 1999.

Dubofsky, Melvyn, and Warren Van Tine, eds. *Labor Leaders in America*. Urbana: University of Illinois Press, 1987.

Dusinberre, William. *Them Dark Days: Slavery in the American Rice Swamps*. New York: Oxford University Press, 1996.

Easton, Pam. "Making Official Holiday of Juneteenth Questioned." *Fort Worth Star Telegram* (June 19, 2004): 3.

Edling, Max M. *A Revolution in Favor of Government: Origins of the U.S. Constitution and the Making of the American State*. Oxford: Oxford University Press, 2003.

Ellis, Joseph J. *His Excellency: George Washington*. New York: Alfred A. Knopf, 2004.

English, June A., and Thomas D. Jones. *Scholastic Encyclopedia of the United States at War*. New York: Scholastic, 1998. For young adults.

Epstein, James. "Understanding the Cap of Liberty: Symbolic Practice and Social Conflict in Early Nineteenth-Century England." *Past and Present* 122 (February 1989): 75-118.

Equiano, Olaudah. *Equiano's Travels: The Interesting Narrative of the Life of Olaudah Equiano or Gustavus Vassa, the African*. Abridged and edited by Paul Edwards. London: Heinemann, 1996.

Fairclough, Adam. *Better Day Coming: Blacks and Equality, 1890-2000*. New York: Viking, 2001.

Farrer, Claire R. *Living Life's Circle: Mescalero Apache Cosmovision*. Albuquerque: University of New Mexico Press, 1991.

———. *Thunder Rides a Black Horse: Mescalero Apaches and the Mythic Present*. 2nd ed. Prospect Heights, Ill.: Waveland Press, 1996.

Fernández-Armesto, Felipe. *Columbus*. Oxford: Oxford University Press, 1991.

Fleming, E. McClung. "From Indian Princess to Greek Goddess: The American Image, 1783-1815." *Winterthur Portfolio* 3 (1967): 37-66.

Fleming, Thomas. *Liberty! The American Revolution*. New York: Viking, 1997. Companion to PBS series; online exhibit at http://www.pbs.org/ktca/liberty/

Flexner, James Thomas. *Washington, the Indispensable Man*. Boston: Little, Brown, 1974.

Foner, Philip S., ed. *We, the Other People: Alternative Declarations of Independence by Labor Groups, Farmers, Woman's Rights Advocates, Socialists, and Blacks, 1829-1975*. Urbana: University of Illinois Press, 1976.

Frank, Mitch. *Understanding September 11th: Answering Questions about the Attacks on America*. New York: Viking, 2002. For young adults.

Franklin, John Hope. "A Century of Civil War Observation." *Journal of Negro History* 47 (April 1962): 97-107.

———. *The Emancipation Proclamation*. Garden City, N.Y.: Doubleday & Company, 1963.

———. *From Slavery to Freedom*. New York: Alfred A. Knopf, 1968.

Freedman, Russell. *Give Me Liberty: The Story of the Declaration of Independence*. New York: Holiday House, 2000. For young adults.

———. *In Defense of Liberty: The Story of America's Bill of Rights*. New York: Holiday House, 2003. For young adults.

Frost, Bryan-Paul, and Jeffrey Sikkenga, eds. *History of American Political Thought*. Lanham, Md.: Lexington Books, 2003.

Fumagalli, Chris. "Festival Celebrates Oñate's Historic Arrival." *Borderlands* [El Paso Community College] 17, 9 (1998-99). Online at http://www.epcc.edu/ftp/Homes/monicaw/borderlands/

Furlong, William Rea, and Byron McCandless. *So Proudly We Hail: The History of the United States Flag*. Washington, D.C.: Smithsonian Institution Press, 1981.

Gantt, Elizabeth. "May Is for Remembrance." *Harrisburg Magazine* [Pennsylvania] (May 2004). Online at http://www.harrisburgmagazine.com/hbgmag_online/0405fea-MEMORIAL-DAY.html

Gelb, Norman. "Reluctant Patriot." *Smithsonian* 35, 6 (September 2004): 66.

Genovese, Eugene D. *Roll, Jordan, Roll: The World the Slaves Made*. New York: Pantheon Books, 1974.

Gerber, Scott Douglas, ed. *The Declaration of Independence: Origins and Impact*. Washington, D.C.: CQ Press, 2002.

Gillis, John R. "Memory and Identity: The History of a Relationship." In his *Commemorations: The Politics of National Identity*. Princeton, N.J.: Princeton University Press, 1994.

Gould, Lewis L. *Grand Old Party: A History of the Republicans*. New York: Random House, 2003.

Gowen, Annie. "In the Name of 9/11 Victims: Crusade Gets Ships Christened for Pentagon, Pennsylvania Dead." *Washington Post* (September 10, 2004): B01.

Grace, Catherine O'Neill, and Margaret M. Bruchac with Plimoth Plantation. *1621: A New Look at Thanksgiving*. Washington, D.C.: National Geographic Society, 2001. For young adults.

Gray, Paul. "The Trouble with Columbus." *Time* 138, 14 (October 7, 1991): 52-56.

Greiff, Constance M. *Independence: The Creation of a National Park*. Philadelphia: University of Pennsylvania Press, 1987.

Guelzo, Allen C. *Lincoln's Emancipation Proclamation: The End of Slavery in America*. New York: Simon & Schuster, 2004.

Gulevich, Tanya. "Macy's Thanksgiving Day Parade." In *Encyclopedia of Christmas and New Year's Celebrations*. 2nd ed. Detroit: Omnigraphics, 2003.

———. *Understanding Islam and Muslim Traditions: An Introduction to the Religious Practices, Celebrations, Festivals, Observances, Beliefs, Folklore, Customs, and Calendar System of the World's Muslim Communities, Including an Overview of Islamic History and Geography*. Detroit: Omnigraphics, 2004. For young adults.

Hakluyt, Richard. *The Principal Navigations, Voyages, Traffiques, and Discoveries of the English Nation*. Edinburgh: E. & G. Goldsmid, 1889.

Halberstam, David. *The Children*. New York: Random House, 1998.

Hallissy, Erin. "Shining Light on History—Mount Diablo Beacon Recalls Sneak Attack." *San Francisco Chronicle* (December 7, 2000): A24.

Hamilton, Lee H. *How Congress Works and Why You Should Care*. Bloomington: Indiana University Press, 2004.

Hampson, Rick. "Americans Rush to Build Memorials to 9/11." *USA Today* (May 21, 2003). Online at http://www.usatoday.com/news/nation/2003-05-21-memorial-cover_x.htm

Handlin, Lilian. "Discovering Columbus." *American Scholar* 62, 1 (winter 1993): 81-95.

Harden, J. David. "Liberty Caps and Liberty Trees." *Past & Present* 146 (February 1995): 66-102.

Harmon, Daniel E. *The U.S. Armed Forces*. Philadelphia: Chelsea House, 2001. For young adults.

Haskins, Jim. *Christopher Columbus: Admiral of the Ocean Sea*. New York: Scholastic, 1991. For young adults.

———. *I Have a Dream: The Life and Words of Martin Luther King, Jr.* Brookfield, Conn.: Millbrook Press, 1992. For young adults.

Heidler, David S., and Jeanne T. Heidler, eds. *Encyclopedia of the American Civil War: A Political, Social, and Military History*. 5 vols. Santa Barbara, Calif.: ABC-CLIO, 2000.

Henderson, Helene, ed. *Holidays, Festivals, and Celebrations of the World Dictionary*. 3rd ed. Detroit: Omnigraphics, 2005.

Hendrickson, David C. *Peace Pact: The Lost World of the American Founding*. Lawrence: University Press of Kansas, 2003.

Hesser, Amanda. "Turkey Finds Its Inner Duck (and Chicken)." *New York Times* (November 20, 2002): F1.

Hewson, Martha S. *The Electoral College*. Philadelphia: Chelsea House, 2002. For young adults.

Hibbing, John R. *Stealth Democracy: Americans' Beliefs about How Government Should Work*. Cambridge: Cambridge University Press, 2002.

Hoffman, Jon T., ed. *USMC: A Complete History*. Quantico, Va.: Marine Corps Association; [s.l.]: H. L. Levin Associates, 2002.

Hogan, David W. *Centuries of Service: The U.S. Army, 1775-2004*. Washington, D.C.: Center of Military History, United States Army, 2004.

Hoig, Stan. *It's the Fourth of July*. New York: Cobblehill Books, 1995. For young adults.

Holland, W. J., Jr., ed. *The Navy*. Washington Navy Yard, D.C.: Naval Historical Foundation; [s.l.]; Hugh Lauter Levin Associates, 2000.

Horwitz, Elinor Lander. *The Bird, the Banner, and Uncle Sam: Images of America in Folk and Popular Art*. Philadelphia: J. B. Lippincott, 1976.

Howard, James H. "The Plains Gourd Dance as a Revitalization Movement." *American Ethnologist* 3, 2 (1976): 243-59.

Hoxie, Frederick E. *Parading through History: The Making of the Crow Nation in America, 1805-1935.* Cambridge: Cambridge University Press, 1995.

Hughes, Richard T. *Myths America Lives By.* Urbana: University of Illinois Press, 2003.

Humez, Jean M. *Harriet Tubman: The Life and the Life Stories.* Madison: University of Wisconsin Press, 2003.

Irwin, Jim. "GOP Turns 150 This Year, But the Question Is Where?" *Seattle Times* (May 2, 2004): A7.

Jackson, Donald Dale. "Hot Dogs Are Us." *Smithsonian* (June 1999): 104.

Johnson, Robert Erwin. *Guardians of the Sea: History of the United States Coast Guard, 1915 to the Present.* Annapolis, Md.: Naval Institute Press, 1987.

Kachun, Mitch. *Festivals of Freedom: Memory and Meaning in African American Emancipation Celebrations, 1808-1915.* Amherst: University of Massachusetts Press, 2003.

Kammen, Michael. *A Machine That Would Go of Itself: The Constitution in American Culture.* New York: Alfred A. Knopf, 1986.

———. *Mystic Chords of Memory: The Transformation of Tradition in American Culture.* New York: Alfred A. Knopf, 1991.

Kayal, Michele. "In Hawaii, Recipes for Thanksgiving Include Blending Customs." *New York Times* (November 28, 2003): A28.

Kazin, Michael, and Steven J. Ross. "America's Labor Day: The Dilemma of a Workers' Celebration." *Journal of American History* 78, 4 (March 1992): 1294-1323.

Keller, Morton. *The Art and Politics of Thomas Nast.* New York: Oxford University Press, 1968.

Kelly, Kate. *Election Day: An American Holiday, an American History.* New York: Facts on File, 1991.

Kennedy, Caroline. *A Patriot's Handbook: Songs, Poems, Stories and Speeches Celebrating the Land We Love.* New York: Hyperion, 2003.

Ketchum, Alton. "The Search for Uncle Sam." *History Today* 40, 4 (April 1990): 20-26.

Keyssar, Alexander. *The Right to Vote: The Contested History of Democracy in the United States.* New York: Basic Books, 2000.

Kielburger, Marc, and Craig Kielburger. *Take Action! A Guide to Active Citizenship.* Hoboken, N.J.: John Wiley & Sons, 2002. For young adults.

Kindsvatter, Peter S. *American Soldiers: Ground Combat in the World Wars, Korea, and Vietnam.* Lawrence: University Press of Kansas, 2003.

King, Coretta Scott. *My Life with Martin Luther King.* Rev. ed. New York: H. Holt, 1993.

King, Martin Luther, Jr. *Letter from Birmingham City Jail.* Philadelphia: American Friends Service Committee, May 1963.

———. *The Measure of a Man.* Philadelphia: Pilgrim Press, 1959.

———. *Strength to Love.* New York: Harper & Row, 1963.

———. *Stride Toward Freedom.* New York: Harper & Row, 1958.

———. *The Trumpet of Conscience.* New York: Harper & Row, 1968.

———. *Where Do We Go from Here: Chaos or Community?* New York: Harper & Row, 1967.

———. *Why We Can't Wait.* New York: Harper & Row, 1964.

Kirk, Elise K. "'Hail to the Chief': The Origins and Legacies of an American Ceremonial Tune." *American Music* 15, 2 (summer 1997): 123-36.

Klingaman, William K. *Abraham Lincoln and the Road to Emancipation, 1861-1865.* New York: Viking, 2001.

Korshak, Yvonne. "The Liberty Cap as a Revolutionary Symbol in America and France." *Smithsonian Studies in American Art* 1, 2 (autumn 1987): 52-69.

Kracht, Benjamin R. "The Kiowa Ghost Dance, 1894-1916." *Ethnohistory* 39, 4 (1992): 452-77.

———. "Kiowa Powwows: Continuity in Ritual Practice." *American Indian Quarterly* 18 (1994): 321-48.

Kroll, Steven. *By the Dawn's Early Light: The Story of the Star Spangled Banner.* New York: Scholastic, 2000. For young adults.

Larson, Kate Clifford. *Bound for the Promised Land: Harriet Tubman, Portrait of an American Hero.* New York: Ballantine Books, 2004.

Least Heat-Moon, William. *Columbus in the Americas.* Hoboken, N.J.: John Wiley & Sons, 2002.

Lemay, J. A. Leo. "The American Origins of Yankee Doodle." *The William and Mary Quarterly* [3rd Series] 33, 3 (July 1976): 435-64.

Levin, Jerome D. *Presidential Elections, 1789-2000.* Washington, D.C.: CQ Press, 2002.

Levine, Ellen, ed. *Freedom's Children: Young Civil Rights Activists Tell Their Stories.* New York: Putnam, 1993. For young adults.

Levine, Susan. "Sharing a Half-Century Salute; Korean War Veterans Descend on Mall for Armistice Commemoration." *Washington Post* (July 28, 2003): B01.

Library of Congress Symposia on the American Revolution. *The Impact of the American Revolution Abroad.* Papers presented at the fourth symposium, May 8 and 9, 1975. Washington, D.C.: Library of Congress, 1976.

Linton, Ralph, and Adele Linton. *We Gather Together: The Story of Thanksgiving.* 1949. Reprint, Detroit: Omnigraphics, 1990.

Litwicki, Ellen M. *America's Public Holidays, 1865-1920.* Washington, D.C.: Smithsonian Institution Press, 2000.

Maddex, Robert L. *The U.S. Constitution A to Z.* Washington, D.C.: CQ Press, 2002.

Mahon, John K. *History of the Militia and the National Guard.* New York: Macmillan, 1983.

Maier, Pauline. *American Scripture: Making the Declaration of Independence.* New York: Knopf, 1997.

———. *From Resistance to Revolution: Colonial Radicals and the Development of American Opposition to Britain, 1765-1776.* New York: Alfred A. Knopf, 1972.

Maisel, L. Sandy, ed. *The Parties Respond: Changes in American Parties and Campaigns.* 4th ed. Boulder, Colo.: Westview Press, 2002.

Marcovitz, Hal. *The Liberty Bell.* Philadelphia: Mason Crest Publishers, 2003. For young adults.

Margolick, David. *Billie Holiday, Café Society and an Early Cry for Civil Rights.* Philadelphia: Running Press, 2000.

Marling, Karal Ann. *Old Glory: Unfurling History.* Charlestown, Mass.: Bunker Hill Publishing in association with the Library of Congress, 2004.

Marrin, Albert. *George Washington and the Founding of a Nation*. New York: Dutton Children's Books, 2001. For young adults.

McClay, Wilfred M. "The Mixed Nature of American Patriotism." *Society* 41, 1 (November-December 2003): 37-45.

McFeely, William S. *Frederick Douglass*. New York: W. W. Norton & Company, 1991.

McKissack, Patricia C. *Martin Luther King, Jr.: A Man to Remember*. Chicago: Children's Press, 1984. For young adults.

McKissack, Patricia C., and Fredrick L. McKissack. *Days of Jubilee: The End of Slavery in the United States*. New York: Scholastic, 2003. For young adults.

———. *Sojourner Truth: Ain't I a Woman*. New York: Scholastic, 1992. For young adults.

McPherson, James M. *Battle Cry of Freedom: The Civil War Era*. New York: Oxford University Press, 1988.

McPherson, James M., ed. *"To the Best of My Ability": The American Presidents*. New York: Dorling Kindersley, 2000.

Meltzer, Milton. *Bread—and Roses; The Struggle of American Labor, 1865-1915*. New York: Knopf, 1967.

———. *There Comes a Time: The Struggle for Civil Rights*. New York: Random House, 2001. For young adults.

Middlekauff, Robert. *The Oxford History of the United States*. Vol. 2, *The Glorious Cause: The American Revolution, 1763-1789*. New York: Oxford University Press, 1982.

Milkis, Sidney M., and Michael Nelson. *The American Presidency: Origins and Development, 1776-2002*. 4th ed. Washington, D.C.: CQ Press, 2003.

"Miller, Chambliss Act to Help Soldiers Become U.S. Citizens." [Editorial] *Gainesville Times* [Georgia] (November 13, 2003).

Mintz, Steven. "Responses to Industrialism." *Digital History*, 2003. Retrieved February 2005 from http://www.digitalhistory.uh.edu/historyonline/us26.cfm

Mires, Charlene. *Independence Hall in American Memory*. Philadelphia: University of Pennsylvania Press, 2002.

Misiroglu, Gina. *The Handy Politics Answer Book*. Detroit: Visible Ink Press, 2003.

Molotsky, Irvin. *The Flag, the Poet and the Song: The Story of the Star-Spangled Banner*. New York: Dutton, 2001.

Moore, John L. *Elections A to Z*. 2nd ed. Washington, D.C.: CQ Press, 2003.

Morgan, Edmund S. *The Birth of the Republic, 1763-89*. 3rd ed. Chicago: University of Chicago Press, 1992.

Morison, Samuel Eliot. *Admiral of the Ocean Sea: A Life of Christopher Columbus*. 2 vols. Boston: Little, Brown, 1942.

Murray, Stuart. *America's Song: The Story of 'Yankee Doodle.'* Bennington, Vt.: Images from the Past, 1999.

Myser, Michael. "Homeland Security 101." *Wired* (August 18, 2004). Online at http://www.wired.com/news/school/0,1383,64608,00.html

National Commission on Federal Election Reform. *To Assure Pride and Confidence in the Electoral Process, Report of the National Commission on Federal Election Reform; Jimmy Carter et al.* Washington, D.C.: Brookings Institution, 2002.

The National Guard: Defending the Nation and the States. Washington, D.C.: U.S. Advisory Commission on Intergovernmental Relations, April 1993.

Newman, Simon P. *Parades and the Politics of the Street: Festive Culture in the Early American Republic.* Philadelphia: University of Pennsylvania Press, 1997.

Nicholson, Philip Yale. *Labor's Story in the United States.* Philadelphia: Temple University Press, 2004.

The 9/11 Commission Report: Final Report of the National Commission on Terrorist Attacks Upon the United States. Authorized ed. New York: W. W. Norton & Company, 2004.

Norton, Bruce H., ed. *Encyclopedia of American War Heroes.* New York: Facts on File, 2002.

Oates, Stephen B. *Let the Trumpet Sound: The Life of Martin Luther King, Jr.* New York: Mentor, 1982.

———. *With Malice toward None: The Life of Abraham Lincoln.* New York: Harper & Row, 1977.

Our Flag [52-page booklet]. Washington, D.C.: Joint Committee on Printing, U.S. Congress, 2003. Online through the Federal Citizen Information Center at http://www.pueblo.gsa.gov/cic_test/misc/ourflag/titlepage.htm

Palmer, Dave Richard. *1794: America, Its Army, and the Birth of the Nation.* Novato, Calif.: Presidio, 1994.

Patriotism in America. Issue of *CQ Researcher* 9, 24 (June 25, 1999): 547-67.

Patterson, Richard S., and Richardson Dougall. *The Eagle and the Shield: A History of the Great Seal of the United States.* Washington, D.C.: Office of the Historian, Bureau of Public Affairs, Department of State, under the auspices of the American Revolution Bicentennial Administration, 1978.

Payne, Charles M., and Adam Green, eds. *Time Longer Than Rope: A Century of African American Activism, 1850-1950.* New York: New York University Press, 2003.

Pflueger, Lynda. *Thomas Nast: Political Cartoonist.* Berkeley Heights, N.J.: Enslow Publishers, 2000. For young adults.

Phillips, William D., Jr., and Carla Rahn Phillips. *The Worlds of Christopher Columbus.* Cambridge: Cambridge University Press, 1992.

Piehler, G. Kurt. *Remembering War the American Way.* Washington, D.C.: Smithsonian Institution Press, 1995.

Pious, Richard M. "The Powers of the Presidency." In *Democracy Papers*, edited by Melvin I. Urofsky. U.S. Department of State, Bureau of International Information Programs, November 2001. Online at http://usinfo.state.gov/products/pubs/democracy/

Pleck, Elizabeth. "The Making of the Domestic Occasion: The History of Thanksgiving in the United States." *Journal of Social History* 32 (summer 1999): 773-89.

Polgreen, Lydia. "Rituals of Grief, on a Day Eased Only by Time." *New York Times* (September 12, 2004): A1.

Prange, Gordon W. *At Dawn We Slept: The Untold Story of Pearl Harbor.* New York: McGraw-Hill, 1981.

———. *Pearl Harbor: The Verdict of History.* New York: McGraw-Hill, 1986.

Provost, Foster. *Columbus Dictionary*. Detroit: Omnigraphics, 1991.

Quarles, Benjamin. "Antebellum Free Blacks and the 'Spirit of '76'." *Journal of Negro History* (July 1976): 229-42.

Reinhold, Meyer. *Classica Americana: The Greek and Roman Heritage in the United States*. Detroit: Wayne State University Press, 1984.

Rice, Earle, Jr. *The Bombing of Pearl Harbor*. San Diego: Lucent Books, 2001. For young adults.

Riis, Jacob. *How the Other Half Lives: Studies among the Tenements of New York*. New York: C. Scribner's Sons, 1890.

Ripley, C. Peter, ed. *Witness for Freedom: African American Voices on Race, Slavery, and Emancipation*. Chapel Hill: University of North Carolina Press, 1993.

Roberts, Robert North, and Scott Hammond. *Encyclopedia of Presidential Campaigns, Slogans, Issues, and Platforms*. Westport, Conn.: Greenwood Press, 2004. For young adults.

Rogers, Donald, ed. *Voting and the Spirit of American Democracy: Essays on the History of Voting and Voting Rights in America*. Urbana: University of Illinois Press, 1992.

Rosenberg, Emily S. *A Date Which Will Live: Pearl Harbor in American Memory*. Durham, N.C.: Duke University Press, 2003.

Rouse, Irving. *The Tainos: Rise and Decline of the People Who Greeted Columbus*. New Haven, Conn.: Yale University Press, 1992.

Rubel, David. *The Scholastic Encyclopedia of the Presidents and Their Times*. 3rd ed. New York: Scholastic, 2001. For young adults.

Santino, Jack. "Yellow Ribbons and Seasonal Flags: The Folk Assemblage of War." *Journal of American Folklore* 105, 415 (January 1992): 19-33.

Schier, Steven E. *You Call This an Election? America's Peculiar Democracy*. Washington, D.C.: Georgetown University Press, 2003.

Schlereth, Thomas J. "Columbia, Columbus, and Columbiana." *Journal of American History* 79, 3 (December 1992): 937-68.

Schlesinger, Arthur M. "Liberty Tree: A Genealogy." *New England Quarterly* 25, 4 (December 1952): 435-58.

Schlesinger, Arthur M., Jr., ed. *The Almanac of American History*. Rev. and updated ed. New York: Barnes & Noble Books, 1993.

———, ed. *History of U.S. Political Parties*. 5 vols. Philadelphia: Chelsea House Publishers, 2002. For young adults.

Schonauer, Scott. "Marines Canceling or Adapting Parties Marking Service's 226th Birthday." *Stars and Stripes* (November 8, 2001). Online at http://www.estripes.com

Schudson, Michael. *The Good Citizen: A History of American Civic Life*. Cambridge, Mass.: Harvard University Press, 1999.

Schwartz, Barry. *George Washington: The Making of an American Symbol*. New York: Free Press, 1987.

Shade, William G., and Ballard C. Campbell, eds. *American Presidential Campaigns and Elections*. 3 vols. Armonk, N.Y.: M. E. Sharpe, 2003.

Shaw, Peter. *American Patriots and the Rituals of Revolution.* Cambridge, Mass.: Harvard University Press, 1981.

Siemers, David J. *Ratifying the Republic: Antifederalists and Federalists in Constitutional Time.* Stanford, Calif.: Stanford University Press, 2002.

Siskind, Janet. "The Invention of Thanksgiving: A Ritual of American Nationality." *Critique of Anthropology* 12 (1992): 167-91.

Smith, Rogers M. *Civic Ideals: Conflicting Visions of Citizenship in U.S. History.* New Haven, Conn.: Yale University Press, 1997.

Smith, Whitney. *The Flag Book of the United States: The Story of the Stars and Stripes and the Flags of the Fifty States.* Rev. ed. New York: William Morrow & Co., 1975.

Sommer, Frank H. "The Metamorphoses of Britannia." In *American Art: 1750-1800, Towards Independence,* edited by Charles F. Montgomery and Patricia E. Kane. Boston: Published for the Yale University Art Gallery and The Victoria and Albert Museum by the New York Graphic Society/ Little, Brown and Company, 1976.

"Southwest Observes First Thanksgiving." *Hispanic Journal* 11, 4 (April 1998): 10-12.

"Special Trees: It's Not the Size or Species, But the Attributes and Emotions We Give Them That Make Our Arboreal Neighbors So Valued." *American Forests* 108, 2 (summer 2002): 5.

Spillman, Lynette P. *Nation and Commemoration: Creating National Identities in the United States and Australia.* Cambridge: Cambridge University Press, 1997.

Statement of the Pullman Strikers, U.S. Strike Commission. *Report and Testimony on the Chicago Strike of 1894.* Washington, D.C.: Government Printing Office, 1895.

Stout, David. "Justices Let Prisoners Sue to Regain Right to Vote." *New York Times* (November 8, 2004).

Streissguth, Thomas, ed. *The Attack on Pearl Harbor.* San Diego: Greenhaven Press, 2002.

Swarns, Rachel L. "Allowing Those Who Fight for Their Country to Be a Part of It." *New York Times* (May 7, 2003): A20.

Sweet, Leonard I. "The Fourth of July and Black Americans in the Nineteenth Century." *Journal of Negro History* 61, 3 (July 1976): 256-75.

Taylor, Charles A. *Juneteenth: A Celebration of Freedom.* Greensboro, N.C.: Open Hand Publishing, 2002. For young adults.

Taylor, Theodore. *Air-Raid-Pearl-Harbor! The Story of December 7, 1941.* San Diego: Harcourt Brace Jovanovich, 1991. For young adults.

Temperley, Howard, ed. *After Slavery: Emancipation and Its Discontents.* London: Frank Cass, 2000.

Thompson, Sue Ellen, ed. *Holiday Symbols and Customs.* 3rd ed. Detroit: Omnigraphics, 2003.

Thorpe, Francis Newton, ed. *The Federal and State Constitutions, Colonial Charters, and Other Organic Laws of the States, Territories, and Colonies Now or Heretofore Forming the United States of America.* Compiled and edited under the Act of Congress of June 30, 1906. Washington, D.C.: Government Printing Office, 1909.

Trachtenberg, Marvin. *The Statue of Liberty.* London: Penguin Books, 1976.

Travers, Len. *Celebrating the Fourth: Independence Day and the Rites of Nationalism in the Early Republic.* Amherst: University of Massachusetts Press, 1997.

"Trees of Liberty." *American Forests* 109, 1 (spring 2003): 20.

Tucker, Spencer C., ed. *Encyclopedia of American Military History*. 3 vols. New York: Facts on File, 2003.

Turner, H. M. "Reminiscences of the Proclamation of Emancipation." *African Methodist Episcopal Church Review* (January 1913): 211-14.

U.S. Department of State, Bureau of Public Affairs. *The Great Seal of the United States*. Washington, D.C., September 1996. Booklet online in PDF format at http://www.state.gov/www/publications/great_seal.pdf

U.S. House of Representatives Joint Committee on Printing. *Our American Government*. 106th Congress, 2d sess., 2000. H. Doc. 106-216. Online at http://www.access.gpo.gov/congress/house/

Vidrine, Jane. "Louisiana Celebrations Rooted in Tradition." An article for the 1989 Louisiana Folklife Festival booklet, published on the web site of the Louisiana Division of the Arts at http://www.crt .state.la.us/folklife/creole_art_celebrations.html

Vile, John R. *Encyclopedia of Constitutional Amendments, Proposed Amendments, and Amending Issues, 1789-2002*. 2nd ed. Santa Barbara, Calif.: ABC-CLIO, 2003.

Wallendorf, Melanie, and Eric J. Arnould. "'We Gather Together': Consumption Rituals of Thanksgiving Day." *Journal of Consumer Research* 18, 1 (June 1991): 13-31.

Ward, Geoffrey C. *The Civil War: An Illustrated History*. New York: Alfred A. Knopf, 1990.

Warren, Charles. "Fourth of July Myths." *William and Mary Quarterly* 2, 3 (July 1945): 237-72.

Watley, William D. *Roots of Resistance: The Nonviolent Ethic of Martin Luther King, Jr.* Valley Forge, Pa.: Judson Press, 1985.

Watson, Robert P., and Colton C. Campbell, eds. *Campaigns and Elections: Issues, Concepts, Cases*. Boulder, Colo.: L. Rienner, 2003.

White, Richard. "Civil Rights Agitation: Emancipation Days in Central New York in the 1880s." *Journal of Negro History* 78 (winter 1993): 16-24.

White, Shane. "'It Was a Proud Day': African Americans, Festivals, and Parades in the North, 1741-1834." *Journal of American History* 18 (June 1994): 13-50.

———. *Stories of Freedom in Black New York*. Cambridge, Mass.: Harvard University Press, 2002.

Wiggins, William H., Jr. "Lift Every Voice and Sing: A Study of Afro-American Emancipation Celebrations." In *Discovering Afro-America*, edited by Roger D. Abrahams and John S. Szwed. Leiden, Netherlands: E. J. Brill, 1975.

———. *O Freedom! Afro-American Emancipation Celebrations*. Knoxville: University of Tennessee Press, 1987.

Wiggins, William H., Jr., and Douglas DeNatale, eds. *Jubilation! African American Celebrations in the Southeast*. [Educator's Guide] Columbia: University of South Carolina Press, 1994.

Williams, Carol J. "Columbus' Remains Are a Bone of Contention." *Los Angeles Times* (December 3, 2003): A1.

Williams, Juan. *Eyes on the Prize: America's Civil Rights Years, 1954-1965*. Introduction by Julian Bond. New York: Viking, 1987. Companion volume to PBS series.

Wills, Anne Blue. "Pilgrims and Progress: How Magazines Made Thanksgiving." *Church History* 72, 1 (March 2003): 138-58.

Wills, Garry. *Inventing America: Jefferson's Declaration of Independence.* New York: Doubleday & Company, 1978.

Winslow, Edward. Letter to George Morton, December 11, 1621. In *Mourt's Relation, or Journal of the Plantation at Plymouth,* edited by D. B. Heath. New York: Corinth Books, 1963.

Witcover, Jules. *Party of the People: A History of the Democrats.* New York: Random House, 2003.

Wolkomir, Richard. "Near and Far, We're Waving the Banner for Flags." *Smithsonian* 28, 3 (June 1997): 70-78.

Wood, Gordon S. *The American Revolution: A History.* New York: Modern Library, 2002.

———. *The Radicalism of the American Revolution.* New York: Vintage Books, 1992.

Woolls, Daniel. "Mystery: Who's Buried in Columbus Tombs?" *Miami Herald* (October 2, 2004): 1A.

Word, Ron. "First Thanksgiving Occurred in St. Augustine, Researcher Says." *The Florida Times-Union* (November 26, 2002). Online at http://www.jacksonville.com

Wright, Robert. *The Continental Army.* Washington, D.C.: Center of Military History, 1983.

Yacovone, Donald, ed. *Freedom's Journey: African American Voices of the Civil War.* Chicago: Lawrence Hill, 2004.

Zelinsky, Wilbur. *Nation into State: The Shifting Symbolic Foundations of American Nationalism.* Chapel Hill: University of North Carolina Press, 1988.

Web Sites

Web Sites

This section includes all web sites listed in the entries in alphabetical order by the names of the sponsoring organizations.

Abraham Lincoln Bicentennial Commission at http://www.lincolnbicentennial.gov
Air Force at http://www.af.mil
Air Force Association at http://www.afa.org/
Air Force Historical Research Agency at http://afhra.maxwell.af.mil
Air Force Sergeants Association at http://www.afsahq.org/
Air National Guard at http://www.ang.af.mil/
American Ex-Prisoners of War at http://www.axpow.org/
American Federation of Labor-Congress of Industrial Organizations (AFL-CIO)
    Labor Day at http://laborday.aflcio.org/aboutunions/laborday/
    Workers Memorial Day at http://www.aflcio.org/yourjobeconomy/safety/memorial/
American Gold Star Mothers at http://www.goldstarmoms.com/
American Labor Museum at http://www.geocities.com/labormuseum/
American Legion at http://www.legion.org/
American Legion Auxiliary at http://www.legion-aux.org/
American Pyrotechnics Association at http://www.americanpyro.com
AMVETS at http://www.amvets.org/
Arizona Memorial Museum Association at http://arizonamemorial.org/
Arlington National Cemetery at http://www.arlingtoncemetery.org
Army at http://www.army.mil
Army and Navy Union, USA at http://www.armynavy.net/
Army Institute of Heraldry at http://www.tioh.hqda.pentagon.mil/
Army National Guard at http://www.arng.army.mil/
Bill of Rights Institute at http://www.billofrightsinstitute.org/
Blinded Veterans Association at http://www.bva.org/
Blue Star Mothers at http://www.bluestarmoms.org/
Civil Rights Movement Veterans at http://www.crmvet.org/
Coast Guard at http://www.uscg.mil
Commission on Presidential Debates at http://www.debates.org/

Cornell University Library, "'I Will Be Heard': Abolitionism in America" at http://rmc.library.cornell .edu/abolitionism/

Corporation for National & Community Service and **USA Freedom Corps**, Martin Luther King Jr. Day of Service at http://www.mlkday.org

Corpus Christi Museum of Science and History at http://www.shipsofdiscovery.org/

Democratic Party at http://www.democrats.org/

Disabled American Veterans at http://www.dav.org/

Election Reform Information Project at http://www.electionline.org/

Flag House & Star-Spangled Banner Museum at http://www.flaghouse.org

Fleet Reserve Association at http://www.fra.org/

Fourth of July Celebrations Database, compiled by James R. Heintze of American University, at http://gurukul.american.edu/heintze/fourth.htm

Free Library of Philadelphia, Centennial Exhibition Digital Collection at http://libwww.library.phila .gov/CenCol/

Gold Star Wives of America at http://www.goldstarwives.org/

Gulf War Veteran Resource Pages at http://www.gulfweb.org/

Harriet Tubman Historical Society at http://www.harriettubman.com

Harriet Tubman Home at http://www.harriettubmanhome.org

Inaugural Committee at http://inaugural.senate.gov/

Independence Hall Association at http://www.ushistory.org

Iraq War Veterans Organization at http://www.iraqwarveterans.org/

Jamestown-Yorktown Foundation at http://www.historyisfun.org

Juneteenth.com at http://www.juneteenth.com

Korean War Veterans Association at http://www.kwva.org/

Library of Congress

"Abraham Lincoln Papers" at http://memory.loc.gov/ammem/alhtml/malhome.html

Abraham Lincoln's Inauguration at http://memory.loc.gov/ammem/today/mar04.html

"African-American Odyssey" at http://lcweb2.loc.gov/ammem/aaohtml/

"After the Day of Infamy: 'Man on the Street' Interviews Following the Attack on Pearl Harbor" (American Folklife Center) at http://memory.loc.gov/ammem/afcphhtml/afcphhome.htm

"Air-Raid on Pearl Harbor" at http://memory.loc.gov/ammem/today/dec07.html

"American Life Histories: Manuscripts from the Federal Writers' Project, 1936-1940" at http://memory.loc.gov/ammem/wpaintro/wpahome.html

"American Women: 'With Peace and Freedom Blest!' Woman as Symbol in America, 1590-1800" at http://memory.loc.gov/ammem/awhhtml/aw05e/aw05e.html

"By Popular Demand: Portraits of the Presidents and First Ladies from 1789-Present" at http://memory.loc.gov/ammem/odmdhtml/preshome.html

"Columbus Day" at http://memory.loc.gov/ammem/today/oct12.html

"Drafting the Documents" at http://www.loc.gov/exhibits/declara/declara2.html

"Elections the American Way" at http://memory.loc.gov/learn/features/election/

"The First Labor Day" at http://memory.loc.gov/ammem/today/sep05.html

"1492: An Ongoing Voyage" at http://www.loc.gov/exhibits/1492/

"Frederick Douglass Papers" at http://memory.loc.gov/ammem/doughtml/doughome.html

"From Slavery to Civil Rights: A Timeline of African-American History" at http://memory.loc
.gov/learn/features/civilrights/flash.html

"George Washington Papers" at http://lcweb2.loc.gov/ammem/gwhtml/gwhome.html

George Washington's Birthday at http://memory.loc.gov/ammem/today/feb22.html

"How Did America Get Its Name?" (July 2003) at http://www.loc.gov/wiseguide/america.html

"'I Do Solemnly Swear . . . ' Presidential Inaugurations" at http://memory.loc.gov/ammem/
pihtml/pihome.html

"I Hear America Singing—Patriotic Melodies" at http://lcweb2.loc.gov/cocoon/ihas/html/
patriotic/patriotic-home.html

"Immigration . . . The Changing Face of America" at http://memory.loc.gov/learn/features/immig/
introduction.html

Inauguration Day at http://memory.loc.gov/ammem/today/jan20.html

"Inaugurations . . . From George W. to George W." at http://learning.loc.gov/learn/features/inaug

"Independence Day" at http://memory.loc.gov/ammem/today/jul04.html

"Martin Luther King Jr. Birthday" at http://memory.loc.gov/ammem/today/jan15.html

"The New Yellow Ribbon Tradition" (American Folklife Center) at http://www.loc.gov/folklife/
ribbons/

"Selected Civil War Photographs" and Timeline at http://memory.loc.gov/ammem/cwphtml/
cwphome.html

"September 11, 2001, Documentary Project" at http://memory.loc.gov/ammem/collections/
911_archive/

"Thanksgiving in American Memory" at http://memory.loc.gov/learn/features/thanks/thanks.html

U.S. Constitution at http://memory.loc.gov/ammem/today/sep17.html

"Veterans Day" at http://memory.loc.gov/ammem/today/nov11.html

"The Veterans History Project" at http://www.loc.gov/folklife/vets/

"Washington in 1809—A Pen-Picture. Diary of Sarah Ridg [Schuyler], January 3 – November 2,
1809" at http://memory.loc.gov/ammem/pihtml/pihome.html

Living Memorials Project at http://www.livingmemorialsproject.net/

Lower Manhattan Development Corporation (World Trade Center site) at http://www.renewnyc.com

Macy's at http://www.macys.com

Marine Corps at http://www.marines.com and http://www.usmc.mil/

Marine Corps History and Museums Division at http://hqinet001.hqmc.usmc.mil/HD/

Marine Corps League at http://www.mcleague.org/

Martin Luther King Jr. Center for Nonviolent Social Change at http://www.thekingcenter.org

Military Order of the Purple Heart at http://www.purpleheart.org/

National Archives and Records Administration

"The Charters of Freedom" at http://www.archives.gov/national_archives_experience/charters
.html

"Congress and the Civil Rights Act of 1964" at http://www.archives.gov/exhibit_hall/treasures
_of_congress/page_24.html

"The Constitution of the United States, The Bill of Rights, and Amendments to the Constitution"
at http://www.archives.gov/national_archives_experience/charters/ constitution.html

"The Declaration of Independence" at http://www.ourdocuments.gov/doc.php?flash=true&doc=2

"The Emancipation Proclamation" at http://www.ourdocuments.gov/doc.php?doc=34

"Joint Address to Congress Leading to a Declaration of War Against Japan" by Franklin D.
Roosevelt at http://www.ourdocuments.gov/doc.php?flash=true&doc=73

"Presidential Libraries" at http://www.archives.gov/presidential_libraries/index.html

"U.S. Electoral College" at http://www.archives.gov/federal_register/electoral_college/

National Association for the Advancement of Colored People at http://www.naacp.org/

National Association of Juneteenth Lineage at http://www.najl.org/

National Association for Music Education, National Anthem Project at http://www.thenational
anthemproject.org

National Civil Rights Museum at http://www.civilrightsmuseum.org/

National Council on Fireworks Safety at http://www.fireworksafety.com/

National D-Day Museum at http://www.ddaymuseum.org

National Guard Association of the United States at http://www.ngaus.org/

National Guard Bureau at http://www.ngb.army.mil/

National Healing Field Foundation at http://healingfield.org

National Hot Dog and Sausage Council at http://www.hot-dog.org/

National Japanese American Memorial Foundation at http://www.njamf.com/

National League of POW/MIA Families at http://www.pow-miafamilies.org/

National Military Appreciation Month at http://www.nmam.org

National Park Service

African-American Civil War Memorial at http://www.nps.gov/afam/index.htm

Flight 93 National Memorial at http://www.nps.gov/flni/

Fort McHenry National Monument and Historic Site at http://www.nps.gov/fomc/index.htm

Independence Hall at http://www.nps.gov/inde/home.htm

Korean War Veterans Memorial at http://www.nps.gov/kowa/index.htm

"The L'Enfant and McMillan Plans," on the design and planning of Washington, D.C., at
http://cr.nps.gov/nr/travel/wash/lenfant.htm

Lincoln Memorial at http://www.nps.gov/linc/index.htm

Martin Luther King Jr. National Historic Site at http://www.nps.gov/malu/

Mount Rushmore at http://www.nps.gov/moru/

Spirit of Freedom African-American Civil War Memorial at http://www.nps.gov/afam/home.htm

USS Arizona Memorial at http://www.nps.gov/usar/

Vietnam Veterans Memorial at http://www.nps.gov/vive/index.htm

Vietnam Women's Memorial at http://www.nps.gov/vive/index.htm

Washington Monument at http://www.nps.gov/wash/index.htm

"We Shall Overcome; Historic Places of the Civil Rights Movement" at http://www.cr.nps.gov/nr/travel/civilrights/

Women in Military Service for America Memorial at http://www.nps.gov/gwmp/wimsa.htm (also http://www.womensmemorial.org/)

World War II Memorial at http://www.nps.gov/nwwm/index.htm (also http://wwiimemorial.com)

National Underground Railroad Freedom Center at http://www.freedomcenter.org

Naval Historical Center

Navy Day and naval history at http://www.history.navy.mil

Pearl Harbor attack at http://www.history.navy.mil/photos/events/wwii-pac/pearlhbr/pearlhbr.htm

Navy at http://www.navy.mil

Navy League at http://www.navyleague.org/

Non-Commissioned Officers Association at http://www.ncoausa.org/

North American Vexillological Association at http://www.nava.org/

Office of U.S. Representative John Conyers Jr., "Reflections on the Significance of Martin Luther King Day" at http://www.house.gov/apps/list/press/mi14_conyers/108_01_19_04.html

Office of U.S. Representative William Lacy Clay, "A Call to Action" at http://www.house.gov/clay/sp030825.htm

Paralyzed Veterans of America at http://www.pva.org/

Pearl Harbor Survivors Association at http://www.pearlharborsurvivorsonline.org/

Pentagon Memorial Project at http://memorial.pentagon.mil

Plimoth Plantation at http://www.plimoth.org

Public Broadcasting Service (PBS)

"African American World" at http://www.pbs.org/wnet/aaworld/

"Africans in America" at http://www.pbs.org/wgbh/aia/

"The American President" at http://www.pbs.org/wnet/amerpres/

"The Rise and Fall of Jim Crow" at http://www.pbs.org/wnet/jimcrow/ and http://www.jimcrowhistory.org/home.htm

Republican Party at http://www.gop.com

Reserve Enlisted Association at http://www.reaus.org/

Reserve Officers Association at http://www.roa.org/

Smithsonian Institution

"The American Presidency: A Glorious Burden" (National Museum of American History) at http://americanhistory.si.edu/presidency/

"Civil War @ Smithsonian" at http://www.civilwar.si.edu/home.html

"Hot Dogs as America" (American Museum of Natural History) at http://www.amnh.org/exhibitions/baseball/hotdogs/

"September 11: Bearing Witness to History" (National Museum of American History) at http://americanhistory.si.edu/september11/

"The Star-Spangled Banner" (National Museum of American History) at http://americanhistory.si.edu/ssb/

"Vote: The Machinery of Democracy" (National Museum of American History) at http://americanhistory.si.edu/vote/index.html

Sojourner Truth Memorial Statue Project at http://www.noho.com/sojourner/

Southern Regional Council, "Will the Circle Be Unbroken?" at http://unbrokencircle.org/

Stanford University, Martin Luther King Jr. Papers Project at http://www.stanford.edu/group/King/

Sussex County Return Day, Inc., at http://www.returnday.org/

Transform Columbus Day Alliance at http://www.transformcolumbusday.org

U.S. Citizen and Immigration Services at http://uscis.gov/

U.S. Department of Defense at http://www.defenselink.mil

U.S. Department of Labor, Labor Hall of Fame at http://www.dol.gov/oasam/programs/laborhall/about.htm

U.S. Department of State

"Democracy Papers" at http://usinfo.state.gov/products/pubs/democracy/

"An Outline of American History" by Howard Cincotta (May 1994) at http://usinfo.state.gov/usa/infousa/facts/history/toc.htm

"United States Elections 2004" at http://usinfo.state.gov/products/pubs/election04/

U.S. Department of Veterans Affairs

Nationwide Gravesite Locator at http://www.cem.va.gov

Veterans Day at http://www.appc1.va.gov/vetsday/

U.S. Election Assistance Commission at http://www.eac.gov/

U.S. Federal Election Commission at http://www.fec.gov/

U.S. Government Printing Office

"Citizenship" at http://bensguide.gpo.gov/6-8/citizenship/index.html

"Election Process" at http://bensguide.gpo.gov/6-8/election/index.html

The Flag. United States Code, Title 4, Chapter 1 at http://www.access.gpo.gov/uscode/title4/chapter1_.html

"Symbols of U.S. Government" at http://bensguide.gpo.gov/3-5/symbols/index.html

Veterans for Peace at http://www.veteransforpeace.org/

Veterans of Foreign Wars of the United States at http://www.vfw.org/

Veterans of the Vietnam War at http://www.vvnw.org/

Vietnam Veterans of America at http://www.vva.org/

Voices of Civil Rights, sponsored by the American Association of Retired Persons, the Library of Congress, and the Leadership Conference on Civil Rights, at http://www.voicesofcivilrights.org

Walter P. Reuther Library at http://www.reuther.wayne.edu/

White House Commission on Remembrance at http://www.remember.gov

White House Historical Association at http://www.whitehousehistory.org

White House, Office of the Press Secretary, "Address to a Joint Session of Congress and the American People" by George W. Bush at http://www.whitehouse.gov/news/releases/2001/09/20010920-8 .html

Women's Army Corps Veterans Association at http://www.armywomen.org/

Photo and Illustration Credits

Photo and Illustration Credits

Cover: Front—American Patriotism © 2000 Comstock Inc.; Spine—Photography American Icons/Eyewire® by Getty Images © 2000 Getty Images.

Title page: American Patriotism © 2000 Comstock Inc.

Patriotism in the United States: American Patriotism © 2000 Comstock Inc. (pp. 18, 23, 35, 40 top, 43); Photography American Icons/Eyewire® by Getty Images © 2000 Getty Images (pp. 29, 31, 40 middle and bottom); Library of Congress (pp. 27, 33, 37, 41); National Archives/www.ourdocuments.gov (p. 30); courtesy of the Boston Public Library, Print Department (p. 32).

Armed Forces Day: Neither the Department of the Navy nor any other component of the Department of Defense has approved, endorsed, or authorized this product (p. 51); Courtesy, United States Marine Corps (p. 53); Courtesy, United States Coast Guard (p. 55); Use of the Air Force Coat of Arms symbol does not indicate endorsement by the Department of Defense or the Department of the Air Force (p. 56).

Citizenship Day: Monticello/Thomas Jefferson Foundation, Inc. (p. 62); National Archives/www.ourdocuments .gov (p. 65).

Columbus Day: Library of Congress (p. 73); Mark Leffingwell/AFP/Getty Images (p. 76); Ed Smith (p. 79).

Election Day and Inauguration Day: AP/Wide World Photos (p. 85); American Patriotism © 2000 Comstock Inc. (p. 88); Sussex County Return Day, Inc. (p. 91); Library of Congress (p. 93).

Emancipation Day and Juneteenth: People & Portraits/Westside Press © 1997 Judson Rosebush Company Inc. (p. 97); Library of Congress (pp. 99, 100, 102, 106); Courtesy of the Galveston Island Convention and Visitors Bureau (p. 109).

Flag Day: American Patriotism © 2000 Comstock Inc. (p. 116); U.S. Department of Veterans Affairs (p. 121); The National Flag Day Foundation, Inc. (p. 122).

Independence Day: Photography American Icons/Eyewire® by Getty Images © 2000 Getty Images (p. 126); Library of Congress (pp. 130, 133 right, 136, 138, 142); People & Portraits/Westside Press © 1997 Judson Rosebush Company Inc. (pp. 133 left and middle, 134); Library of Congress (p. 140); MPI/Getty Images (p. 146); courtesy, American Antiquarian Society (p. 152); American Patriotism © 2000 Comstock Inc. (p. 155); National Park Service (p. 163); Parades of the World © Corel Corporation (p. 165).

Labor Day: Library of Congress (p. 176); Kathy McKinley (p. 181).

Martin Luther King Jr. Birthday: AFP/Getty Images (p. 186); Library of Congress (p. 188); copyright © Bettmann/CORBIS (p. 193); Cecil Stoughton, LBJ Library (p. 195); copyright © Bettmann/CORBIS (p. 197).

Memorial Day: Historic American Sheet Music, "O'er graves of the loved ones plant beautiful flowers," Music #45, Duke University Rare Book, Manuscript, and Special Collections Library (p. 206); Ron Sachs/Consolidated News Pictures/Getty Images (p. 212).

National Pearl Harbor Remembrance Day: National Park Service (pp. 218, 220, 222).

Patriot Day: AP/Wide World Photos (pp. 226, 232); Department of Defense (p. 231).

Thanksgiving: Parades of the World © Corel Corporation (p. 236); Photography American Icons/Eyewire® by Getty Images © 2000 Getty Images (p. 240); AP/Wide World Photos (p. 245).

Veterans Day: *Detroit News* Collection/Walter P. Reuther Library, Wayne State University (p. 250); National Park Service/courtesy Dwight D. Eisenhower Library (p. 253); Ricardo E. Magdaleno/City of Houston (p. 258); Georgia Veterans Day Parade Association of Atlanta (p. 261).

Washington's Birthday: Library of Congress (pp. 265, 270).

Index

Index

A

abolition movement, 100-03, 150-53

Adams, Abigail, 86

Adams, John, 20, 25, 90, 127, 136, 137, 138, 138 (ill.), 150

Adams, John Quincy, 25, 150

Adams, Samuel, 132, 133, 133 (ill.)

Afghanistan, 228, 348

AFL-CIO. *See* American Federation of Labor and Congress of Industrial Organizations (AFL-CIO)

African Americans
civil rights movement, 108, 186, 190, 191-98, 200, 342, 353-56
segregation and discrimination faced by, 108, 187-89, 191-92, 354
under slavery, 137-38, 150-53
voting rights, 85-86, 189, 194, 196, 353

Air Force, 56-57
See also U.S. armed forces

al Qaeda, 228-29, 348, 349

Alabama, 108, 112, 192, 260

Alaska, 167

Albany Congress, 135

Albany, New York, 135, 201

Albany, Oregon, 258

Alexandria, Virginia, 272

All Veterans Day, 252
See also Veterans Day

Allied powers, 221

Altgeld, John P., 327, 329, 330-33

Alvarez Piñeda, Alonzo, 78

"America," 108

American Civil War. *See* Civil War

American Colonization Society, 153

American Court Gossip, 321-23

American Federation of Labor and Congress of Industrial Organizations (AFL-CIO), 180

American flag, 30
folding, 121 (ill.)
history of, 117-19
laws and regulations, 121, 336-41
Pledge of Allegiance, 120, 256, 324, 325, 336
songs honoring, 119

American Indian movement, 77
See also Native Americans

American Legion Auxiliary, 210

American Railway Union, 179, 327, 328

American Revolution. *See* Revolutionary War

American Tribute, 155

"American's Creed," 28-29

Ames, Mary Clemmer, 320-21

"Anchors Aweigh," 52

Ann Arbor, Michigan, 201

Anniston, Alabama, 112

Anthony, Susan B., 159, 160

Anti-Federalists, 66, 146, 267

Antietam, Maryland, Battle of, 104

Apache Girls' Puberty Ceremonial, 159

Appleton, Wisconsin, 123

Arizona, 69, 111, 168

Arkansas, 112, 169

Arlee, Montana, 168

Arlington National Cemetery, 212, 256, 320

Arlington, Virginia, 234, 261

Armed Forces Day, 47-61
observances of, 57-59